SKY GUARDIANS

SKY GUARDIANS

Britain's Air Defence
1918–1993

MICHAEL J. GETHING

ARMS AND
ARMOUR

Arms and Armour Press
A CASSELL IMPRINT
Villiers House, 41-47 Strand,
London WC2N 5JE.

Distributed in the USA by
Sterling Publishing Co. Inc., 387 Park Avenue
South, New York, NY 10016-8810.

Distributed in Australia by Capricorn Link
(Australia) Pty. Ltd, P.O. Box 665, Lane Cove,
New South Wales 2066.

British Library Cataloguing-in-Publication Data:
a catalogue record for this book is available from
the British Library

ISBN 0-85368-946-6

Cartography by Peter Burton

Designed and edited by DAG Publications Ltd.
Designed by David Gibbons; layout by Anthony
A. Evans; edited and indexed by Jonathan
Falconer; printed and bound in Great Britain by
The Bath Press, Bath, Avon.

The publishers and author are grateful to the
Controller of HMSO for permission to repro-
duce the photographs on pages 70, 108, 142,
144, 190, 195 and 196.

Dedication:

To the memory of military personnel from
all services who gave their lives in the air
defence of Great Britain since air warfare
first threatened these shores.

On a personal note, I would like to link this
dedication to the memory of my adopted
mother, Betty Gething (1918-78), without
whose support for my fanatical interest in
the RAF during my formative years, I would
never have been in a position to produce
this book.

Michael J. Gething

CONTENTS

Introduction, 7   Air Defence Evolves, 11

The emergence of the Royal Air Force (RAF) as an independent service on 1 April 1918 was the final admission that air power had emerged as an independent and credible force. It could render fixed lines of emplaced ground defences ineffective and, over water, the strike range of aircraft was far in excess of any ship-based naval gun. The aircraft, whether heavier or lighter than air, was a force to be reckoned with. Of course, for every military development, in this case the striking power and range of the aircraft, there is a counter. Against the bomber, the fighter was developed.

In 1914, aerial warfare was in its infancy yet, in four years, it advanced from rudimentary concepts of artillery spotting and general reconnaissance to encompass the embryo elements of air superiority, ground attack, naval strike, tactical and strategic reconnaissance, maritime surveillance (including anti-submarine warfare) and strategic bombing. The air defence of the home base evolved as a series of responses to threats, real and imaginary. Considering the means available, sharpened by trial-and-error and the courage of pioneer air fighters, by 1918 the UK's air defence force was a tolerably efficient organisation.

Between the two World Wars, the RAF based its strength on the number of aircraft in service with its French equivalent -the only numerical 'threat' to the UK at the time. It was not suggested that France would *ever* go to war against this country; it was just that the *Aéronautique Militaire* was the only half-credible "yardstick" against which the RAF's air defence could be measured. Once German re-armament became a reality, UK air defence needs were still underestimated until the late-1930s. Only then did the world see the build-up of the RAF and the introduction of, first, Hurricanes and, then, Spitfires, as has been noted in many other works, "only just in time". These aircraft, their pilots, groundcrew and the support personnel in what is now referred to as "the command and control" chain, were responsible for ensuring that the RAF did not lose what Winston Churchill described as "The Battle of Britain".

The Second World War saw the rapid development of fighter aircraft, the development of the gas turbine the jet engine and the introduction of radar, both ground-based and airborne. Air defence was developed and refined. While some of the lessons of the war were learnt and expanded, others were not. During the so-called "Cold War", air defence became very much a "numbers game" until, in the late-1950s, the guided missile appeared.

The guided missile was the solution to very many problems. It was so much cheaper than manned aircraft that it could be bought in vast quantities. However, the fighter aircraft, with the wealth of radar and avionics on board, was becoming an expensive asset and, while being singularly more effective than the older generation of aircraft it replaced, its cost meant that aircraft were no longer replaced on a one-for-one basis.

The infamous Duncan Sandys Defence White Paper of 1957, foresaw the end of the manned interceptor fighter and the rise of the anti-aircraft missile, known today as the surface-to-air missile or SAM. The Lightning was to be the RAF's last manned interceptor fighter, scheduled for withdrawal in the mid-1960s. The guided missile was, however, unable to live up to its expectations. Now, over 35 years later, the manned interceptor, or air defence fighter, is still with us. The Lightning itself continued in service for 27 years, with first an Anglicised American F-4 Phantom and, most recently, the trinational Tornado Air Defence Variant (ADV) complementing and replacing the type. Now that the European Fighter Aircraft (EFA) has survived its crisis and assumed a new identity (Eurofighter 2000), manned fighters will continue to be flown by the world's air arms well into the 21st Century.

Since 1945, the ways and means of detecting intruding and unwanted aircraft in UK airspace has evolved. Reliability and effectiveness of ground-based radars has increased and the need for a more secure command and control system which responded to the threat has been realised. Airborne early warning systems, looking for low-level targets over the horizon, were adopted and air-to-air (AAR) refuelling - developed for use with the V-bomber deterrent force - was found to give fighters an increased time on station for their combat air patrols (CAPs).

During the late-1960s and 1970s the RAF was involved in the search for a replacement aircraft for its offensive V-bomber force following the successive debacles of TSR-2, F-111K and AFVG. The Multi-Role Combat Aircraft (known initially by its acronym of MRCA then christened Tornado) filled the vacancy. Developed jointly by Italy, West Germany and the UK, the Tornado finally went into production and air defence took a back seat. It was not until the late-1970s that the next plan to overhaul and update the UK air defences was initiated. It is the fruit of this most recent improvement that forms a major part of this book.

However, in order to appreciate the problems of today, one must still look to the lessons of the past. My initial approach to the subject was to present brief "Snapshots" of the state of the UK's air defences at 10-year intervals, commencing in 1918 when the RAF was formed by the amalgamation of the Royal Flying Corps and the Royal Naval Air Service. However, the tale grew in the telling. Initial background had to be presented to put the whole concept into perspective and, although the "Snapshots" approach has been retained, their content has increased in length from the original concept. Events and developments over the decades, not least the Second World War, cannot be totally ignored and, so, are described in brief, where required, in order to give the overall picture.

The end result is more of a progressive history with fixed points for evaluation and comparison, concluding with an account of the UK's air defences in 1993 and some plans and thoughts for the future. The latter part of this book sets out to explain the workings of the multifarious processes and systems which come together to provide the Air Defence of Great Britain. There is a whole chain of command which stretches from HQ of RAF Strike Command in High Wycombe all the way out to the pilot and navigator of a Tornado F3 fighter sitting on combat air patrol over the North Sea.

It is opportune that this book is published in the 75th Anniversary Year of the formation of the RAF. This book presents the background against which air defence measures happened. It also presents the reader with the position today and how, should a similar need arise, the RAF is equipped to, and how it would, fight such a battle today.

In 1918, the air defence fighter (to use today's parlance) was equipped with the most basic of systems - two 0.303in machine guns and the pilot's intelligence was a verbal briefing using information that came from visual observation. Today, the Tornado F3 is armed with a 27mm cannon, four beyond-visual-range Sky-flash air-to-air missiles and four shorter range, infra-red-seeking Sidewinder missiles. It is equipped with a Foxhunter airborne interception radar with multiple target capability; radar and missile warning receivers; active and passive means to decoy enemy radar and missiles; and secure, real-time communications.

To ensure the fighters are in the air, there are ground-based, three-dimensional, phased array radars (supplemented by Boeing E-3 airborne early warning aircraft); while to back up the airborne defences, there are ground-based Rapier SAMs (with a replacement for the Bloodhound under evaluation) and radar-guided Oerlikon 35mm anti-aircraft guns (courtesy of former-Argentine President Galtieri). All of these are interconnected by a complex, secure Command, Communications, Control and Intelligence (C3I) network, known as the Air Defence Ground Environment (ADGE).

Since 1945, the UK has been referred to as "an aircraft carrier anchored off the continent of Europe". As a member of the NATO alliance, the UK's role as an off-shore base, should another European war have broken out, was paramount. In the last few years, since Mikhail Gorbachev introduced the words "glasnost" and "perestroika" to the English language and Boris Yeltsin concluded the START 2 agreement with outgoing US President George Bush, the chances of direct warfare between NATO and what was the Warsaw Pact have been drastically reduced.

Yet the reader must be under no illusions. One of the several reasons that peace has reigned in Europe for over 40 years is that the RAF, as part of the NATO alliance, was able to respond to the air threat to the UK in such a manner that aerial attacks against this country would be too costly for a potential aggressor to contemplate. Even though we may expect to see the nuclear missile threat reduced and, hopefully, be eliminated, the threat of maverick missiles has emerged. Likewise the threat of conventional warfare against NATO, and the UK base, still exists. Attack by air is a major part of that threat. It may have become a cliche but the ancient Roman dictum of *"Si Pacem Vis Para Bellum"* remains a truism. Great Britain still needs its Sky Guardians.

ACKNOWLEDGEMENTS

In preparing this book, I have tapped many sources and, in specific areas, called upon acknowledged references and colleagues with more expertise than I, to explain how certain equipment and systems work or were developed.

To the following "willing souls" who were subjected to a range of specific questions at various time, I offer thanks: Richard Allen, Malcolm English, Bill Green, Bill Gunston, Chris Hobson - Librarian of the RAF Staff College, Bracknell, Paul Jackson, Arnold Nayler and the Library staff of the Royal Aeronautical Society, the Library staff at the RAF Museum, Hendon, Martin Streetly, Gordon Swanborough, John W. R. Taylor, Dick Ward, Mike Witt and my colleagues, past and present, on *Defence* magazine.

I must also thank the public relations staffs of the Frazer Nash Division of Airscrew Howden, Boeing Aerospace, British Aerospace, GEC-Marconi Avionics, Marconi Radar & Command Systems, Oerlikon Contraves, Siemens Plessey Defence Systems and Short Brothers. Your names are too numerous to mention but you know who you are. My thanks to you for putting up with what may, at the time, have seemed like infuriating questions of minor detail.

To Don Parry and Ian V. Hogg I offer my particular thanks. Without their invaluable contributions, this book would not have been possible. Similarly, I thank the patience of Rod Dymott and Arms & Armour Press in awaiting this tome. To my wife Carol and children, David and Charlotte, I salute your forebearance and understand your frustrations (not always supressed) while I was working on this book.

Finally, I must acknowledge the wholehearted cooperation of the Royal Air Force itself. Michael Hill, Command Public Relations Officer of RAF Strike Command, in particular, was instrumental in allowing me access to a variety of personnel and arranging many of the flying facilities I was allowed and to him I shall be forever grateful. To all ranks at all levels who came across me over the past six years, who heard of this book in preparation and who offered their unstinted support, I thank you.

However, in the end, it is the author who has brought them together and with whom responsibility for accuracy, presentation and interpretation of all the facts remains.

Michael J.Gething
Cowfold, West Sussex.
January, 1993

Above: On the night of 16/17 June 1917, a DH2 (similar to the example illustrated), flown by Captain Saundby, made the second of three attacks on Zeppelin *L48*, which subsequently crashed at Holly Tree Farm, Theberton. (Author's Collection)

Below: In the war against the Zeppelin airships, the BE2c was used with success against five airships. (Via Ian Hogg)

AIR DEFENCE EVOLVES

In order to illustrate the way in which the British air defences were developed, built-up and eroded in successive peaks and troughs, the reader is presented with a series of historical "Snapshots". These commence in 1918, the year that the RAF was formed as an independent service. It was also the year which saw the end of "The Great War" - as the First World War was then known - and may seem a curious place at which to begin the story of the Air Defence of Great Britain. Yet 1918 was both an end and a beginning: the end of a war and the beginning of an evolution in air power.

The four years of the First World War saw the emergence of two threats: first, the airship (perceived before the war) and, second, the manned, strategic bomber (an alien concept in 1914). By the time of the Armistice, both threats had evolved, been applied and had been countered, although not without supreme efforts from the pilots at squadron level and much inter-service rivalry between the Royal Naval Air Service (RNAS) and the Royal Flying Corps (RFC). However, in order to comprehend the nature of air defence, it is necessary to set the scene before moving to the first of these "Snapshots".

Early moves

In 1908, the Committee of Imperial Defence was charged with examining the threat posed by airships and aeroplanes and considering any advantage which Britain might derive from their use. In July 1912, after evaluating the potential menace of the German Zeppelin force, it reported that:

"It is possible that aeroplanes, owing to their superior mobility, may be found capable of destroying airships, but this has yet to be proved. Having regard to the great speed of modern airships (47 miles per hour), to the conditions as compared with aeroplanes, to the fact that they carry guns and firearms for purposes of defence, and to the difficulty of destroying them by shells or explosives, it is by no means proved that aeroplanes are likely to have the better of an encounter, though they can travel faster and ultimately rise higher than the present type of airship, which is some compensation for the greater time taken in rising.

"It appears probable that, for the immediate present, the surest method of attacking airships would be by a superior force of armed airships."

While the benefit of hindsight might allow us some mild amusement at the possibility of this vision of H. G. Wells' *War in the Air* becoming a reality, the truth was to be very different.

There was a tradition that defence against any enemy incursion on British soil was the responsibility of the Army. With the advent of aviation, this principle was extended to the airspace above the British Isles, consequently in August 1912 the RFC Military Wing was tasked with providing the aircraft to defend ports and other key objectives. The Army - in the form of the War Office - was more concerned with the use of aircraft for reconnaissance and failed to produce any plans for the air defence of the home base. The Royal Navy, however, with a view to working with the Fleet and individual ships, did establish a series of coastal airfields. These would also have a value in the future air defence plans as they evolved.

By November 1913, the Navy's responsibility was extended to protecting important naval targets in the vicinity of their bases. Even so, the War Office retained responsibility for air superiority over the British Isles. While experiments in night-flying and the use of airborne illumination were conducted, the emphasis was still on reconnaissance for the British Expeditionary Force (BEF) that might be expected to be deployed to France in the event of a European war.

Armament experiments were conducted, with No 3 Squadron concluding that of various machine guns tested on aircraft, the Lewis gun offered the greatest promise. The RNAS trialled an anti-airship weapon devised by the Royal Aircraft Factory, Farnborough, - a large grappling iron with an explosive charge, known as the "Fiery Grapnel". The iron would be lowered from an aircraft by cable and, having "caught" the airship and - hopefully - punctured the gasbag, an explosive charge would ignite the leaking hydrogen gas. A RNAS armaments expert also recommended that all the major airfields should have two machine-gun-armed aircraft available to deal with any enemy raiders.

During the period of international tension that arose between the Archduke Franz Ferdinand's assassination on 28 June 1914, and Britain's declaration of war on 4 August, a number of precautionary measures were taken. Naval aircraft touring the UK were recalled to base in July; First Lord of the Admiralty, Winston Churchill, decreed on 29 July that naval aircraft must regard defence against aerial attack as their prime responsibility; and, on 30 July, No 4 Squadron RFC, was temporarily detached from BEF duties to bolster the home air defences.

Unprepared
Although the threat of air attack from the outbreak of war was considered strong in both public and official circles, the War Office failed to take the matter seriously. With virtually all front-line aircraft committed to the BEF, only the second-line aircraft - principally a few, unarmed Farmans, Bleriots and early models of the BE2 - were available for home defence. Their offensive capability was pitiful, amounting only to revolvers and rifles with some anti-airship "darts". Should these weapons fail to destroy the airships, some aircrew were even instructed, albeit obliquely, to take "other measures" to destroy any intruding Zeppelins. The commander of Hendon (a RNAS base) was more forthright and went so far as to issue an order which contained the following paragraph :

"If the aeroplane fails to stop the airship by the time all the ammunition is expended, and the airship is still heading for London and shows no sign of being turned from her objective, the the pilot must decide to sacrifice himself and his machine and ram the airship at the utmost speed."

Meanwhile, the RNAS did, at least, possess several aircraft with development potential and one aircraft which might, honestly, be called a fighter - the Vickers FB5 Gunbus, which had been under development since 1912. It was powered by a pusher engine, which allowed the installation of a machine gun in the nose. In service, the Gunbus was used mainly by the RFC.

Once war was declared, the Army still showed reluctance to assume the responsibility of air defence, suggesting that "the

aeroplane would not be a suitable form of defence for use over London". It also suggested to the Navy that "the stationing of aeroplanes on the east coast with a view to the interception of dirigibles is a more desirable method of defence". The implications were clear. The Royal Navy had assumed an air defence role and, after discussions between Churchill and Lord Kitchener, Secretary of State for War, it was agreed in Cabinet that they would assume responsibility for home defence from 3 September 1914.

In August 1914, the Royal Navy had positioned three "anti-aircraft" guns (a previously unheard-of role for artillery) and a dozen searchlights in central London, to protect major government buildings. The Third Sea Lord, Rear Admiral F. C. T. Tudor, was given overall command of gunnery matters, once the Navy had assumed responsibility for air defence, and he also headed a committee to produce an air defence plan.

Working on the principle that attack was the best form of defence, the RNAS adopted the "Nelson Touch" with a raid on the German city of Dusseldorf, which destroyed the German Zeppelin *LZ25*. There followed, on 21 November 1914, the famous raid against the Zeppelin works at Friedrichshafen on the shores of Lake Constance - a distance of some 250 miles from Belfort in eastern France, near Basle. Three RNAS Avro 504s, each armed with four 20lb bombs, managed to cause damage out of all proportion to the effort expended. One Zeppelin was destroyed, the workshops were badly damaged and a gas plant was put out of action. One of the Avros was shot down and its pilot taken prisoner; the other two returned safely to base.

However, as the Germans advanced, further operations of this nature became impractical. Of course, this also meant that German air resources were in a better position to raid Britain and the raids soon began. The first recorded attack on the UK was on 21 December 1914, when a single Friedrichshafen FF 29 floatplane of the Imperial German Navy appeared off Dover and dropped two bombs (to no effect). By the time news of the incident had reached the "proper authorities", the raider was long gone.

Enter the Zeppelin
The first Zeppelins appeared on the night of 19 January 1915. Two out of the three which set off, Zeppelins *L3* and *L4* of the Imperial

German Navy, arrived over East Anglia in appalling weather. They dropped their bombs "blind" and succeeded in killing two people in Great Yarmouth and three in King's Lynn. There was no action to counter this enemy raid.

Thereafter, as the larger "P" class Zeppelins entered service, during the spring of 1915, they became a constant thorn in the East Coast's defences. The first Zeppelin "kill" was finally made by Flight Sub-Lieutenant R. A. J. Warneford on the night of 7 June 1915. Flying in a Morane-Saulnier Type L parasol monoplane, armed with six 20lb HE bombs, he was detailed to bomb the airship sheds at Evere. However, at about 03.00hr, he spotted LZ37 over Ostend. He succeeded in climbing above the airship and he released his bombs. The airship exploded and crashed in flames near Ghent; but the Morane was caught in the blast, sustaining some damage. This forced Warneford to land to fix a broken petrol pipe. He managed to get airborne once more, after effecting temporary repairs, and returned to base. It was the first completely successful air interception in history and won Warneford the Victoria Cross. The fortunes of war, sadly, dictated he would die just 10 days later.

During the remainder of 1915, German airships continued to raid Britain while, within Whitehall, inter-service rivalry surfaced on the question of responsibility for Britain's air defence. All that the War Office and Admiralty appeared to agree on was that night-flying was not an easy task and that early detection of enemy airships was practically impossible. Meanwhile, the pilots of both services strove to counter the threat with inadequate aeroplanes and insufficient

resources. The learning curve was not rising quickly enough.

As "penny packets" of aircraft were dispersed around the East Coast and London, many varied forms of weaponry were developed - none of them operationally effective - while flares and small searchlights were also tried out as means of detecting the incoming airships. Standing patrols were not rated as effective, yet waiting for sightings usually meant the enemy was out of reach before the air defenders arrived on the scene.

Public awareness of the airship threat to London was heightened with the raid of the night of 13/14 October 1915, when five Zeppelins, much dispersed, met an organised attempt at interception. In order to engage the raiders before they reached the capital, many RFC aeroplanes had flown a sortie and were on the ground as the airships crossed various parts of Greater London. Unfortunately, no provision for overlapping patrols had been made. Prearranged signal rockets were not seen by pilots in the air and the searchlights in and around the capital, with one exception, were unsuccessful in catching the Zeppelins. The illumination of L15 was ineffective as no aircraft were in the air. It was curious that no RNAS aircraft were ordered into this action and this led to recriminations. The Royal Navy reiterated its official view that to attempt the interception of Zeppelins which were not visually identified, was useless.

By January 1916, the War Office and the Admiralty were, once more, engaged in a battle of responsibility. After some delicate negotiations, almost upset upon Kitchener's return from abroad, Arthur Balfour (who had taken over as First Lord of the

Right: The remains of Zeppelin *L15* sinking off the Kent coast on 1 April 1916. (Via Ian Hogg)

Admiralty in May 1915) and Kitchener agreed a compromise, formally endorsed by the War Committee on 10 February. This allowed the Royal Navy responsibility "to deal with all hostile aircraft attempting to reach [the UK]" while the Army undertook "to deal with all such aircraft which reach these shores". As a rider, it was further agreed that the Army (responsible for all defence arrangements on land) "would also provide the aeroplanes required to work with the home defence troops" as well as protecting garrisons and important potential targets. Inter-service co-operation was urged to ensure any unnecessary duplication of effort.

Air Defence Emerges

This agreement came into effect at noon on 16 February 1916 with the Commander-in-Chief Home Forces, Field Marshal Lord French assuming responsibility for the air defence of London, with the rest of the country following on 22 February. In anticipation of the handover, the War Office had prepared plans the previous December for the anti-aircraft defence of London and the rest of the country.

For London, the War Office adopted the plan put forward by Admiral Sir Percy Scott prior to the transfer of responsibility. A double ring of guns was proposed at five and nine miles radius from Charing Cross, with some slight distortion to take in the Woolwich Arsenal, the Royal Small Arms Factory at Enfield and the Royal Gunpowder Factory at Waltham Abbey. Beyond the gun rings a further ring of searchlights was established and intended, initially, to guide defending aircraft by signalling, with its beam, in the direction of reported raiders. Ground-based observers were also employed using the telephone system for communications. The ground-based part of the AA defence plan demanded 487 guns and 490 searchlights, yet in June there were only 271 guns and 258 searchlights in the whole of the UK, most of the former being were totally inadequate for the job.

Airfields were established at Croydon, Farningham, Hainault, Hounslow, Joyce Green, Northolt, Sutton's Farm and Wimbledon Common, each with a pair of BE2cs to be flown by experienced night-flying pilots drawn from reserve squadrons. Naval aircraft from Chingford and Hendon assisted the RFC until the official take-over, thereafter the RFC would also base a night-fighting element at Hendon. Three BE2cs were also deployed north, for the defence of Teeside, being based at Cramlington. Plans were also drawn up to counter attacks against other major UK cities. The RFC's tactics remained unchanged: pilots would fly within visual range of their bases and attempt to deal with any airships which crossed their paths.

By 1 February 1916, the BE2c detachments became elements of No 19 Reserve Aeroplane Squadron (RAS), headquartered at Hounslow. Although still ostensibly a training unit, the night fighter detachments' pilots were assigned the home defence duties as their sole responsibility. As good as this was for the defence of London, the home defence units deployed in the provinces were not so fortunate and instructions as to what action to take against Zeppelin raids, when no suitable aircraft were available, did not inspire confidence.

Even before the official hand-over of responsibility was made, the revised defences were put to the test on the night of 31 January/1 February 1916. Nine German naval airships made their biggest raid to date against the UK. Although targeted against Liverpool, early sightings led the War Office to assume that London was the target. In bad weather, fog and mist, many of the intruders were scattered and none reached their target despite claims to the contrary. The places actually hit by the 205 high explosive and 174 incendiary bombs which were dropped that night were Burton-on-Trent, Derby, Ilkeston, Loughborough, Scunthorpe and the Tipton-Wednesday-Walsall area. Some 70 people were killed and 113 injured. Although Zeppelin *L19* was lost at sea on its return journey, the remainder survived. Only one 4.7in round was fired from the AA guns and 16 aircraft sent against the raiders (of which eight were damaged and two pilots killed - both experienced squadron commanders - and three injured). It was one of the biggest fiascos in the history of the UK's air defence.

As might be expected, reorganisation followed - rapidly. One officer was appointed to command all aircraft engaged in the defence of London, yet he still had to supervise the training squadron at Hounslow! The scattering of "penny packets" of aircraft was to prove ineffective and, by May 1916, these became grouped together into three flights of No 39 Squadron at Sutton's Farm, Hainault Farm and Hounslow. By June, a new Home Defence Wing of the RFC had been formed

and during July and August the number of squadrons grew (reaching 11 by the end of the year), while further refinements were made to the organisation.

During the first six months of the new regime, there were 17 Zeppelin raids and nine hit-and-run aeroplane raids. Still, it was a period of consolidation and by the end of the year, despite losing resources to the Western Front, the airship menace had receded. The German authorities had realised, as early as autumn 1916, that the airship was no longer a viable "strategic" bomber. The German Army Airship Service discontinued its airship missions after the raid of 16 February 1917.

Three months later, twin-engined Gotha bombers began a series of daylight raids on London and its suburbs which were to prove a "prequel" to the Blitz of the Second World War. Germany had been preparing for these raids for several months and they were to be carried out by the *Kampfgeschwader der Obersten Heersleitung 3* (Battle Squadron 3 of the Army High Command), usually shortened to Kagohl 3, and later re-titled *Bombengeschwader 3* (Bogohl 3).

The London Raids

The German rationale behind the winged-bomber raids on London was later analysed by the historian, Major Frhr von Bulow, who noted:

"The main purpose of the bombing attacks was the intimidation of the English people, the crippling of their will to fight and the preparation of a basis for peace. The sec-
ondary purpose of the raids was to disrupt the British war industry, disorganise the communications between the coastal ports and London, attack supply dumps of the coastal ports and hinder transport of war materials across the Channel. The target of the raids was confined principally to London because it was the heart of England, the operational headquarters of the Allies and the centre of the war industry."

Despite this grand strategy, it became obvious that tactical success in the destruction of targets was considered more important than the primary aim of destroying British morale. Had Germany continued the long-range raids, they would have been more profitable than the short-range, tactical raids on the Western Front that the Gothas and Giants were later to undertake. However, we are jumping slightly ahead of the narrative.

The Gotha daylight raids began on 25 May 1917, when 21 Gothas - two having turned back with mechanical trouble - made a daylight raid intending to reach London. However, heavy cloud obscured the capital and they bombed Folkestone and Shornecliffe instead, inflicting 97 fatalities and 195 injuries. Both the RFC and RNAS sent up air defence sorties, with virtually no effect. One Gotha was shot down on its return journey by RNAS Sopwith Pups operating out of Dunkirk, France. The first daylight raid to reach London was mounted on 13 June by 20 Gothas, of which two turned back with engine trouble and only 18 attacked. In all, 162 people were killed and

432 injured and, of 92 sorties mounted against the intruders, not one British fighter managed an interception on the outward journey.

The public outcry following the raid was loud and bellicose, causing plans to be put in hand to strengthen the Home Defence Force and redistribute the anti-aircraft guns. Although the British commanders took measures such as re-deploying No 56 Squadron (SE5s) and No 66 Squadron (Sopwith Pups) back to England from the Western Front, they returned to France by 6 July. With an amazing stroke of timing, the Gothas reappeared on 7 July and, although the defences made a better showing - 30 aircraft making contact and only one Gotha shot down (on its return trip) - it emphasised to the public that the air defence of London and the South East of England was not all it should be.

With the public now crying for blood - almost - the War Cabinet sanctioned the return of two fighter squadrons from France. The C-in-C of the British Expeditionary Force, Field Marshal Sir Douglas Haig, protested this action would prejudice imminent and important operations but, in the end, a typical British compromise was reached. On 10 July, No 46 Squadron, equipped with Sopwith Pups, arrived at Sutton Farm from France; and 24 new Sopwith Camels, earmarked for re-equipping two squadrons in France, were brought into the Home Defence Force.

The follow-up action of the War Cabinet on 11 July was, predictably enough, the formation of a committee. Nominally under the chairmanship of the Prime Minister, David Lloyd George, it was effectively led by Lieutenant-General J. C. Smuts, whose brief was to examine air defence and the overall air organisation. His report, submitted on 19 July, was one of the fundamental documents which led to the establishment of an independent Royal Air Force just under a year later. However, the rational thinking of Smuts' analytical mind soon got to the heart of the matter.

His report highlighted that the major shortcoming of the system, as it existed, was that it had been developed to combat the threat of the airship, in many respects an easy target. It was easily located by and held in the beam of a searchlight; it presented a large and vulnerable target for the anti-aircraft guns; and once intercepted by even a single aircraft, armed with explosive or incendiary bullets, it was as good as destroyed. Aeroplanes, he maintained, were totally different. They were faster and more agile than the airship and, therefore, harder for searchlights to find and follow; more difficult for the guns to hit; and, when attacked by a single fighter, because of their practice of flying in formation (wherever possible), were able to defend themselves much more efficiently. The Smuts solution was to fire great barrages of anti-aircraft shells into the track of the bombers, in an attempt to break up the formation, and for the fighters to attack in groups, isolate individual bombers and, thus, pick them off while providing mutual protection. His recommendations included the appointment of a senior officer, with air experience, to be placed in charge of a London Air Defence Area (LADA) which included all regions within range of the Gothas, under the command of C-in-C Home Forces, Field Marshal Lord French.

The Air Defence of London

The man chosen for this task - a political hot potato - was Major-General Edward Bailey Ashmore, who had learned to fly in 1912 and had alternated his postings in the Army between the Royal Artillery and the RFC. He was judged to be an excellent choice for the post, having proven efficiency, personal charm and the aptitude to get along with most people. He also possessed that vital quality for people in such positions - a sense of humour. As he observed in his memoirs, entitled *Air Defence* (Longmans, 1929):

"We of the Expeditionary Force were inclined to look on the troubles of London somewhat lightheartedly. The fact that I was exchanging the comparative safety of the front for the probability of being hanged on the streets of London did not worry me."

Ashmore assumed his new role at noon on 8 August 1917. His command consisted of six Home Defence squadrons (37, 39, 50, 51, 75 and 78 Squadrons), plus three being formed as a direct result of the Smuts Report (44, 61 and 112 Squadrons); all fixed and mobile anti-aircraft guns and searchlights between Harwich and Dover; and aircraft observation posts east of a line between Grantham and Portsmouth. He set up a barrier line of anti-aircraft guns some 20 miles east of London, in order to leave the fighters free to attack raiders coming over the coast (to the east of the gun-line) or engage the bombers individually as their formations were broken up after passing through the gunfire barrage. Ground signals, in the form of large, moveable arrows - easily visible from the air - were provided for the searchlight and gun sites, which were to be pointed at enemy aircraft in sight. A final innovation was to use wireless-equipped (Morse sets, not voice) aircraft "trackers" to shadow the intruders and, periodically, to signal their course and position to the ground. (These aircraft were, in effect, the precursors of the E-3D Sentry airborne early warning aircraft now in RAF service.)

Although the new organisation took time to settle down, on 12 August a formation of nine Gothas, having made landfall over Southend instead of Chatham, found 15 Camels of No 44 Squadron rising to intercept them. In the best traditions of Falstaff, they executed a 180 degree turn, jettisoned their bombs and fled. One of the Gothas was shot down by an RNAS Pup. On 22 August, a force of 10 Gothas which crossed the coast near Margate was badly mauled by the guns and, abandoning hopes of reaching London, looked for targets of opportunity. Three were shot down: one by an RNAS Camel over Dover; one by antiaircraft guns in the Thanet area and the third was most likely destroyed by the guns, although this was hotly disputed between the RNAS and the RFC. Certainly, the whole formation was pursued by a constant stream of gunfire while over England. This, effectively, marked the end of daylight raids.

However, before entering the realms of night operations, let us round off the airship saga. We have noted the cessation of the German Army's airship raids in February 1917 and the service was formally disbanded on 31 July. What of the German Navy and their Zeppelins ? The furore created by the Gotha raids tended to overshadow the airships, in which the German naval staff maintained their faith. The advantage offered by the airship was the altitude at which it could fly and drop its bombs, usually between 18,000 and 20,000ft. The German Navy maintained that flying at this height, its airships were virtually immune from fighter attack. The results of a night raid on 16/17 June 1917 tended to confirm this contention, yet both played a part in the effective removal of the airship as a threat to the UK.

The decision by the commander of the German Naval Airship Division, *Korvettenkapitan* Peter Strasser, to mount a raid on London during that short midsummer night in an effort to regain the faith of his superiors in the airship as a strategic weapon was, to say the least, imprudent. Only two of the four Zeppelins dispatched reached England and one of those was destroyed.

One of the two which reached England was *L48*, the first of the new five-engined "U" class Zeppelins designed to operate from 20,000ft. After crossing the coast, it appeared *L48* was having engine trouble and, after dropping her bombs north of her target, Harwich, she descended to 13-14,000ft to take advantage of stronger tailwinds at this height. A BE2c and an FE2b took off to intercept *L48* from the experimental station at Orfordness, which had been allocated a home-defence commitment. Although the BE2c could only reach 11,000ft, the FE2b, flown by Lt F. D. Holder with Sgt S. Ashby as gunner, was at some 14,200ft and, although unable to reach *L48*, still fired on her. Tailing the Zeppelin, Holder and Ashby were able to fire again when she began to descend.

Later, a DH2 - again from Orfordness and flown by Capt R. H. M. S. Saundby - was able to fire into *L48* as she was limping towards the coast. A third attack was made by Lt L. P. Watkins of No 37 Squadron, flying a BE12, firing from 2,000ft closing to 500ft. A fire started in the tail, spreading quickly and at 0330hr on 17 June, *L48* crashed at Holly Tree Farm, Theberton. Although each of the three aircraft could, legitimately, claim one third of a kill, it was awarded to Watkins on the rationale that credit should been given to a dedicated Home Defence squadron, rather than the part-time efforts of Orfordness.

While *L48* effectively demonstrated that descent to a lower altitude invited fighter attack, it was left to the other Zeppelin, *L42*, to confirm that maintaining height was a distinct advantage. An RNAS Sopwith Baby chased *L42* for 70 minutes but was unable to get within range. Shortly after seeing *L48* go down, two RNAS Pups sighted *L42* flying at some 16,000ft but could just not reach her to attack. A Curtiss H-12 flying boat also chased *L42* for 95 minutes and, again, was unable to gain sufficient altitude to attack.

Although, subsequently, there were other raids by German Navy airships, the experience of *L48* was instrumental in the removal of the Zeppelins from raids over England. On 17 August 1917, the Kaiser decreed that the German Navy be limited to 25 airships, with a prime role of reconnaissance, and that the production rate of new Zeppelins be reduced from two per month to one every two months. The Zeppelin menace was practically over... but the night raids by winged aircraft were about to begin.

Night Operations

As the RFC's air defences stiffened, the German losses in the daylight raids became intolerable. The slow speeds and low attack altitudes prevented the Gothas from evading the ever-improving British air and ground defences. The switch to night operations became inevitable. Although the night attacks began on 2/3 September 1917, the first Gotha raid, on Chatham, was carried out on 3/4 September with a raid on London the next night. Of 11 Gothas dispatched, five reached their targets: on the ground, some 152 fatalities and 177 injuries were sustained as a result of the attack.

Again there was public outcry and, again, the War Cabinet summoned General Smuts to report and recommend. His comments were rather disparaging against the night fighters: "...they find it impossible to see the enemy machines even at a distance of a couple of hundred yards" he commented. The description "nightfighter" had come in at the end of August 1917, as the Home Defence squadrons had been categorised into either day or nightfighter units. The former were those equipped with the higher performance aircraft of the force, while the latter had the older, more sedate and stable machines. These, it was hoped, could rise to meet any Zeppelin threat, despite being incapable of dealing with the Gothas by day.

Smuts was of the opinion that by using more powerful searchlights, the bomber crews could be dazzled and he also proposed a new form of balloon barrage. This involved a line of balloons carrying an "apron" of wire in the sky. This, he suggested, would cause the bombers to fly higher and decrease the accuracy of their bombing.

The "apron in the sky" was not entirely new, having been suggested in several forms to the Munitions Inventions Department at earlier dates. The form it eventually took was to connect, with long horizontal cables, a number of spaced-out balloons and suspend a screen of vertical wires from those connecting cables. Although 20 such "aprons" were proposed,

only 10 were actually installed. Each apron, of five balloons, was strung along a line between Tottenham, Wanstead, Barking, Plumstead and Lewisham. The other aprons were never installed when, following a raid in May 1918, the intruders were severely mauled by the defences and the Air Council (the governing body of the newly-formed RAF) were of the opinion that the existing defences were sufficient.

Meanwhile, a new system of gun barrages had been worked out and initiated. The sky over London was divided into squares and patterns of barrage were calculated so as to produce a "curtain" of shells, some 2,500ft deep, at various heights within each square. These squares were then declared "off limits" to defending aircraft, so that any aircraft within was assumed to be hostile and could be fired on without question.

This scheme was further improved upon, albeit unofficially in the first instance, by a Colonel Thompson of the Thanet Gun Defences. He devised a system of height observation and control and, on its first "showing", shot down two Gothas. This success invited an immediate rebuke from the War Office for using an unauthorised system. There followed a series of exchanges with Ashmore accepting responsibility and the War Office retaliating by forbidding the use of the new gun barrage system and the (somewhat childish) response of not providing some gunsites with telephones. Eventually Lord French intervened in favour of Ashmore, and the Thompson system became standard. Indeed, it remained in use until replaced by radar during the latter half of the Second World War.

Returning to the nightfighter scene, the myth of the "inability" of aircraft, such as the Sopwith Camel, to operate safely at night, due to their "instability", was dispelled by another unofficial action by an officer "at the sharp end". During the raid of 3/4 September, the acting commanding officer of No 44 Squadron (equipped with Camels), Capt G. W. Murlis Green, pressured the Home Defence Brigade and extracted permission to take-off. With two other Camels, he took-off with the aid of an improvised flarepath, patrolled over the Thames estuary for an hour (sadly, to no effect) and landed in perfect safety. While accepting that the Camel needed to be treated correctly, night operations *per se* did not add to the risk. Later, Ashmore was to describe this operation as "perhaps the most

Right: One of the novel forms of passive air defence instituted by Major-General Edwin Ashmore, following the raid on London on 4 September 1917, was a balloon apron defence line just outside London and inside the aircraft patrol lines. By the middle of 1918, 10 of these aprons were in position, suspended at almost 10,000ft. (Via Ian Hogg)

important event in the history of air defence". During some 200 subsequent night patrols by Home Defence Force Camels, there was not one fatal accident.

Even so, the success of nightfighters during the night raids was not particularly encouraging. During the course of 157 patrols there were only nine sightings. Although not proven, it is widely believed that a Sopwith 1½ Strutter from No 78 Squadron accounted for the loss of one Gotha on the night of 25/26 September. It is thought the aircraft was forced to ditch after

losing fuel from tanks punctured by the Sopwith's gunfire. German sources attribute the loss to anti-aircraft fire.

At this stage in the air war by night, a new German bomber entered the lists. Designated by the letter "R" (for *Riesenflugzeug* - giant aeroplane), it was soon dubbed the "Giant". They were almost double the size of the Gothas, which belonged to the "G" class (from *Grossflugzeug* - large aeroplanes). These "R" class Giants were flown by *Riesenflugzeugabteilungen* (Rfa) 501, which had been withdrawn from the Eastern Front in the summer of 1917, to work-up for operations over England under the operational control of Kaghol 3. The first Giant raid, consisting of two aircraft, took place on the night of 28/29 September and, although 1,800kg of bombs were dropped, no casualties were sustained.

Unlike the daylight raids, the night raids were not flown in tight formations and the Giants were only deployed in small numbers per raid. On 18/19 December 1917, the first Giant reached London, dropping a single 300kg bomb, to no effect, in Eaton Square. Later that night, Maj Murlis Green (who, it will be remembered, pioneered the night use of the Camel) attacked one of the accompanying Gothas over east London, damaged an engine and caused it to ditch in the sea off Folkestone. It is perhaps fitting that the pioneer of Camel night-flying should also provide evidence of its success as a nightfighter.

However, success was very much the exception rather than the rule. As Ashmore commented, "a large number of pilots were risking their necks for pitifully small results". Once in the air, he went on, the aviators were as efficient as was expected. He concluded they were being let down by poor support on the ground. This led him to reorganise the observation/reporting system on the ground (the air defence ground environment in today's parlance) and was to prove the basis for his work in setting up the Observer Corps (now the Royal Observer Corps) in 1924. As an adjunct to this, much work was carried out on sound location systems, especially around the Channel coast. Work on the balloon screens was hastened and new patrol lines for fighters, crossing the most likely approaches, were set up with the area below emptied of guns but saturated with searchlights.

The scene is now set for the first of our "Snapshots" -1918.

Left: The Gotha GV was the final production version of this series of German bombers and could carry six 110 lb bombs a distance of some 305 miles. The Gothas were considered a more formidable threat that the Zeppelins. (RAeS Library)

Left: The wreckage of a Gotha bomber shot down over Essex on 28 January 1918. (Via Ian Hogg)

Left: The Bristol F2B fighter, known affectionately as "the Brisfit" and similar to the type illustrated, entered service with the Home Defence Force in September 1917, with five squadrons being equipped with the type by 1918. (RAeS)

"SNAPSHOT" 1918

This section is the lead "Snapshot" of the historical background and is the only one within the book that considers a wartime situation. This is intentional for, as the author was once told (perhaps apocryphally), fighting a war gets in the way of the work of the air force.

In order that the reader can evaluate the progress (or lack of it) in each "Snapshot", it is inevitable that some crossover may occur under the separate headings. Where this happens, the main thrust will be in the appropriate section.

THE THREAT

As military commanders have always found, many potential threats become non-existent when the "shooting war" begins, while other developments, which have been known of, appraised and not considered hostile, become threats. By the same token, a potential means of countering that threat may, when attempted, be ineffective yet another means, previously rejected, can succeed. War is a great catalyst for what we now call lateral thinking.

By 1918, as has been described in the introductory chapter, the airship as a credible threat had almost been eliminated. There were isolated attacks but nothing serious. The airborne threat to the UK was vested in aeroplane raids conducted by the Gotha and Giant series of bombers.

Gotha GII to GV

The Gotha series of twin-engined bombers were designed and built by Gothaer Waggonfabrik AG and formed the mainstay of German *Bombengeschwadern*. They were also built by Luft-Verkehrs Gesellschaft (LVG) – who delivered most of their machines to Austria with locally designed and built engines – and the Siemens-Schuckert Werke.

The GII was the first in the series, appearing early in 1916. It was a three-bay, swept-wing biplane with a single fin and rudder, of wooden frame and fabric construction and powered by two 220hp Benz pusher engines. It was armed with two Parabellum 7.92mm Light MG14 machine guns on ring mounts, one in the nose and one aft of the wings. This weapon had a firing rate of 750 rounds/min and was fed with 250-round belts. It is generally acknowledged as the most flexible aircraft gun of the First World War. The GII was only built in small quantities.

The Gotha GIII was similar, only the powerplant was changed to a pair of 260hp Mercedes DIVa engines. The GIII did, however, introduce an innovation which was to be improved upon in the later G models: a tunnel through the centre of the fuselage, whereby the gunner could fire his weapon rearwards beneath the tail. Again, this version only saw limited production.

The major production versions in the series were the GIV and GV. Although they retained the Mercedes DIVa engines, the wings featuring cut-outs in the trailing edge of the lower mainplane, to allow clearance for the pusher propellers. Twin mainwheels were positioned under each engine nacelle and, on later machines, a pair of smaller, raised wheels was located ahead of the mainwheels, to counter the Gotha's tendency to nose-over on landing.

Data: Gotha GV

Powerplant	two 260hp Mercedes DIVa six-cylinder, in-line, water-cooled engines
Span	77ft 9.25in
Length	38ft 11in
Height	14ft 1.25in
Wing area	966.6sq ft
Empty weight	6,028lb
Loaded weight	8,745lb
Maximum speed	87.5mph at 12,000ft
Time to height	9,840ft in 28min
Service ceiling	21,320ft in 52.5min
Combat range	305 miles
Armament	two Parabellum 7.92mm Light MG14 machine guns on flexible mounts; the usual bomb load for the daylight raids over the UK being six 110lb bombs

Zeppelin Staaken R "Giants"

Originally designed and manufactured by Baumann, Hirth and Klein at the Versuchbau Gotha-Ost (VGO) or East Gotha Experimental works (the company subsequently becoming Zeppelin Werke Staaken), the "Giant" series of bombers were remarkable on two counts. They were, for their day, huge aircraft – the RVI had a wingspan of over 138ft and, although many versions were only built in very small numbers (single examples in some cases), they were all used operationally, both on the Western and Eastern fronts.

The first example was a tri-motor design, the VGO I, powered by 245hp Maybach MbIV engines, which made its maiden flight on 11 April 1915. This was followed by the generally similar VGO II. These two aircraft proved to be underpowered and a third design, the VGO III, was powered by six 160hp Mercedes DIIIs – the wing-mounted engines being in tandem, one driving a tractor and one a pusher propeller; while the third pair of engines were mounted side-by-side and, together, drove a tractor propeller.

The fourth example initiated the R-series of designations – R for *Riesenflugzeug* or Giant Aeroplane – and the second and third machines were retrospectively re-designated RII and RIII. The RIV, produced in 1917, differed from the RIII in having 220hp Benz engines in the wing nacelles. Through the models, armament had been increased to reach six or seven machine guns in the RIV, but was reduced to five on the RV – one being mounted in a wooden fairing over the leading edge of the upper mainplane centre-section. The RV was powered by five Maybach engines, the same type as used used on the VGO I, being mounted in tandem on the wings but with a single engine in the nose.

The only design to be put into anything like quantity production was the RVI: one by the parent company, seven by Luftfahrzeugbau Schutte-Lanz, six by Automobil und Aviatik AG and four by Ostdeutsche Albatros-Werke GmbH. It was powered by four Maybach or Mercedes engines, wing-mounted in tandem. The armament consisted of one Parabellum 7.92mm machine gun in the nose, two dorsally-mounted and one in the ventral position plus up to 18 x 220lb bombs carried internally. It carried a crew of seven and the landing gear consisted of four wheels under each nacelle and two in the nose. RVIs were used in raids over France and the UK.

The first R-planes of Rfa 501 were deployed to the Western front in August 1917 with their first raid (of two aircraft in company with some Gothas) being carried out on the night of 28/29 September 1917. Targeted against London, they dropped their 3,968lb bomb load over London and Sheerness with no casualties. On 16/17 February 1918, the first 2,205lb (1,000kg) bomb was dropped by *R39* hitting the Royal Hospital, Chelsea, during a raid which spread over London, Deal and Dover. The next night, a lone raider, *R25* captained by Lt Max Borchers, made a successful raid on St Pancras Station in London, killing 21 people and injuring 32.

In all, the Giants of Rfa 501 completed 11 raids over Great Britain, with another two raids, targeted at England, ending up being raids on French towns. The final Giant raid was on the night of 19/20 May 1918, when three aircraft dropped 7,055lb of bombs over London/Chelmsford, killing 49 and injuring 177. This raid saw the third (and last) dropping of a 1,000kg bomb, again carried by *R39*.

The series continued to develop in dribs and drabs with a single RVII, three RXIVs, one RXIVa, three RXV and a lone RXVI. Interestingly, an RVI was developed as a seaplane for naval use by the provision of large metal floats. Only one was built and it was written off during trials.

Data: RVI

Powerplant   four 245hp Maybach MbIV or 260hp Mercedes DIVa six-cylinder, in-line, water-cooled engines

Span	138ft 5.625in
Length	72ft 6.25in
Height	20ft 8in
Wing area	3,572sq ft
Empty weight	17,426lb
Loaded weight	26,066lb
Maximum speed	84.35mph at sea level
Time to height	9,840ft in 43min
Service ceiling	14,170ft
Endurance	7-10hrs
Armament	four Parabellum 7.92mm

light MG14 machine guns on flexible mounts; plus a maximum of 4,409lb of bombs, 2,205-2,645lb being the norm

DETECTION AND IDENTIFICATION

The implied military threat of the balloon or flying machine was recognised almost from the very beginning of their development. At the Hague Conference of 1899, it was declared that the discharging of projectiles or explosives from aircraft was prohibited. This was accepted by the major powers and

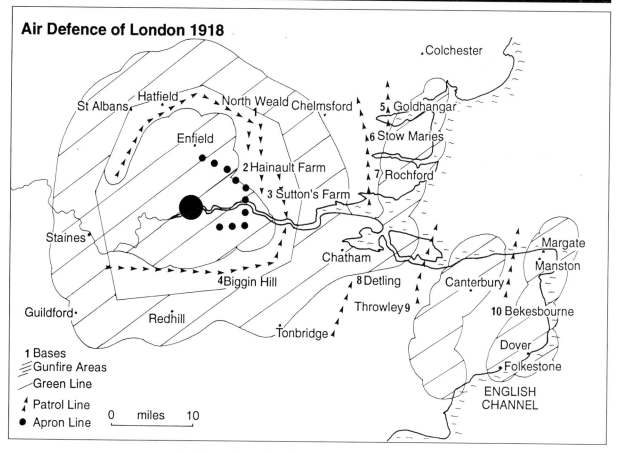

Air Defence of London 1918

Colchester

St Albans · Hatfield · North Weald · Chelmsford

5 Goldhangar

Enfield

6 Stow Maries

2 Hainault Farm

7 Rochford

3 Sutton's Farm

Staines

Margate
Manston

Chatham

4 Biggin Hill

8 Detling
Canterbury

Guildford ·

Throwley 9

10 Bekesbourne

Redhill

Tonbridge

Dover

Folkestone

ENGLISH
CHANNEL

1 Bases
Gunfire Areas
Green Line
Patrol Line
Apron Line

0   miles   10

was nominally in force for five years. Yet over those years, events were moving fast and, by 1907, a different picture prevailed and the Conference of that year was rather more ambiguous. It was no longer unanimously agreed that the earlier resolution should be maintained.

Technology was advancing in other areas and two developments, both of which were to have momentous effects upon aviation, were emerging from theory into practice. Firstly, the opportunity of communicating with an aircraft in flight, from a ground station, by wireless was an exciting prospect and one that had been occupying minds among the Royal Engineers at Aldershot. Work had begun as early as 1907 and was followed by experiments with a tethered balloon. In May 1908 a free run was made in the balloon *Pegasus* carrying a wireless receiver. While the balloon was over Petersfield, signals were received from Aldershot, 20 miles away. These experiments were quickly followed by attempts at sending messages from the balloon. In 1910, radio was used for the first time to communicate with an aircraft in flight, from a

ground station, during trials in the United States. The first air-to-ground transmission in England was made in 1911.

These matched experiments in other European countries and even earlier work had led to the discovery, in 1886, that radio waves had reflecting properties. By 1904, an experiment had indicated that this property might be used for the detection of objects. Consequently, the early days of this century indicated trends that were to be the basis of an eventual air defence system capable of providing detection, identification and a method of ensuring a system of command and control.

The airship was becoming a highly practical aircraft and, even as early as 1907, there were many who foresaw the threat of such a machine and accepted the likelihood that they could bomb the UK. By 1908, the Germans carried out wireless telegraphy trials in an airship, the aim of which was to ascertain if this would prove to have any dangerous effects upon the crew. Of course, there were no problems and a similar conclusion was reached through other experiments in France and Belgium. It was even

Order of Battle, November 1918

London Air Defence Area (LADA)

Wing	Squadron	Flight	Aircraft	Base
47	51	A	FE2b/d	Mattishall, Norfolk
		B	&	Tydd St.Mary, Lincs
		C	Sopwith F1 Camel	Marham, Norfolk
49	39		Bristol F2B Fighter	North Weald, Essex
	44		Sopwith F1 Camel	Hainault Farm, Essex
	78		Sopwith F1 Camel	Sutton's Farm, Essex
	141		Bristol F2B Fighter	Biggin Hill, Kent
50	37	A		Stow Maries, Essex
		B	Sopwith F1 Camel	Stow Maries, Essex
		C		Goldhangar, Essex
	61		Sopwith F1 Camel	Rochford, Essex
	75	A	Bristol F2B Fighter,	Hadleigh, Suffolk
		B	Sopwith F1 Camel	Elmswell, Suffolk
		C	& Avro 504K	Elmswell, Suffolk
53	50		Sopwith F1 Camel	Bekesborne, Kent
			SE5a *	Bekesborne, Kent
	112		Sopwith F1 Camel	Throwley, Kent
			& Sopwith Pup	
	143		Sopwith F1 Camel	Detling, Kent
			& SE5a	

Northern Air Defence Area (NADA)

Wing	Squadron	Flight	Aircraft	Base
46	36	A	Bristol F2B Fighter	Usworth, Co Durham
		B	&	Ashington, North'b'l'd
		C	Sopwith Pup **	Seaton Carew, Durham
	76	A	Bristol F2B Fighter	Copmanthorpe, Yorks
		B	&	Helperby, Yorks
		C	Avro 504K ***	Catterick, Yorks
	77	A		Whiteburn, Berwick
		B	Avro 504K	Penston, Midlothian
		C		Penston, Midlothian
48	33	A		Brattlesby, Lincs
		B	Avro 504K	Kirton-in-Lindsey, Lincs
		C		Elsham, Lincs
	90****	A		Leadenham, Lincs
		B	Avro 504K	Buckminster, Leics
		C		Wittering (Stamford), Northants

Notes:

*	SE5a received from November 1918
**	About to re-equip with Avro 504K
***	Some BE12b aircraft flown as well
****	Formed, initially, from a flight of 38 Sqn

being suggested, by 1909, that airships could be remotely controlled via radio links.

Whatever the politics of the time, the new technology was well on the road to war. Electromagnetic detection would take a few more years to evolve but radio was to revolutionise many aspects of the coming struggle.

Although 1918 was to prove to be the last year of the Great War, it was one of mixed fortunes for the Allies. April of that year marked a crisis in the land campaign in France and the following month saw the

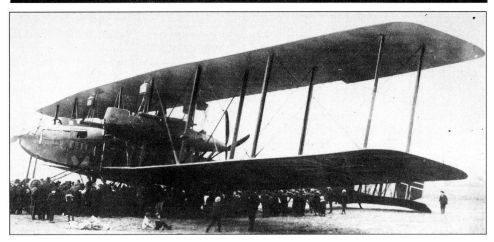

Right: This Zeppelin Staaken bomber was designated the RIV, R signifying *Riesenflugzeug* or Giant Aeroplane. Even by modern standards it is a large aircraft, as this picture shows. (RAeS)

heaviest German air raid of the war against London. It also proved to be the last against that city.

Over the previous four years, starting from a position of total unpreparedness, a defensive system had slowly been built up from hard-won experience, improved reliability of engines, improved ground facilities and a better approach to overall training. By the latter stages of the war, a more mature attitude to night flying also prevailed and a greater respect given to meteorological conditions. Airfield lighting was improving and the provision of gas-fired beacons offered a primitive homing aid. Flare-path techniques had evolved and patterned to give an indication of wind direction. The lighting had originally been a bucket of burning petrol but this had later given way to asbestos wound on a metal frame, dipped in paraffin and lit. Known as the Money Flare, it was to remain in service for many years.

An appreciation of the problems associated with night flying had led to the beginnings of instrument flying techniques. Aircraft were being fitted with landing lights and even a crude form of "electric" altimeter, whereby a trailing wire could activate a cockpit warning light at a certain height above the ground. Variable instrument panel lighting had also been developed. Flares were provided, both fixed to the aircraft and parachute-deployed, to assist the pilot in the event of a forced landing by night.

While these difficulties were being addressed, it still left the basic problem of actually detecting the incoming aircraft or airship. Interception of radio messages was a form of early warning and later in the war jamming was used to prevent the enemy airships receiving Direction Finding (DF) fixes. A body of ground observers was established,

initially using the police forces, but by the end of 1915 observer cordons provided by the local military were being established. Observer posts were set up to detect and attempt to track approaching intruders through visual and audible means. Such sites included lightships and lighthouses to offer the maximum warning, although this advantage was often lost through the communication links. Of course, this process had certain limitations due to meteorological variations and the airships could run their engines at idle power and take advantage of favourable winds to drift over the coast. Some of the observers' listening posts were partially staffed by volunteer, blind persons who were considered to have above-average aural acuity. By operating in pairs and communicating via land line, it was possible to obtain a fairly accurate fix on an approaching aircraft.

Searchlights offered a chance, on fairly clear nights, to pin-point the target for the anti-aircraft guns and also signal the position to patrolling British aircraft. The first airship to be actually illuminated over Britain was *LZ38*, which took part in a coastal raid on the night of 16/17 May 1915. Attempts were made to equip aircraft with some form of external lighting for target detection but these were not successful. Later attempts were made to develop a parachute-borne star shell which would enable ground gunners to provide the necessary illumination and an indication of the intruders' presence.

The need to improve the range of audible detection led to an experiment whereby a 16ft parabolic sound reflector was sited in a chalk cliff in Kent. Tests indicated that this could roughly halve the time of detection. More problematical was the continuing search for methods of communicating with the pilot. Radio technology was advancing but, in the interim, a number of ideas were put forward for ground signalling. By 1916, the Ingram "T" system was introduced. This involved a large letter "T" (the head measuring 20ft x 4ft , the tail 40ft x 4ft) being laid on the ground which could, by positioning up to three 8ft diameter discs in any of 40 positions, convey a message for the pilot to see. This system was fine for daylight but it still left the problem of communication at night. A lightweight airborne receiver eventually came along, together with complaints that its operation could interfere with the Royal Navy's DF stations. In retrospect, this seems to be a poor reason for objection in what should have been a matter for joint consultation and maximum co-operation.

A series of trials took place during the second half of 1916 using a number of different frequencies, the equipment was improved and plans were made for the use of airborne radio in the defence scheme. This was not yet to be, as the dawn of 1917 seemed to indicate a lessening of the Zeppelin threat to a point where cuts were made in the Home Defence organisation. Inter-service rivalry also appeared to have inhibited the more rapid application of radio techniques in an airborne role.

This optimism was soon shown to be misplaced, when improved versions of the German airships, able to operate at higher altitudes, entered service. Then, on 25 May, with complete surprise, a force of Gotha GIVs attacked Folkestone. This led to considerable recrimination with vociferous complaints about the lack of warning. Some blame was put upon inefficient ground communication links and raised, once more, the question of radio communication with the defending aircraft. Significantly, a new phase of daylight air attacks on Britain had begun.

The inevitable post-mortem and subsequent daylight attacks led to a wider use of radio and the opening of a transmitter, sited at Biggin Hill, which was the Wireless Experimental Establishment's test site. Two BE12s were fitted with transmitters which enabled them to indicate the position of enemy aircraft, allowing a tracking system to be established. The first recorded operational use of this system was in August 1917, during a Gotha daylight raid on coastal towns. Before the end of the year, the first night sighting had also been achieved. Despite these successes, in practical terms,

the aircraft lacked the necessary performance to intercept the intruders in time. Consequently, procedures for rapid notification of an evolving attack remained unsatisfactory, but it was another step along the way to what we now know as Airborne Early Warning (AEW) and Airborne Warning And Control System (AWACS) aircraft.

The Biggin Hill facility was also concerned with developing efficient direct-speech communications for both ground-to-air and air-to-air applications, as well as the creation of a training school.

Even though daylight, theoretically, aided visual detection, it could prove difficult as the aircraft now tended to fly higher and haze often made sighting difficult. At least one popular publication of the time suggested that it might be possible to treat the surfaces of a machine so that, when some distance from the ground, it would be practically invisible against the background of the sky. During 1917, the German Linke-Hofmann RI had a fuselage covered with transparent Cellon material, although there is no record of the effectiveness of such a covering in terms of camouflage.

As the improved air defences began to offer an increased effectiveness, the German tactics changed once more – to night attacks. It was back to the old problems of night flying techniques and good intelligence about the developing attacks. It also gave another stimulus to the use of sound-location techniques. A system was introduced which featured two large conical horns, rather in the manner of the classical ear trumpet. The operator used simple stethoscope ear pieces to pick up the magnified sound waves.

A four-horn version was also produced and both systems offered improved audible detection, giving a rough, though serviceable, indication of position in both azimuth and elevation. Experiments with large sound reflector surfaces were revived and a number of different types were deployed with some success. Greater use was being made of searchlights and the military was becoming increasingly aware of the need to integrate all of these different methods and ideas to create a more effective response to the night bomber. Real progress was slow but as the Great War entered its final year, improvements were added including more powerful searchlights, new gunfire tactics and gradually improving communication links.

By 1918, much of the early work in airborne radio communications was beginning to show practical results. This resulted in a greater use of receivers in aircraft and, also, a growing number of transmitters, though the latter were initially only fitted to flight commanders' aircraft. The creation of an effective command and control system was now a reality, with designated callsigns for both airfields and squadrons.

This process also led to reorganisation and improvements in the whole London Air Defence Area (LADA) and the emergence of a central operations room complete with plotters. Special dedicated telephone lines were connected to 25 sub-control rooms throughout the area. Each of these had direct links with the airfields, as well as gun and searchlight batteries, balloon sites and observer posts. At the main centre, Gun Liaison and Fighter Liaison officers were in attendance and a Police representative liaised with his own organisation and the fire brigades.

It was an impressive development which made full use of direct-voice communications and came into being just as the air-raids came to an end. It was never really tested in anger and, despite the years of neglect that then followed, it laid the foundations for an organisation that would evolve into the command and control system which proved so decisive in 1940.

RESPONSE: AIRCRAFT AND ARMAMENT

The descriptions and data presented on the aircraft relate to this year (1918). Basic early history is outlined for the model in service, but any subsequent developments and variants are not discussed.

Avro 504K

Better known as a training aircraft than a fighter, the Avro 504 series of aircraft also served in bomber and reconnaissance roles. The type's maiden flight was on 20 September 1913 and several versions were built before the 504K came along. Derived from the 504J, the main feature of the K-model was the ability to interchange engines between a 130hp Clerget, 110hp Le Rhone or the 100hp Gnome Monosoupape.

Early in 1918, the decision was made to equip the northern Home Defence squadrons with Avro 504Ks, powered by the 110hp Le Rhone engine, which gave it a ceiling of some 18,000ft. Flown as single-seat aircraft from the rear cockpit (the front cockpit being, invariably, faired over), its armament consisted of a single Lewis gun on a Foster mounting above the upper wing centre-section, with flare brackets fitted under the lower wings. The gravity fed fuel tank was moved from the centre section to the inboard section of the port wing, to make room for the Foster gun mounting. Some of these aircraft were fitted with the V-strut undercarriage, similar to that used on the Avro 521, in order to improve performance. Over 200 of the Home Defence 504Ks were produced.

Data: Avro 504K single-seat fighter variant

Powerplant	110hp Le Rhone
Span	36ft 0in
Length	29ft 5in
Height	10ft 5in
Wing area	330sq ft
Empty weight	1,231lb
Loaded weight	1,829lb
Maximum speed	95mph at sea level, 87mph at 8,000ft
Time to height	5min to 3,500ft, 16min to 10,000ft
Service ceiling	18,000ft
Armament	one 0.303in Lewis machine gun, plus flares

Bristol F2B

Otherwise known as the Bristol Fighter, "Brisfit" or "Biff", the F2B became one of the mainstays of the RAF in its formative years. Its origins in 1915, however, began as a replacement for the BE2c in the corps reconnaissance and artillery-spotting role (for which the RE8 was also conceived).

Designed by Frank Barnwell, as the R2A, it was a tandem two-seat, equal-span biplane powered by a 120hp Beardmore engine. The pilot was given a forward-firing fixed Lewis gun and the observer another Lewis gun on an Eteve rotating mounting. A refinement, designated R2B, was powered by the 150hp Hispano-Suiza engine, had unequal-span wings with strut-braced extensions.

A further re-design saw the 190hp Rolls-Royce Mk I engine installed and the wings revert to equal span. The fuselage was re-designed, giving a downward curve towards the tailplane. The engine installation, with two tall flank radiators at the rear of the engine, was considered clumsy. While the observer's Lewis gun was retained (but with a Scarff-mounting), the pilot was given a fixed Vickers gun, firing through a tunnel in the forward petrol tank, down the centreline of the aircraft. This third variant was designated F2A, reflecting the change of emphasis in role to fighter-reconnaissance, making its maiden flight on 9 September 1916. Two prototypes and 50 production aircraft were ordered.

The first prototype F2A (A3303) saw action on 7 July 1916, when it became one of some 90 aircraft which were sent to attack the German Gotha formation which attacked London that day. Although both aircrew (pilot Lt F. D. Holder and observer Lt F.W. Musson) fired their guns at the enemy, they were unable to close in and abandoned the chase through lack of fuel. Production aircraft eventually went to France in March 1917.

There, they were used in the classic two-seater role, with disastrous results. However, some pilots began to use the F2A in the manner of a single-seater, concentrating on the forward gun and leaving the observer to protect the rear, and these tactics proved successful. The aircraft came to be referred to as the Bristol Fighter.

By December 1916, the second prototype F2A had been further modified, improving the pilot's forward vision and allowing for the installation of a larger, upper petrol tank and an ammunition box for the Vickers gun. A lower centre-section plane was also created. These modifications were incorporated for the second batch of 200 aircraft ordered, being re-designated F2B.

The first 150 F2Bs had the Rolls-Royce Mk I engine (later christened the Falcon I) but the 200hp Falcon II and 275hp Falcon III versions followed, as they became available. During mid-1917, an improved tailplane, of smaller size but higher aspect ratio was fitted. Other engine options were trialled and it had been decided to standardise on the 200hp Sunbeam Arab but the war was over before quantity deliveries were available.

The Bristol F2B entered service with the Home Defence force, with No 39 Squadron RFC, in September 1917 and, subsequently, with four other RAF units in 1918. Interestingly some of these aircraft used a system of sighting the observer's gun by the pilot, by means of a special sight mounted on the centre section. Illuminated gun sights were also used at this time. Some 4,747 F2Bs were built up to September 1919. After the war, the RAF flew the F2B up to 1927 at home and 1932 abroad (the last unit being No 6 Squadron in Iraq).

Data: Bristol F2B

Powerplant	275hp Rolls-Royce Falcon III
Span	39ft 3in
Length	25ft 10in
Height	9ft 9in
Wing area	405.6sq ft
Empty weight	1,934lb
Loaded weight	2,779lb
Maximum speed	104mph at 10,000ft, 94mph at 15,000ft
Time to height	14min 25sec to 10,000ft, 25min 45sec to 15,000ft
Service ceiling	17,000ft
Armament	one 0.303in Vickers machine gun; one or two 0.303in Lewis machine guns on Scarff ring mounting; up to 12 x 25lb Cooper bombs

Royal Aircraft Factory BE12b

The Royal Aircraft Factory (which subsequently became the Royal Aircraft Establishment, then the Royal Aerospace Establishment and now merged with several other government R&D establishments to form one corporate organisation entitled the Defence Research Agency – DRA) produced a series of aircraft under the designation Bleriot Experimental (BE) by way of acknowledgement of Bleriot's expertise as the leading pioneer of tractor aeroplanes.

The BE2 series was designed by Geoffrey de Havilland (who subsequently founded his own company) and the BE2 flew before the outbreak of the First World War, on 11 February 1912. It was a biplane of conventional format with a 60hp Renault engine. The BE12 was essentially a BE2c model fitted with the Royal Aircraft Factory's 140hp Mk 4a engine and a V-type undercarriage. It made its maiden flight on 28 July 1915. The BE12a was a similar modification on the BE2e airframe. By 1916, a number of BE12s had been allocated to the Home Defence force and on 17 June 1916, Lt L. P. Watkins of No 37 Squadron RFC, shot down the Zeppelin L48 in aircraft No 6610.

By September 1917, although the Royal Aircraft Factory was installing a 200hp Hispano-Suiza engine, as used on the SE5a, into a BE12 so, too, was the Southern Aircraft Repair Depot (SARD), also located at Farnborough. An agreement was reached, whereby the SARD would proceed, with assistance from the Royal Aircraft Factory.

The added power enabled the aircraft to reach the altitudes to which the Zeppelins were regularly ascending in order to escape British fighters. As the Hispano-Suiza engine was in short supply, the allocation of the BE12b to Home Defence emphasised the seriousness of the situation. It was planned that 150 out of 200 BE12a's would be completed as BE12b's. In the event only 36 BE12bs were issued to the Home Defence forces by 1918 and it is not known if – but considered doubtful – the type ever saw action against German Gotha or Giant bombers.

Data: BE12a

Powerplant   140hp RAF Mk 4a (No official performance trials of the BE12e are thought to exist, although – compared with the BE12 – it was understood to be "quite spectacular".) Known data on the BE12/a/b is annotated accordingly)

Span	(BE12/12b)	37ft 0in
Length	(BE12/12b)	27ft 3in
Height	(BE12)	11ft 1.5in
Wing area	(BE12b)	371sq ft
Empty weight	(BE12a)	1,610lb
Loaded weight	(BE12a)	2,327lb
Maximum speed	(BE12a)	105mph at sea level, 91.5mph at 6,500ft, 80.5mph at 10,000ft
Time to height	(BE12a)	9min 10sec to 5,000ft, 24min 15sec to 10,000ft
Service ceiling	(BE12)	12,500ft
Endurance	(BE12)	3hrs
Armament	(BE12b)	one or two

0.303in Lewis machine guns, plus facility to carry bombs

Royal Aircraft Factory FE2b/d

The designation FE refers to Farman Experimental, acknowledging Henri Farman's expertise in pusher aircraft (in the same way as BE acknowledged Bleriot). The FE2, originally designed by Geoffrey de Havilland, was a biplane with accommodation provided for two pilots in tandem in a central nacelle, powered by a 50hp Gnome engine, in pusher configuration, behind them and twin booms joining at a rectangular tailplane mounted above the upper booms. Having the propeller arc aft of the crew meant that forward-firing weapons could be mounted on the aircraft. The first FE2 flew on 18 August 1911.

The FE2a was a new and larger aircraft with three-bay wings, a wide-span centre-section and outer wing panels common to the BE2c. The entire trailing edge of the upper centre-section could be lowered as an airbrake, while the main undercarriage was a substantial oleo type, with a small nose-wheel. The initial powerplant was a 100hp Green six-cylinder, in-line, water-cooled engine; but this gave way to a 120hp Austro-Daimler (Beardmore) engine of similar configuration (as used on the RE5). The pilot sat in the upper, rear seat, with the observer in the lower forward cockpit, armed with a single Lewis gun on a No 2 Mk I mounting.

On the FE2b, the airbrake flap on the centre-section was deleted and a simpler gravity petrol tank of 33gal capacity (three gallons smaller that the FE2a) was installed. A 160hp Beardmore engine was later installed, together with an extra 18gal tank below the pilot's seat. While the oleo undercarriage was sturdy, the V-type was also used on a number of aircraft, as was a development by Lt Trafford Jones of No 20 Squadron, which removed the nosewheel and took its horizontal struts up to the lower nacelle longerons.

Several different gun mountings were used on the FE2b, culminating with the No 4 Mk IV mounting and, between the two cockpits, an Anderson telescopic mounting, enabling the observer to stand up and fire rearwards over the wing. This was to prove somewhat risky at times although he was secured to the aircraft by a safety strap. For use by the Home Defence squadrons, some of the FE2bs were converted to single-seat configuration and armed with a variety of weapons. Despite trialling double-yoked twin Lewis guns, a 0.45in Maxim gun and a Vickers 1-pdr quick-firing gun, sometimes known as the "pom-pom", the single Lewis gun remained the standard armament. The Vickers pom-pom, however, was used by five aircraft of No 51 (Home Defence) Squadron. These aircraft had the 160hp engine and a much-modified nacelle to accommodate the heavier weapons and the 40-round belts of ammunition. One aircraft (A781) was fitted with a searchlight with a Lewis gun mounted on either side, the intention being to keep the target illuminated during firing. Electrical power was provided by a small, air driven generator mounted beneath the nacelle.

The other major variant of the FE2 series used for Home Defence was the FE2d, essentially a 2b powered by a 250hp Rolls-

Royce engine. Its performance was not found to be good enough to counter the various German airships. On the night of 13 March 1918, an FE2d of No 36 Squadron – flown by 2/Lt E. C.Morris, with 2/Lt R. D. Linford as observer – reached 17,300ft over Hartlepool during an attack on a Zeppelin (*L42*). Although both aircrew fired on the airship, they could not close the distance between them to attack effectively. This typical experience of the FE2d explains why it saw only limited employment with the Home Defence squadrons.

Nevertheless, the fact that the FE2b and 2d were still in service in 1918, having been in continual development throughout the war, is a testimony to the type's ruggedness. Although it does not fall within the context of this work, it must be said that the FE2 also served as a bomber.

Data: Common to FE2b and 2d

Span	47ft 9in
Length	32ft 3in
Height	12ft 7.5in
Wing area	494sq ft

FE2b with 160hp Beardmore engine

Empty weight	2,061lb
Loaded weight	3,037lb
Maximum speed	91.5mph at sea level, 81mph at 6,500ft, 76mph at 10,000ft
Time to height	7min 24sec to 3,000ft, 39min 44sec to 10,000ft
Service ceiling	11,000ft
Armament	one or two 0.303in Lewis machine guns; up to 350lb of bombs

FE2d with 250hp Rolls-Royce Mk I engine

Empty weight	2,509lb
Loaded weight	3,469lb
Maximum speed	94mph at 5,000ft, 88mph at 10,000ft
Time to height	7min 10sec to 5,000ft, 18min 20sec to 10,000ft
Service ceiling	17,500ft
Endurance	3.5hrs
Armament	one or two fixed 0.303in Lewis machine guns; one or two free-mounted Lewis guns; up to six 20lb or 25lb bombs

Royal Aircraft Factory SE5a

History is unsure of the exact origins of the SE5. Some sources suggest that the Royal Aircraft Factory at Farnborough was invited, by General Sir Sefton Brancker, to design a single-seat fighter around the Hispano-Suiza engine, to a specification set out by Major-General Hugh Trenchard early in 1916. Other sources suggest that the Factory had already designed such an aircraft, initiated by Frank Gooden and later refined by H. P. Folland. Whichever version is true, no doubt remains that Folland assumed overall design responsibility early in the project. Certainly the catalyst was a British order for 50 engines, following the recommendation of Lt-Col H.R.M. Brooke-Popham who had inspected the engine in Paris during the summer of 1915.

The basic design work had been completed by June 1916 and was a simple but classic single-bay biplane, with a tail unit adapted from the contemporary FE10. The equal-span wings had raked tips and the airframe was wire-braced and fabric-covered. Although no armament was fitted to the first example, which made its maiden flight on 22 November 1916, a single fixed Vickers machine gun was mounted on the forward, port decking of the fuselage, firing through the propeller which was synchronised by a Constantinesco hydraulic mechanism, with a single Lewis gun on a Foster overwing mounting. A large windscreen was fitted and, after using a leading-edge fuel tank initially, an overwing gravity tank was accepted as standard.

The first production SE5, of a batch of 50 aircraft, was delivered to the Aircraft Experimental Establishment at Martlesham Heath. There, its lateral control was criticised. Wingspan was reduced and the aileron control improved as a result. At the same time, the 200hp Hispano-Suiza 8BCa engine was fitted and these three modifications between them bought forth the SE5a, deliveries being made from July 1917. All existing SE5s were later converted to the new configuration, using the Hispano-Suiza engine or British-built versions. The SE5a entered large scale production in February 1917.

There were several problems with the various engine configurations, but these were eventually resolved and the 200hp Wolseley Viper was extensively used by aircraft deployed to France. Other airframe modifications were made to the fin and mainplane trailing edges and undercarriage struts but, again, these were resolved. The SE5a went on to acquire a first-class reputation as a stable gun-platform and for its strength. Only three Home Defence squadrons were equipped with the type yet, in France, many of the leading fighter pilots, including Bishop and Mannock, flew and fought in it with success. The aircraft was considered to be less than suitable in the home defence role because the liquid cooled engine required a longer ground run-up than the air cooled engines, thereby increasing its reaction time for a quick take-off.

Data: SE5a

Powerplants 150hp then 200hp Hispano-Suiza 8BCa, 200hp Wolseley Viper, 200hp Wolseley Adder I (not all engine options are shown)

Span	(originally) 27ft 11in, (later) 26ft 7.4in
Length	20ft 11in
Height	9ft 6in
Wing area	(originally) 249sq ft, (later) 244sq ft
Empty weight	(150hp Hispano-Suiza) 1,399lb
Loaded weight	(150hp Hispano-Suiza) 1,953lb (200hp Wolseley Adder) 2,048lb
Maximum speed	(150hp Hispano-Suiza) 114mph at 10,000ft, 98mph at 15,000ft; (200hp Wolseley Adder) 126mph at 10,000ft, 116.5mph at 15,000ft
Armament	one fixed 0.303in Vickers machine gun and one overwing Foster mounted 0.303in Lewis machine gun, plus four 25lb Cooper bombs

Sopwith Type 9700 – the 1½-Strutter

Originally designed for the Admiralty, the Sopwith Type 9700, powered by a 110hp Clerget 9Z engine, used a W-form cabane bracing arrangement originally seen on the company's "Sigristbus". The aeroplane was more usually known by its unofficial nickname of the "1½-Strutter". This two-seater featured widely separated cockpits, yet was originally designed to be armed with only a single Lewis gun in the rear cockpit. This was to be fitted on a rotating and elevating mounting, which would allow the gunner to fire forward over the upper wing.

The prototype was completed in December 1915 and, unusually for its time, was considered small and compact. It was equipped with airbrakes on the trailing edge of the lower centre-section of the wings, in anticipation of the flat-glide characteristics expected. It was ordered into production almost immediately in both two-seat fighter and single-seat bomber configuration. Flight testing began in January 1916 and a report on its speed trials was passed to the RFC. While some doubt was expressed regarding its structure, its flying qualities were praised. It was ordered for the RFC in March 1916. About this time, a Vickers gun was fixed in a forward-firing mounting, using interrupter gear, and the concept of the two-seat fighter as epitomised by the Bristol F2B was born.

The events taking place in France, which led to the Somme offensive in July 1916, prompted the RFC to request more aircraft and many 1½-Strutters were transferred from the RNAS to the RFC. Some aircraft were improved by fitting a 130hp Clerget 9B engine. Problems were experienced when mounting the Vickers gun on the aircraft, which were eventually overcome, and a Scarff mounting was adopted for the rear Lewis gun. Once in combat, however, the 1½-Strutter was found to be

Below: Some 56 examples of the Sopwith LCT, alias the "1½ Strutter", were pressed into Home Defence service in 1917, having been outclassed as a fighter on the Western Front. (BAe)

outclassed as a fighter and many were modified as bombers but, without an adequate bomb sight, this version did not see operational service.

During the summer of 1917, some 56 two-seat and three single-seat 1½-Strutters were allocated to Home Defence squadrons. At least one of the two-seaters was converted to single-seat configuration, the pilot occupying what had been the rear cockpit. The armament varied on and within the squadrons: some using a single Lewis gun, others a double-yoke arrangement on a Foster over-wing mounting. These converted aircraft became known, somewhat irreverently, as Sopwith "Comics".

Data: 1½-Strutter

Powerplant	110hp Clerget 9Z
Span	33ft 6in
Length	25ft 3in
Height	10ft 3in
Wing area	346sq ft
Empty weight	1,259lb
Loaded weight	2,149lb
Maximum speed	100.5mph at 6,500ft,
	96.5mph at 10,000ft
Armament	one 0.303in Vickers

machine gun and one 0.303in Lewis machine gun plus four 25lb bombs. Home Defence aircraft had either two Lewis guns or one Vickers and one Lewis gun

Sopwith Pup

Originally developed from Harry Hawker's Runabout, this new Sopwith fighter was powered by an 80hp Le Rhone engine and armed with a single, forward-firing and synchronised Vickers machine gun. The prototype was passed for flight on 9 February 1916 and details passed to the RNAS, with a copy to the RFC.

The RFC ordered the Sopwith Scout (as it was officially known, being designated Type 9901 by the Admiralty) in April 1916 but the aircraft soon became known, unofficially, as the "Pup" and the name stuck. It entered RFC service in late August/early September 1916 and first examples were sent to France in December 1916.

Initially fitted with a variable-incidence tailplane, from January 1917 Pups were being delivered with fixed tailplanes. Stronger centre-section mainplane struts were soon found to be needed and were fitted. Although only modestly powered, the Pup was found to be exceptional in maintaining height during dog-fights and this manoeuvrability was one of the reasons for keeping numbers in service long after they had been outclassed in France.

In April 1917, a 100hp Gnome Monosoupape was installed in a Pup, on the assumption that more power would improve performance and many Pups were so-modi-

Below: The Sopwith Pup, illustrated here by a preserved example still flying, was considered to be underpowered. Use of the Pup by the Home Defence force was limited. (BAe)

fied. Even so, operational use of this version of the Pup appears to have been limited to the Home Defence squadrons equipped with the type, as the extra 20hp did not drastically improve the performance over the standard Pup, though it improved its rate of climb which enhanced its role as an interceptor. However, attempts to fit a Lewis gun to fire over the top of the wing proved unsuccessful.

Data: Pup

Powerplants	80hp Le Rhone 9C or 100hp Gnome Mono-soupape
Span	26ft 6in
Length	19ft 3.75in
Height	9ft 5in
Wing area	254sq ft
Empty weight	787lb (Le Rhone), 856lb (Gnome)
Loaded weight	1,225lb (Le Rhone), 1,297lb (Gnome)
Maximum speed	111.5mph at sea level (Le Rhone), 102mph at 10,000ft (Le Rhone), 104mph at 10,000ft (Gnome)
Time to height	6min 25sec to 5,000ft (Le Rhone), 16min 25sec to 10,000ft, 5min 12sec to 5,000ft (Gnome), 12min
Service ceiling	24sec to 10,000ft 17,500ft (Le Rhone), 18,500ft (Gnome)
Endurance	3hr (Le Rhone), 1.75hr (Gnome)
Armament	One 0.303in Vickers machine gun; sometimes a single 0.303in Lewis machine gun; plus some provision for 25lb Cooper bombs

Sopwith F1 Camel

When flown by an experienced pilot, the Sopwith F1 Camel was an effective and manoeuvrable fighter aircraft, yet inexperience or incompetent handling led to an unforgiving reputation. It became the First World War's equivalent of the Spitfire.

The first design of the Sopwith F1, powered by a 110hp Clerget 9Z engine, with the pilot hunched under the upper mainplane centre-section – giving a squat appearance – was passed on 22 December 1916. Armed with a pair of forward-firing, Vickers machine guns, it bore a similarity to the Pup but with a deeper fuselage. Two prototypes were delivered to the Admiralty and one, designated F1/3, to the RFC. The latter had been tested by February 1917. Problems were discovered with upward vision (and a rectangular hole was eventually cut into the centre-section to remedy this) and also with the feed mechanism of the starboard gun.

Below: The Sopwith F1 Camel, retrospectively known as "the Spitfire of the First World War" and a successful fighter over the Western Front, only saw limited use in Home Defence and had been withdrawn by the summer of 1918. (BAe)

Production began in April 1917 and RFC Camels were powered by either a 110hp Le Rhone or 130hp Clerget engine (supply problems were encountered with this powerplant); the RNAS received aircraft powered by the 150hp Bentley BR1 engine. By the middle of the year, Camels of all persuasions were being deployed to France and, despite the enthusiasm for its fighting qualities, its performance fell below official figures, especially with the Clerget-powered variants.

The Camel was earmarked for the Home Defence force from July 1917, as a response to the German air attacks on London on 13 June and 7 July that year. Initially Clerget-powered aircraft were delivered, but later the Le Rhone-powered Camel became standard.

Despite its sensitive flying qualities, it was successfully flown by night. However, it was soon discovered that once pilots fired the guns, the muzzle flash "blinded" their night vision. This rather basic problem was overcome with the development of a new variant with the cockpit moved further aft and a pair of Lewis guns fitted above the upper wing on a special double Foster mounting. To improve visibility for the pilot the centre section cut-out was enlarged and in some cases, additional cut-outs were made in the lower wing roots, though these modifications inevitably affected the aircraft's performance.

Data: Camel

Powerplant	110hp Le Rhone 9J or 130hp Clerget 9B
Span	28ft 0in
Length	18ft 8in (Le Rhone)
Height	8ft 6in
Wing area	231sq ft
Empty weight	962lb (Clerget)
Loaded weight	1,482lb (Clerget), 1,422lb (Le Rhone)
Maximum speed	108mph at 6,500ft (Clerget), 97.5mph at 15,000ft (Clerget), 111.5mph at 15,000ft (Le Rhone)
Time to height	6min 40sec to 6,500ft (Clerget), 5min 10sec to 6,500ft (Le Rhone), 23min 15sec to 15,000ft (Clerget), 16min 50sec to 15,000ft (Le Rhone)
Service ceiling	18,500ft (Clerget), 24,000ft (Le Rhone)
Armament	two 0.303in Vickers

machine guns or (in the Home Defence night-fighter) two 0.303in Lewis guns; plus up to four 25lb Cooper bombs

Sopwith 5F1 Dolphin

Although it did not enjoy the fame or ubiquity of either the Camel or the SE5/5a, the Sopwith 5F1 Dolphin was probably the most potent fighter the RFC received prior to the establishment of the RAF.

During initial manufacturer's trials on 22 May 1917, powered by a 200hp Hispano-Suiza engine, it recorded an indicated air speed of 116-118kts (some 143.88 – 146.18mph) at a height of 5,000ft: startling figures for its day. Indeed it was a startling aircraft. Sopwith designer, Herbert Smith, began with the premise of placing the pilot's head in the middle of the open centre-section of the upper wing and, as a result, he adopted a negative stagger on the mainplanes. The pilot got his superlative view and his twin Vickers machines guns were close to hand (for unjamming in flight, when necessary). The tail unit was reminiscent of the Camel.

First impressions of the aircraft were good. Capt W. A. (Billy) Bishop, who flew the first prototype in June 1917, said of its "handiness"..."the machine is extraordinarily quick on turns and very handy". Of the view, he commented that it was... "very good", while of the speed ..."with the engine only giving 2,000 revolutions the speed at 2,000ft was 106kts which is equal to 122mph". Even so, Trenchard was of the opinion that the SE5 should stand as the RFC's primary fighting scout, although he requested the Dolphin as a better option than the French 200hp Spad ..."provided that the delivery is not later than the 200 Spad would be". Perhaps the look of the Dolphin belied its performance.

That said, some 500 Dolphins were ordered in mid-June with further contracts being awarded up to September 1918. The Aircraft Experimental Establishment at Martlesham Heath had criticised the Dolphin's radiator configuration and considered improvements were needed in its rudder control. Three more prototypes were built, the fourth representing the production configuration, which included provision for one or two upward firing Lewis guns forward of the cockpit but aft of the Vickers guns, thereby making it the first British multi-gun fighter.

As the aircraft began to be flown to France, they were greeted with enthusiasm by all the pilots who flew them. Typical is the reaction of Maj Sanday of No 19 Squadron, who began to receive the aircraft from November 1917, and who reported that it ..."seems to handle perfectly at all heights, and does not lose any of its controllability at 15,000ft, the view is perfect and the machine easy to fly. Twelve pilots of this squadron have flown it and were delighted with the machine." The squadron had re-equipped from the Spad 7 by 9 January 1918. By May 1918, three units (Nos 19, 23 and 79 Squadrons) had been equipped with the aircraft. Although 12 squadrons were planned, only one more unit (No 87 Squadron) took the Dolphin to war in France.

By January 1918, the front main spar butt attachments were being strengthened on all aircraft, as a result of an accident due to failure of a lower wing attachment. No subsequent Dolphin was structurally suspect after this modification. Some minor problems continued with the radiator, but were solved. The engine problems of the SE5a (oil leaks, specifically) continued to plague the Dolphin and a direct-drive Hispano engine was fitted, to make this the Dolphin III. The Dolphin II, powered by a 300hp Hispano-Suiza, was adopted by France but never entered service.

Seven Dolphins were allocated to No 141 Squadron of the Home Defence force early in 1918 but, unfortunately, were not popular for night flying due to the temperamental nature of the Hispano-Suiza engine, its protracted warm up time due to liquid cooling and an increased risk of overturning at night. This was the one drawback of the Dolphin that was never, properly, rectified, although an escape hatch for the pilot, for just such an eventuality, was incorporated in the port fuselage and half hoops of steel tubing mounted above the top wings to offer protection for the pilot's head.

Data: Dolphin

Powerplant	200hp Hispano-Suiza 8Ba
Span	32ft 6in
Length	22ft 3in
Height	8ft 6in
Wing area	263.25sq ft
Empty weight	1,350lb (1st prototype)
Loaded weight	1,880lb (1st prototype), 2,003lb
Maximum speed (1st prototype);	112.5mph at 10,000ft
(1st prototype);	116mph at 15,000ft
(1st prototype);	119.5mph at 15,000ft
Time to height	5min 30sec to 6,500ft
(1st prototype);	6min 25sec to 6,500ft, 11min 0sec to 10,000ft, 20min 12sec to 15,000ft
Service ceiling	21,500ft (1st prototype)
Endurance	2.25hrs (1st prototype)
Armament	two fixed 0.303in Vickers machine guns; one (occasionally two) semi-free 0.303in Lewis machine gun; plus four 25lb Cooper bombs

RESPONSE: ANTI-AIRCRAFT ARTILLERY

The London Air Defence Area began 1918 with a grand total of 323 searchlights and 249 guns (see accompanying table for breakdown). By April, the number of searchlights had increased to 353 (including those distributed below the aeroplane patrol lines) and the guns to 266, plus 35 sound-locators.

It was a far cry from the first pieces of British artillery ever to be specifically installed for air defence in 1912 – two 6in, 30cwt siege howitzers emplaced close to Chattenden Ammunition Depot, Kent. These unlikely weapons were selected simply because they were the only artillery which could elevate sufficiently to threaten an aircraft. Anti-aircraft artillery (later to become known within the military by its acronym, AAA – "Triple-A") was another branch of military technology which was to make prodigious steps forward during the First World War.

AAA-fire was more universally referred to by the aircrew of that war, and beyond until 1939, as "Archie". How anti-aircraft fire (and, by association, the guns themselves) obtained this affectionate nickname is explained by one of the leading authorities on artillery, Ian V. Hogg, in his book *Anti-Aircraft – a history of air defence.*

"The story goes that a young British pilot flying over the German lines used to express his distain for the shells which burst all around him by using the 'punchline' from a music-hall song of the day; as his aircraft rocked to the blast, he would sing out 'Archibald – certainly NOT!'. The story got about, as such stories do, and before long, all anti-aircraft guns were known as 'Archibald', shortened, in due course, to 'Archie'."

However in 1912, before AAA became commonplace, the Royal Gun Factory at Woolwich Arsenal began work on a 3in anti-aircraft (or, as it was then known, "High Angle") gun, which entered service in March 1914 as the 3in Mk 1. Due to the later proliferation of various types of 3in guns, in 1915, this became the "3in 20cwt", the latter value being the weight of the barrel and breech. It was introduced as a "common service" – ie, Army and Navy – weapon and large numbers were installed in warships.

In August 1914, there were 33 anti-aircraft guns in British service: one 4in, four 3in, and 28 1pdr Maxim "Pom-pom" guns. During the course of the war, almost every possible gun was tried as an air defence weapon – from the "Pom-pom" to 6in naval guns – and the private gun-makers turned out their store rooms to contribute many peculiar designs.

At the end of the First World War, the total number of guns delivered on regular contracts (ie, excluding the odds and ends produced out of stock by gunmakers) were as follows: 13pdr 9cwt – 724; 3in 20cwt – 541; 4in – 55. To these figures should be added the 302 13pdr 9cwt and 53 3in 20cwt guns which had been repaired and put back into service. As an example of the quantity of ammunition demanded by AAA, the 13pdr 9cwt guns had swallowed some 2,458,500 high-explosive shells, 1,361,400 shrapnel shells and 33,400 incendiary shells by November 1918.

The guns listed below are those which were "approved armament" and existed in some numbers.

75mm Autocannon
This was the French 75mm field gun with a high-angle mounting, equipping a DeDion-Bouton lorry. The reason for its adoption was that, in 1915, no British gun could fire high-explosive (HE) shells due to the absence of a suitable bore-safe time fuze. The swiftest solution to the need for AAA was to adopt the French gun.

About 12 of these French-made guns were brought to the UK late in 1915 for the defence of London. A number of barrels and recoil systems were also bought and the Coventry Ordnance Works mounted most of them on British lorries. A few guns were fitted to revolving-platform mountings and emplaced in various sites close to London. It was retained in service until 1920.

Data: 75mm Autocannon
Calibre	75mm
Type of mounting	vehicle

Weight in action	not known
Max elevation	70°
Effective ceiling	not known
Weight of shell	12.25lb
Type of shell	HE (Melinite)
Muzzle velocity	ca 1,900ft/sec
Rate of fire	12rds/min

3in 5cwt Mk 1
Like most gunmakers, Sir William Armstrong's Elswick Ordnance Company had been experimenting with anti-aircraft guns before the war. In 1915, when the War Office asked all gunmakers for any suitable designs which they might have, Elswick offered four of these light guns on pedestal mountings. They were tested in July 1915 and, found suitable, they were adopted and more were requested. Eight more were built and issued in 1916.

Of the 12 guns in service, six were mounted on lorries and the remainder were ground-emplaced. All were primarily used for the defence of Naval Dockyards. Their performance was marginal, at best, and all were scrapped as soon as the war ended.

Data: 3in 5cwt Mk 1
Calibre	3in
Type of mounting	pedestal
Weight in action	18cwt
Max elevation	79°
Effective ceiling	not known
Weight of shell	12.5lb
Type of shell	time-fuzed shrapnel
Muzzle velocity	1,640ft/sec
Rate of fire	10rds/min 3in

20cwt Mks 1 to 3
As noted above, these were the first "purpose-built" British anti-aircraft guns to be designed and were built in large numbers. The first patterns were quite advanced for their day, and featured a semi-automatic sliding block breech mechanism and a wheeled travelling platform with stabilising outriggers. Many were also installed on lorries and on naval mountings for shipboard use.

The original design was somewhat too elegant for rapid wartime production and several manufacturing modifications appeared with a total of 16 "Marks", or patterns, eventually seeing service. Originally firing a time-fuzed shrapnel shell, it was later given HE and "anti-Zeppelin" (incendiary) projectiles. Wartime ammunition production totalled 976,800 HE, 240,100 shrapnel and 75,700 incendiary shells.

Data: 20cwt Mks 1 to 3

Calibre	3in
Type of mounting	pedestal static, cruci-form mobile or lorry
Weight in action	5 ton 19cwt on mobile platform
Max elevation	90°
Effective ceiling	23,500ft with 12.5lb shell
Weight of shell	12.5lb or 16lb
Type of shell	HE (12.5lb) or shrapnel (16lb)
Muzzle velocity	2,500ft/sec
Rate of fire	12rds/min

13pdr 6cwt AA Gun Mk 3

This was the standard Royal Horse Artillery field gun, selected because it threw a useful size of shell and because they were less and less needed on the Western Front, where the 18pdr field gun became the standard. The mounting was a simple pedestal in the back of a Peerless or other lorry. Introduced in November 1914, they remained in service throughout the war. Those which survived were re-converted back into field guns in 1919; some are still in use today with The King's Troop, RHA, for ceremonial purposes.

Data: 13pdr 6cwt AA Gun Mk 3

Calibre	3in
Type of mounting	pedestal on motor lorry
Weight in action	7 tons inc lorry
Max elevation	70°
Effective ceiling	17,000ft
Weight of shell	13lb
Type of shell	Shrapnel
Muzzle velocity	1,700ft/sec
Rate of fire	12rds/min

13pdr 9cwt AA Gun Mk 1

An attempt to convert the 18pdr field gun in the same way as the 13pdr was a failure, due to the ballistic unsuitability of the shell. So in order to obtain greater velocity, the 18pdr was reduced in calibre from 3.3in to 3in by the insertion of a barrel-liner, while a new round of ammunition, using the 13pdr shell and the 18pdr cartridge, was developed. This became the 13pdr 9cwt gun and was a very good weapon.

Introduced in November 1916, it remained in British service until 1921 (and continued in Canadian and Dutch service until the early 1930s). The mounting was a pedestal on a motor lorry, like the 13pdr 6cwt, but stronger. A variant model, the 13pdr 9cwt "A" gun, was the same gun but on a mounting derived from the 3in 20cwt. Only a few were built before the war ended.

Data: 13pdr 9cwt AA Gun Mk 1

Calibre	3in
Type of mounting	pedestal on motor lorry
Weight in action	7.5 tons inc lorry
Max elevation	80°
Effective ceiling	19,000ft
Weight of shell	13lb
Type of shell	shrapnel
Muzzle velocity	2,150ft/sec
Rate of fire	12rds/min

12pdr 12cwt Mk 1* High Angle

This was a coastal defence anti-MTB (Motor Torpedo Boat) – or fast attack craft in today's parlance – weapon with modifications made to its standard pedestal mounting to allow it the required high elevation. It was used on static mountings and, also, on a two-wheeled platform with outriggers for

Right: The lorry-mounted 13pdr/9cwt AA gun, seen here in action at night, was first used in 1916 and remained in British service until 1921. (Via Ian Hogg)

mobile deployment. It was introduced late in 1915 and remained in service until 1920, after which the guns were re-converted back to their original role.

Data: 12pdr 12cwt Mk 1* High Angle

Calibre	3in
Type of mounting	pedestal on mobile, cruciform mounting
Weight in action	5 tons
Max elevation	85°
Effective ceiling	20,000ft
Weight of shell	12.5lb
Type of shell	HE
Muzzle velocity	2,200ft/sec
Rate of fire	10rds/min

Ordnance QF 3.6in Gun Mk 1

Had the war continued, this would have been the standard AAA gun in British service. Developed to meet a 1917 demand for a new gun, it was an outstanding weapon for its day. As it was, only four were made before the war ended and postwar penury soon stopped further production; probably no more than a dozen were completed.

There were two versions: a static pedestal mounting and a mobile version on a tracked trailer with outriggers. Formally introduced in September 1918, it was declared obsolete in November 1927.

Data: Ordnance QF 3.6in Gun Mk 1

Calibre	3.6in
Type of mounting	pedestal static or tracked mobile
Weight in action	not known
Max elevation	85°
Effective ceiling	25,000ft
Weight of shell	25lb
Type of shell	HE
Muzzle velocity	not known
Rate of fire	ca 15rds/min

4.5in Gun Mk 5

This was another powerful naval and coastal defence gun adopted for AAA use. Again, fitted to a pedestal mounting, it was emplaced, principally, around Naval bases and dockyards. All AAA versions were dismantled and returned to their original use in 1919.

Data: 4.5in Gun Mk 5

Calibre	4.5in
Type of mounting	pedestal static
Weight in action	6 tons 16cwt
Max elevation	80°
Effective ceiling	28,750ft

Weight of shell	31lb
Type of shell	HE
Muzzle velocity	2,350ft/sec
Rate of fire	8rds/min

Distribution of AAA & Searchlights within LADA, January 1918

Location	Guns	Lights
London		
Northern	13	30
Location	*Guns*	*Lights*
Central	10	19
Eastern	14	30
Western	18	34
Outer Barrier		
Epping	27	18
St. Albans	23	20
Staines	19	19
Redhill	25	20
Harwich	13	33
Chatham and Sheerness	26	45
Dover	27	38
Mobile Brigade in Kent	18	9
Mobile Brigade in Essex	16	8
TOTALS	249	323

RESPONSE: TACTICS

By the summer of 1918, Ashmore had brought together all the elements of his air defence system: gunsites, searchlights, balloon aprons, observer posts and aerodromes with both day and nightfighters. Many were part of the newly-formed Royal Air Force, but some elements remained Army and the observers were either police, coastguards or medically-downgraded soldiers.

This air defence system worked about as well as the technology of the time would allow. All the elements were connected by a direct telephone line to 25 "sub-control points", without being diverted through an exchange. There would be no chance of a "disconnection". Each sub-control point was equipped with a table-mounted, large scale map surrounded by a number of "plotters". Each plotter was connected to a group of observers and as sound or sight of aircraft was reported, markers would be placed on the table to correspond, and were kept updated as information came in.

Above the map sat "tellers" who were in direct telephone communication with the LADA control room. This mirrored the sub-control point, but with a map covering the whole LADA area. Each of these plotters was in contact with two or three tellers. The markers were colour-coded, each code relat-

Below: This view of the 3.6in AA gun, mounted on a tracked trailer, shows the difficulty in re-loading when firing at high angles.(Via Ian Hogg)

ing to a different segment of the key clock-face. As the minute hand of the clock passed into a new colour segment, the markers corresponding to this would be used. Thus, watchers over the table could identify fresh information from old.

Overlooking the whole room sat General Ashmore and his staff controlling the gun defences and fighter aircraft, with repre-

sentatives of the police and fire services. From the picture built up on the table, instructions could be immediately sent to the guns, balloons and fighter stations.

There was even the first form of fighter control, in the form of a wireless transmitter which could relay instructions to the few selected aircraft (the flight commanders') in the air. In daylight, it was sufficient to get the fighters within visual range of intruders. For night operations, an additional short-range transmitter was placed in each individual flight commander's aircraft and receivers in each fighter, so that commands issued by LADA control would be with the airborne fighters at "the sharp end" in a relatively short time – a matter of minutes.

In the air, following the experience of Maj Murlis Green, the fighters had taken to mounting upward-firing machine guns in addition, or as an alternative, to their forward firing Vickers guns. New sights were developed to provide an illuminated ring which was just filled by a Gotha's wingspan at 100ft. The rings were later adapted to accommodate the Giant's wingspan of 138ft. Flash eliminators were fixed to the gun muzzles, so that the pilot's night vision would not be destroyed. For the same reason, engine exhausts were modified to damp down the flames. Even the colour scheme of the aircraft was changed to a dark olive green and the national marking became plain red/blue roundels, with the white intermediate ring removed.

The training of pilots, too, was to reach a fine pitch. They were required to complete some 24hrs solo including four hours at night. Cross-country flights were made, in daylight, with the pilots wearing dark goggles to simulate the impression of flying by night. This was to avoid training by night, away from the usual patrol lines, which might, it was thought, be certain to cause false alarms. The student pilots were also required to pass severe tests of aerial combat by day and night, as well as completing a course of wireless telephony before they were graded as First Class Operational Pilots.

Ashmore comments, in his memoirs... "Notwithstanding the long time required for this training [not specified], the 6th Brigade was able to keep up the establishment of Home Defence Units, and, in addition, to form and send to France a complete night-fighting squadron."

The techniques of nightfighting can best be left to our previously-mentioned pioneer,

Sqn Ldr Murlis Green, who described his methods in a paper to the RAF Staff College in 1923.

"On a dark night with no moon the exhaust flames of a stationary engine machine [ie, a non-rotary engine] will usually be seen before the outline of the machine itself, but on a clear moonlight night the outline of the machine is generally first seen.

"After patrolling for an hour or so in the dark without seeing anything there is a tendency, when a hostile machine is seen at last, to dive straight at it firing both guns. This method seldom leads to success as the flash of the machine-guns, even when shielded, usually impairs the pilot's sight to such an extent that after the first few rounds have been fired he loses the target.

"The method found most successful up to now is as follows. Once you have seen your objective you must not take your eyes off him until he is destroyed or you wish to break off the fight. Turn your machine quickly into the same direction as he is going and get behind and slightly below him. If you have a 45 degree mounting use it. If your guns fire in line of flight close up until almost colliding, throttle back and open fire.

"There are two reasons why it is important not to open fire until extremely close range has been reached. Firstly, it is difficult to distinguish friend from foe at night, as of course crosses cannot be distinguished from circles, so that one has to rely entirely upon silhouettes. Secondly, range is very deceptive at night."

The whole organisation was honed to a fine edge by frequent exercises but, sadly in one respect and fortunately in another, it was never to be put to the ultimate test. The German bombers had flown their last mission over England on 19/20 May 1918. It was their biggest raid yet – 38 Gothas and three Giants – and their costliest. Only 19 bombers penetrated the London area and just 13 managed to reach over the City. Ashmore's new organisation, although not yet complete and working in total harmony, was able to destroy six of the bombers – three by the guns and three by the nightfighters. Admittedly the half-light of an approaching summer assisted in the identification of the targets, but it was indicative of the improvements in the air defences. Had

the raids continued, then the revitalised LADA would have made the Germans pay a high cost.

In August 1918, the German High Command had decided against further attacks on London (and Paris). The bombers were to be diverted to the support of German forces over the Western front, in an effort to avoid the impending defeat. Just before this decision was implemented, the German Navy made its final fling on the night of 5/6 August. Ignoring impending bad weather, Strasser, the head of the Navy Airship Service, boarded the latest Zeppelin, *L70* and, in company with four other airships, set out to raid the Midlands. *L70* was the first "X" class "Super Zeppelin", some 694ft long, powered by seven engines giving a top speed of 81mph and a bomb load of 8,000lb.

Even before crossing the coast, the formation had split and when two (*L56* and *L63*) of the five were spotted from Great Yarmouth, two DH4 bombers were hastily launched, followed by another dozen aircraft, including five Camels, from Yarmouth, Burgh Castle and Covehithe. Losing the pair of Zeppelins in the air, one of the two DH4s broke cloud to see *L70* and the two others (*L53* and *L65*) above. Flown by Maj Egbert Cadbury, with Capt Robert Leckie as gunner, the DH4 climbed to 16,000ft, closed on *L70* and Leckie raked her with his Lewis gun, firing Pomeroy explosive ammunition. Thus Germany's most powerful Zeppelin was shot down in flames into the sea off Great Yarmouth (the target of Germany's first air raid on the UK). Had not Leckie's gun jammed at the crucial moment, *L65* would also have become a victim. It was the last German raid of the war against England.

However, *L70* was not the last Zeppelin to be shot down. Although no longer used for bombing raids, Germany continued using the Zeppelin for reconnaissance and on 11 August, *L53* was on patrol over the North Sea. Below them was a destroyer, HMS *Redoubt* which was towing a lighter on which resided a Camel and its pilot, Lt S. D. Culley. Seeing *L53*, the destroyer went to full speed and the Camel soared into the sky. Climbing to 19,000ft, Culley attacked the airship and shot her down. It was a target of opportunity rather than a concerted effort by the organised air defence. Nevertheless, *L53* had the dubious distinction of being the last of 29 airships to be destroyed in the First World War.

CRITIQUE

Hindsight is a wonderful facility and it will be deployed to the full in this, and subsequent, sections of this book. What must be obvious to anyone is that, within the limits of technology prevailing at the time, the air defence organisation that existed in 1918 was second to none. It had all the elements of the system which were used in 1940, ensuring the victory of the Battle of Britain, less one – radar.

The evolution of air defence, as I believe has been shown, was fraught with misconceptions, provision of inadequate equipment (at least in the early stages) and petty but far-reaching "trade demarcation disputes" between the British Army and the Royal Navy. Yet evolve it did, thanks to some clear thinking and common-sense provided by General Smuts at staff level. Operationally, the contribution by Major-General Ashmore – integrating the many elements which gave the UK its first air defence organisation – cannot be ignored. Finally, at "the sharp end", there were the many contributions made by the aircrew themselves, drawn from the hard school of experience.

While, like all elements of the air defence organisation, the guns, searchlights and sound-locators took time to evolve, they had, by 1918, reached a high standard of competence. The development of the 3in 20cwt gun was particularly important, although many were diverted to naval use that might have been better deployed in the role for which they were intended. It is also interesting to note that had the 3.6in QF Mk 1 gun been produced in quantity after the war, it might well have prejudiced the development of the later 3.7in gun.

One the aircraft side, it was not until aero-engines of sufficient power became available that the defending fighters were able to reach the intruders. Similarly, while it required the advent of interrupter gear, allowing the pilot to "point" his aircraft and shoot at the same time, attacks in this manner could not be conducted in squadron, or even flight, strength at night until the very end of the war – after the threat had receded.

Although it was proved that the standard, single-seat day fighters of the time could be safely operated at night and the nightfighter as a concept was born, the two-seater (with a rear gunner) was also to prove effective. Yet as Sqn Ldr Murlis Green pointed out in the same Staff Paper quoted earlier, "Only half the armament of the machine can be used when firing a broadside".

The Murlis Green paper became something of a classic of its time and it made an interesting recommendation – the adoption of a twin-engined nightfighter with a crew of two gunners and the pilot. This configuration, he maintained, could have a better forward view and, with the two gunners "slightly raised behind [the pilot] and just above the top plane [wing], so that they can both fire all round on their own level and upwards to an angle of 45°'" much better arcs of fire. The larger machine, he continued "is more suitable for fitting larger types of guns, wireless telephones and other paraphernalia necessary for night fighting". His recommendation was for 0.5in calibre guns. The one big disadvantage of a twin-engined aircraft at that time was its limited manoeuvrability but, even so, he suggested "a Home Defence twin-engine fighter could be made much handier than the present type of twin-engine bombers", such as the DH10.

If, as has been said, the detection of the intruders and the means to direct them was as efficient as could be achieved at the time, the final problem remained as one of physical interception, especially at night. Both single-seat and two-seat fighters, however, suffered from a poor forward view which was essential. Sqn Ldr Murlis Green again: ..."a pilot flying at night is practically stone deaf and very short sighted ..."

The greatest gift to nightfighters – airborne radar – was not to come for another 20-odd years. For the time being, the wireless telephone was the best form of guidance available to the air defenders of 1918. To take full advantage of the system, aircraft had to be in the air on their established patrol lines – combat air patrols in today's jargon – and trust to luck that the wireless message directed them to an area within easy sight of the enemy. In the end, it was left to the "Mark One Mod Zero" eyeball to make a visual contact. Murlis Green confirms this: ..."once [the pilot] has seen the enemy there is a very good chance of success".

The RAF had done a good job and, as history relates, after a lean period post-1918, it went on to grow in strength and purpose to become the totally essential third dimension of the British armed forces.

Left: The Breguet 19 saw extensive service with France as both a bomber and reconnaissance aircraft, as well as being widely exported. The version illustrated, fitted with a Hispano Suiza engine, served with the Spanish Republican forces during the Spanish Civil War. (Greenborough Associates)

Left: The Farman 60 series (illustrated here by the Goliath civil version) entered French service during the closing stages of the First World War. The final bomber variant, the F63 BN4 served with the 22nd Air Regiment at Chartres. (Greenborough Associates)

Left: The Loire et Olivier LeO 20 BN3, powered by licence-built Bristol Jupiter engines, served as a night bomber for many years. (Greenborough Associates)

1928

The creation of the Royal Air Force on 1 April 1918 (All Fool's Day) was viewed with suspicion and when peace "broke out" in November, the need for a Home Air Defence plan became academic. On Armistice Day, the RAF possessed its largest-ever inventory of aircraft: 22,647, of which 3,300 were frontline types and 103 were airships. Its personnel strength was 27,333 officers and 263,837 other ranks, plus some 25,000 members of the Women's Royal Air Force.

The end of the Great War was greeted both by relief and a deep feeling of revulsion over what war had become. Never before had so great a sacrifice been demanded of any of the participating nations and while many ordinary people found it difficult to comprehend its meaning, there was a universal belief that it had been a "war to end all wars". This simple phrase was not yet a cliche in the years immediately following the war, but a heartfelt conviction that never again would such a catastrophe befall Europe. The need for an air force in peacetime was soon being questioned.

It is not surprising, therefore, that during 1919, the service shrank to the proverbial shadow of its former self. It had been reduced to a minor force with little long term planning and subject only to minimal investment. In summary, during the 1920s, the RAF's role was very much that of aerial policeman in many of the more remote areas of an increasingly dissident Empire. Although this type of operation often proved effective, it was of little relevance to a European scenario and was carried out by increasingly venerable aircraft, often with a critical shortage of spares. In India, according to no less a person than Marshal of the RAF Sir Arthur Harris, aircraft were operated on single ignition engines because of financial stringency.

Yet in the years following the Armistice, with Sir Hugh Trenchard as Chief of the Air Staff, the independence of the service was assured and the foundations laid for its eventual expansion in the run-up to the Second World War.

Life in Great Britain adopted a pedestrian pace, which did little for the morale of many of those who had survived the carnage. During these bleak years for air power, there was one shining example of hope and that was in the form of the RAF's Central Flying School (CFS). This unit became a "Centre for Excellence" and an organisation that retained a questing investigative spirit of aviation, laying the foundations for future technical growth.

At the same time, it was accepted that defence spending was not altogether popular with the tax payer and in an early RAF public relations exercise the RAF Tournament was held at Hendon in 1920. This proved popular with the public, being repeated as an annual event, becoming known as the RAF Pageant and, then later, the RAF Display.

Many people, both within and outside the RAF, were aware of its deficiencies and felt helpless in view of the political apathy which was bolstered by the absurd, self-regenerating "10-Year Rule". Such an outlook stifled enterprise and inhibited development and research with its cosy acceptance of a continuing *status quo*.

Air Defence did not, initially, come into the planned peacetime organisation of the RAF. On 11 December 1919, the plan for the permanent peacetime organisation was presented to both Houses of Parliament. It made provision for, at home: two squadrons (increasing to four) as a striking force; one Army co-operation flight per Army Division; one or more squadrons for artillery co-operation; one reconnaissance and spotting squadron, half a torpedo squadron, an aeroplane fighting flight, a flying-boat flight and a float seaplane flight (eventually in-creasing to three aeroplane and two seaplane squadrons) for Fleet co-operation. Overseas the deployment was eight squadrons and one Depot in India; seven squadrons and one Depot in Egypt; three squadrons and one Depot in Mesopotamia (now Iraq); one seaplane flight in Malta; one seaplane flight in Alexandria; and one seaplane flight on a seaplane-carrier in the Mediterranean.

The aeroplane fighting flight, for Fleet co-operation, was the nearest to an air defence fighter unit planned in 1919. Yet only four years later, in 1922, the first murmurings over the need for air defence were heard. Such was the level of concern expressed, that a special committee was set up under Lord Salisbury to consider the whole question of national and imperial defence. It reported that ..."in addition to meeting the essential air power requirements of the Navy, Army, Indian and overseas commitments, British Air Power must include a Home Defence air force of sufficient strength adequately to protect us against air attack by the strongest air force within striking distance of this country." At that time, the only country capable of launching an air attack on the UK was France and this was considered highly unlikely. Yet, British diplomacy was not always in step with France and, it was considered, it could be hampered by a weakness of British arms.

Already a paper plan, based on the report of the Steel-Bartholomew Committee on the Air Defence of Great Britain, was in existence. This proposed the expansion of the RAF at home to 23 squadrons, for both offence and defence. For air defence, a line of sound locators would be positioned on the coast, backed-up by ground observer posts. Next in the layered defences would be

an 'outer artillery zone', behind which was a 15-mile deep 'aircraft fighting zone', stretching from Salisbury Plain, around London into Cambridgeshire. Central London would be covered by an "inner artillery zone", while searchlights would be deployed in the outer artillery and aircraft fighting zones. The report was presented in April 1923.

This principle of the Salisbury committee was accepted by the new Prime Minister, Stanley Baldwin, who said on 26 June 1923 "the Home Defence force should consist of 52 squadrons to be created with as little delay as possible". The plan called for 17 fighter squadrons (some 200 aircraft) to be deployed, together with 400 bombers, keeping the RAF on a par with French airforces. The modest 23-squadron expansion had been overtaken.

Sadly, other Cabinet decisions at this time (and over the next few years) did not match this plan. Particularly the Rule that estimates of the three Service Departments must be based on the assumption that no major war would occur for the next 10 years. This limited resources allocated to the services, already stretched to the utmost to

London Defences 1928

- ▲ Fighter Station
- – – Boundary of Observer Corps Area
- —— Boundary of Aircraft Fighting Zones
- ≡ Outer Artillery Zone
- ▨ Inner Artillery Zone
- – · – Coastal Gun Defended Area
- △△ Restricted Flying Area

Cambridge
Duxford ▲
Harwich Defence
Henlow ▲
Harwich
Chelmsford
▲ North Weald
Sutton's Farm ▲
Shoeburyness & Sheppey Defence
Northolt ▲
Greenwich ▲
Chatham
Devizes
Upavon ▲
Kenley ▲
Biggin Hill ▲
Maidstone
Aldershot
Hawkinge ▲
Dover Folkestone
Dover Defence
Southampton
Portsmouth
Portsmouth Defence

meet the other inescapable commitments, such as defence of India, mentioned above. Indeed, plans included dispatch of 24 Home Defence squadrons to India, in the event that India was threatened. In effect, the Home Defence units were treated as a "general reserve" to reinforce the RAF worldwide.

However, such ambitious plans were bound to be affected by the economic conditions prevailing at the time. The original completion date of the 52-squadron plan was April 1928, but by November 1923, the Committee of Imperial Defence had postponed this to 1930. In December 1925, a Cabinet committee, under the Earl of Birkenhead, recommended a further delay to 1935-36. While the committee recognised the need for a Home Defence force and had no complaint as to its planned size, they considered progress could be safely retarded (ie, slipped), especially since financial economy was so desirable.

The definition of the organisation of the Air Defence of Great Britain called for by the 52-squadron plan, was deputed to a committee under Major-General Romer, which included Major-General Ashmore among its members. The interim report was presented in May 1924 and, adapting aspects of the Steel-Bartholomew Report, was to lay the foundations of the air defence organisation in place during the Battle of Britain in 1940. The first AOC-in-C of the new Air Defence of Great Britain was Air Marshal Sir John Salmon, whose appointment was announced in January 1925. Its operational headquarters at Hillingdon House, Uxbridge, was opened in June 1926.

THE THREAT

With hindsight it is easy to see the reality behind the dream but, at that time, it was enough to allow belief in a better future and fertile ground for the growth of a remarkable degree of political naivety. Before the start of the new decade the seeds of future conflict were already being sown. The so-called peace negotiations were based on retribution, rather than long term goodwill, and even the lesser allies, like Italy and Japan, began to feel isolated and the victims of broken promises.

There were other political changes in process: the relationship between Britain and France had cooled and in March 1922 a newspaper article offered for general consumption something that had been a growing cause for concern among the more aware. The article itemised the strength of the French Air Force as 300 bombers and 300 fighters of up-to-date design and with a formidable strike capability. In contrast, the RAF had a home defence force of just some 40 aircraft. There was also a growing feeling among politicians in the UK that France was using this military influence to dictate policy in Europe, which was displeasing to the British government - a situation that was further exacerbated by the French occupation of the Ruhr.

Such shocks are often good for a nation slipping into self delusion and the flurry of activity that followed the newspaper publication led to the creation of the Home Defence Air Force in 1923. Even this good intention was to be inhibited by the growing economic problems and faced near disaster as a consequence of the infamous "Geddes Axe" and its swingeing cut-backs in public spending. There was also a marked resistance among the public to military service and recruitment was difficult. In addition, there were signs of an element of defeatism entering the British psyche when considering aerial attack, which was later enshrined in the phrase "the bomber will always get through".

While there was no evidence that France was likely to be an aggressor, it is always necessary for the military mind to recognise a "perceived" threat. As Germany was of no consequence in this role at that time, France was seen as the only likely nation to have the capability and this had been emphasised by the 1922 newspaper report. Whatever may now be thought, the disposition of the UK's bomber and fighter airfields, at that time, indicated the accepted scenario.

At a time when technical innovation in military aircraft was at a very low ebb in the UK, the French industry was looking ahead and investigating the use of new configurations and materials. In 1925 the *Société Blériot Aéronautique* developed a four-seat escort fighter, powered by two Lorraine engines of 400hp and indicated the way ahead for heavily armed, aerodynamically efficient monoplanes.

It was the sort of technical awakening that the British press had intended in its disclosures of French aviation advances in 1922. At least one effect was the introduction of the Air Estimates for 1923-24 which contained an increase in funding of more than £1 million. In presenting the State-ment, Sir Samuel Hoare, the Secretary of State for Air, remarked that in 1922 only 200 aeroplanes, civil and military, had been built in the UK while 300 civil and 3,000 military types had been built in France. At that time the French aviation industry employed more than 9,200 workers while the UK figure was just 2,500.

As much as anything it was a state of mind. It is arguable that the French nation is naturally air-minded, while the British are more akin to the sea. Communication links between Britain and its Empire were still almost entirely dependent upon surface ships whereas the French, even before the end of the First World War, were considering the development of an aerial service to Morocco as the first step in the introduction of an air mail service to South America.

Such positive thinking affected the development of aviation at a critical time and established a suitable climate, both in public opinion and commercial confidence, to take advantage of technical advances. When considering the "perceived threat" of the time the following examples are an indi-cation of what the French were producing during the 1920s. Although never seriously imagined as an actual threat, they provided the subject matter of many an RAF Staff College envisaged scenario, along with con-sideration of how the UK would handle the French influences in the Mediterranean area!

So if, in 1928, the French Air Force was considered the yardstick against which the air threat to the UK was measured, it is appropriate here to outline the size and potency of this "perceived threat".

Breguet 19

The prototype of this two-seat biplane was introduced at the 1921 Paris Salon. It fea-tured sesquiplane wings with only a single interplane strut on each side and a circular cross-section fuselage. First flown in May 1922 powered by a Renault engine, the Breguet 19 was eventually produced in a number of different versions with a variety of engine powers. The type remained in ser-vice for almost 15 years.

It proved popular as an export product and by the end of 1926 more than 1,100 units of both reconnaissance (A2) and bomber (B2) versions had been built for the French Air Force and overseas customers, including Argentina, Belgium, Bolivia, China, Greece, Persia, Poland and Serbia.

Licence production was also granted to Belgium, Greece, Japan, Spain and Yugo-slavia. A special "one-off" version made the first, successful crossing of the North Atlantic from east to west.

Data: Breguet 19 B2

Powerplant	one 450hp Lorraine engine
Span	48ft 8in
Length	31ft 2.5in
Height	10ft 10.5in
Wing area	538sq ft
Loaded weight	4,850lb (max T/O)
Maximum speed	141mph
Service ceiling	22,000ft
Range	800 miles
Armament	one forward-firing 0.303in

Vickers machine gun, twin rear-mounted 0.303in Lewis guns and one ventrally-mounted 0.303in Lewis gun. Plus 30 x 22lb or eight 110lb bombs internally or two 440lb bombs on underwing racks

Dewoitine D1

This was the first aeroplane to be produced by the Toulouse-based company and it made its first flight on 18 November 1921. It set the trend for a series of parasol-wing mono-planes from the company, all featuring light-weight metal airframes covered with fabric.

The D1 was extensively demonstrated in a number of countries and orders were received from Yugoslavia, Switzerland and Japan. As a portent for the future, a licence was granted to Ansaldo of Italy for indige-nous production and a total of 126 were constructed, designated AC1. The French ordered 29 for naval use.

Powered by a single 300hp Hispano Suiza engine, the D1 had a maximum speed of 156mph and could climb to 16,000ft in just over 15min. By December 1924, the air-craft had captured three world speed records.

Data: Dewoitine D1

Powerplant	one 300hp Hispano Suiza engine
Span	36ft 11in
Length	24ft 3.75in
Height	9ft 0.25in
Loaded weight	2,751lb (max T/O)
Maximum speed	156mph
Time to height	15min 6sec to 16,400ft
Service ceiling	28,000ft
Range	440 miles
Armament	two forward-firing machine guns

Farman F60 Series

The Farman F60 Series began as a large night bomber in the closing stages of the Great War. It was a successful aeroplane that was also to make a valuable contribution to civil aviation as the Goliath. In 1923 the F60M was introduced, powered by two 310hp Renault 12 engines and served as a night bomber with the 21st Air Regiment based at Nancy. Two years later a number of these aircraft, fitted with 380hp Jupiter engines, served in Morocco against the Riffs.

Other versions included the F63 BN4, also with Jupiter engines for the bomber role, equipping the 22nd Air Regiment at Chartres. The final version, the F68, was a three-seat night bomber, some 32 of which served with the Polish Air Force.

In an attempt to fully exploit the potential of the basic design, a four-engined version was produced in 1923 and designated F140. It was capable of carrying a large load and established a number of world records for endurance and altitude following its first flight in 1924. Although six of these were ordered for experimental duties, the aircraft did not enter squadron service with the French.

A new range of Farman biplane bombers succeed the F60 series from 1928, known as the F160 series. The ultimate, the F168, powered by a pair of 480hp Jupiter engines, served with the French Air Force for many years.

Data: F60

Powerplant	two 380hp Gnome-Rhone GR 9Aa Jupiter engines
Span	87ft 0in
Length	47ft 7in
Height	17ft 4in
Loaded weight	12,786lb (max T/O)
Maximum speed	90mph
Service ceiling	18,000ft
Range	340 miles
Armament	machine guns and bombs

Liore et Olivier LeO 7, Leo 12, LeO 20

The LeO 7/2 was a three-seat, twin-engined biplane bomber which entered production in 1922. A machine gunner/observer was seated in the nose, with a pilot seated towards the centre section and another gunner to the rear in armoured cockpits. An experimental batch of 20 aircraft was built. A larger, marine version, the LeO7/3, was also developed and 12 were produced, although this variant did not prove to be a success.

This aircraft was followed by the LeO 12 which flew in May 1924, another twin-engine biplane type which was often demonstrated using the power of just one engine. Five were built and put into squadron service on an experimental basis.

The LeO 122, a LeO 12 powered by a pair of Jupiter engines, served as a prototype for the LeO 20 of which 320 were delivered to the French Air Force, equipping their night bomber squadrons for many years. Although similar to the LeO 12, the LeO20 was slightly larger than its LeO 122 prototype. It was armed with five defensive machine guns, one of which was mounted in a retractable, streamlined fairing under the fuselage.

Data: LeO 7, LeO 12, LeO 20

	LeO 7/2	LeO 20
Powerplant	two 300hp Hispano Suiza 8Fb engines	two 420hp Gnome Rhone 9 Ady engines
Span	61ft 0in	72ft 0in
Length	38ft 0.75in	45ft 3.75in
Height	13ft 2.25in	13ft 11.75in
Loaded weight	6,614lb (max T/O)	12,037lb (max T/O)
Cruise speed	106mph at 16,400ft	N/A
Maximum speed	126mph	123mph
Service ceiling	23,000ft	18,900ft
Range	N/A	620 miles
Armament	Five (?) machine guns plus bombs	Five machine guns plus 1,100lb of bombs

Nieuport 29

Although originally intended for use in the Great War, the streamlined Nieuport 29 was produced too late and, instead, became the standard fighter in a number of postwar air forces. With a true monocoque fuselage mounting a Hispano Suiza V-type engine, it was armed with a pair of machine guns on the engine cowling.

In 1921 the design underwent considerable change and the improved version, designated Nieuport-Delage (ND) 29 C1, made its debut at the 1922 Paris Salon. It served with the French Air Force until 1928, during which time it was used against the Riffs in Morocco where a number were converted to fighter bombers, carrying light bombs in addition to machine guns. The ND29 C1 was also used by Belgium (where it was built

under licence), Italy, Japan, Spain and Sweden.

An experimental version, the ND40, was also developed, with a supercharged engine, for a high-altitude fighter role. Although not accepted by the French Air Force, this example set up a new world altitude record of 36,565ft in October 1923.

Data: Nieuport ND29

	ND29 C1	ND40
Powerplant	(both) one 300hp Hispano Suiza 8 Fb	
Span	32ft 1.25in	32ft 0in
Length	21ft 9.75in	21ft 8in
Height	8ft 4.75in	7ft 10.5in
Wing area	289sq ft	?sq ft
Loaded weight	2,535lb (max T/O)	2,623lb (max T/O)
Maximum speed	146mph at sea level,	143mph
Time to height	10min 59sec to 21,325ft	N/A
Service ceiling	26,200ft	26,200ft
Range	360 miles	372 miles
Armament	(both) two machine guns	

Nieuport-Delage 42

Designed as a high altitude fighter, the prototype ND42 appeared in 1924 as a parasol monoplane. A two-seat, sesquiplane version appeared at the same time, with a machine gun fitted in the observer's cockpit for defence of the rear sector.

By the time the single-seater took part in the 1925 fighter competition it, too, had the sesquiplane configuration. Distinguishing itself as the fastest of the competitors there, an order by the French Air Force for 25 followed. The production ND42 C1 ver-

sion featured one machine gun firing through the propeller and two more mounted in the wing.

Data: Nieuport-Delage 42

Powerplant	one 500hp Hispano Suiza 12 Hb engine
Span	39ft 4in
Length	24ft 7in
Height	9ft 10in
Wing area	286.7sq ft (prototype)
Loaded weight	3,986lb (max T/O)
Maximum speed	165mph at sea level, 140mph at 24,600ft
Time to height	32min 36sec to 24,600ft
Service ceiling	26,900ft
Range	528 miles
Armament	three 8mm machine guns

Wibault 7 and 72

Earlier Wibault designs were developed in metal construction, both for airframe and skinning, to offer a very rugged military aircraft. Biplane designs were abandoned in 1923 in favour of parasol monoplanes. The result of these evolving concepts was the Wibault 7, flown for the first time in 1924. Three prototypes were developed with differing powerplants the third of which, prophetically, carried the name of *Rafale*. A competitor in the French fighter competition of 1925, the Wibault 7 came out top, mainly as a result of its outstanding rate of climb (10min 56sec to 13,125ft). Production versions of the Wibault 7 entered service with the French Air Force in 1926, initially with the 32nd Air Regiment at Dijon, as high altitude fighters.

A later version, designated Wibault 72, featured an improved undercarriage and was

Left: Produced too late to enter French service during the First World War, the streamlined Nieuport 29 was finally withdrawn from home service in 1928. (Greenborough Associates)

Right: The Wibault 72 C1 parasol monoplane fighter served with the French Air Force until 1936. (Greenborough Associates)

fitted with two Vickers machine guns firing through the propeller and two Darne machine guns mounted in the wing. Some 60 of this variant were ordered for the French Air Force. The strong construction of these aircraft led to a long period of service which lasted until 1936.

Data: Wibault 72

Powerplant	one 420hp Gnome-Rhone GR9 Ac Jupiter engine
Span	36ft 0in
Length	24ft 9in
Height	9ft 9in
Loaded weight	3,350lb (max T/O)
Maximum speed	156mph
Service ceiling	27,900ft
Range	370 miles
Armament	two 0.303in Vickers machine guns and two 8mm Darne machine guns

DETECTION AND IDENTIFICATION

While the spectre of a French threat was appearing, technology continued to be developed in laboratories. There was increasing use of the electromagnetic spectrum, though without any real goad for military applications.

Wartime techniques were still used as such and rudimentary ideas for such necessary applications as cross-country navigation, at night, were still very much in their infancy. In theory, directional wireless navigation techniques were available to supplement dead reckoning techniques. One of these was simple Direction Finding (D/F), based on wartime artillery spotting, while

the second was rather more experimental, using continuously-emitting beacons. In practice the problems of detecting a signal, applying corrections and accurately plotting the result ensured a poor standard of precision.

In fact, a record of a night exercise in a Handley Page O/400 of the period gives an indication of the reality of the times. The intention was to fly from a base in southern England to Belfast, then across to Hull and return. Despite a crew which included a dead-reckoning navigator and two directional wireless navigators they became completely lost. After some considerable time, it was decided that the were over the Irish Sea and needed to turn West for a landfall near Dublin. The sea was seen through cloud and eventually the coast was sighted and a landing made, only to find that the aircraft was in the vicinity of Ipswich! Clearly there was a great deal to be done.

Once need for a Home Defence Air Force had been established, the plan for its disposition was set by the Romer Committee. A number of measures were adopted that were to affect the structure of the future Fighter Command. With France considered to be the "threat", the air defence system assumed the direction of air attack to be from across the English Channel, towards London and South East England. Certainly the method of detecting, and then tracking, an enemy airborne attack had changed little since the days of the Gotha raids.

The basic principle which had been realised during the war, and remains equally true today, is to establish a form of early warning that will allow the effective deployment of the defending forces. A further inhibiting factor in a situation which called for the earliest possible warning, was the rate-of-climb performance of the defending fighter aircraft.

By far the most common-sense measure initiated was the resurrection of ground observer posts, covering the area south of a line running from the Bristol Channel to the Humber. All Observation Posts were to be linked directly, by land line, to the Observer Centres and each centre linked, in turn, to the Fighting Area Headquarters, with some centres also linking to adjacent Aircraft Sectors.

This was a logical extension of the system devised by General Ashmore in 1918. Between August and September 1924, he supervised preliminary trials of the new Observation System. This trial found that the course of an aircraft could be plotted with speed and accuracy, both by day and by night. Records of courses flown agreed with the log books of the pilots who participated. By June 1925, two Observation Areas had been established over Kent, Sussex and part of Surrey and a recommendation made that they be extended into Hampshire to the west, as well as the eastern counties. The Committee of Imperial Defence (CID) approved these suggestions on 29 October 1925. Thus was the Observer Corps (later the Royal Observer Corps – ROC) established.

Initially, the Romer Committee had recommended that the provision of personnel and their training should be an Army responsibility. However, as the information supplied by the Observer Corps was, essentially, air intelligence, it was recognised that the Romer view had be modified to reflect this reality. Accordingly, in October 1928, it was proposed – and approved – through the CID, that control of the Observer Corps should be transferred from the War Office to the Air Ministry. This became effective from 1 January 1929.

Among the other defensive measures embodied in the Romer plan was the provision of sound locators based on the coast, although it was accepted they had considerable limitations. Both inner and outer anti-aircraft artillery zones were re-established, as in 1918.

While sound locators were the best aid to the Observer Corps at the time, some people were beginning to look at other methods of detection using electrical solutions. Such electrically-based experiments had been carried out over a fairly wide range of military applications, both in Europe and the United States. It was recognised that communication and detection were the very essence of military tactics.

Following the successes of radio in the Great War, experiments continued in peace time, particularly with the use of higher frequencies to permit long range communication with both ships and aircraft. Work also continued on methods of jamming hostile transmissions, a technique which had been in use since the early part of the century, but one that was now being refined into the redoubtable weapon of Electronic Warfare. Other experiments covered use of radio teleprinters, photo facsimile transmission and, even, television. Following from

Order of Battle, June 1928
(extracted from *The Air Force List*)

Sqn	Aircraft	Base
1	Armstrong Whitworth Siskin IIIA	Tangmere, Sussex
3	Hawker Woodcock II	Upavon, Wilts
17	Hawker Woodcock II	Upavon, Wilts
19	Gloster Grebe	Duxford, Cambs
23	Gloster Gamecock	Kenley, Surrey
25	Gloster Grebe	Hawkinge, Kent
29	Armstrong Whitworth Siskin IIIA	North Weald, Essex
32	Gloster Gamecock	Kenley, Surrey
41	Armstrong Whitworth Siskin IIIA	Northolt, Middx
43	Gloster Gamecock	Tangmere, Sussex
56	Armstrong Whitworth Siskin IIIA	North Weald, Essex
111	Armstrong Whitworth Siskin IIIA	Sutton's Farm, Essex (Hornchurch)

wartime experiments, radio-controlled aircraft and flying bombs were also considered and tried out to some degree. Significantly, it was recognised that such innovation demanded a form of defence and the first indications of countermeasures began to be considered.

Forward thinking minds could appreciate that electrical ideas, enhanced by thermionic principles, were leading towards a new technology that bore the first seeds of a new type of detection of aerial targets. Consideration was given to picking up the infra-red radiation emitted by aircraft engines; the detection of various types of electromagnetic emissions from onboard systems and the application of techniques later to become known as radar. Perhaps one of the most prophetic of these considerations was a memo written in August 1926 in which an O.F. Brown, of the Department of Scientific and Industrial Research, suggested the use of a cathode ray tube oscilloscope in anti-aircraft research, to the Committee of Imperial Defence.

At about the same time it became fashionable to talk of "death rays", an idea sparked no doubt by the emerging technology of electronics, but which helped to prepare the ground for the acceptance of advanced ideas. In 1928, L.S.B. Alder of the Royal Navy's Signals School put forward a suggestion for using radio waves to detect ships and a provisional specification for this idea was filed in March 1928.

So, while the initial work which would spawn the development of radar was being investigated, albeit in sporadic directions, the primary – and most effective – means of detection and identification of enemy air attacks at this point remained the Observer Corps.

Below: The Armstrong-Whitworth Siskin III was the first RAF fighter of all-metal construction. The Siskin IIIA illustrated was one of a batch built by Gloster Aircraft. (Glosters)

RESPONSE: AIRCRAFT AND ARMAMENT

Armstrong Whitworth Siskin IIIA

The post-Great War economies had seen the RAF reduced in strength and the wartime Snipe remain in service with home defence squadrons for nearly five years. The first new fighters the RAF received – the Siskin III and Grebe (*see overleaf*) – began to enter service in 1924 and, even then, it was 1926 before the last Snipes were replaced.

The Siskin III was generally similar to the original Siddeley Siskin of 1919, which was a biplane of wooden construction powered by a 340hp ABC Dragonfly radial engine. The Siskin II was built in both single-seat fighter and two-seat trainer variants with a metal fuselage, wooden wings and parallel interplane struts.

The Siskin III was the first RAF fighter to be largely of metal construction and was powered by a 325hp Armstrong Siddeley Jaguar III radial engine. It retained the wartime armament of two synchronised Vickers guns, firing through the propeller arc. Although the prototype (which made its maiden flight on 7 May 1923) had the parallel interplane struts of the Siskin II, production aircraft introduced "vee" interplane struts. The first production aircraft flew in March 1924 and the first RAF unit, No 41

Squadron, formed at Northolt in May 1924. Some 62 Siskin IIIs, including 32 of the two-seat III DC trainers, were built.

The Siskin IIIA was built in much greater numbers, 412-including 47 dual-control trainers. It was distinguished from the III by the absence of the underfuselage fin and the installation of the more-powerful Jaguar IVS engine of 420-450hp, depending on whether it was normally aspirated or supercharged. The first IIIAs entered service with No 111 Squadron at Hornchurch in September 1926 and, in all, 11 RAF squadrons were equipped. The last unit to fly the Siskin IIIA was No 56 Squadron at Biggin Hill, which gave up its aircraft in October 1932.

Data: Siskin IIIA

Powerplant	420-450hp Armstrong Siddeley Jaguar IVS
Span	33ft 2in
Length	25ft 4in
Height	10ft 2in
Wing area	293sq ft
Empty weight	2,061lb
Loaded weight	3,012lb
Maximum speed	156mph at sea level, 142.5mph at 15,000ft
Time to height	3min 30sec to 5,000ft, 10min 30sec to 15,000ft
Service ceiling	27,000ft
Armament	two synchronised 0.303in

Vickers machine guns; with provision for four 20lb bombs under the wings

Gloster Grebe

With the Siskin III (*see above*), the Grebe was the first of a post-Great War generation of fighters to enter RAF service. It was derived from the Nieuport Nighthawk, for which Glosters had the design rights in 1920, together with the services of its designer, H. P. Folland. Development of what became the Gloster Grebe began with the Grouse I (with a Bentley rotary engine) and the Grouse II (with a Lynx radial engine). The Grebe was of wooden construction. It was fitted with an upper mainplane of high-lift aerofoil section and a lower mainplane with a medium-lift aerofoil section. The armament consisted of a pair of Vickers guns.

Three prototypes were constructed, being powered by a 325hp Jaguar III radial engine, the maiden flight of which was in May 1923. The first production version, the Grebe II, powered by the 400hp Jaguar IV, flew in August 1923, and featured an oleo undercarriage and redesigned fuel tanks. The mountings for the ailerons was considered unusual: the upper mainplane ailerons were hinged parallel with the tapering trailing-edge of the outer wing, while the ailerons on the lower mainplane were hinged at right-angles to the airflow.

Trials at the A&AEE Martlesham Heath in the autumn of 1923 drew the comments from pilots that the Grebe (also known, initially, as the Thick-wing Nighthawk) was far superior to any existing fighter type. The

Left: This Gloster Grebe II was the first production aircraft and was issued to No 25 Squadron. (Greenborough Associates)

Above: The Gloster Gamecock had the distinction of being the RAF's last wooden fighter aircraft. This aircraft is seen in No 23 Squadron markings. (Author's Collection)

first aircraft entered RAF service with one flight of No 111 Squadron at Duxford in 1923, with the first full squadron (No 25) equipping with the type in October 1924. In 1926, two Grebes were successfully launched from the airship *R33*, flying at 2,000ft and, during trials, it became the first British fighter to survive a terminal velocity dive of 240mph. The aircraft was, however, prone to chronic wing flutter on the upper mainplane and "vee" struts were introduced on many aircraft to brace the upper wing extensions.

In all, some 112 Grebe II fighters were built for the RAF, 412 including 20 dual-control trainers. Indeed, the Grebe was one of the first RAF fighters for which a two-seat trainer version was produced. Five squadrons, plus the one flight, were equipped with Grebes and the last unit to fly the type, No 25 Squadron, exchanged them for Siskins in June 1929.

Data: Grebe

Powerplant	400hp Armstrong Siddeley Jaguar IV
Span	29ft 4in
Length	20ft 3in
Height	9ft 3in
Wing area	254sq ft
Empty weight	1,720lb
Loaded weight	2,614lb
Maximum speed	152mph at sea level, 145mph at 10,000ft
Time to height	23min to 20,000ft
Service ceiling	23,000ft
Endurance	2.75hrs
Armament	two synchronised 0.303in Vickers machine guns with 1,200 rounds

Gloster Gamecock

Again designed by H. P. Folland, the Gamecock was similar to the Grebe, but with a more rounded fuselage, new ailerons and was powered by the Bristol Jupiter engine. The armament, comprising two Vickers machine guns, was sunk in blast troughs on either side of the forward fuselage. It made its maiden flight in February 1925, powered by a Jupiter IV, but the production-standard Jupiter VI was fitted to the third prototype. It was to be the last RAF fighter of wooden construction.

The first RAF unit to take delivery of the Gamecock was No 43 Squadron at Hendon in March 1926, closely followed by No 23 Squadron in April. Indeed, No 23 Squadron was to retain its Gamecocks long after other units had been re-equipped. The other RAF units equipped with the Gamecock were Nos 3, 17 and 32 Squadrons.

As might be expected of a close descendent of the Grebe, the Gamecock also suffered from wing-flutter troubles. This led to the installation of a "vee" strengthening strut between the wing extensions and the interplane struts in later years of service. Pilots were also warned to avoid right-hand spins. In spite of these vices, the pilots were very fond of the Gamecock and the public were thrilled at the aircraft's aerobatic performances at the Hendon air day. The type was withdrawn from squadron service in September 1931.

Data: Gamecock

Powerplant	425hp Bristol Jupiter VI
Span	29ft 9.5in
Length	19ft 8in
Height	9ft 8in
Wing area	264sq ft
Empty weight	1,930lb
Loaded weight	2,863lb
Maximum speed	155mph at 5,000ft, 145mph at 10,000ft
Time to height	7min 36sec to 10,000ft, 20min to 20,000ft
Service ceiling	22,000ft
Armament	two synchronised 0.303in Vickers machine guns

Hawker Woodcock II

The Woodcock was the first fighter to be produced by the H. G. Hawker Engineering Company, as successor to the famous Sopwith firm. It was designed to meet RAF Specification 25/22, which called for a single-seat interceptor nightfighter to replace the obsolete Snipe.

The first prototype was a wood and fabric biplane of two-bay configuration, powered by an Armstrong Siddeley Jaguar II radial engine of 358hp. Poor rudder control and wing flutter discovered during its early flights in 1923 led to a redesign. The second prototype, the Woodcock Mk.II, was a far superior aircraft: it went to single-bay configuration and the powerplant was changed to a Bristol Jupiter IV of 380hp, later uprated to 420hp. This radial engine featured metal "helmets" over each of its cylinders, in an effort to reduce drag. Both prototypes were fitted with an unusually-wide undercarriage, which was to prove popular with pilots.

The Woodcock II was put into production and between May 1925 and April 1927, 62 aircraft were delivered to the RAF. The first aircraft entered service with No 3 Squadron at Upavon in July 1925, replacing their Snipes. The second RAF unit to receive the type was No 17 Squadron in March 1926, again replacing Snipes. Both squadrons were tasked with the nightfighter role.

Although its top speed of 141mph and armament of twin Vickers machine guns were no great improvement over the Snipe, a 1918-vintage aircraft, the Woodcock was considered a useful boost to the RAF air defences. It was replaced in No 17 Squadron during January 1928 but soldiered on in No 3 Squadron until September that year. The Gamecock replaced the Woodcock in both squadrons.

Below: The Woodcock was the first aircraft to come from the Hawker company (successor to Sopwith). These Woodcock IIs are from No 17 Squadron. (BAe)

Data: Woodcock II

Powerplant	420hp Bristol Jupiter IV
Span	32ft 6in
Length	26ft 2in
Height	9ft 11in
Wing area	346sq ft
Empty weight	2,014lb
Loaded weight	2,979lb
Maximum speed	141mph at sea level, 115mph at 20,000ft
Time to height	8min 48sec to 10,000ft, 16min 24sec to 15,000ft, 30min 54sec to 20,000ft
Service ceiling	20,000ft
Armament	two synchronised 0.303in Vickers machine guns

RESPONSE;
ANTI-AIRCRAFT ARTILLERY

In November 1918, the anti-aircraft (AA) gun defences of Great Britain comprised 48 AA companies of the Royal Garrison Artillery, 31 AA Battery HQs, 225 AA sections and three mobile AA brigades. In 1919, this was drastically reduced to one regular AA brigade of three batteries, and one Royal Engineer (RE) searchlight battalion, despite the protests of General Ashmore. No Territorial Force AA brigades had ever been established.

As a result the AA gun defences of Great Britain went into stagnation. Regular soldiers with AA experience were redistributed or demobilised with only a small "tail" support force which, by November 1922, had become a sub-division of the Field Artillery, merging with the coast defence branch for administration purposes.

Although the report of the Steel-Bartholomew Committee had been accepted by the Government, it remained as a planning document only and was not fully implemented. The War Office, however, did establish four Territorial Army (TA – as the Territorial force had become in October 1921) AA gun brigades in the Home Counties in 1923, after publication of the first findings of the Committee. A fifth was later added. These were loosely grouped as the London Air Defence Area. As regular units were reserved for overseas deployment, the TA brigades were the effective home defence force.

By 1928, there were two regular AA brigades within the Royal Artillery: 1 Brigade with three batteries, headquartered at Blackdown; and the similar-sized 2

Brigade at Portsmouth. With four guns per battery, this meant only 24 AA guns in service, being the 3in 20cwt, described in the previous "Snapshot". All other types had been scrapped or returned to their original role. If one realises that the TA batteries were on a cadre training basis, each of the three batteries with the TA brigades probably held no more than one weapon each; the total number of weapons within the TA was no more than 15, 20 at the most.

Although the number of AA guns was not large, the interwar period did see improvements in the training of AA gunners and the development of better fire control mechanisms. The publication of a War Office *Textbook of AA Gunnery* in 1925 did establish the preferred characteristics of a future AA weapon system. All but one of the main points, set out below, were introduced into service before or during the Second World War.

- *The need for AA ammunition with better ballistic performance, high-explosive fillings and mechanical time fuzes*
- *The adoption of automatic loading gear for increased rates of fire*
- *The need for better height-finding equipment, using a longer optical base for improved accuracy*
- *The provision of better fire control at battery level, using tachymetric or plane-prediction instruments to apply corrections relating to the conditions of the moment*
- *Application of a simple tachymetric sighting system to mobile AA guns*
- *The design of improved sound-locating instruments to aid searchlights and for use in directing barrage fire*

In 1927 the Vickers No 1 Predictor, a tachymetric instrument which needed target height from an external source to complete its calculations, was introduced into service. It was the first instrument to produce corrected firing data for direct application for AA guns (previous methods having only produced "aim-off" or deflection values to aiming over open sights. Initially matched to the 3in 20cwt AA gun, the No 1 Predictor could cope with targets travelling at up to 250mph and at heights up to 24,000ft. Later modifications allowed these limits to be raised.

At this time, as a result of the Romer Committee recommendations, the specification for a new anti-aircraft gun was in the process of being agreed by the Royal

Artillery Committee. This was to become the 3.7in Mk 1 gun and is described in the 1938 "Snapshot".

It is also, perhaps, worth mentioning the 18pdr Birch Gun in this context. It was the first British self-propelled fieldgun and was also capable of anti-aircraft use. While the original 1925 version had the gun mounted in a turret, carried on a Vickers tank chassis, the second (1926) version had the gun in an open barbette mounting. This allowed it to elevate to 85°, so that it could double as a forward-area air defence weapon, in addition to its field role. A battery of these guns were built and issued to the Experimental Armoured Force (EAF) in 1927. However, after the 1928 manoeuvres, the EAF was disbanded and, by 1934, all the Birch Guns had been scrapped.

CRITIQUE

The state of the UK air defences in 1928 may, perhaps, be best summed up by the phrase "the spirit was willing but the purse was small". The RAF was a shadow of its former self and its fighter aircraft, although shiny silver and great performers in public, barely a match for their French equivalents in both performance and numbers. The detection, command and control facilities were only just up to the standards of the previous decade, while the anti-aircraft artillery was virtually non-existent.

The seeds for improvement had, however, been sown. These were to be another 10 years in coming to fruition. The principle reason must surely be the "certainty" that another war was at least 10 years away. The British may have had their differences with the French, but the thought of actually going to war against them was not really credible.

There was a certain amount of "air-mindedness" being generated in the nation's public, much of which affected the school-boys of the time and was to pay dividends 10 years later. However, the funding allocated to air defence remained comparatively small. A lasting peace was still considered feasible and great faith was placed in the League of Nations to resolve disputes before they degenerated into conflict.

Indeed, the mentality of the Great War was, not unnaturally, still firmly entrenched within the minds of most of the industrial and service hierarchy of the period. The RAF stuck to the biplane fighter while the French, at least, were flying monoplanes, albeit of the parasol type which was used in the First World War. Science and technology was evolving, but slowly. It would take another 10 years and the emergence of a real threat to the UK to bring the embryo concepts into functioning equipment. Even so, the benefit of hindsight allows us to suggest that the forthcoming developments only arrived "in the nick of time".

Below: The 3in 20cwt MkI AA gun, seen here in a Mounting, AA, MkIV, on a Peerless lorry, was the standard AA gun in service from 1917 to 1939. (Via Ian Hogg)

1938

During the previous decades, the true state of the UK's aerial preparedness had become obvious to those in authority, but not always recognised by those in politics. The relatively basic demands of the 1920s reviews had been inhibited to some degree by financial stringency but also by an attitude that did not wish to prejudice – some would say offend – the deliberations of the Disarmament Conference at Geneva. The final demise of this conference in November 1934 offered an opportunity to direct popular attention towards the reality.

Certainly many of the British public were still totally opposed to war and refused to acknowledge that it might once again be necessary to face conflict. Typical thinking of the times led to a refusal by a local council to grant permission for the establishment of an aerial bombing range in Berkshire in 1930. Perhaps this was understandable, but it seemed to be less so when the request was repeated in November 1939 and received the same rebuttal.

In 1938, the threat of Nazi Germany was a reality and Great Britain was in the throes of rearmament. The Munich Crisis in September came and went, leaving a scant year's breathing space before the outbreak of war. The air defence of the country was in a much better state than 10 years previously and during the late-1930s, a dose of reality arrived.

Earlier, in June 1933, it had been decided to postpone the completion of the 52-squadron Home Defence Air Force plan until 1939-40. Then, in March 1934, Prime Minister Stanley Baldwin assured the House of Commons that if the Disarmament Conference failed, steps would be taken to bring about an Air Disarmament Con-ference. If that, too, failed, the Government would proceed to bring RAF strength up to that of the strongest air force within striking distance of the UK. He announced provision for six new squadrons.

In July 1934, the further expansion had been approved. A Metropolitan Air Force was to be set up, raising the number of squadrons from 52 to 75, of which 28 were to be fighters. The Auxiliary Air Force, formed as part of the Air Defence of Great Britain in 1925, began converting from bombers to fighter aircraft. On 30 July, it was announced that the government intended to develop precautionary measures to protect the civilian population and safeguard essential services against bombing.

A further step was taken when, in December 1934, a sub-committee was formed to consider the re-orientation of the country's air defences. The threat of 10 years previously had been seen as coming from the coast of France; now, Germany was the potential enemy. A Memorandum signed in 1934 by Air Marshal E. R. Ludlow-Hewitt, Deputy Chief of the Air Staff, on the re-orientation of the air defence system reasoned thus:

"With a change in the direction of attack from the South East to the East, combined with the great increases which have recently been made in the ranges of bombing aircraft, a much larger part of this country has become exposed to air attack. Aircraft operating from the North Sea Coast of Germany can now deliver effective attacks on the industrial centres in the neighbourhood of the Tyne and the Tees, the big industrial areas in Lancashire and Western Yorkshire, the industrial centre in the Midlands in and around Birmingham. All these places fall within an arc of which the centre is on the North Sea Coast of Germany in the neighbourhood of Emden, and of which the radius is 375 miles."

The Memorandum continued: "Hence...aircraft operating from Germany can now attack the great industrial centres in the Midlands and in the North of England without coming within reach of the existing air defences." It also noted that: "...the important objectives in the London Area will remain the principal objective of enemy air forces, particularly if the enemy aircraft were able to operate from the Low Countries, where they would be strategically very well placed to develop the maximum offensive against the capital".

The superior performance of aircraft was not ignored in the calculations. "Whereas in 1923 we only had to consider a speed of night bombers of about 80mph, they already have a speed of 160mph and a further increase to 200mph has already been realised and will soon become normal." Such "high speeds", it was acknowledged, "render it impossible for fighting aircraft to make contact [within the searchlight zones] before the enemy aircraft has disappeared into the darkness beyond the range of the searchlights".

In summary, the Memorandum stated:

"The changed direction and conditions of air attack now require the provision of defences for North-Western England and the Midlands as well as for London. The wider arc in which the attackers may now choose their objective entails the lengthening of our defensive system by some 100 miles. The width of the lighted zone necessary to enable the fighters to intercept and engage the night bombers, will require to be increased by 5-10 miles."

After discussing the pros and cons of either a continuous aircraft and outer artillery zone defence plan, or a discontinuous system covering the most important centres only, the opinion of the Air Staff was that "there is...no effective alternative to the establishment of a continuous defence zone from the Tees, around the Eastward of London to Southampton."

This Memorandum stirred matters up. In April 1935, the Boyd Commission recommended the expansion of the Observer Corps to cover most of Great Britain; and in June, the Government approved a scheme for a Metropolitan Air Force of 120 squadrons, of which 35 would be fighter units, by 1937. This number of 35 fighter squadrons was reduced to 30 in April 1936, owing to the increased establishment of aircraft for each squadron. By July 1936, the Metropolitan Air Force had been reorganised and split into four functional Commands: Bomber, Fighter, Coastal and Training. The Air Officer Commanding appointed for Fighter Command was Air Marshal Sir Hugh Dowding. In the same month, air exercises were held to give collective training to the Metropolitan Air Force and it was assumed, for the first time, that the attacking forces would come in over the South East coast. It was also the first real test of the effectiveness of the Observer Corps. In November 1936, the scheme for providing Balloon Barrages was announced.

On the equipment side, January 1937 saw the introduction into service of the RAF's last biplane fighter, the Gloster Gladiator, going to Nos 3 and 72 Squadrons. By December, the first monoplane fighter for the RAF, the Hawker Hurricane, armed with eight machine guns in the wings, entered service with No 111 Squadron at Northolt. The first Supermarine Spitfires entered service with No 19 Squadron at Duxford in June 1938. Following the Munich Crisis, the formation of Mobilisation Pools was ordered on 27 September 1938.

THE THREAT

The decade between 1928 and 1938 had been one of growing realisation that a very real threat did exist and that it was Nazi Germany. At the same time it was the decade of belief in disarmament, peace movements and latterly appeasement. Over it all, there remained the growing conviction, now being passed onto the man in the street, that the bomber was somehow invincible.

War between Japan and China tended to confirm the horrors of modern aerial bombardment and this was often reflected in the media and through popular entertainment in the cinema or in highly imaginative novels. The Spanish Civil War brought the reality closer to home and seemed to reinforce the conviction of the bomber's invincibility.

In February 1934, the Defence Requirements Committee (established in 1933) estimated that the potential of German military aircraft, by October 1935, would be 504 aircraft with 172 in reserve, the majority of which would be bombers. By 1938, no-one could deny that the air threat to the UK was the German *Luftwaffe*. Propaganda was widely used by both sides to incite and allay fears.

So, what was the exact nature of the air threat poised against the UK in 1938? The following details the major German bombers and principle fighters which might be expected to escort them.

Dornier Do17

Known as the "Flying Pencil", the prototype Dornier Do17c made its maiden flight on 20 November 1934, powered by a pair of 700hp BMW VI-7.3 12-cylinder liquid-cooled engines, and a conventional single fin configuration. Despite official statements that the aircraft was designed as a six-seat high-speed mailplane for *Deutsche Luft-*

Above: Typical of the early models of Dornier Do17 is this Do17 V-8, the prototype for the Do17F-1 reconnaissance version. (Greenborough Associates)

hansa, it was intended to be a bomber from the start. After evaluation by the *Reichsluftfahrtministerium* (RLM), three more prototypes were ordered in 1935, with a twin endplate fin-and-rudder configuration. The fuselage was of all-metal construction and the shoulder wings of metal construction with fabric covering with a fully-retractable undercarriage. A seventh prototype carried defensive armament.

A non-standard version, the Do.17M V1 powered by two Daimler-Benz DB601A engines adapted to run on special high octane fuel, appeared at the International Military Aircraft Competition in Zurich in July 1937. Its performance there far outstripped that of the fastest European fighter then in service, the French Dewoitine D.510. This caused quite a stir in international aviation circles at the time, as it was alleged this version was the standard then entering *Luftwaffe* service.

The first production versions, the Do17E-1 bomber and its F-1 photo-reconnaissance counterpart, were in *Luftwaffe* service by spring 1937, being powered by BMW VI-7.3 engines, uprated to 750hp, and armed with two or three 7.9mm MG15 machine guns plus (for the E-1) 1,100 lb of bombs (although 1,650 lb could be carried for reduced-range missions). Examples of these aircraft saw service with Condor Legion squadrons participating in the Spanish Civil War. A more heavily-armed export version, with four machine guns and one 20mm cannon plus 2,200 lb of bombs, was produced for Yugoslavia as the Do17K. These were supplied by Germany and also built under licence.

The 536 Do17E/F models were followed by an improved but interim standard of bomber, the Do17M, powered by BMW-Bramo 323A radial engines. The airframe featured a wing covered with Duraplat, an extra fuselage fuel tank, protection for all fuel tanks and an electro-mechanical undercarriage actuation mechanism. The reconnaissance equivalent of the M-model was the Do17P.

The first example, Do17M V1, was subsequently re-engined and used on the trials in Zurich referred to earlier. The shortcomings of the Do17E, as revealed in Spain (limited warload and poor defence from below and to the rear) were not totally remedied with the Do17M. These "defects" had to wait for the Do17Z to be addressed.

In 1938, the Dornier Do17 series was a potent threat. Further improved versions of the type were to be developed (with over 500 examples of the Do17Z being built) and the design spawned the Do215, Do217 and Do317 variants.

Data: Do17E

Powerplant	two 750hp BMW VI-7.3 engines
Span	59ft 0.67in
Length	53ft 3.75in
Height	14ft 2in
Wing area	592sq ft
Empty weight	9,920lb
Loaded weight	15,520lb
Maximum speed	193mph at 13,120ft
Service ceiling	16,730ft
Range	932 miles (without bombload
Tactical Radius	310 miles (with max. bomb load)
Armament	two or three 7.9mm MG 15 machine guns; with 1,650lb of bombs

Heinkel He111

Destined to bear the brunt of the *Luftwaffe*'s bombing offensive over the UK in 1940, the Heinkel He111 was conceived in 1933 and designed from the outset to be both a bomber and commercial transport. Officially unveiled as a 10-seat civil airliner for *Deutsche Lufthansa* in 1936, the prototype He111a had actually flown a year early on 24 February 1935. Despite this propaganda subterfuge, the elliptically-winged He111 was also being developed as a bomber. (The commercial development of the He111 has been omitted from this account.)

The He111a (later re-designated He111V-1) was, structurally, a state-of-the-art metal, stressed-skin monoplane powered by a pair of BMW VI-6.0Z engines. It slim, streamlined fuselage culminated in a glazed nose for the bombardier. Defensive armament consisted of a nose-mounted 7.9mm MG15 machine gun, with similar weapons in an open dorsal position and a retractable ventral "dustbin" position, while 1,763 lb of bombs could be carried vertically in an eight-cell magazine in the central fuselage.

The initial production model, the He111A-0, derived from the second bomber prototype He111b (later V-3) with an extended glazed nose, was authorised into pre-series production late in 1935. The bomb load was increased to 2,205 lb and with a slightly increased gross weight of 16,976lb was considered underpowered. As such it was rejected for *Luftwaffe* service.

From 1936, the the Daimler Benz DB 600A engine in the 1,000hp class was substituted for the He111B-0 and B-1 versions, from late 1936, and the DB600CG on the He111B-2, produced from May 1937. With a crew of four, the He111B carried four 551lb bombs. As with other contemporary *Luftwaffe* combat aircraft, the He111B-2 was deployed to Spain with the Condor Legion, where it gained a reputation for outstripping opposing fighters. The 58 survivors were later absorbed into the Spanish Air Force.

With the appearance of the 1,050hp DB 600Ga engine, this was tested on a B-0 airframe, leading to the pre-production He111D-0 variant. For this, the whole engine installation was cleaned-up and, despite an increase in normal loaded weight to 19,423lb, these engines added 25mph to the aircraft's maximum speed at 13,120ft. However, as production models of the D-1 came on line in late 1937, supplies of the DB600Ga dried up as they were diverted to Messerschmitt Bf.109 production. This led tosuspension of the D variant and a search for a substitute engine,which was found in the 1,075hp Junkers Jumo 211A-1 engine. Both the pre-production He111E-0 and production E-1 versions appeared in January 1938, having been laid down as D-models. The bomb load for the E-0 was increased to 3,748lb and in the E-1 to 4,410lb. Examples were, again, despatched to the Condor Legion in Spain.

The F-model, which followed, used the straight-tapered wings developed for the unsuccessful He111G civil version. Again powered by the Jumo 211, the He111F-1 was built exclusively for the Turkish Air Force, while the *Luftwaffe* took 40 He111F-4 versions, fitted with internal and external bomb stowage of the E-4 version. This was an interim order, built in parallel with the He111J, powered by the DB 600CG, available again by early 1938. The He111J was developed as a torpedo bomber and did not feature internal bomb stowage until later in its career.

Official figures for September 1938 indicate that almost half of the *Luftwaffe*'s first-line bomber strength of 1,235

Left: This view shows three of the second-generation Heinkel He111P-1s of III/KG55 in the spring of 1939. By this time, the stepped cockpit and glazed nose of the earlier versions had given way to the wholly-glazed nose design, which typified the genre. (Greenborough Associates)

twin-engined bombers comprised 570 He111, of which 468 were operational. These were made up from 272 He111Bs, 171 Es29 Fs and 88 He111Js.

The first of a second generation of Heinkels, the He111P-0, appeared in January 1938. In addition to the new wing design, it featured a continuous-curved contour, glazed nose (doing away with the conventional stepped windscreen) and an underfuselage "canoe-shaped" ventral gun position – to be the norm on all subsequent He111 models. Still armed with three 7.9mm MG15 machine guns, it carried a maximum bomb-load of 4,410lb and was powered by two 1,050hp DB601Aa engines. Trials continued during 1938 and first examples of the production He111P-1 began to enter *Luftwaffe* service in the earlyspring of 1939.

Development of the He111 series continued throughout the Second World War, with the most developed version being the H-model, which went to 23 sub-variants. Spain undertook licence-production of the He111H-16, continuing after the war as the CASA C.2111, powered by Rolls-Royce Merlin engines – an ironic twist of fate – remaining in service until the late 1960s.

Data : He111B-2

Powerplant	two 950hp Daimler Benz DB600CG 12-cylinder engines
Span	74ft 1.75in
Length	57ft 5in
Height	14ft 5.25in
Wing Area	942.92sq ft
Loaded weight	18,960lb (normal) – 22,046lb (max. T/O)
Maximum speed	230mph at 13,120ft
Service ceiling	22,965ft
Range	1,030 miles (with 1,653 lb bomb load)

Armament	three 7.9mm MG15 machine guns; with up to 3,307 lb of bombs.

He111P-4

Powerplant	two 1,175hp Daimler Benz DB601A-1 12-cylin der engines
Span	73ft 9.8in
Length	53ft 9.6in
Height	13ft 1.5in
Wing Area	931.11sq ft
Loaded weight	29,762 lb (normal)
Maximum speed	200mph at 16,405ft (with 3,439 lb bomb load)
Service ceiling	24,692ft (He111P-1)
Range	1,224 miles
Armament	six 7.9mm MG15 machine guns; with up to 4,410lb of bombs, internally and externally.

Junkers Ju86

As with the He111, the Junkers Ju86 saw its origins in aparallel development of bomber and commercial airliner. The first Ju86ab1 prototype made its maiden flight on 4 November 1934, powered by a pair of Siemens SAM22 air-cooled radial engines as the Jumo 205 diesel engines were unavailable. The initial pre-series aircraft, the Ju86A-0 powered by 600hp Jumo 205 andthe Ju86B-0 with 845hp BMW 132Dc engines were, respectively, bomber and 10-seat airliner. The A-0 bombers were used as development aircraft.

The first bomber for the *Luftwaffe* was the Ju86A-1 which entered service in the early summer of 1936. However, after a continuing longtitudinal stability problem was solved by the addition of a wedge-shaped extension replacing the tailcone, aircraft with this modification were re-designated Ju86D-1. Only a score of A-1 models were built as such. Its initial armament was three

Right: A pre-series Junkers Ju86E-0, which rectified some of the shortcomings of the Ju86D series aircraft, seen in its civil registration although the camouflage gives away its more warlike role. (Greenborough Associates)

Left: A classic view of the airborne arm of the Blitzkrieg, the Junkers Ju87B-2 "Stuka" dive bomber. Greenborough Associates)

MG15 machine guns and up to 2,200lb of bombs. Sweden ordered 37 equivalent Ju86Ks (powered by Pegasus engines) to be manufactured under licence by SAAB but only 16 were built.

Like other *Luftwaffe* aircraft of the time, the Ju86D saw service in Spain with the Condor Legion. It proved inadequate when pitted against the fighter opposition so it was quickly withdrawn in favour of the He111B. Attempts to improve the performance led to the BMW 132F engined- bomber, designated Ju86E-1. Fuel capacity was increased to 330Imp gal and other modifications led to improved serviceability. These interim aircraft entered *Luftwaffe* service from late summer 1937. Further improvements saw the cockpit moved forward and a new fully-glazed nose fitted to produce the Ju86G-1. This was only built in small numbers and used as an aircrew trainer.

Later development saw the pressurised, high-altitude version, the Ju86P-1. Use of two 880hp Jumo 207 engines and an increase of 10ft in wing span enabled it to fly at higher altitudes and while the bomb load remained constant, the armament was reduced to a single MG17 machine gun. Even so, the speed of 224mph remained too low for a modern bomber. This model was further improved with an even greater wing-span (30ft over the original) and the 950hp Jumo 207B-3, to produce the Ju86R series. These were eventually employed as reconnaissance aircraft, a role in which they entered the Second World War. The projected four-engined Ju186 and the six-engined Ju286 were never built.

The number of Ju86s in *Luftwaffe* service was at its peak in autumn 1938, with 235 on strength, 200 of which were operational. These comprised 159 Ju 86A/Ds, 43 Ju86Es and 33 Ju86Gs. A year later, the *Luftwaffe* only had about 30 Ju86Gs in service and these were withdrawn by the end of the Polish campaign.

Data : Ju.86

Powerplant	two 880hp Junkers Jumo 205C-4 six-cylinder engines (Ju86D) or two 799hp BMW 132F nine-cylinder engines (Ju86E)
Span	73ft 9⅞in
Length	58ft 7⅛in
Height	15ft 5in
Wing area	882.67 sq ft
Empty weight	12,786lb (Ju86D)
Loaded weight	17,687lb (max T/O for Ju86D) or 18,078 lb (max T/O for Ju86E-1)
Maximum speed	202mph at 9,840ft (Ju86D) or 224mph at 14,765ft (Ju86E)
Service ceiling	19,360ft (Ju86D) or 25,265ft (Ju86E)
Tactical radius	354 miles (Ju86D) or 286 miles (Ju86E)
Armament	three 7.9mm MG 17 machine guns; with either four 551lb bombs or 16 110lb bombs carried internally

Junkers Ju87

The most famous of all *Luftwaffe* dive-bombers or *Sturzkampfflugzeug*, the

Right: Illustrative of the line of many Messerschmitt Bf109s is this Bf109 V-20, originally a Bf109E-08, seen fitted with a trial installation of an engine-mounted 20mm cannon. (Greenborough Associates)

Junkers Ju87 was tagged with the name "Stuka", contracted from its German type description, early in the Second World War.

Design began in 1934 with the maiden flight of the Ju87V-1 being made by the end of 1935. This aircraft was powered by a 640hp Rolls-Royce Kestrel V engine and featured an inverted gull wing, fixed and heavily-"trousered" main undercarriage, and a twin tail-plate fin and rudder. Tail flutter during a steep dive resulted in the destruction of the machine and required a complete redesign of the tail assembly. The second prototype, Ju87V-2, with a large angular fin and rudder appeared early in 1936, powered by a 610hp Jumo 210Aa. It also featured special dive brakes, developed by Junkers engineers. Comprising slats mounted aft of the wing leading edges, it was anticipated these would reduce the dive speed, enabling a closer pull-out to the target and, thus, increased accuracy of delivery of its bombs.

The German Air Ministry was evaluating the concept of the dive bomber as a mobile weapons system, able to replace heavy artillery. Thus, the Ju87 found itself competing with the Arado Ar81, the Hamburger Flugzeugbau Ha137 and Heinkel He118 and, surprisingly, winning selection. First production Ju87A-1s were delivered to the *Luftwaffe* in the spring of 1937 and the type was evaluated in combat with the Condor Legion in Spain. There it was found to be most effective with little opposition and this was later confirmed by the *Blitzkrieg* of 1939-40.

Small refinements were made and the Ju87B model was put into mass production for the *Luftwaffe*, Italy and other countries. The B-model entered service in summer 1938 and featured a re-designed cockpit canopy, a second wing-mounted machine gun, more streamlined spats to the main undercarriage and the 1,100hp Jumo 211Da engine.

Although it continued to be refined during the Second World War, the Ju87 was only effective when the *Luftwaffe* possessed air superiority and there was little or no opposition. The myth of the Ju87's invulnerability was to be shattered in 1940 during the Battle of Britain but, in 1938, the threat was considered real enough.

Data: Ju87B

Powerplant	one 1,150hp Junkers Jumo 211D engine
Span	45ft 3.25in
Length	36ft 3in
Height	12ft 9.5in
Wing area	343.3sq ft
Empty weight	6,085lb
Loaded weight	9,370lb
Maximum speed	240mph at 13,500ft
Service ceiling	26,248ft
Range	370 miles (with 1,100lb bomb).

Armament two 7.9mm MG17 machine guns, one in each wing; one 7.9mm MG15 machine gun in the rear cockpit; plus either one 1,100lb bomb under the fuselage or one 550lb under the fuselage and four 110lb bombs under the wings

Messerschmitt Bf109

When, in 1934, the RLM placed a development contract for a monoplane fighter with *Bayerische Flugzeugwerke* (whence the designator prefix "Bf" originated) few would have suspected over 35,000 of the resulting aircraft would be built over the next 25 years. Even after the company was reconsti-

tuted as Messerschmitt GmbH in July 1936, the fledgling 109 (and the twin-engined 110 design) continued to be designated with the "Bf" prefix.

William Green, in his definitive history of the Messerschmitt Bf109 (*Augsberg Eagle*, Aston Publications,1987) describes the aircraft as "a supreme example in the development of the single-seat fighter" being a "marriage of the all-metal stressed-skin monocoque structure with the low-wing cantilever monoplane configuration, and the embellishment of this union with cockpit canopy and retractable undercarriage".

The *Luftwaffe*'s requirement for a fighter, Green relates "demanded the monoplane configuration, an armament of two 7.9mm MG17 machine guns, emphasised high rates of roll and turn, complete integrity in a power dive, and also stressed the importance of perfect spinning behaviour". Work on the design began in 1934, despite official discouragement resulting from personal animosity between Willy Messerschmitt and the German State Secretary of Aviation, Erhard Milch. Nevertheless, work continued and the resulting aircraft was evaluated against several competitors, notably Heinkel's He112.

Although intended to be designed around the 610hp Jumo 210A engine, this engine was not available for the prototype Bf109a (later re-designated Bf109V-1). For its maiden flight,in late May of 1935, the Bf109a was powered by a 695hp Rolls-Royce Kestrel V. The second prototype, V-2, flew in January 1936, powered by the Jumo engine. The third prototype (intended as a pattern for the production A-model, which was never built) was the first to carry the two 7.9mm MG17 machine guns in the upper nose cowling, firing through the propeller arc, with provision for another MG17 firing through a cropped spinner. This was later changed to a 20mm MG FF/M (Oerlikon) cannon, thus endowing the Bf109 with a longer-range armament than its British contemporaries.

Official attitudes to the Bf109 were not favourable in the beginning but with the results of initial flight tests, this attitude warmed. By June 1936, the company had a contract for 10 pre-production Bf109B models for evaluation. These were, later, officially assigned to the development programme. The first pre-series Bf109B-0 entered pre-service evaluation in the spring of 1937, being fitted with the 610hp Jumo 210B engine, followed closely by the pro-

duction Bf109B-1, with a 635hp Jumo 210D. This version entered *Luftwaffe* service with II *Gruppe's Jagdgeschwader (JG) 132* "Richtofen", replacing obsolete He51 biplanes, early in 1937.

In July 1937, two B-1s, a B-2 and model V-13 were sent to Zurich for the International Flying Meeting. There, five of Germany's "new wonder fighter" – not one a standard production example – suitably impressed the world's military observers. The Bf109V-8, powered by the Jumo 210Ga engine, won the 228-mile Circuit of the Alps at an average speed of 241mph; the team event over the same circuit was won by the V-7, V-8 and V-9 (all Jumo-powered) with an average speed of 233.5mph; the V-8 madefour circuits of a 31.4 mile course, with an average speed of 254.54mph; while the V-13, fitted with a 960hp Daimler Benz DB600Aa engine, climbed to 9,840ft and back down to 500ft in 2min 5.7secs.

These impressive results gave the German Propaganda Ministry a field day and helped their misinformation that the Bf109 was in large scale production. The year was crowned for Germany and the Bf109 when, on 11 November 1937, the Bf109V-13 fitted with a specially-boosted DB601 engine delivering 1,650hp for short periods and smaller aerodynamic refinements including a new cockpit hood, flown by Hermann Wurster, raised the world air speed record for landplanes to 379.38mph.

It was inevitable that the Bf109 would join the Condor Legion in Spain and II/JG 132 (with 16 aircraft) was rapidly posted to Spain in March 1937. Although they enjoyed considerable success, the armament was still considered poor. For the Bf109C-0/C-1 models, the number of MG 17s were increased by two wing-mounted guns, to four, with a fifth gun, firing through the propeller boss, going on the C-3 model. Deliveries of the *Clara* began in early spring of 1938 and a dozen Bf109C-1s were sent to Spain in August 1938.

Production of the *Clara* was limited, to be followed by the Bf109D or *Dora* which was the Jumo-engined version produced in the largest numbers. It reverted to the Jumo 210Da engine of the B-series but retained the four-gun armament of the Bf109C-1. Examples were shipped to Spain in August 1938, while examples were also supplied to Hungary and Switzerland.

Sufficient D-1 models were produced to equip one *Gruppe*, before giving way to the E-model (*Emil*) fitted with the 1,100hp

DB601 engine with fuel injection. The first prototype was V-14, flown during the early summer of 1938. The pre-production E-0 models and the initial production Bf109E-1, appearing late in 1938, were armed with four MG17machine guns, but for the E-3 model, the two wing-mounted machine guns were replaced by the 20mm MG FF cannon.

The *Emil* was to be the prime *Luftwaffe* fighter for the first 18 months of the Second World War. History went on to record that the Bf109E was superior in performance and manoeuvrability over all types but the Spitfire in the campaigns in Poland, Czechoslovakia, France, Belgium, the Netherlands and during the Battle of Britain. It was also widely exported to Bulgaria, Hungary, Romania, Switzerland and Yugoslavia, with single-figure numbers also going to Japan and the Soviet Union.

However, on 19 September 1938, there was a total of 583 Bf109s (of all types) on *Luftwaffe* strength, of which 510 were serviceable. Substantial numbers had still to be issued to frontline units and the main productions models in service were the Bf109B, C- and D-models. The Bf109 continued to be developed during the Second World War, through F, G, H and K models. It comprised more than 60% of German fighter production between 1936 and 1945, fighting on every front in the war.

After the war, production continued in Czechoslovakia (S-99 and S-199) and Spain (HA 1109 and HA 1112), Czech examples being flown by Israeli pilots during the Israeli War of Independence in 1948. Finland retained its Bf.109G-10s in service until 1954; in Spain, the Merlin-powered HA 1112 *Buchon* remained in service until 1967.

Data : Bf 109C-1

Powerplant	one 700hp Junkers Jumo 210Ga engine
Span	32ft 4.5in
Length	28ft 0.66in
Height	8ft 0.5in
Wing area	174.053sq ft
Empty weight	3,522 lb
Loaded weight	5,026 lb (max. T/O)
Maximum speed	261mph at sea level, 292mph at 14,765ft
Maximum range	405 miles
Service ceiling	27,560 ft
Time to height	8.75min to 16,400ft
Armament	four 7.9mm MG 17 machine guns, two in the wings, with 420rpg, and two nose-mounted, with 500rpg.

Data : Bf 109E-3

Powerplant	one 1,175hp Daimler Benz DB 600Aa engine
Span	32ft 4.5in
Length	28ft 4.5in
Height	8ft 2.33in
Wing area	174.053sq ft
Empty weight	4,189 lb
Loaded weight	5,875 lb
Maximum speed	290mph at sea level 348mph at 14,560ft
Maximum range	410 miles
Service ceiling	34,450ft
Time to height	7.75min to 19,685ft
Armament	two wing-mounted 20mm MG FF cannon, with 60rpg, plus two mounted 7.9mm MG17 machine guns, with1,000rpg.

DETECTION & IDENTIFICATION

Aerial exercises in the early 1930s did little to dispel the concern over the bomber's effectiveness and only served to emphasise the need for early warning. Much experimentation had continued with acoustic devices and sound mirrors had grown in size but with little increase in effectiveness, which at the very best had only been able to give a range of some 24 miles. Aircraft, such as the Hawker Hart, also had problems of communication with ground controllers, using Wireless Telegraphy (W/T), and usually only the squadron commander carried a wireless operator.

Meanwhile, experimental technology was advancing and new techniques in manufacture, more highly powered engines

Below: Large, ponderous and vulnerable, the pioneer Chain Home RDF (radar) stations were a far cry from the technology of today. (Marconi Radar)

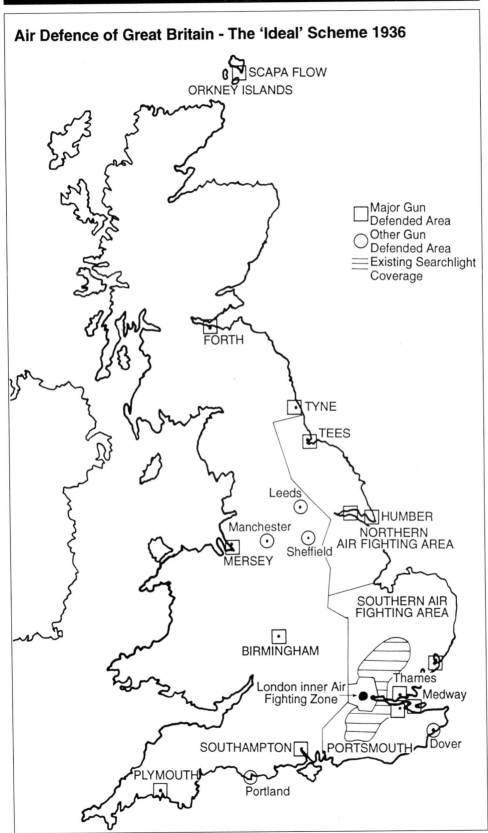

Air Defence of Great Britain - The 'Ideal' Scheme 1936

SCAPA FLOW
ORKNEY ISLANDS

☐ Major Gun
Defended Area
○ Other Gun
Defended Area
≡ Existing Searchlight
Coverage

FORTH

TYNE

TEES

Leeds

Manchester

MERSEY

Sheffield

HUMBER
NORTHERN
AIR FIGHTING AREA

SOUTHERN AIR
FIGHTING AREA

BIRMINGHAM

Thames

London inner Air
Fighting Zone

Medway

SOUTHAMPTON

PORTSMOUTH

Dover

PLYMOUTH

Portland

supercharged for performance and using high grade fuels, enhanced materials and rapid advances in electronics were all laying the foundations for a very new form of air force. In retrospect, it can be recognised that there were a number of dedicated personnel in the RAF, industry and, even, politics who were facing up to the technical challenges and succeeded in suddenly changing the biplane atmosphere of the mid-1930s into the all-metal, high performance monoplane RAF that was emerging by 1938.

At the same time the infrastructure of a modern expanding service was being established. In 1934, the first of eight expansion schemes was announced, together with the issuance of Air Ministry Specification F5/34, from which sprang the Hurricane and Spitfire. The following year saw the setting up of a Scientific Survey of Air Defence and this was followed by the establishment of the Command system in the RAF, placing of orders in the United States, instituting the revolutionary process of "ordering off the drawing board" and the creation of shadow factories. In 1937 the formation of the Royal Air Force Reserve was announced.

Of course, technology knows no frontiers and it was obvious to many that Germany was creating a remarkable aeronautical expertise, some of which was masked by an apparent commercial application. Germany was also making rapid progress in electronics, the development of blind flying techniques, electronic navigation and precision landing systems. Work was also proceeding on radar techniques with a particular application to anti-aircraft guns.

The threat was becoming more serious: not only were the new generation of aircraft faster in terms of cruising speeds, but with a far greater capability for operating in poor weather which would offer an element of protection. The problem of early warning was now critical and a system was needed that could detect approaching raiders long before they reached the coast.

Perhaps one of the most significant of the new ideas was the introduction of the Committee of Scientific Research on Air Defence, which held its first meeting in January 1935. This was one of the first occasions on which it was formally noted that future war would require considerable scientific assistance in order to achieve ultimate victory. The committee undertook to consider all kinds of ideas that could conceivably be used and these included the ever popular "death ray". As a result, the Committee sought the advice of R. A. Watson-Watt, who was the then Superintendent of Radio Department at the National Physics Laboratory, Slough, concerning the use of electromagnetic radiation to damage an aircraft or incapacitate the crew. Consideration was also being given at the time to the use of infra-red techniques and it was considered by many scientists as the more likely technology in the context of the times. As in all scientific endeavour, such thinking was being applied in other parts of the world, including the United States, France, Germany and Japan, and was to lead to the emergence of radar.

It has already been mentioned that techniques, which were later to be identified as radar, were already being proposed. In 1931 members of the UK Signals Experimental Establishment proposed a method of ship detection and informed the War Office of their experiments. Other straws in the wind included a report from the General Post Office which covered the problem of interference to radio signals by aircraft. Engineers, concerned with an experimental VHF radio link between Colney Heath and Dollis Hill, noticed that problems of "flutter" arose when aircraft from Hatfield were in the vicinity.

During 1934, demonstrations were carried out in the United States which included the use of a parabolic reflector operating with wavelengths of around 9cm. Just two years later, researchers in the United States and France were filing patent applications for so-called detectors which were supposed to offer indications of distance, azimuth bearing, elevation and speed of targets.

Certainly the pace of technology was accelerating and, in early February 1935, Watson-Watt submitted a report to the Air Ministry on the "Detection and Location of Aircraft by Radio Methods". This was the beginning, in the UK, of what was first called Range and Direction Finding (RDF) and which later became known as radar. It is noteworthy that in the same year *Société Française Radioéléctrique* (now known as Thomson-CSF) fitted a radar on the French liner *Normandie* for detecting icebergs .

Later in that month, Watson-Watt and his team carried out a demonstration with a device using the BBC transmitter at Daventry as an illuminator. This trial showed that radio signals could be reflected from aircraft, the "target" in this instance being a Handley Page Heyford of the RAF.

The Reorientation of the Air Defence of Great Britain 1938

Limit of Range of
Bombers Operating
in the Low Countries

Newcastle
Usworth▲

Catterick▲

Leeds•

Liverpool
Sheffield
Manchester

▲ Digby

Boundaries of
Aircraft Fighting
Zones
▲ Fighter Stations
Inner Artillery
Outer Artillery
Zone Boundary

▲ Wittering

Birmingham•

Division between
North/South Aircraft
Fighting Zones

Duxford ▲
Hendon
Northolt ▲   ▲ North Weald

Harwich

Kenley▲ ▲ Biggin
Hill

Dover
Hawkinge

▲ Tangmere

Portsmouth

Limit of range of
bombers operating in
Germany

Although this was a very rudimentary piece of equipment, the experiment was enough to convince senior officers of the RAF that it could provide an answer to the problem of detection and even the government's purse strings were loosened to allocate the research team an initial £10,000 to continue with the work.

This was soon to show results, with a set working by June and detecting aircraft at a maximum range of 42 miles; by September the range had increased to 58 miles and by early in the following year 62 miles had been achieved. It was then decided to put the latest version, operating in the 20-55MHz band, into production in order to establish a defensive radar coverage known as Chain Home (CH). At the same time the British team was equally aware of the inherent weakness of electromagnetic systems when faced with deliberate interference or jamming. It was a significant portent for the future and an actual in-flight jamming test took place in 1938.

At the same time an element of public education was being attempted with the introduction of air-raid precautions and of camouflage and smoke screen equipment, as well as a degree of control over BBC broadcasts which would be used in the public interest.

Meanwhile, work was continuing in the United States and Germany. American researchers were detecting aircraft at 50 miles in 1934. The work seemed of particular interest to the US Navy, where it had been recognised that the fleet needed some form of early warning system. By 1937, a destroyer was fitted with a radar which detected aircraft at 20 miles and this performance was quickly improved upon. American experiments also included a series of tests using a combined radar and infrared detection system with a searchlight.

The prototype Chain Home station was built at Bawdsey and was handed over to the RAF in March 1937. This became the world's first operational radar station and, during aerial exercises in April 1937, was found to be capable of plotting targets as far as 80 miles. As the Chain became established ranges of up to 120 miles were achieved and by the time of the Munich Crisis additional operational stations were sited at Colchester, Southend, Canterbury and Dover.

The significance of these early stations was soon appreciated in operational terms and further production orders were placed for radar sets to enable an extended chain to be built covering the entire east coast of the UK.

An interesting social trend also became apparent at this time, when it was suggested that women could be more psychologically suited to be RDF operators than men. It is accepted that women often demonstrate a consistently higher standard of performance in a given task and have a delicacy of touch that was deemed perfect for operation of the new equipment. This was later recognised in the aircraft manufacturing industry where the wiring department was often almost totally composed of female operatives. In the case of Britain's air defence, this trend led to the sight of WAAFs playing a prominent part in the events about to unfold.

It was recognised that the use of RDF would require a number of new techniques, not least of which would be the need to educate fighter pilots into accepting an element of ground control. In August 1936 the "Biggin Hill Experiment" was begun using Gloster Gauntlets. It must be appreciated that RDF was still both highly secret and experimental at this time, which tended to inhibit explanation to many of those taking part. Lessons learned laid the foundation for the operational framework that would evolve and also accepted the fact that the ground controller could "eyeball" the evolving tactical situation and make interception assessments with remarkable precision and this became accepted practice right up until the 1960s.

Perhaps, most importantly, the "Experiment" had demonstrated that it was now possible to have a more effective method of defensive fighter deployment than the standing patrols, which were the traditionally-accepted procedure. At the same time communications were being streamlined and the use of code words introduced to reduce message traffic congestion and prevent ambiguity. "Angels One Five" had entered the operational vocabulary.

While the new technology became established, another important element had also been in course of enhancement – the Observer Corps, later to receive the "Royal" prefix. From its beginnings in the Great War, this dedicated, voluntary service had continued to provide effective support to the air defence structure. In 1929, it was brought under the control of the Air Ministry and, by 1936, it was deployed as 10 groups, each of which operated under its own main air defence station. Observation posts were located in areas of interest and were able to keep in touch with the plotters at headquarters by telephone. As war approached their numbers increased greatly and, eventually, the Observer Corps comprised more than 1,000 observation posts and some 30,000 observers.

As the public became ever more curious about the strange pylon-like structures that were being built to serve as RDF aerials, the RAF also appreciated that warfare was becoming a much more scientific process and this indirectly led to the beginning of a philosophy which was to have a significant effect upon all aspects of the RAF's operations over the next six years. It can be appreciated that the early radar sets were semi-experimental and required a considerable amount of firsthand technical assistance if they were to be used to best advantage. In order to achieve the optimum operational results a team of scientists was seconded to the station at Bawdsey and placed at the disposal of Fighter Command headquarters. The primary role of this team was to assess the operational efficiency of the system and to make recommendations for improvements. Thus, was Operational Research born.

At the same time, work had also been proceeding on the development of a radar that could be used with anti-aircraft gun batteries, to provide medium range warning and accurate rangefinding. This was of considerable interest to the Army and, in October 1938, orders were placed for 500 production versions of these sets, operating in the 54-84MHz band and which were designated Gunlaying Mk 1.

Consequently, 1938 was a true watershed year, marking the introduction of an effective, long range, detection system and the growing maturity of an air force

equipped with the new eight-gun fighters. A technological revolution had been achieved, the lean years were past and the RAF could face the future with growing confidence. The stage was set for war.

RESPONSE: AIRCRAFT & ARMAMENT

The following section highlights that the transition being made from four-gun biplane fighters to eight-gun monoplanes was underway, but not yet widespread. It does not include details of aircraft in No 22 (Army Co-operation) Group, which later became Army Co-operation Command, or details of the balloon defences.

Bristol Blenheim IF

The Bristol Blenheim IF was a simple modification of the light bomber for the night-fighter role. Its origins began with the Bristol Type 142 six-passenger executive aircraft designed for Lord Rothermere, named *Britain First*. Flying in 1935, this civil aircraft reached 280mph, some 40mph faster than the best fighters of the day. Presented to the Nation, it was developed into a high-speed medium bomber and the first Blenheim prototype made its maiden flight on 25 June 1936.

Of all-metal construction, this twin-engined monoplane was fitted with a retractable undercarriage. An integral bomb-bay in the fuselage was able to accommodate up to 1,000lb of bombs. The Blenheim bomber was armed with a forward-firing machine gun and another in a semi-rotatable dorsal turret. The first Blenheim bombers entered RAF service in 1937.

The main difference between the bomber and the Blenheim IF fighter was the

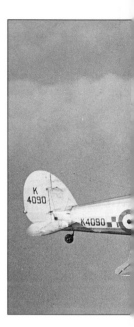

Left: The Bristol Blenheim If was a relatively simple modification to the short-nose Blenheim bomber to fit it for the night-fighter role, involving the installation of a tray in the belly housing four 0.303in forward-firing machine guns. (Crown Copyright)

Above: The Gloster Gauntlet (seen here in the markings of No 19 Squadron) was the last of the RAF's open-cockpit fighter aircraft, designed in the manner of a First World War fighter. (Rolls-Royce via Derek James)

installation of four Browning machine guns in a belly pack, mounted on the bomb-bay doors. Of the 1,552 aircraft produced, 200 were converted to IF configuration. These were the first British aircraft to be equipped with airborne interception (AI) radar and went on to serve during the "Blitz" of 1940-41, during which they were found to have insufficient speed for interception work.

The first operational RAF unit with the Blenheim IF was No 25 Squadron in December 1938, although conversion to type on this squadron and No 600 Squadron, AAF, began slightly earlier in the year. Although unable to excel in the night-fighter role, the Blenheim IF did pioneer night intruder operations in December 1940, with No 23 Squadron.

Data: Blenheim Mk IF

Powerplant	two 840hp Bristol Mercury VIII radial engines
Span	56ft 4in
Length	39ft 9in
Height	9ft 10in
Wing area	469sq ft
Empty weight	8,839lb
Loaded weight	12,500lb
Maximum speed	260mph
Rate of climb	1,540ft/min (initial)
Service ceiling	27,280ft
Range	1,125 miles
Armament	five 0.303in Browning

machine guns, one fuselage mounted and four in a belly gun pack; plus one 0.303in Vickers K gun in the dorsal turret

Gloster Gauntlet

The Gauntlet was the RAF's last open-cockpit fighter biplane. Originally designated SS19B, the prototype Gauntlet was developed from Gloster's experimental SS18 and SS19 six-gun fighters of 1932, making its maiden flight in late 1933. It was accepted as the replacement for the Bulldog to meet RAF Specification 24/33 and 24 aircraft were ordered.

Of metal construction, with fabric covering, equal-span twin-bay wings were adopted with Frise-type ailerons. Great care was taken in the finish of the aircraft, particularly with regard to its streamlining. A fixed undercarriage was fitted and the aircraft was powered by a 645hp Bristol Mercury VIS2 air-cooled, radial engine. The six-gun armament had been reduced to two fixed Vickers guns, mounted in troughs on either side of the nose and firing through the propeller arc.

The first Gauntlet Mk Is entered RAF service with No 19 Squadron at Duxford in May 1935. Improvements followed swiftly, with the adoption of a new type of wing and fuselage construction, a more powerful engine and, on some later aircraft, the use of a Fairey three-bladed, fixed-pitch metal propeller in place of the original wooden two-bladed type. This version was designated the Gauntlet Mk II and 204 were built between 1936 and 1937. At the time it was the RAF's fastest fighter and the type eventually flew with 22 different RAF squadrons, with its peak in 1937 when 14 Fighter Command squadrons flew the Gauntlet.

Fitted with two-way radio equipment, the Gauntlet became the first RAF fighter to effect a ground radar-controlled interception. During early trials of RDF (as it was then known), an aircraft of No 32 Squadron was successfully homed onto an airliner flying over the Thames in November 1937.

By 1938, the Gauntlets were being replaced by Gladiators and Hurricanes, and it was finally withdrawn during 1939. The Gauntlet served overseas until 1940, the last unit so-equipped being No 430 Flight in East Africa, fighting the Italians.

Data: Gauntlet II

Powerplant	one 650hp Bristol Mercury VI radial engine
Span	32ft 9in
Length	26ft 2in
Height	10ft 4in
Wing area	315sq ft
Empty weight	2,775lb

Loaded weight	3,970lb
Maximum speed	230mph at 15,500ft
Time to height	9min to 20,000ft
Service ceiling	35,500ft
Range	460 miles
Armament	two 0.303in Vickers machine guns

Gloster Gladiator

The Gladiator had the dual distinction of being the RAF's last fighter biplane and its first fighter with a fully-enclosed cockpit. Making its maiden flight in September 1934, the Gladiator was a further refinement of the Gauntlet. The first RAF unit to equip with the Gladiator was No 72 Squadron in February 1937, yet by the outbreak of war almost all Fighter Command Gladiator squadrons had been re-equipped.

Using a fuselage and tail unit virtually the same as the Gauntlet, the equal-span wings were of single-bay configuration. The "V"-strut main undercarriage of the Gauntlet was replaced by a low-drag, cantilever mounting with internally-sprung wheels. Designed as a private venture, the SS37 (as the type was then designated) conformed to RAF Specification F7/30 and, after a competition against Blackburn and Westland biplane designs and the original gull-winged Spitfire proposal, it was ordered into production in July 1935.

The SS37 prototype was powered by the 645hp Mercury VIS2 and was armed with a pair of nose-mounted Vickers guns and underwing Lewis guns. For the production Gladiator Mk I, the powerplant was changed for the more-powerful Mercury IX and, as Browning guns became available, these were substituted for the original weapons.

The Gladiator Mk II featured the Mercury VIII engine with an automatic mixture control carburettor, a Vokes air cleaner and an electric starter, allowing cockpit control. A Fairey three-bladed metal propeller replaced the original two-bladed wooden type.

In all 527 Gladiators, plus 60 naval Sea Gladiators, were built, 216 of which were for export. The RAF at home equipped 14 regular squadrons with Gladiators as well as five Auxiliary squadrons. Four Sea Gladiators, including the legendary "Faith", "Hope" and "Charity", were the sole fighter defence of Malta between 11 and 28 June 1940. The last RAF unit to fly the type, No 6 Squadron in Egypt, gave up its aircraft in January 1942.

Data: Gladiator Mk I

Powerplant	one 840hp Bristol Mercury IXS radial engine
Span	32ft 3in
Length	27ft 5in
Height	10ft 4in
Wing area	323sq ft
Empty weight	3,450lb
Loaded weight	4,750lb
Maximum speed	253mph at 14,500ft
Time to height	9.5min to 20,000ft
Service ceiling	33,000ft
Endurance	2hrs
Armament	four 0.303in Browning machine guns; two in the nose, one under each lower wing

Hawker Demon

The 1930 Air Exercises proved somewhat of a shock to the RAF when its Hawker Hart light bombers proved faster than the defending interceptors. The Hart was then considered as the platform for re-introducing the two-seat fighter concept, neglected since the Bristol F2B fighter. In March 1931, No 23 Squadron accepted one flight of Hart fighters for comparative evaluation against two flights of Bulldogs.

The experiment was a success and, after some improvements to the rear gun position, the Hart fighter – now christened the Demon – went into production in 1932. The Demon was of all-metal construction with fabric covering. The unequal-span, staggered wings were of single-bay configuration and the trailing edge of the upper wing centre-section was cutaway to improve the pilot's vision. Both the centre-section and N-type interplane struts were splayed outwards. The main undercarriage was of cross-axle "V"-

Above: Derived from the Gauntlet, the Gloster Gladiator was the RAF's last fighter biplane in service. This example, a Mk II, is displayed at the Battle of Britain Museum at Hendon. (Author)

type with oleos on the forward struts. Early Demons were powered by the 485hp Kestrel IIS engine but, from 1936, later machines had the derated 580hp Kestrel V or 640hp Kestrel VI engines. Its armament consisted of two forward-firing Vickers guns, mounted in troughs on each side of the engine, firing through the propeller arc, plus a Lewis gun in a rear cockpit which was cutdown in a forward slope. Later Demons featured an early form of gun turret. In order to protect the gunner from a slipstream of some 200mph, Fraser-Nash developed a hydraulically-powered, "lobster-back" shield to protect the gunner. This version was known as the Turret-Demon.

A total of 308 Demons was built by Hawker and Boulton Paul, including a general-purpose version (with more on-board equipment) for the Royal Australian Air Force. The Demon served with Nos 23, 25, 29, 41 and 63 Squadrons RAF, and Nos 600, 601, 604, 607 and 608 Squadrons AuxAF, at home, and also saw service abroad with Nos 64 and 74 Squadrons, plus deployments of Nos 23 and 41 Squadrons to the Middle East during the Abyssinian crisis. It was withdrawn from frontline service during 1939.

Data: Demon I

Powerplant	one 584hp Rolls-Royce Kestrel V(DR) in-line supercharged engine
Span	37ft 3in
Length	29ft 7in
Height	10ft 5in
Wing area	348sq ft
Empty weight	3,067lb or 3,336lb with turret
Loaded weight	4,464lb or 4,668lb with turret
Maximum speed	155mph at 3,280ft, 182mph at 16,400ft
Time to height	2.1min to 3,280ft, 16.9min to 19,680ft
Service ceiling	27,500ft
Endurance	2.5hrs
Armament	two forward-firing 0.303in Vickers machine guns in the nose, one 0.303inLewis gun in the rear cockpit; with provision for light bombs under the wings

Hawker Fury

The first RAF fighter which exceeded 200mph to enter squadron service, the Hawker Fury was developed from the Mercury-engined F20/27 of 1928 and the Hornet of 1929. It was evaluated against the Fairey Firefly IIM and chosen as the new RAF interceptor, offering more speed and climb than contemporary day- and night-fighters, but with less endurance. The first Fury made its maiden flight on 25 March 1931 and the type entered service with No 43 Squadron at Tangmere in May 1931.

With its unequal-span, staggered, single-bay wings, the Fury's family resemblance to the Hart is noticeable. The wings featured metal spar, wooden ribs and fabric covering, with ailerons on the upper wing only. The fuselage was of a metal box girder construction with bracing, faired to an oval shape, fabric covered to the rear and with detachable metal cowling panels. The undercarriage was of the conventional cross-axle "V"-type with oleo/rubber shock absorbers on the front legs. The powerplant was a single 525hp Rolls-Royce Kestrel IIS in-line engine. The twin Vickers guns were mounted above the engine and fired through the propeller arc.

The Fury I proved popular with the RAF pilots who flew it, in terms of speed, rate-of-climb and manoeuvrability. The RAF ordered 117 Fury Is and these aircraft equipped Nos 1 and 25 Squadrons, in addition to No 43 Squadron. They remained in service until 1939. A further 30 Fury Is were exported.

Not content with the performance of the Fury I, Hawker began to refine the design in 1932, which offered better performance. Essentially the improvements were the addition of spats to the wheels and the installation of the Kestrel VI, which offered a 20% increase in power. An early Fury I was converted to act as a prototype for the Mk II and, during initial trials at A&AEE Martlesham Heath, reached 228mph and showed a 34% increase in rate-of-climb.

The RAF ordered the Fury II to Specification 14/32 in 1935 and Hawker

Below: Derived from the Hart day bomber, the Hawker Demon became a classic two-seat fighter in the mode of the Bristol F2b. However, in 1934, the RAF adopted a "lobster-back" power-operated turret for the aircraft, designed and built by Frazer Nash, the prototype of which is illustrated. (Frazer Nash)

<table>
</table>

Above: The Hawker Fury was the first RAF fighter to exceed 200mph in 1931. The later Fury II (illustrated by aircraft of No 25 Squadron) entered service in 1937 but were withdrawn during 1938. (BAe)

Order of Battle, September 1938
Fighter Command – HQ: Bentley Priory, Stanmore, Middx

No 11 (Fighter) Group – HQ: Hillingdon House, Uxbridge, Middx

Sqn	Aircraft	Base
1	Hawker Fury I	Tangmere, Sussex
3	Gloster Gladiator I	Kenley, Surrey
17	Gloster Gauntlet II	Kenley, Surrey
25	Gloster Gladiator II	Northolt, Middx
29	Hawker Demon (Turret)	Debden, Essex
32	Gloster Gauntlet II	Biggin Hill, Kent
43	Hawker Fury I	Tangmere, Sussex
54	Gloster Gladiator I	Hornchurch, Essex
56	Hawker Hurricane I	North Weald, Essex
65	Gloster Gladiator I	Hornchurch, Essex
74	Gloster Gauntlet II	Hornchurch, Essex
79	Gloster Gauntlet II	Biggin Hill, Kent
85	Gloster Gladiator I (converting to Hawker Hurricane I)	Debden, Essex
87	Hawker Hurricane I	Debden, Essex
111	Hawker Hurricane I	Northolt, Middx
151	Gloster Gauntlet II	North Weald, Essex
600	Hawker Demon (converting to Bristol Blenheim If)	Hendon, Middx
601	Hawker Demon	Hendon, Middx
604	Hawker Demon	Hendon, Middx

No 12 (Fighter) Group – HQ: Hucknall, Notts

Sqn	Aircraft	Base
19	Gloster Gauntlet I (converting to Vickers-Supermarine Spitfire I)	Duxford, Cambs
23	Hawker Demon (Turret)	Wittering, Cambs
41	Hawker Fury II	Catterick, Yorks
46	Gloster Gauntlet II	Digby, Lincs

Order of Battle, September 1938 (continued)

Sqn	Aircraft	Base
64	Hawker Demon	Church Fenton, Yorks (with a detachment at Martlesham Heath)
66	Gloster Gauntlet II	Duxford, Cambs
72	Gloster Gladiator I	Church Fenton, Yorks
73	Hawker Hurricane I	Digby, Lincs
213	Gloster Gauntlet II	Wittering, Cambs
607	Hawker Demon	Usworth, Co Durham
608	Hawker Demon	Thornaby, Yorks

No 22 (Army Co-operation) Group – HQ: S Farnborough, Hants

2	Hawker Hector (re-equipping with Westland Lysander I)	Hawkinge, Kent
4	Hawker Hector	Odiham, Hants
13	Hawker Hector	Odiham, Hants
16	Westland Lysander I	Old Sarum, Wilts
26	Hawker Hector	Catterick, Yorks
53	Hawker Hector	Odiham, Hants
59	Hawker Hector	Old Sarum, Wilts

No 30 (Balloon) Group – HQ: Kelvin House, London

No 1 Balloon Centre – Kidbrooke
Nos 901, 902, 903 Sqns, AAF

No 2 Balloon Centre – Hook
Nos 904, 905 Sqns, AAF

No 3 Balloon Centre – Stanmore
Nos 906, 907 Sqns, AAF

No 4 Balloon Centre – Chigwell
Nos 908, 909, 910 Sqns, AAF

built 23 aircraft before handing over production to the General Aircraft Company, which built another 89 between 1936-7, including 19 for export. Production aircraft also included an extra fuel tank in the forward fuselage to maintain endurance but which reduced top speed to 223mph. The first Fury II flew in December 1936 and the type entered service with No 25 Squadron at Hawkinge in October 1937, remaining operational until 1938.

The Fury II should not be confused with the High Speed Fury, which was fitted with a 700hp Goshawk engine and, later, the PV-12, which would become the famous Merlin.

Data: Fury II

Powerplant	one 640hp Rolls-Royce Kestrel VI in-line engine
Span	30ft 0in
Length	26ft 8.75in
Height	10ft 2in
Wing area	252sq ft
Empty weight	2,743lb
Loaded weight	3,609lb
Maximum speed	223mph at 16,500ft
Time to height	3.8min to 10,000ft, 8.6min to 19,680ft
Service ceiling	29,500ft
Range	260 miles
Armament	two 0.303in Vickers machine guns, mounted in the upper decking of the nose

Hawker Hurricane I

Although the Hurricane was to become legendary during the Battle of Britain, its initial claim to fame was as the RAF's first monoplane fighter armed with eight machine guns. Hawker began work in 1933 on a Fury Monoplane powered by a Rolls-Royce Goshawk, with a fixed spatted undercarriage. By 1934, the design was being refined to accommodate the PV-12 engine (later named Merlin), the undercarriage was made to retract inwards and an enclosed cockpit was introduced.

The concept so impressed the RAF that Specification F36/34 was drafted around the design and it was immediately adopted for production, meeting, as it did, the specification exactly! The prototype, powered by a Merlin C engine driving a two-bladed propeller, made its maiden flight on 6 November 1935. Initial handling trials confirmed its performance and, in June 1936, 600 aircraft were ordered and this had increased to 1,000 by November 1938.

The first unit to exchange their biplane fighters (Gladiators) for the Hurricane was No 111 Squadron at Northolt, in December 1937. In February 1938, Sqn Ldr J. W. Gillan, OC No 111 Squadron, entered the record books by flying from Edinburgh to Northolt at an average speed of 408mph, flying at 17,000ft with a strong tail wind. By September 1938, five units had re-equipped with the Hurricane – Nos 3, 56, 73, 87 and 111 Squadrons.

The Hurricane's method of construction, which differed little from the Hart or Fury, was a major factor in achieving a short delivery time. The low cantilever wings were of two-spar construction, a metal leading edge and fabric-covered. This, however, was later changed to metal covering from the 682nd Mk I (N2423). Each wing contained four Browning guns, firing outside the propeller arc. The fuselage was of tubular metal, rectangular Warren-girder construction with cross-bracing, with metal panels forward and a fabric-covered rear fuselage (which never changed throughout production).

Apart from the introduction of metal wing skins, the Hurricane I was later improved by the addition of the Merlin III engine with triple ejector exhaust manifolds and a two-pitch, thee-bladed propeller. Although the Hurricane I was refined further, the Mk II did not fly until June 1940. This, and subsequent versions, are outside the scope of this text. In all, 12,950 Hurricanes of all marks were built in the UK, (production ceasing in September 1944) plus a further 1,077 in Canada.

Data: Hurricane Mk I

Powerplant	one 1,030hp Rolls-Royce Merlin II/III
Span	40ft 0in
Length	31ft 5in
Height	13ft 1.5in
Wing area	257.5sq ft
Empty weight	4,670lb
Loaded weight	6,600lb
Maximum speed	324mph at 17,500ft
Time to height	6.3min to 15,000ft
Service ceiling	34,200ft
Range	460 miles
Armament	eight 0.303in Browning machine guns, four in each wing

Vickers-Supermarine Spitfire I

The Spitfire became a legend within two years of entering RAF service. It maintained its reputation, through successive versions, throughout the Second World War and long afterwards. It was one of the few British aircraft to remain in production throughout the war. The format of this book allows the reader to look at the Spitfire in its original form (here) and its later variants (in the "Snapshot" for 1948), perhaps emphasising the advances made over 10 years. For this reason, a full history between the Mk I and the F14 is not given: other books address this subject in greater detail.

The origins of the Spitfire begin with R. J. Mitchell's Schneider Trophy seaplanes, culminating in the S6B which won the trophy outright for Great Britain in 1931 and set the World Speed Record for seaplanes at 407mph. Mitchell then designed a monoplane fighter, designated F7/30, powered by a 600hp Rolls-Royce Goshawk engine and with a cranked wing, having anhedral on the inner and dihedral on the outer mainplanes. Although satisfying RAF specifications, Mitchell felt he could do better and he produced another design with an enclosed cockpit and retractable undercarriage, again using the Goshawk engine.

The design was submitted to the Air Ministry in 1934 and accepted, but with certain modifications. Specification F5/34 called for the installation of eight wing-mounted machine guns and the use of the new Rolls-Royce PV12 engine, subsequently named Merlin. After some intensive re-design work, the prototype Spitfire, built to Specification F37/34, made its maiden flight on 5 March 1936.

From its very first flight the Spitfire proved a thoroughbred, with its performance staggering everyone who witnessed its demonstrations. An initial production contract for 310 aircraft was placed in June 1936. Production began in 1937 and the early Mk I models differed from the prototype very little. The Merlin II replaced the Merlin C engine, a tailwheel replaced the

Above: Later to be the workhorse of the RAF in the Battle of Britain, the Hawker Hurricane I was the first low-wing, eight-gun monoplane fighter in the RAF, entering service in 1937. (BAe)

fighter, fighter-bomber and photo-reconnaissance aircraft, being continually improved to the extent that the ultimate version, the F24, was virtually a different aircraft.

Data: Spitfire Mk IA

Powerplant	one 1,030hp Rolls-Royce Merlin II/III
Span	36ft 10in
Length	29ft 11in
Height	12ft 7.75in
Wing area	242sq ft
Empty weight	4,341lb
Loaded weight	5,820lb
Maximum speed	355mph at 19,000ft
Time to height	9.4min to 20,000ft
Rate of climb	2,500ft/min (max)
Service ceiling	34,000ft
Range	395 miles (includes allowance for take-off climb and 15min combat)
Armament	eight 0.303in Browning machine guns, four in each wing

RESPONSE: ANTI-AIRCRAFT ARTILLERY

tailskid and ejector exhausts were fitted in place of flush ones.

Although early production aircraft were fitted with a two-bladed propeller, a de Havilland three-bladed, variable-pitch airscrew appeared later, which was ultimately replaced by a constant-speed propeller. Later Spitfire Mk Is were given a domed canopy, to improve all-round vision. Early Spitfires entered service with only four guns but, once the A-wing became available, the intended eight-gun armament was fitted, becoming the Mk IA.

The first RAF Spitfires to enter service went to No 19 Squadron at Duxford in August 1938, where they served as an intensive flying trials unit. Some 300 flying hours were completed within a short period of time and corrective action taken on a number of minor defects which appeared. In all, 1,566 Mk Is were built, mostly IAs, but 30 were delivered with the B-wing, with two 20mm Hispano cannon and four Browning machine guns, as the Mk IB.

The Spitfire went on to serve with distinction in practically every theatre of the war. It served the RAF as an interceptor

As the series of international crises during the mid-1930s concentrated the politician's minds, reality began to assert itself. Germany and Italy (along with Japan) were re-arming and the possibility of an air attack on Great Britain was once more considered a reality.

As a result of recommendations from the Reorientation Committee formed in February 1934 (later known as the Air Defence of Great Britain Committee), an expanded Steel-Bartholomew concept was implemented. The AA element of this plan was the decision to give certain key industrial areas their own AA and searchlight defences. The first stage of this (planned for completion by 1940) involved 17 gun batteries and 42 searchlight companies.

In 1936, a "New Ideal" plan raised the total requirement of heavy AA guns to 608 (76 batteries) and 2,547 searchlights (108 companies) with the additional AA units being TA-manned. Almost half of the new units were to be raised in the London region, with the rest in the Midlands and the north of England. By 1938, a regional command system had been created and the responsibilities for searchlights transferred from the Royal Engineers to the Royal Artillery (RA).

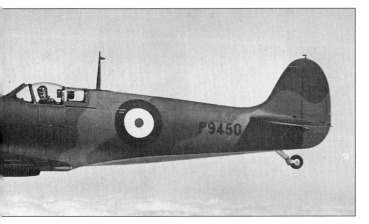

Below: The classic lines of the Supermarine Spitfire I, designed by R.J. Mitchell, first entered service with No 19 Squadron in August 1938. (Greenborough Associates)

The distribution of RA units and its command structure was very similar to that proposed for the Air Defence of Great Britain of 1936. There were two AA Groups: the 1st Group in the Aldershot Command, headquartered at Blackdown, with VI Brigade (comprising three heavy and one light AA gun batteries); and the 2nd Group in the Western Command, headquartered at Lichfield, with I and II Brigades (I Bde – three heavy and four light, II Bde – three heavy and two light gun batteries) all being British-based. Other units within these formations were based abroad. There were 24 brigaded TA-manned AA units in existence by 1938.

With another war imminent and the AA gun defences were being built up once more, it was realised that future production of guns and equipment would be slow. The acquisition of the 40mm Bofors AA gun from Sweden and Poland, together with the Sperry AAA Computer are instances of "buying-in" to cover shortfalls in domestic production. Also, in 1935, the Research Department of the Woolwich Arsenal was asked to investigate the possible use of rockets as a cheap and effective anti-aircraft weapon.

By late 1937, the 3in model of rocket projectile (known as "unrotated projectiles" or "UPs" for secrecy) with an 18lb warhead, had been selected as a future AAA weapon and development continued. Trials were conducted in early 1939 but, due to service insistence that the projector design incorporate a closed breech, the back-flash of the rocket motor disturbed the airflow around the rocket tail fins, causing erratic flight. The problem proved insoluble and the project was abandoned.

The air defence guns in service and in production are described below:

3in 20cwt

As described in the 1918 "Snapshot", this gun was still in service in considerable numbers. No significant changes had been made to the weapon itself. However, better-designed shells, with more reliable and longer-burning fuzes had improved the effective ceiling of the gun to about 25,000ft.

It is worth noting here that even when the 3.7in guns (see below) began appearing in greater numbers during the Second World War, the Army was reluctant to part with the 3in gun, since it was lighter and more easily moved and emplaced than the 3.7in weapon. Consequently, the 3in remained in

place until even its "best friends" had to admit that it could no longer cope with the threat of modern aircraft; the last guns were declared obsolete in 1946.

3.7in Mks 1 and 3

Based on the specification drawn up in 1928, this gun was developed by Vickers during the early-1930s and entered service in April 1937. An extremely advanced weapon, it was designed for laying by data transmission from a predictor and did not have open sights. The Mk 1 guns were mobile mountings – four-wheel platforms with outriggers; the Mk 2 models were static pedestal mountings; the Mk 3 were wartime economy mobile models. All had the same ballistic performance and were originally hand-loaded.

Later, in 1943, the Machine Fuze Setting No 11 (an automatic fuze-setter and loader) appeared and speeded up the rate-of-fire by obviating hand fuze setting and loading. Although more powerful guns appeared in later years, the 3.7in gun remained in service until 1959. This was due to its mobility; all the more powerful weapons were static.

Data: 3.7in Mks 1 and 3

Calibre	3.7in
Type of mounting	pedestal static or platform mobile
Weight in action	20,541lb mobile; 23,000lb static
Max elevation	80°
Effective ceiling	32,000ft
Weight of shell	28lb
Type of shell	HE
Muzzle velocity	2,600 ft/sec
Rate of fire	10 rds/min by hand; 20 rds/min with MFS

Below: Still in service in August 1938, this 3in/20cwt AA gun is seen here being put through its paces in Hyde Park. (Via Ian Hogg)

Right: The unusual angle of this view shows the gun layer's position on the Bofors Mk I 40mm AA gun. This weapon became synonymous with AA guns the world over and served the UK for almost 40 years. (Via Ian Hogg)

40mm Bofors Mk 1

Initially introduced in 1937, the first 100 guns were bought direct from Sweden. A further batch were bought from Poland (who had a licence to manufacture) and, before the end of the year, the UK obtained its own licence to make them.

Although there were various marks of gun and carriage, the basic data remains unchanged. The standard mounting was a four-wheeled platform with outriggers, but there were also static mountings, tank mountings and, of course, naval mountings. All were designed to operate with either open sights or predictors. (The gunners rarely used the predictor until radar became available, late in the Second World War.) The figures below pertain to 1938, although performance improved gradually during the war as refinements were made to both sights and ammunition.

Data: 40mm Bofors Mk 1

Calibre	40mm
Type of mounting	cruciform platform, four wheel
Weight in action	4,368lb
Max elevation	90°
Effective ceiling	5,000ft (restricted by sights and predictor); 23,500ft maximum
Weight of shell	2lb
Type of shell	HE impact-fuzed, with self-destruct after 3,500-5,500yd flight, depending on the tracer
Muzzle velocity	2,700 ft/sec
Rate of fire	120 rds/min in clips of four

4.5in Gun Mk 2

This heavy gun was used for the defence of vulnerable points against high-flying aircraft. The naval calibre of 4.5in was adopted for commonality of ammunition supply, as most of these weapons were emplaced around naval bases and ports where 4.5in naval ammunition was readily obtainable. It was only used on static mountings.

Data: 4.5in Gun Mk 2

Calibre	4.5in
Type of mounting	Static pedestal with shield
Weight in action	14.75 tons
Max elevation	80°
Effective ceiling	34,500ft
Weight of shell	54lb
Type of shell	HE
Muzzle velocity	2,400ft/sec
Rate of fire	8rds/min

CRITIQUE

It has been said that the year between the Munich Crisis and the commencement of hostilities in September 1939 proved vital in the re-armament of Great Britain and the preparation of its air defences. While in general this is true, this decade was one where, although the military planners and technicians came up with solutions, the politicians almost left it too late to implement them.

The RAF's fighter force was all-biplane until the Hurricane entered service, followed a year later by the Spitfire. The AA gun defences were equally, woefully, underestimated until Treasury purse-strings were slowly loosened in the the late-1930s. Even then, mobilisation plans were far from efficient, as the call-out following the invasion of Czechoslovakia in September 1938 was to prove. It proved the deficiencies highlighted in Parliament by a Member serving in a TA AA regiment the previous May. The Government only just survived a vote of censure and it was this which put the rearmament programme into top gear.

Although obvious now, the attitudes of the time may be considered complacent. The British public was not as fortunate then, as they are today, with having as wide a specialised press dealing with defence and military aviation matters. In 1938, as far as aviation was concerned, there was only *The Aeroplane* and *Flight* to which the public could turn for comment on events and capabilities. Even then, what was published was slanted heavily on the strength of the RAF and its ability to defend this country, combined with an-almost patronising view that bombers were not the great threat they were made out to be. Investigative journalism by knowledgeable comentators, as we know it today, was never considered.

Commenting on the aviation press of the time the respected author Bill Gunston suggests "these stalwart magazines saw as their mission a spirited defence of all things British, concentrating on what seemed to be the good things and ignoring the bad or the missing. To a very large degree editorial policy was dictated by the overriding wish to please the people who exerted power over the magazine, such as the Air Ministry Press Section, the Royal Aero Club and, above all, the advertisers."

Typical of such coverage is the article by Maj F. A. de V. Robertson published in *Flight* on 22 September 1938. It reflects the somewhat blinkered approach of the time. Entitled "What of the Air Menace?", the article examines "the potentialities of attack and defence ... in the light of the Present Situation". While correctly defining the two principle roles of the bomber to act as long-range artillery to attack military objectives and to terrorise a civilian population into demanding its Government should sue for peace, the author takes the view that the bomber threat is not as great as has been made out. In countering Baldwin's con-

tention that "the bomber always gets through" – a remark the author considers "ill-considered" – he notes that "Madrid, Valencia and Barcelona were never forced into surrender by air raids, even when they had practically no air defences". He maintains that "A city which has strong defences and is practised in air raid precautions is in far less jeopardy".

While one must accept that such an undercurrent of optimism was the norm at the time, there was a questionable lack of realism. "When aiming his bombs, the bomber must fly, if even for only a brief period, on a straight and level course. The defence will be waiting for that moment, and either guns or fighters will be ready for it. The guns can make very good shooting when the bomber flies straight and level." Maj Robertson's article also reflects the view of the time that France provided a significant buffer against German air-raids and, should they occur, increase the warning time for the RAF.

Against this background of "public information", one might have expected an honest appreciation of the *Luftwaffe's* equipment to be carried in a journal such as *Flight*. In the issue of 13 October 1938, leading an article entitled "Germany's Air Arm", the un-named writer begins: "It is regretable ... that more information on its equipment is not available. However a certain amount of data have filtered through to this country by devious means ..." In-country reportage by a staff writer or correspondent could have been arranged, for better coverage in the UK is just what the Nazi leaders wanted. Gunston maintains "nearly all doors would have been opened" and cites a visit to the Messerschmitt works at Augsberg he made as a child with a German-speaking uncle. He met Willy Messerschmitt and "saw lots of aeroplanes including DB600-engined Bf109s and the prototype Bf110". Roy Fedden of Bristol and Charles Linbergh both made visits to Germany and saw most of the *Luftwaffe's* capability. The information was available.

However, it must be said that once war was declared a year later, the country's air defences were better prepared to meet the foe than in September 1938. Once the reality that Hitler was not content with the annexation of part of Czechoslovakia, then the build-up which followed was vital. Yet it still took the defeat of France to ensure the state-of-mind required to win the Battle of Britain in 1940.

1948

"SNAPSHOT" – 1948

In the intervening 10 years since 1938, the Second World War had been fought and the greatest air defence battle of all time, the Battle of Britain, won by the RAF. It is not the purpose of this book to describe this and the many other air defence battles of this war: many, more-learned tomes have addressed this subject.

Suffice it to say, here, that the major technical innovations to come out of the Second World War, as far as the RAF air defender was concerned, were the jet engine; improvements in radar, both on the ground and in the air; the beginnings of electronic warfare (EW) and the very first guided missiles. Of these, only the first two developments had reached operational service with the RAF, along with some elements of EW. The others would come.

Of more importance in the immediate postwar years was how the British armed forces, particularly the RAF, would be restructured in a peacetime environment, and to what level the air defence element would be reduced. In autumn 1947, the Labour Government announced that defence spending would be limited to £600 million per year. This was a considerable sum in its day but less than the services had expected. The RAF's share of the budget was £173 million for 1948-49, compared with £255 million in 1946-47 and £214 million for 1947-48.

It was some consolation to the RAF however, when, in October 1947, the Minister of Defence, A. V. Alexander, told the House of Commons that the Government's first priority was to fund the research required to develop the weapons of the future. The second priority was "to maintain the structure of the RAF and its initial striking power". This followed the decision in January 1947 to fund and develop a British atomic weapon. In the 1948 Defence Statement, these priorities were confirmed, with the Royal Navy coming second in ascendancy and the Army last.

Such prioritising was, unfortunately, a necessity, given the state of the UK's financial and industrial weakness at this time. It was assumed that a major war would be unlikely in the five years to 1952 and only slightly more likely in the following five years. Having endured six years of global war and coming out on the winning side, such assumptions were met with popular approval.

With the declared policy and reduced funding, the RAF was forced to concentrate on essentials. Bomber and Fighter Commands would reap the most benefits, followed by Coastal Command with Transport Command and the "tail" elements becoming the "Cinderellas" of the service. That said, the Air Staff had long acknowledged the need for a broader-based establishment, with the accent on squadron mobility and the transport element was required to ensure the concept's success.

The RAF had been looking at ways of achieving this aim since 1943 and several plans had been made, none of which received official sanction, until Plan E of summer 1947. With a firmer idea of the responsibilities of the service and the resources available, Plan E was thought to be adequate for the RAF's needs. Under Plan E, the RAF had a target of 165 squadrons (some 1,500 aircraft), of which 51 squadrons (536 aircraft) were fighters. While most of the squadrons were to be UK-based, 24 would be deployed in Germany, 18 in the Middle East and 18 in the Far East. It should also be pointed out that, at this time, the term "fighter" encompassed both the pure air defence aircraft (essentially radar-equipped nightfighters) and dual-role fighter-bombers without the benefit of radar (used as "dayfighters" or "fighter, ground attack" as circumstances dictated). The latter being types that, today, we know as pure ground-attack aircraft.

However, the target strengths of Plan E were still required to be adjusted, downwards, to meet the new limits on defence spending. As might be expected, the main reductions were achieved in the transport field, although the bomber force was cut by 16 aircraft and Coastal Command lost its anti-shipping strike squadrons. The fighter force was the only element of Plan E to survive virtually intact.

Following the end of hostilities, there was the equally thorny problem of manpower to consider and the need to demobilise many thousands of personnel. Among the "demobbed" men were many valuable and experienced personnel and, despite the still considerable number of men under training, there was a distinct lack of balance in the skilled aircrew and tradesmen required within the RAF. It was acknowledged, in 1948, that the RAF was under a considerable strain and that lack of trained men was disorganising the work of many units. It was not until 1949 that stability and balance returned to the RAF, allowing more normal levels of efficiency to be achieved.

The provision of aircraft and other equipment was another factor in the imbalance of the transitional period between war and peace establishments. In 1945, many of the RAF's aircraft consisted of types supplied under the Anglo-US Lend-Lease Act of 1941. With the exception of the Douglas Dakota transport aircraft, it was decided that all Lend-Lease aircraft were to be given-up (ie, returned to the United States or destroyed) and be replaced by British types. This was explained in the 1946 Defence Statement, which stated that existing stocks of British aircraft would be used, wherever possible, with only a limited number of modern replacements. The policy was clarified in the 1947 Defence Statement which referred to the progressive rearmament of Fighter Command with the most modern type of jet fighter. (It also stated that Transport Command would receive small numbers of British designed-and-built aircraft.)

So, in June 1948, the RAF found itself with a considerably smaller force than that proposed in Plan E. There were 80 regular squadrons based in the UK, plus 20 Royal Auxiliary Air Force (RAuxAF) squadrons – the prefix "Royal" having been conferred on the Auxiliaries in December 1947. Of these, Fighter Command had 25 squadrons – some 207 aircraft – which included Air Observation Post (non-fighter) types. Based overseas were 33 more full squadrons and six cadre squadrons (of all types). Although the Germany-based forces were beginning to receive jet-powered fighters, the Middle and Far East air forces had to rely on Second World War designs such as the Spitfire, Tempest and Beaufighter.

THE THREAT

As has been stated, the general assumption was that no major war would be fought in

the period to 1952 and it was unlikely that one would be fought in the five years thereafter. Events in Europe and the Far East (communist insurgency in Malaya and the events which led to the Korean War) were to bring crises that would temper this postwar optimistic view.

With the Axis powers defeated, it was the former ally of the UK and United States – the Soviet Union – who emerged as the perceived threat. In June 1948, all hopes of a trouble-free and peaceful Europe were shattered when the Soviet Union severed ground lines of communication to Berlin, in defiance of an international agreement. Murmurs of the Soviet threat had been heard ever since 1945 and the first indications of a potential blockade of Berlin became apparent early in 1948. Once this blockade was imposed, an air-bridge to the city – to become known as the Berlin Airlift – was initiated. Although the Soviets did not precipitate open conflict, their hand was revealed.

By the end of 1948, the Allies had effectively beaten the Berlin blockade (although it was to continue into 1949). It was the first "battle" of the so-called Cold War and it was the Soviet Union's first defeat. As yet, the Soviet Union did not possess nuclear weapons, but they were not far off. As far as the UK was concerned, the Soviet's long-range manned bomber force was emerging as a potential threat, yet in 1948 it possessed neither sufficient effective bombers nor the nuclear weapons it would have in later years.

To understand the situation regarding the role of the long-range bomber within the Soviet armed forces strategy, one must turn back the pages a little. Russia has had a long tradition of strategic bombers. In 1917, the Imperial Russian Air Force equipped a long-range bomber force with the world's first four-engined heavy bomber. This was the *Il'ya Muromets* designed by Igor Sikorsky (later to win fame as the designer and builder of pioneering flying boats and as "Father of the Modern Helicopter"). Yet the economic chaos which followed the Bolshevik revolution, in the aftermath of the First World War, retarded the development of strategic aircraft.

Even so, the TB-series of heavy bombers was developed, culminating with the TB-3 which, in 1932, was the world's first force of all-metal, four-engined, long-range bombers. A separate strategic air force was constituted in 1937 but, as support of the ground forces took precedence over long-range bombardment, this eventually became a tactical force during the Second World War (or the Great Patriotic War, as it was known in the Soviet Union). Soviet air strategy was not treated as being "independent" but rather as an adjunct to the land battle, being the third dimension of combined-arms warfare. From 1941, the central objective of the Soviet Union was to defeat Nazi Germany and expel the *Wehrmacht* from Soviet soil.

However, it is interesting to note that, during the Teheran conference of 1943, Stalin is reported to have asked a number of "intelligent questions" regarding US long-range bombers. This interest was followed-up by the request, a year later, for over 500 American B-17 Flying Fortress and B-24 Liberator four-engined bombers under the Lend-Lease Act. Such aircraft would have, in addition to taking the bomber offensive into Germany from the East, have made a substantial amount of what we today call "technology transfer" available to the Soviets. His request was refused.

Later, on 31 July 1944, Stalin had his pattern for the future when the first of three Boeing B-29 Superfortress bombers force-landed in Siberia after long-range operations over Japan. A fourth was acquired after a crash-landing. These aircraft were to serve as patterns for a reverse-engineering programme, enabling the Soviets to acquire current generation instruments, mechanisms and systems. The Tupolev design bureau was tasked with duplicating the airframe and Shvetsov, the Wright R-3350 Cyclone radial engines, which were designated ASh-73TK. The first model took to the air in July 1947. Over 1,000 of the copied aircraft, designated

Tu-4 (later assigned the NATO codename "Bull") were ordered. After 1949, when the first Soviet air-delivered atomic bombs became available, Stalin had his nuclear bomber force and Soviet industry had leapt a generation in bomber development.

Meanwhile, prior to the arrival of the B-29s, the groundwork on an independent bomber force was again being prepared. In 1946, the bomber regiments of the Soviet Air Force were reconstituted as the *Dal'naya Aviatsiya* (DA), otherwise known as Long Range Aviation, the title it would bear for the next 35 years.

The DA also possessed small numbers of other aircraft, such as the Il-4 and the Pe-8, but these were the remnants of the Second World War bomber force and, in the context of an air attack on the UK, may be discounted.

Tupolev Tu-4 "Bull"

The arrival of the Boeing B-29s have already been described, together with the allocation of airframe development of the Tu-4 to Tupolev and the ASh-73TK engine development to Shvetsov. An initial order was made for 20 "Chinese copies" of the B-29, production of which began in 1945. The first three aircraft, indistinguishable from the originals, except for a whip radio aerial beneath the rear fuselage, were displayed at the Soviet Aviation Day display at Tushino in 1948.

The ASh-73TK engines were less powerful than the R-3350 originals but this, to a degree, was compensated for by the lower weight of the Tu-4 airframe. The engines drove four-bladed propellers of Soviet design. The armament was concentrated in four remotely-controlled, twin-gun turrets,

Below: The Soviet Tupolev Tu-4 "Bull" was a copy of the American Boeing B-29 produced by "reverse-engineering" and armed with Soviet guns and powered by the ASh-73TK engines. (Greenborough Associates)

two above and two below the fuselage, plus three in the tail position. Initially, they were fitted with the 12.7mm BS machine gun, equivalent to the US 0.50in weapon, but later these were changed to the 23mm NS cannon, with one tail gun being deleted. However, the Tu-4 lacked the radar bomb sights and long-range navigation equipment of its American pattern, making night and bad weather operations all the more difficult.

The Tu-4 began to enter service in 1948-49 and, by 1955, was being replaced by jet-powered bombers with all frontline aircraft having been replaced by 1960. Some continued in service as aerial refuelling tankers, paratroop transports and maritime reconnaissance aircraft. In all, some 1,200 Tu-4s were built, of which 400 were later supplied to the People's Republic of China. As far as 1948 is concerned, the Tu-4 "Bull" represented the promise of an appropriate airborne delivery system and, in the next few years, was to give the Soviet Union the chance to climb the learning curve associated with the technical and operating experience that had lapsed during the Great Patriotic War.

Data: Tu-4 "Bull"

Powerplant	four 2,300hp Shvetsov ASh-73TK 18-cylinder radial engines
Span	141ft 4in
Length	99ft 1in
Height	27ft 9in
Wing area	1,680sq ft
Empty weight	75,000lb
Loaded weight	104,940lb (max T/O)
Maximum speed	360mph at 33,000ft
Service ceiling	36,745ft
Range (combat)	3,050 miles (with full bomb load)
Armament	10 x 23mm NS cannon,

plus up to 11,000lb of bombs in two internal bays

DETECTION AND IDENTIFICATION

The decade between 1938 and 1948 witnessed one of the most intensive periods of technical innovation in history. Under the goad of war, a complete new science emerged and electronically-based systems became the very foundation of the air defence system. Aircraft detection had developed and the accompanying need for communication had progressed from HF to VHF to ensure clarity and efficiency in controlling the fighter force.

Technology really had been decisive in the Battle of Britain and, for almost 20 years, the Chain Home pylons were a feature of the British landscape. Good Friday 1939 proved to be a significant date for, on that day, a regular 24hr watch of the skies was commenced, which continues to this day. When war was declared on 3 September 1939, a total of 19 Chain Home radars were operational. In the months that followed, further stations were planned and, by the end of 1941, the entire coastlines of Great Britain and Northern Ireland were covered. At the same time, the radar equipment was continually improved to offer good performance and reliability. Rapid advances in technology also meant that "gap fillers" to deal with low level attacks were also introduced and other types of radar antennae became common across the country. However, the original Chain Home system continued to be the primary early warning system throughout the war, some stations serving until the 1950s.

In the wider role, electronics were used in all types of operation ranging from personal radar beacons for locating aircrew in case of bailout, through an increasing range of Electronic Warfare (EW) systems, to navigation and blind bombing aids.

For the defensive role, the dayfighter had become more effective, thanks to radar. However, the *Luftwaffe's* change of tactics to night bombing had caused problems for the fighter in actually finding the aircraft that it was being vectored towards. Early attempts at nightfighting had been fraught and, often, it was just luck that the "Mark One, Mod Zero" eyeball detected a flash of exhaust, or moonlight and a lack of cloud made the effort easier.

The answer was to be found in Airborne Interception (AI) radar. Simple in theory but very difficult in practice. The Chain Home used high power and covered an appreciable area in which to set up the complete system. The attempt to put a radar inside an aeroplane required a completely new approach in which the first consideration was the use of a much shorter wavelength.

This type of application had been envisaged in the mid-1930s and an early associated experiment, using a Handley Page Heyford once again, was conducted in 1937. Power requirements posed a major problem and it was not until the latter part of 1938 that a suitable thermionic device could be provided. By the following year a system was in being and, though still highly experimental, it was designated AI Mk I and first flew in May 1939 in a Fairey Battle.

Discussion followed as to the best type of aircraft for its combat use and, in the context of the times and state of development of the AI, it was decided to use a converted Blenheim Mk I bomber/dayfighter. In July 1939, a Minute was raised to call for the installation of 21 AI Mk II sets, which was the production version of the first equipment. The first of the aircraft were delivered in November 1939 and were used for initial trials and training. Inevitably, difficulties abounded as the new equipment was tested in service conditions with recurring problems of ambiguity. This led to the development of AI Mk III which gave a good indication of targets at a range of three to four miles.

Difficulties persisted and there was even an indication that some senior figures in the military were prepared to abandon the idea completely. Other ideas of combating the night bomber were suggested, including bombing from above though this still posed a problem of detection and location and the use of airborne searchlights. This latter concept became a reality in the form of the Turbinlite.

Basically it was not possible, even with AI, to effectively use the Chain Home system to place a nightfighter in optimum range of the target. There was a need for a system that could offer an instantaneous indication of the relative position of both the fighter and its target. This requirement was passed to the Air Ministry Research Establishment (AMRE) and, as a result of their work, a production Ground Control Interception (GCI) radar was available by the end of 1940. But on the night of 22/23 July 1940 an AI-equipped Blenheim NFI succeeded in destroying a Dornier Do17 off the South Coast.

In addition to the rapid development of these various radar-based techniques, it is apposite to note that, from December 1939, the RAF had begun to monitor German radio traffic. In February 1940, the first listening post was established at Hawkinge, in what became known as the "Y" Service. This was an important operation which allowed the RAF to gather a great deal of intelligence about the enemy's order of battle as well as collating callsigns and assigned frequencies. The service was supplemented by D/F which provided further useful infor-

mation to the Fighter Controllers. This service was closely allied with the intelligence-gathering operation at Bletchley Park and the exploitation of the German Ultra signal decoder.

The intelligence information was invaluable to the Fighter Command organisation and its main operations room at Bentley Priory. Communication was largely dependent upon a comprehensive telephone network, backed up by a number of emergency lines and by a teleprinter network.

The problems of AI were continually being addressed and such was the tempo of the times that each new "Mark" was separated by weeks rather than years, such as would be normally expected. The Mk IV made its debut and overcame many of the earlier problems and it was fitted in a new aeroplane – the Bristol Beaufighter NFI.

By the time that the war was over, radar had undergone considerable refinement with the introduction of centimetric radar and an ever-increasing capability. The threat of aerial bombardment on Great Britain had gradually declined as the war progressed, to a point where the civilian population was taking a very relaxed attitude to the subject of Air Raid Precautions. Sporadic attacks were harassed by an increasingly-effective nightfighter force; they faced well organised anti-aircraft gun systems; were decoyed by false fires and, even, suffered interference with their external navigation systems. German results were poor and their bomber attrition rate was high. Then, in June 1944, there was a rude interruption as the V-1 "Doodlebug" offensive began, to be followed by V-2 rockets (of a type now referred to as surface-to-surface missiles). This presented a new face to warfare and provided an indication of things to come.

With the ending of the war in 1945, the RAF found that it was now operating at a "frontline" deep within Europe. Once again it seemed that a European threat to Britain was overcome but, unlike 1918, there was not quite the same speed of operational rundown and worrying political trends suggested that a complex new European scenario was developing in which Russia, our wartime ally, was to become the perceived threat for the next 40 years. In addition, the emergence of self determination ambitions among many of the nations that were still thought of as part of the British Empire, demanded an element of military power to contain the situation, though many of these became local wars of attrition and a contin-

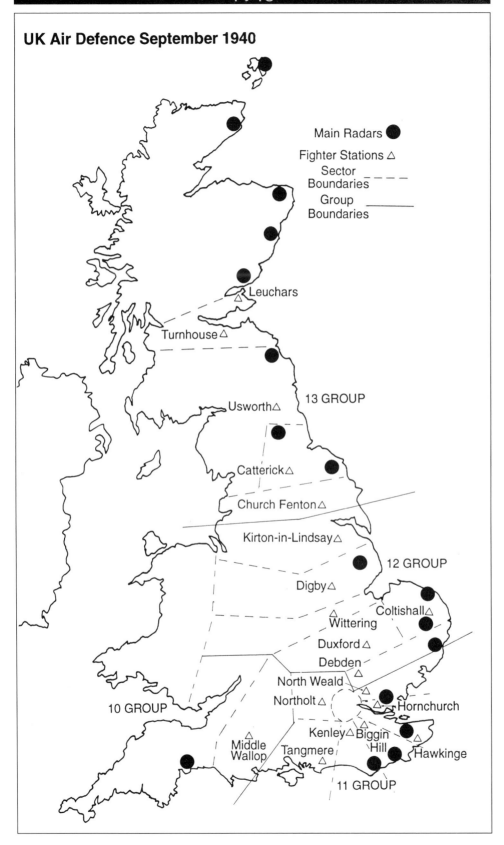

UK Air Defence September 1940

Main Radars ●
Fighter Stations △
Sector Boundaries − − −
Group Boundaries ——

Leuchars △
Turnhouse △

13 GROUP

Usworth △
Catterick △
Church Fenton △
Kirton-in-Lindsay △

12 GROUP

Digby △
Coltishall △
Wittering △
Duxford △
Debden
North Weald
Northolt △
Hornchurch
Kenley △ Biggin Hill
Middle Wallop △
Tangmere △
Hawkinge

10 GROUP

11 GROUP

uing drain on the UK's resources. Meanwhile, Europe was being increasingly spoken of in terms of East and West and the words "Iron Curtain" and "Cold War" entered the language.

Of course, there was the inevitable contraction in defence contracts and companies sought other ways of using the new technology. In terms of radar, it was necessary to address the needs of a new air transport network and the establishment of an airways system. The "GEE box", that had been used to navigate British bombers during the night offensive, was now fitted in airliners and airfield control radars made their appearance. Although the next decades saw the growth of massive civilian radar systems, they were also capable of assisting the RAF in monitoring British airspace and should not be ignored in military terms.

In the decade from 1938, the speed and operating capabilities of aircraft had increased considerably and the jet engine was now seen as the powerplant of the future. Once again, Britain was faced by the threat of the bomber and although the "bomber will always get through" philosophy had lost its most potent effect, it was realised that the potential threat was now very real.

In 1946, a senior RAF officer was given the task of considering future requirements and to make recommendations. These were duly delivered and reflected the increasing scale of the problem by suggesting that the whole of the UK be divided into just six sectors, rather than the previous multiplicity of sectors. It was also suggested that a clear distinction be made between tactical control and interception control, this latter task to be under the control of GCI stations in the particular sector. New, dedicated GCI buildings were erected and featured the by-now traditional plotting table, supported by the inflow of intelligence from Chain Home stations, Observer Corps reports and the sector's own radars. The system was a direct development of that used during the war and a descendent of the final system established at the end of the Great War. It was just that it covered a larger area and was on a 24hr basis in all weathers.

By the end of 1948, it was obvious that a strong defensive posture would have to be maintained for some considerable time. Long range rocket systems were already in being, aircraft could operate in all weathers at extended ranges and the shadow of the nuclear age was soon to reach Britain.

RESPONSE: AIRCRAFT & ARMAMENT

While the jet-powered fighter had now become operational, the propeller-driven fighter was not yet extinct. Continual development of Second World War aircraft accounted for all the major types in service in this year.

The advent of airborne radar had also seen the nightfighter take on a renaissance. With Airborne Interception (AI) radar, the nightfighter could be vectored onto the enemy aircraft, but left to its own devices to close individual targets. The dayfighter, as yet not equipped with AI radar, while having ground radar for vectors, still relied on the "Mark One, Mod Zero" eyeball for target discrimination and guns for its killing power.

For *aficionados* of aircraft nomenclature, it must be noted that official Air Ministry numbering of aircraft marks above Mk XX (ie, 20) in Roman numerals was changed to Arabic numerals in February 1942, at which time role prefix letters were also introduced. From 1947, all mark numbers were expressed in Arabic numerals.

de Havilland Mosquito NF30/36

Built of non-strategic materials – basically plywood – de Havilland's "Wooden Wonder" was developed for many operational roles: bomber, fighter, photo-reconnaissance; and adapted for numerous secondline duties with the RAF. Parallel naval versions were also produced. Of the 7,781 Mosquitoes built, only 1,071 were built after the end of hostilities.

The first DH98 Mosquito made its maiden flight on 25 November 1940, in bomber configuration. The first fighter version, the NFII, was included in the first batch of 50 aircraft ordered in March 1940. It was armed with four 20mm Hispano cannon in the front fuselage belly and four 0.303in Browning machine guns in the extreme nose and was fitted with AI Mk IV or Mk V radar. These aircraft were powered by two Rolls-Royce Merlin 21 (1,480hp) or Merlin 23 (1,390hp) engines. The first two Mosquito fighter units were Nos 23 and 157 Squadrons, which formed in May 1941.

The NFXXX (NF30) was introduced in 1944 most of which were fitted with Merlin 76 (1,710hp) engines for high altitude operation. This was the last nightfighter variant to see wartime service and more than 350 were built. By May 1945 seven squadrons were used for home defence duties, with a further six squadrons operating in support of bomber operations. Eight Fighter Command squadrons (Nos 23, 25, 29, 141, 151, 219, 264 and 307 Squadrons) and four AuxAF units (Nos 605, 608, 609 and 616 Squadrons) flew the NFXXX.

One of the last versions of this private-venture aircraft, the Mosquito NF36, was first flown in May 1945 and 163 were built. Derived from the NFXXX, it was powered by Merlin 113 engines, equipped with US-built AI Mk X radar and armed with four 20mm cannon. Six Fighter Command units (Nos 23, 25, 29, 141, 219 and 264 Squadrons) flew the NF36 and the type remained in frontline service until 1953.

Data: Mosquito NF36

Powerplant	two 1,690hp Rolls-Royce Merlin 113/114/113A/114A engines
Span	54ft 2in
Length	41ft 9in
Height	15ft 3in
Wing area	435sq ft
Empty weight	15,400lb (all weights and performance figures are for Mk XXX)
Loaded weight	22,300lb
Maximum speed	407mph at 28,000f
Time to height	7.5min to 15,000ft
Service ceiling	39,000ft
Range	1,300 miles or 1,1770 miles with auxiliary tanks
Armament	Four 20mm Hispano cannon

de Havilland Hornet F1 and F3

Like its illustrious forebear the Mosquito, de Havilland's DH103 Hornet was also a private-venture development. Designed as an island-hopping, long-range fighter for the Pacific campaign, the Hornet made its maiden flight on 28 July 1944, but was too late to see service during the war. The first RAF unit to equip with the Hornet was No 64 Squadron, Horsham St Faith, in May 1946.

Of wood and metal construction, the single-seat Hornet was a much more graceful aircraft than the Mosquito. Combined with a pair of Merlin engines, a 130 to port and a 131 to starboard, the prototype reached a top speed of 485mph. Once the armament of four 20mm cannon and other operational equipment had been installed to produce the production F1 version, this top speed was reduced to 472mph.

During the handling trials of September-October 1945, the Hornet F1 was criticised at A&AEE Boscombe down for deficiencies in longitudinal stability. To correct this problem, a dorsal fin was introduced and, together with an increase in internal fuel capacity from 360 to 540gal, this became the Hornet F3. A&AEE handling trials between July 1947 and May 1948 cleared this version for service. In all, 209 Hornets were built for the RAF, most of which were the F1/3 model but five were the PR2 version and 12, the FR4.

Only four Fighter Command units were equipped with the Hornet: No 64 Squadron (previously mentioned) was the first, moving via Church Fenton to Linton-on-Ouse in

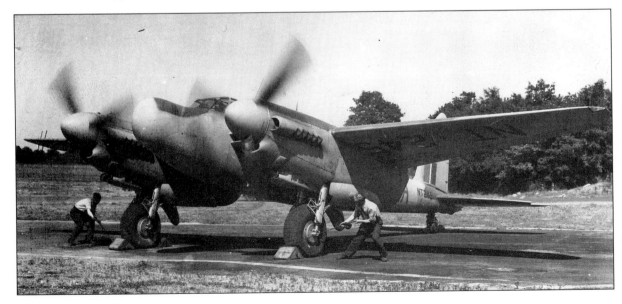

Below: The penultimate fighter version of the genre, the wartime de Havilland Mosquito NF30 was still in service with six RAuxAF squadrons as a night fighter in 1948. This aircraft is seen at West Malling in August 1947. (Via Phil Birtles)

Above: The fastest piston-engine fighter ever produced for the RAF, the de Havilland Hornet F3 only ever served with four RAF units within Fighter Command, a No 41 Squadron aircraft being illustrated. (Via Phil Birtles)

1947, being joined by No 65 Squadron later the same year. The second Hornet unit to form was No 19 Squadron at Church Fenton in 1946, which was joined by No 41 Squadron in 1947. All four units exchanged their F1 models for the Hornet F3 sometime during 1948. These aircraft remained in service until replacement by Meteor F8s during 1951. Three other Hornet squadrons were formed within the Far East Air Force, where they were used for rocket strikes against terrorists in Malaya and the last of these, No 45 Squadron, gave up their aircraft in June 1955. The Hornet had the distinction of being the fastest piston-engined fighter ever used by the RAF.

Data: Hornet F3

Powerplant	two 2,030hp Rolls-Royce Merlin 130/131 engines
Span	45ft 0in
Length	36ft 8in
Height	14ft 2in
Wing area	361sq ft
Empty weight	12,880lb
Loaded weight	20,900lb
Maximum speed	472mph at 22,000ft
Rate of climb	4,000ft/min (initial)
Service ceiling	35,000ft
Range	3,000 miles
Armament	four 20mm Hispano

cannon in nose, plus provision for 2,000lb of rockets or bombs beneath the wings

de Havilland Vampire F1 and F3
The second jet-powered fighter in the RAF, the de Havilland DH100 Vampire entered service in April 1946 with No 247 Squadron at Odiham. Initially known as the "Spider-Crab", the design of the Vampire to Specification E6/41 began in 1941. Unlike the Meteor (see below), de Havilland opted

for single-engined configuration and the twin-boom layout was adopted in order to reduce the length of the jetpipe, thus keeping power losses to a minimum. The prototype DH100 made its maiden flight in September 1943, powered by a Goblin centrifugal-flow turbojet, rated at 2,700lb st. This aircraft had tall, pointed fins but production aircraft standardised on a square-cut fin.

A contract for 120 production Vampire F1s was placed in May 1943, subcontracted to English Electric at Preston, and this was later increased to 300 two years later. The first production Vampire F1 flew from Samlesbury on 20 April 1945, powered by the same engine as the prototype (as were the subsequent 39 production aircraft). From the 41st Vampire F1, the uprated Goblin GN2 was adopted, together with provision for auxiliary drop tanks under the wings. From the 51st Vampire, a pressurised cockpit and bubble canopy were adopted.

The Vampire F3 replaced the F1 in production after 170 examples of the earlier model had been built. The F3 model had the fuel capacity increased from 202 to 326gal, with provision for two 100- or 200gal drop tanks. It also had a redesigned tail assembly, with the tailplane lowered and the finshape reverting to the traditional "DH" type of fin-and-rudder. These changes increased the loaded weight of the aircraft to 11,970lb, but they also improved the range (at 30,000ft) from 730 miles to 1,390miles (with 200gal drop tanks). The prototype Vampire F3 flew on 4 November 1946 and 117 production aircraft were built.

The first Vampire F1 unit (No 247 Squadron) was followed by No 130 Squadron in June 1946 and, in January 1947, was renumbered as No 72 Squadron

89

at Odiham. There it was joined by No 54 Squadron which, together with No 247 Squadron, made up Fighter Command's first Vampire Wing. In July 1948, Vampires of No 54 Squadron became the first RAF jet aircraft to cross the Atlantic, flying via Iceland, Greenland and Labrador. The RAuxAF received its first Vampire F1s (its first jet-powered aircraft) in July 1948, when No 605 (County of Warwick) Squadron exchanged its Mosquito nightfighters for Vampires. A dozen RAuxAF squadrons were equipped with Vampire F1/3s.

Fighter Command began to exchange the Vampire F3s at Odiham for the FB5 fighter-bomber version from late 1949, reflecting a slight change of role. Later versions of the Vampire served with the RAF in Germany, the Middle East and the Far East. The last Vampires were replaced by the Venoms in 1955-56.

Data: Vampire F1

Powerplant	one de Havilland Goblin D Gn.2 centrifugal-flow turbojet, rated at 3,100lb st
Span	40ft 0in
Length	30ft 9in
Height	8ft 10in
Wing area	266sq ft
Empty weight	6,372lb
Loaded weight	10,480lb
Maximum speed	540mph at 20,000ft
Rate of climb	28,500ft
Range	730 miles
Armament	four 20mm Hispano cannon

Gloster Meteor F4

The Meteor had the distinction of being both the first jet-powered fighter in RAF service and the only Allied jet fighter to see service during the Second World War. Having designed and produced the first British jet aircraft, the experimental E28/39, which first flew on 15 May 1941, it was only natural for Glosters to be tasked with developing a jet fighter.

Work on the aircraft, to Specification F9/40, began in 1940 and eight prototypes were authorised, with a production contract for 20 aircraft being placed in September

Left: Gloster's Meteor had the distinction of being the first jet-powered fighter in RAF service. This Meteor F4, armed with four 20mm cannon, entered service with Fighter Command in 1947. (BAe)

Below: The de Havilland Vampire F1 was the first fighter in the world to exceed 500mph and, although it was too late for war service, No 247 Squadron of the

Odiham Wing was re-equipped by June 1946 as the first RAF unit with the type. (Via Phil Birtles)

1941. The twin-jet configuration was selected as the jet engines of the time could not deliver sufficient power. Indeed, it was the fifth prototype which actually became the first Meteor to fly, on 5 March 1943, powered by Halford H1 turbojets (which

later became the de Havilland Goblin). The powerplant for production Meteors was the Rolls-Royce W2B/23 Welland, rated at 1,700lb st.

The first Meteor Mk Is entered service with No 616 Squadron in July 1944 and were soon based at Manston in use against the V-1 flying bomb. However, it was the Mk III that was the first variant to enter quantity production, with some 280 being built. The first 15 Meteor IIIs were powered by Wellands but subsequently the R-R Derwent was fitted, from aircraft No 16 onwards. Apart from the engine change, internal fuel capacity was increased and a rearwards-sliding cockpit canopy was introduced in place of a sideways-opening hood. After hostilities ended, Fighter Command equipped five fighter squadrons (No 74, 222, 234, 245 and 263 Squadrons) with the F3 (as the new nomenclature designated the "old" Mk III). In August 1948, the first Meteors to join the RAuxAF reached No 500 (County of Kent) Squadron at West Malling.

Making its first flight in July 1945, the Meteor F4 differed from the F3 by having the uprated Derwent 5 turbojets and, although initially having the original 43ft wingspan, it was distinguished by having "clipped" wings with a 5ft 10in reduction in span, retrofitted to most of the first 100 long-span F4s built. The clipped wing improved the aircraft's rate-of-roll to more than 80°/sec but required higher take-off and landing speeds.

The Meteor F4 was chosen to equip the RAF's re-formed High Speed Flight late in 1945 and, on 7 November 1945, Gp Capt H.

J. Wilson, flying EE454 *Britannia*, raised the World Speed Record to 606mph. Eventually, on 7 September 1946, Gp Capt E. M. "Teddy" Donaldson flew EE549 to a record of 616mph.

The first Meteor F4s began to enter RAF service in November 1947, equipping Nos 245 and 263 Squadrons at Horsham St Faith. This version went on to equip 22 Fighter Command squadrons, including seven RAuxAF units. It was a popular aircraft with pilots and proved a valuable addition to the RAF's postwar inventory. The much-improved Meteor F8, first flown in October 1948, began to replace the F4 (and also Vampire FB5s) in frontline squadrons from June 1950. In all, some 489 Meteor F4s were built by Glosters, plus 46 by Armstrong Whitworth, of which 465 entered RAF service.

Data: Meteor F4

Powerplant	two Rolls-Royce Derwent 5 turbojets, rated at 3,500lb st
Span	37ft 2in
Length	41ft 4in
Height	13ft 0in
Wing area	350sq ft
Empty weight	11,217lb
Loaded weight	14,545lb
Maximum speed	585mph at sea level, 550mph at 30,000ft
Rate of climb	7,350ft/min (initial)
Time to height	5min to 30,000ft
Service ceiling	44,500ft
Range	420 miles at 30,000ft with full internal fuel; 680 miles with full internal fuel plus drop tanks; 1,000 miles

Left: First flown in 1948, the Gloster Meteor F8 featured a new tail and outer wing panels. Although replaced by Hunters in 1957, this example served until the late 1970s as a target tug, seen here at Brawdy in July 1976. (Richard E. Gardner)

with full internal, fuselage and wing tanks

Armament four 20mm Hispano cannon, with 780 rounds, mounted two on either side of the cockpit

Vickers-Supermarine Spitfire

As can be seen from the Order of Battle at the end of this "Snapshot", the Spitfire was still very much in evidence with the RAuxAF squadrons in 1948. Following a decision in 1947, the RAuxAF squadrons were in the process of converting to all-day-fighters, with a secondary ground-attack capability. The data below presents a comparison of the three major variants in service in this year.

It has been said in the 1938 "Snapshot" that this book is not the place for a detailed history of the Spitfire. However, in order to clarify the evolution of the type, the following summary of all versions of Spitfire (excluding Seafire, Spiteful and Seafang) is presented.

Mks I, II & V: progressive engine changes with increase in power and rated altitude of the Merlin
Mk III: a "cleaned-up" airframe with Merlin XX engine, only two prototypes built
Mk IV: a redesigned airframe, powered by a two-stage Griffon II engine; became Mk X.
Mk VI: a development of the Mk V with pressurised cabin and extended wingtips
Mk VII: an extended redesign; with a two-stage Merlin, strengthened airframe, redesigned cooling system, an improved pressure cabin, and retractable tailwheel
Mk VIII: an unpressurised Mk VII
Mk IX: a Mk V with the Merlin 61 engine, used as an interim type before Mks VII/VIII
Mk X: the redesignated Mk IV
Mk XI: a photo-recce version of the Mk IX
Mk XII: a Mk V airframe, powered by Griffon II engine, with clipped wings, retractable tailwheel and strengthened fuselage
Mk XIII: a Mk V converted for low-level photo-recce work
Mk XIV: see text below

Left: The penultimate Supermarine Spitfire, the bubble-cockpit F22, was still in RAuxAF service in 1948. (Greenborough Associates)

Data: Spitfire

	F/FR14/e	LF16e	F22
Powerplant	2,050hp Rolls-Royce Griffon 65	1,720hp Packard Merlin 266	2,050hp Rolls-Royce Griffon 61/64/85
Span: standard	36ft 10in	36ft 10in	36ft 11in
: clipped	32ft 7in	32ft 7in	N/A
Length	32ft 8in	31ft 4.5in	32ft 11in
Height	11ft 8in	11ft 7.75in	11ft 9.75in
Wing area:			
standard	242sq ft	242sq ft :	244sq ft
clipped	231sq ft	231sq ft	N/A
Empty weight	6,376lb	5,610lb	7,160lb
Loaded wt : F	8,475lb	7,500lb	9,900lb
:FR	9,000lb	N/A	N/A
Max T/O weight	10,280lb	9,500lb	11,350lb
Maximum speed	404mph at 11,000ft	408mph at 25,000ft	449mph at 25,000ft
Rate of climb	4,580ft/min	4,100ft/min	4,900ft/min
Time to height	7min to 20,000ft	5.7min to 25,000ft	8min to 20,000ft
Service ceiling	43,000ft	43,000ft	43,000ft
Range:			
int fuel	460 miles	434 miles	580 miles
ext tank	850 miles	980 miles	965 miles
Armament	2 x 20mm cannon and 4 x 0.303in Browning M/Gs	2 x 20mm cannon and 2 x 0.50in Browning M/Gs	4 x 20mm cannon

Notes: N/A = not applicable; M/Gs = machine guns

(extracted from SD161 Location of RAF Units, June 1948)

Fighter Command – HQ: Bentley Priory, Stanmore, Middx

No 11 Group – HQ: Uxbridge, Middx

Sqn	Aircraft	Base
1 (Cadre)	Gloster Meteor F4	Tangmere, Sussex
25	DH Mosquito NF36	West Malling, Kent
29	DH Mosquito NF36	West Malling, Kent
54 (Cadre)	DH Vampire F3	Odiham, Hants
56 (Cadre)	Gloster Meteor F4	Thorney Island, Hants
63 (Cadre)	Gloster Meteor F4	Thorney Island, Hants
66 (Cadre)	Gloster Meteor F4	Duxford, Cambs
72 (Cadre)	DH Vampire F3	Odiham, Hants
85	DH Mosquito NF36	West Malling, Kent
92 (Cadre)	Gloster Meteor F4	Duxford, Cambs
222 (Cadre)	Gloster Meteor F4	Tangmere, Sussex
247 (Cadre)	DH Vampire F1	Odiham, Hants
266 (Cadre)	Gloster Meteor F4	Tangmere, Sussex
500 RAuxAF	DH Mosquito NF30 (converting to Gloster Meteor F3)	West Malling, Kent
501 RAuxAF	V-S Spitfire LF16e	Filton, Gloucs
600 RAuxAF	V-S Spitfire F21/22	Biggin Hill, Kent
601 RAuxAF	V-S Spitfire LF16e	Hendon, Middx
604 RAuxAF	V-S Spitfire LF16e	Hendon, Middx
614 RAuxAF	V-S Spitfire LF16/F22	Llandow, Glamorgan
615 RAuxAF	V-S Spitfire F22	Biggin Hill, Kent

No 12 Group – HQ: Newton, Notts

Sqn	Aircraft	Base
19	DH Hornet F3	Church Fenton, Yorks
23	DH Mosquito NF36	Coltishall, Norfolk
41	DH Hornet F3	Church Fenton, Yorks
64	DH Hornet F3	Linton-on-Ouse, Yorks
65 (Cadre)	DH Hornet F1	Linton-on-Ouse, Yorks
74 (Cadre)	Gloster Meteor F4	Horsham St Faith, Norfolk
141	DH Mosquito NF36	Coltishall, Norfolk
245 (Cadre)	Gloster Meteor F4	Horsham St Faith, Norfolk
257 (Cadre)	Gloster Meteor F4	Horsham St Faith, Norfolk
263 (Cadre)	Gloster Meteor F4	Horsham St Faith, Norfolk
264	DH Mosquito NF36	Coltishall, Norfolk
502 RAuxAF	V-S Spitfire F22	Aldergrove, N.I.
504 RAuxAF	DH Mosquito NF30 (converting to V-S Spitfire F22)	Hucknall, Notts
602 RAuxAF	V-S Spitfire F21/22	Abbotsinch, Renfrew
603 RAuxAF	V-S Spitfire F22	Turnhouse, Midlothian
605 RAuxAF	DH Mosquito NF30 (converting to DH Vampire 1)	Honiley, Warks
607 RAuxAF	V-S Spitfire FR14/F22	Ouston, Durham
608 RAuxAF	DH Mosquito NF30 (converting to V-S Spitfire F22)	Middleton St. George, Durham

No 12 Group – HQ: Newton, Notts (cont)

Sqn	Aircraft	Base
609 RAuxAF	DH Mosquito NF30 (converting to V-S Spitfire LF16e)	Yeadon, Yorks
610 RAuxAF	V-S Spitfire F14/F22	Hooton Park, Cheshire
611 RAuxAF	V-S Spitfire FR14/F22	Woodvale, Lancs
612 RAuxAF	V-S Spitfire LF16e	Dyce, Grampian
613 RAuxAF	V-S Spitfire F14/F22	Ringway, Cheshire
616 RAuxAF	DH Mosquito NF30	Finningley, Yorks

Mk XV: reserved, then number used in Seafire series

Mk XVI: see text below

Mk XVII: reserved, then number used in Seafire series

Mk XVIII: Mk XIV with strengthened wings and undercarriage plus increased fuel tankage

Mk XIX: a Mk XIV with modified Mk V wings, used for photo-recce work

Mk XX: an experimental type, being a Mk IV with a Griffon IIB engine

F21: Derived from Mks IV/XX with a new wing (with 4 x 20mm Hispano cannon), a longer undercarriage with wider track, a larger fin and rudder, and powered by a two-stage Griffon 61 engine

F22: see text below

F23: an unbuilt project, being an F22 with improved wing section

F24: an F22 with rear fuselage fuel tanks

Before moving on to the three specific versions in service in 1948, the F/FR14/14e (Mk XIV), the LF16e (Mk XVI) and the F22, it is worthwhile adding one further note. The Mks I, II and V all appeared with various suffix letters – A, B or C. These refer to the wing/armament combination fitted to the type. The A-suffix indicates eight 0.303in Browning machine guns; the B-suffix means two 20mm Hispano cannon plus four 0.303in Browning machine guns; and the C-suffix refers to the universal armament wing, which was developed for the Mk III, and could be fitted with four Hispanos or two Hispanos and four Brownings of either 0.303in or 0.50in calibre. Thus, the Spitfire Mk I (without any suffix) indicates the original armament of four 0.303in Brownings with which it entered service (*see 1938 "Snapshot"*).

In 1948, Air Ministry policy decreed that all Auxiliary squadrons be re-equipped to undertake the dayfighter role. With insufficient jet-powered aircraft available, the later marks of Spitfire were assigned to the role. Of the three Spitfire variants in service

with the RAuxAF, let us first look at the last of the Merlin-engined versions, the Mk XVI.

Put simply, the Mk XVI was a Mk IX with a US-built Packard Merlin 266 engine in place of the UK Merlin 66. Indeed, from September 1944, Spitfires were built as Mk IXs or XIVs, depending on the source of the engine. Although the Mk XVI was available with standard wings, it was more usual to see them with "clipped" wings, which gave better manoeuvrability at low level. Late production aircraft (from February 1945) were built with rearview fuselages and a bubble hood. The Mk XVI entered RAF service with the Second Tactical Air force in 1944. In all, 1,054 Mk XVIs were built and, postwar, saw service with Nos 5, 17, 65, 66 and 595 Squadrons RAF; and Nos 501, 601, 604, 607, 609, 612, 614 and 615 Squadrons RAuxAF.

The first of the Griffon-engined Spitfires to enter large-scale production was the Mk XIV (F/FR14). Intended as an interim type until the Mk XVIII was made available, it became a major variant in its own right with 957 examples being built. Intended for high altitude work, the Griffon 65 engine drove a five-bladed airscrew. The installation of the Griffon increased the length of the nose, which was compensated for by an increased fin area. The ailerons were moved inboard slightly to improve lateral control. Later production models featured the bubble hood and modified rear fuselage. The FR XIVE (FR14e) was a fighter-reconnaissance version, with a clipped universal wing, extra fuel tanks in the rear fuselage and provision for oblique recce cameras. The Mk XIV entered service with No 610 Squadron in January 1944 and saw postwar service with Nos 2, 17, 20, 26, 41, 132, 152, 155, 268, 322, and 350 Squadrons RAF; and Nos 600, 602 and 612 Squadrons RAuxAF.

The Spitfire F22, the penultimate production variant, was a refined F21 which, according to Joseph Smith, Chief Designer to Supermarine from 1938, in a paper presented to the Royal Aeronautical Society in London in December 1946, "represented the highest stage of development of the Spitfire family". The F22 differed from the F21 by having the rear vision hood, a completely new empennage (designed for and fitted to the Spiteful) on late production aircraft and a 24-volt electrical system. Some F22s featured the Griffon 85 engine, with contra-rotating propellers, in place of the Griffon 61. (The introduction of rear fuselage fuel tanks to the F22 produced the final production version, the Spitfire F24.) Although 627 F22s were ordered, only 260 were built with production beginning in March 1945. Although the F22 was the mainstay of the RAuxAF between 1946 and 1951, serving with Nos 502, 504, 600, 602, 607, 608, 610, 613, 614 and 615 Squadrons, only one regular unit, No 73 Squadron RAF, based in Malta, was equipped with the type.

While Spitfires of various marks remained in secondline training units well into the 1950s, 1948 was probably the height of its postwar service. The first Meteors began to filter through the system, replacing Spitfires in the RAuxAF from 1949. The last operational RAF sortie involving a Spitfire – a PR19 of No 81 Squadron in Malaya – was flown on 1 April 1954.

RESPONSE:
ANTI-AIRCRAFT ARTILLERY

This was the immediate postwar period where technology was advancing and threats were changing. In the field of AAA, most work was concentrated on improving the weapons in service or under development in 1945. The guided weapon in the form of the surface-to-air missile (SAM) was still a decade away from service: guns still remained supreme.

Bofors 40mm L/60
Very little changed from the Bofors Mk 1, described in the previous "Snapshot", slight operating improvements but very little ballistic changes had been made, except that powered mountings had been introduced. These were developed by the Bristol Aircraft Company and saw the Mk 1 system, fitted with a barrel 60 times the length of its calibre (60 x 40mm = 2,400mm) – hence L/60 in the designation – mounted on a carriage with a small petrol-driven generator provid-ing power. This improved the tracking rate of the system, with the gunlayer operating a small joystick rather than handwheels.

Data: see 1938 "Snapshot"

3.7in Mks 1 and 3
The weapon itself was virtually unchanged. Its effectiveness, however, was improved by the adoption of proximity-fuzed ammunition. The new ammunition removed the fuze running-time restrictions on ceiling and, thus, pushed the effective ceiling of the system up to 40,000ft.

Data: see 1938 "Snapshot"

3.7in Mk 6
This system, developed during 1942, was the basic 4.5in gun with a 3.7in calibre barrel liner. This enabled the gun to fire the 3.7in shell with a 4.5in cartridge. It employed special rifling and shell design to obtain maximum muzzle velocity and minimum drag in flight.

It was, according to Ian Hogg, former Master Gunner of the Royal Artillery and ordnance expert, "undoubtedly the best anti-aircraft weapon ever built by anyone". Being derived from the 4.5in gun it was used on static mountings only. By 1948, all Home Defence 3.7in guns were the Mk 6 type, the Mks 1 and 3 being confined to field army mobile use.

Data

Calibre	3.7in
Type of mounting	static pedestal
Weight in action	17.12 tons
Max elevation	80°
Effective ceiling	45,000ft with mechanical fuze, 56,000ft with proximity fuze
Weight of shell	28lb
Type of shell	HE
Muzzle velocity	3,425ft/sec
Rate of fire	19rds/min with auto-loader

4.5in Gun Mk 2
There was no change to this weapon as described in the previous Snapshot and, by 1948, only a few remained to protect dockyards and naval installations. Most 4.5in weapons had been replaced by the 5.25in system (see below). No proximity fuze was ever developed for these weapons and, therefore, their performance never changed.
Data: see 1938 "Snapshot"

5.25in Gun Mk 1

This weapon was originally developed as a naval gun and entered Royal Navy service in 1939, placed in twin-mountings on warships. In January 1941, the War Office, searching for a more powerful air defence gun, selected the 5.25in system but had to wait until 1942 when the Navy's initial requirements were fulfilled, before three twin-guns were available for trials.

Two single-gun mountings were then developed: one shielded and the other in a power-operated, armoured turret. The latter allowed dual employment of the weapon: either in the coast defence role or the anti-aircraft role. The turreted mount, which became the standard, had an underground magazine from which ammunition was supplied by hoist, and an engine room which provided hydraulic power for operation of the gun ammunition supply. These weapons were certainly the most complex air defence gun mountings developed anywhere in the world and, in the 1950s, it was said that each gun, with its full installation, cost £250,000.

The 5.25in gun began replacing the 4.5in guns in 1944, being used principally in defended ports and naval bases, including the Thames, Humber, Tyne, Plymouth and Portsmouth. Installation continued after the war, until the arrival of the SAM led to the gun's obsolescence in 1959. A battery of these guns can be still be seen today, preserved in Gibraltar.

Data

Calibre	5.25in
Type of mounting	emplaced turret
Weight in action	49.5 tons
Max elevation	70°
Effective ceiling	43,000ft with time fuze, 54,000ft with proximity fuze

Below: The naval origins of the 5.25in AA gun are apparent in this view of the battery preserved at Gibraltar. (Ian Hogg)

Weight of shell	80lb
Type of shell	HE
Muzzle velocity	2,800ft/sec
Rate of fire	10rds/min

CRITIQUE

This was the stage of the RAF's development when the reality of another potential threat to Great Britain was realised. The Berlin Air Lift was required because the Soviet Union was showing its muscles and although not yet total, the potential to strike at the British Isles was evident.

A new control and reporting system had been established in 1946 and, during 1948, this was still being "fine-tuned". The Royal Observer Corps and the radar stations fed their data into a master radar station located at each of the Fighter Command sectors. These were located at Patrington (for the Yorkshire sector), Neatishead (Eastern), Trimley Heath (Metropolitan) and Sopley (Southern). The new system was workable but, given the resources becoming available to the Soviet Union, open to saturation.

The aircraft of Fighter Command were a curious mix of late marks of Second World War piston-engined fighters and early marks of jet fighters. The RAF was a force in transition. Fighter production was being doubled and the RAuxAF was to be brought up to strength, with jet-powered aircraft. Yet in 1948, the RAuxAF was still awaiting the arrival of the jets. As noted elsewhere, it was the postwar zenith of Spitfire service in the UK.

Aircraft and propulsion design technology was being driven to new limits and the "Sound Barrier" was being touched. Yet, it was to be 1952-53 before the RAF acquired its first swept-wing jet fighters, the CL-13 Sabre F4, the Canadair-built version of the North American F-86 Sabre.

The reason that Great Britain did not possess such aircraft was a result of insufficient action and resources allocated to high-speed flight after cessation of hostilities and a failure to capitalise on the German high-speed and jet engine technology captured in 1945. The United States made more of this work for, as they had initially lagged behind in jet engine technology, they felt they had to seize the intitiative in the postwar years and catch up with Great Britain. In the event, few would disagree with the statement that they overtook British developments during the 1950s (and have continued to do so). Not so many people are aware that Great Britain handed over the work that had been done to the United States in 1946.

Britain could have beaten the United States to supersonic flight but a series of developments were cancelled. The reader is referred to Derek Wood's excellent work *Project Cancelled* for the full, sad history of how Great Britain gave up its lead in fighter development in the late 1940s. However, it must be stated that following the cancellation of the Miles M52 in 1946, the Ministry of Supply handed over all the technical information and wind tunnel results of the M52 project to the United States. This windfall to the Americans was to set British fighter technology back five years and the industry 10 years.

The decision to opt out of supersonic aircraft development was pushed by the need to save money and was, thus, purely political. A year later, in 1947, approval was given to send a small batch of Rolls-Royce Nene jet engines to the Soviet Union. This became the RD-45 engine (which powered the MiG-15 fighters encountered by US and British aircraft in Korea in 1950-52) and started Soviet jet engine development after the Second World War.

So, as a result of two political acts – one of parsimony and one of altruism – the British Government of the day did much to put the future defence of the country under potential threat. By 1948, the effects of these actions were beginning to be realised and it would take some 20 years for them to be, in part, neutralised.

1958

"SNAPSHOT" – 1958

The intervening decade was one of expansion for the RAF's air defence force as it strove to update its fighter force and the control and reporting (C&R) system. The Korean War had emphasised how outdated British fighters were, compared with the new Soviet MiG-15, and the inability of the RAF to police UK airspace effectively. No RAF combat fighters were deployed to Korea, although RAF pilots flew on exchange tours with both the USAF (on F-86 Sabres) and the RAAF (with Meteor F8s, mostly in the ground-attack role). In fact, the only British-operated fighters involved in the conflict were Sea Furies of the Fleet Air Arm, flying from carriers off the Korean coast.

By the mid-1950s, the first generation of jet fighters, the Meteor, Sabre (a Canadair-built version of the USAF's F-86, procured to give the RAF experience with swept-wing fighters), Vampire and Venom, were well on the way to being replaced by the home-grown Hunter, Javelin and Swift. The latter was, however, a failure as a dayfighter and it was only after much modification that it went on to achieve limited success as a reconnaissance fighter in RAF Germany. The C&R network had also been improved and No 81 (Fighter) Group reformed within Fighter Command in 1952, to control its training units.

Fighter Command reached its peak postwar strength in 1956 with 35 squadrons and 600 frontline aircraft: 16 Hunter and two Meteor dayfighter squadrons, eight squadrons each of Meteor and Venom nightfighters and the first squadron of Javelin all-weather fighters. The RAuxAF establishment remained unchanged from 1948, except that by then 10 squadrons were equipped with the Meteor F8 dayfighter and nine with the Vampire FB5 in the ground-attack role. The disbandment of the RAuxAF in 1957, on the grounds of cost-savings and the increasing complexity of second-generation jet fighters, deprived Fighter Command of useful fighter resources. In the same round of cut-backs, 81 Group was disbanded, together with two of its Operational Conversion Units (OCUs).

The vehicle for these cut-backs was the now-infamous Defence White Paper of 1957. Against a background of economies in peacetime and increased reliance on the nuclear deterrent (in the form of the V-bomber force and, later, Thor IRBMs), the air defence requirement concentrated on defending the bomber bases. This was to be effected by a small, highly-efficient, manned interceptor force rather than an extensive air defence organisation. The new English Electric Lightning would replace the Hunters and Javelins, and the air-to-air missile (AAM) their cannon armament. Indeed, it was prophesied (falsely, as it turned out) that the surface-to-air missile (SAM) would eventually replace the manned interceptor and that the Lightning would be the last of the *genre* as far as the RAF was concerned.

By 1958, Fighter Command was well into the shrinking process with only 320 frontline aircraft. (This shrinkage was to continue to 1965, when the strength was down to 60 fighters.) Despite such savage reductions in capability, Fighter Command was still required to reinforce overseas commands in emergencies (as they had done with the deployment of two Hunter squadrons to Cyprus during the Suez campaign). Yet, the first of the new systems entered service in this year: the Firestreak AAM entered service (on Javelins) and the first Bloodhound Mk 1 SAM unit was formed. The RAF had entered the missile age.

THE THREAT

By 1958, the Cold War was reality and the Soviet Union had firmly assumed the role of "the bad guys", with the means at its disposal to present a credible threat. However, the exact nature of that threat was not as great as was supposed at the time. The *Dal'naya Aviatsiya* (DA) had reached a plateau and, although potential existed for the long-range bomber force to be further improved, other factors had come into play.

There was contention within the Soviet Union as to what exact role the DA would play in a future war. The development of the inter-continental ballistic missile (ICBMs) and the submarine-launched missile (initially of a type we now refer to as cruise missiles, although nowhere as sophisticated as today's systems) offered cheaper solutions for the delivery of nuclear weapons. The DA, it was argued, working in conjunction with the strategic rocket forces and a nuclear-powered navy, could achieve the main strategic goals of a future war. Soviet doctrine was based on the all-arms concept of defeating an enemy militarily. This contrasted with the Western (specifically United States) view that deterrence was based on massive retaliation against the enemy heartland. The DA was far from being an independent strategic force.

So, while being a relatively small force, compared with the manned bombers in USAF service, the DA bombers still represented a threat to the UK. Attempting to gauge the exact numbers in service in this particular year is difficult, even in today's era of *glasnost* but Alfred L. Monks of the University of Wyoming, writing in *Soviet Aviation and Air Power* (Brassey's, London 1978), states that in late-1961 the Soviet long-range bomber force consisted of some 190 aircraft, 70 Tu-95 "Bears" and 120 M-4 "Bisons", some 50 of the latter being used as tanker aircraft for the air-to-air refuelling of other "Bisons". The balance is right and the strengths for 1958 are probably in the order of 75% of the 1961 figures.

While the main target for the DA was the continental United States, Western Europe (including the UK) could expect some interest from these types, in the event of a war. Western Europe was also susceptible to the Tu-16 "Badger", a medium-range jet bomber with European range.

Estimates of the potency of these Soviet bombers, originally made on their "discovery" in the early 1950s, were reduced downwards after observing the aircraft more closely and, by 1958, it was clear the threat to the United States would come from ICBMs rather than manned bombers. For Europe and the UK, however, a mix of missiles and bombers was still a distinct possibility.

Myasishchev M-4/201 "Bison"

considered as one of the Soviet aviation industry's greatest achievements of the early 1950s. The M-4 was the first Soviet jet bomber. Its origin lay in an instruction from Stalin to Myasishchev in 1949 to design a bomber to fly missions to North America. This was interpreted as being able to fly 9,950 miles in still air, with an 11,000lb bomb load. At the time, it was considered that only propeller-driven aircraft could achieve such a range, but as Tupolev was working on the prop-driven Tu-88 (put into production as the Tu-16 "Badger"), Myasishchev reluctantly looked at the only available jet engine, the Mikulin AM-3.

Design went ahead but with the realistic view that the range requirement would be

Left: The first Soviet jet bomber, the Myashishchev M-4 "Bison" entered service in 1956. Built in relatively small numbers, this aircraft was later converted to the aerial tanker role. (Author's Collection)

Above: The first of the Soviet Union's jet bombers, the Tupolev Tu-16 "Badger-A", entered service in 1954. This initial version followed the Tu-88 prototype and led to a production run of around 2,000 (not counting Chinese H-6 production). (Via John W. R. Taylor)

unfulfilled. The prototype flew in 1953 and made its public debut in the flypast over Red Square on 1 May 1954. Despite the reduced range, production was authorised in 1955 and the first M-4s (NATO codename "Bison-A") entered service in 1956, with the popular Russian name of *Molot* (Hammer). By Soviet standards, the limited production run of 200 was small.

The M-4 was designed with typical 1950s aerodynamics: a shoulder-mounted, high aspect ratio wing with a 35° sweep; a circular fuselage with a pressurised forward crew compartment for six of the seven aircrew, with the seventh in the tail-gunner position, also pressurised; a conventional swept, variable-incidence tailplane and swept fin; and the four AM-3D engines buried in the wing roots. The main undercarriage was mounted under the fuselage, fore and aft, each with a tandem pair of two-wheel bogies with small, twin-wheel outrigger gear on the wingtips. The defensive armament of eight 23mm cannon were located in pairs, three being in remotely-controlled turrets, one above the fuselage and two below, with the fourth pair being in the tail. Some aircraft also had a nose-mounted 23mm cannon.

Later versions of the M-4, now redesignated the 201M ("Bison-B" and "Bison-C"), were fitted with Soloviev D-15 turbojets, each rated at 28,500lb st, nose radar and provision for air-to-air refuelling. These were used almost exclusively by the Soviet naval air arm, the AV-MF, for maritime reconnaissance. Many "Bisons" of all versions were equipped as aerial tankers.

Data: M-4 "Bison-A"

Powerplant	four Mikulin AM-3D turbo jets, each rated at 19,180lb st
Span	165ft 7.5in
Length	154ft 10in
Height	34ft 3in (approx)
Wing area	3,326sq ft
Empty weight	154,323lb
Loaded weight	352,730lb
Maximum speed	620mph at 36,000ft
Service ceiling	45,000ft
Range (combat)	3,480 miles (with full bomb load)
Armament	eight 23mm NR-23 cannon, plus up to 12,000lb of bombs in three internal bays

Tupolev Tu-16 "Badger"

The longevity of Western combat aircraft in this half of the century is fast becoming commonplace. Anyone who doubts the effectiveness of Soviet aircraft need look no further than the Tu-16 "Badger": ordered in 1950; flown (as the Tu-88 prototype) in 1954; entered service in 1955; still in front-line Russian service at the time of writing (1993), but only just!

The Tu-16 is the smaller of two Tupolev designs undertaken in parallel (the other being the Tu-20/95/142 – see below) it was classed as a medium bomber, rather than long-range. A contemporary of the British V-bombers, its design was a mixture of new thoughts in design with a dose of proven technology. The fuselage was a logical extension of the Tu-4, as was the defensive armament. The wings were highly swept, starting at 42° for the inner section going on to 35° for the outer wing. Its bogie main undercarriage retracted rearwards into trailing edge-pods, while the nosewheel was forward in the fuselage, allowing space for the weapons bay.

Some 2,000 Tu-16s were built, of which the "Badger-A" is the main bomber version. Over 200 of these remain in service. However, the Tu-16 was to prove a versatile and fatigue-free aircraft, being adapted to other specialised roles including aerial tankers, using a unique wingtip-to-wingtip system, as well as the conventional probe-and-drogue method. Other versions are described in subsequent "Snapshots".

Data: Tu-16 "Badger-A"

Powerplant	two Mikulin AM-3M turbo jets, each rated at 20,950lb st
Span	108ft 0.5in
Length	114ft 2in
Height	35ft 6in
Wing area	1,772.3sq ft
Empty weight	82,000lb
Loaded weight	158,730lb (normal T/O)
Maximum speed	616mph at 19,700ft
Service ceiling	40,350ft
Range	3,000 miles (with 8,360lb of bombs)
Combat radius	1,800 miles (on internal fuel)
Armament	seven 23mm NR-23 cannon, plus up to 19,800lb of bombs in internal bay

Tupolev Tu-95 (Tu-20) "Bear"

Developed in parallel competition with the M-4 "Bison", the Tu-95 was a true descendent of the Tu-4 and achieved a similar longevity to its smaller, jet-powered brother, the Tu-16. To meet the requirement of intercontinental range (which eluded the M-4 "Bison"), the selection of turboprop powerplants was the logical solution and, indeed, the Tu-95 was preferred and produced in slightly larger numbers than the M-4.

Design was finalised in 1952 and followed the configuration of the Tu-4 with a circular fuselage cross-section and three compartments for the eight aircrew, with a tunnel connecting the fore and aft compartments. It differed from the Tu-4 by having swept wings (37° inner, 35° outer) and NK-12 turboprop engines. Originally armed with five pairs of 23mm cannon, on produc-

tion aircraft this was reduced to two pairs in remotely-controlled dorsal and ventral turrets and a manned pair in the tail.

The maiden flight of the Tu-95 took place in September 1954 and seven prototypes were seen at the Aviation Day flypast in 1955. The first production "Bear-A's" entered service the same year, with the Soviet DA service designation of Tu-20 (but for clarity, we shall use the manufacturer's designation, Tu-95). Its appearance caused a stir in Western defence circles, as most of the night/all-weather fighters in service could not reach the altitudes at which the Tu-95 flew. However, by 1958, the advent of SAMs and advanced radar-equipped fighters with AAM armament negated this height advantage, making the Tu-95 obsolete as a strategic bomber.

However, the Tu-95 was found to be as versatile as the Tu-16, seeing service with the AV-MF as well as the DA. Subsequent "Snapshots" will detail the specialised versions as applicable.

Data: Tu-95 (Tu-20) "Bear-A"

Powerplant	four 14,795hp Kuznetsov NK-12M turboprop engines
Span	167ft 7.75in
Length	162ft 4.75in
Height	39ft 9in
Wing area	3,342sq ft
Empty weight	190,000lb (approx)
Loaded weight	340,000lb (max T/O)
Maximum speed	575mph at 41,000ft
Service ceiling	41,000ft
Combat radius	5,150 miles (on internal fuel)
Armament	six 23mm NR-23 cannon, plus up to 22,000lb of bombs in two internal bays

DETECTION & IDENTIFICATION

In retrospect, it can be recognised that the decade between 1948 and 1958 was one of transition. National interests were being sublimated in mutual pacts, with NATO now offering a joint process of defence. National independence in development of systems in the West was also under review, with much of the advanced equipment being supplied under the Mutual Defence Assistance Programme. A typical product of this latter programme being the American Airborne Interception (AI) system supplied for the Meteor NF14 nightfighter.

Right: Developed in parallel with the M-4 "Bison", Tupolev's Tu-95 "Bear-A" was powered by turboprops, seen as being the best solution for long-range. Yet by 1958, its high altitude profile rendered it obsolete as a strategic bomber. (US DoD)

It was becoming increasingly recognised that Northern Europe's traditional bad weather periods were no longer an opportunity for respite in war. It was necessary to face an airborne threat 24hrs a day, 365 days a year. By 1950, the RAF was introducing new standards of instrument flight training under an Instrument Rating Scheme that would categorise pilot proficiency according to experience and training.

Apart from the changes in technology and the introduction of the jet bomber, other advances were taking place in electronics as the beginnings of the "electronic revolution" became apparent. This was to lead to a capability and degree of miniaturisation that would establish completely new standards of reliability and revolutionise airborne systems. It was about this time that the word "avionics", a contraction of aviation electronics, was coined.

The introduction of the atomic bomb, followed by the nuclear weapon, had also changed the perception of war. Meteors still carried out fighter affiliation exercises with Lincoln bombers, while the revolutionary new jet-powered Canberra was often artificially restricted in its performance, during exercises, in order to allow the contemporary fighter an opportunity to intercept it successfully and make the exercise more "realistic". At the same time, it was necessary to reconsider defence organisation in the light of the atomic age and the growing influence of long range missiles.

Much of the new thinking created concern among the military, especially in the way that future conflict would reflect changes in long established traditions.

Inevitably this led to much public discussion and, too often, the sad spectacle of inter-service rivalries which often suggest a reluctance to face up to change.

The "atomic equation" created other problems, particularly that of survival of key defensive installations during such an attack. The answer was stated in a project known as "Rotorplan" and which took place between 1951 and 1954. The complete network of air defence systems, apart from antennae, was placed underground in high structural-strength bunkers. It called for considerable amounts of work, in engineering and electronic installations, to create air-conditioned and fully-survivable areas properly fitted with communication and sensor links. At the same time, the Chain Home stations were closed down to give way to a new long range search radar (Type 80), which could detect targets at 200 miles range and at heights of up to 40,000ft. The new radar also possessed much better resolution, offering higher standards of precision to the fighter controllers. As the new system settled down, the threat was still perceived to come from the East and the defensive configuration underlined that concept.

At the same time, the RAF was still faced with the original problem of air defence. How, in the face of emerging technologies, could the defender be able to achieve early warning of the enemy's intentions, the ability to track an approaching attack and the means of positively identifying the enemy in order to launch the appropriate defensive measures?

At this point it may be appropriate to consider the continuing development of

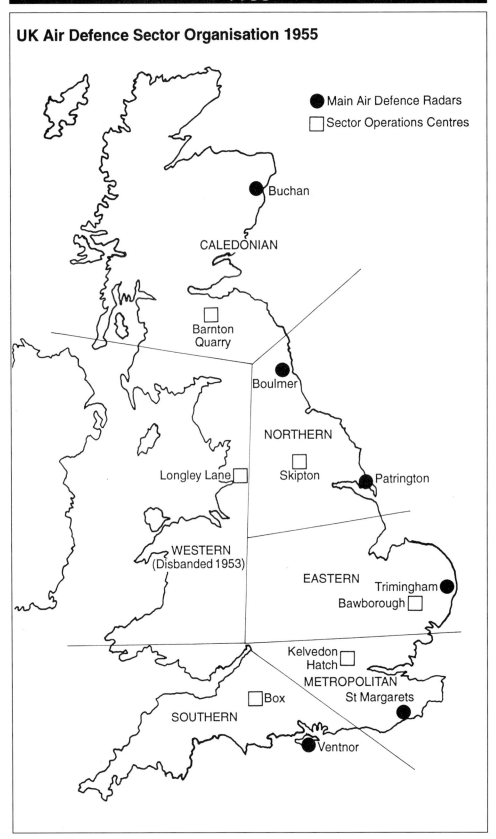

UK Air Defence Sector Organisation 1955

● Main Air Defence Radars
☐ Sector Operations Centres

● Buchan

CALEDONIAN

☐
Barnton
Quarry

● Boulmer

NORTHERN

☐
Skipton

Longley Lane ☐

● Patrington

WESTERN
(Disbanded 1953)

EASTERN

Trimingham ●

Bawborough ☐

Kelvedon ☐
Hatch

METROPOLITAN
St Margarets

☐ Box

●

SOUTHERN

● Ventnor

radar in the air defence role. The early Chain Home system has comprised large antenna structures set to face the direction of the threat. Since then antennae had become more compact and could be rotated to cover a wide area, while the height finding radars were characterised by the rocking motion of the tilted antenna. Evolving techniques had been introduced to reduce the clutter that is generated by ground objects, sea, thunderstorms, rain or thick cloud.

The trick is to be able to get rid of this interference without affecting the wanted signal and this is usually achieved by electronic recognition of some distinct target characteristic. This process has led to one of the most successful of these ploys known as Moving Target Indication (MTI). This makes use of the well known Doppler effect, whereby a moving target appears to change frequency in relation to a fixed target. By use of signal processing techniques the moving targets of interest can be retained while the fixed targets are filtered out.

Electronic techniques using Secondary Surveillance Radar (SSR) in which the target must be co-operative had also been developed. In this case the radar operates in conjunction with a transponder on board the target aircraft and is the basis of identification in a system called Identification, Friend or Foe (IFF). The concept of such a system dated back to the early days of radar development and had been widely used by Bomber Command in the Second World War.

The introduction of the jet bomber had placed further constraints of the defence system, especially in its attempts to gain an early warning benefit. In the closing stages of the Second World War, an Airborne Early Warning (AEW) radar was developed and fitted in a B-17 Flying Fortress. Other versions were to follow and it was of particular interest to navies which faced considerable problems of attempting to extend the radar horizon which was usually limited by the height of the tallest ship's mast!

This combination of radar and the growing influence of computer techniques, now formed the basis of the air defence system. In 1954, the first L-band radar was introduced (FPS-3) supplied by the United States under the Military Aid Programme. Its advanced PPI presentation provided much more "real-time" information and overcame the inherent shortcomings of the old manually plotted sector table. By combining both early warning and tactical inter-

ception data on the one indicator, it enabled the time interval to be tightened, with the result that interceptions were being made further away than had previously been possible.

Fighter aircraft were increasingly being equipped with missiles instead of the machine gun or cannon; and airborne interceptor radar was evolving into an air combat radar in which computer signalling techniques were beginning to supersede the human input. In order to control the growing complexity of the sensor system, an increasingly complex system of communication had also evolved. The overall result was a massive outpouring of electromagnetic emissions from aircraft, all of which are potentially liable to interference and exploitation by external sources – in other words, Electronic Warfare (EW).

The basis of efficiency in an air defence system is the speed with which information can be passed from the sensors to the command authority. Although new techniques had considerably speeded-up this process, it had been largely offset by the increased speed of the attacking force. Typically it can take several minutes from detecting a potential target, establishing its flight path and correctly interrogating its IFF to establish its identity. Meanwhile, the approaching aircraft will have covered a considerable amount of ground. By use of EW techniques in the form of Electronic Countermeasures (ECM) deployed by the enemy, this flow of information can be seriously degraded to further increase the time interval and reduce the optimum time for retaliation.

Correctly applied, ECM techniques can have serious effects upon search radars and height finders, IFF and the communication links. In reply, it is possible to reduce the effectiveness of enemy ECM by a number of measures which are based upon a sound understanding of the techniques and a high standard of training. This introduced an element of "aggressiveness" in the defence system operators. It became paramount to maintain an electronic chess mentality in order to reduce the effects of ECM, as early as possible, in order to retain the maximum possible interval between initial detection and positive identification.

A typical ploy is good frequency management. If two similar radars are sited relatively close together, it is good practice to allocate the operational frequency of each site at opposite ends of their frequency band. Similarly voice broadcasts can be helped by the introduction of channel rotation procedures. These techniques were the beginnings of systems that are today to be found in frequency agility and frequency hopping techniques.

Training and practice was also the basis of a system whereby a jammed search radar, providing only azimuthal information, could be supplemented by use of a height finder to detect range by being aligned along the relevant azimuth.

This increasingly sophisticated technology was affecting all aspects of military thinking and much was being made, at that time, of "push-button warfare" and a growing fashion to consider robotic techniques. Politicians seemed remarkably susceptible to this idea and to accept, too readily, the possibility of missile attack and defence to the detriment of manned vehicles. History has now proved the shallowness of that concept, but it represented a dangerous path at the time.

It must be said that these were the days when it was becoming ever more necessary to consider war in two forms -conventional and nuclear. The first was acceptable and conventional methods were tolerated, but in the case of nuclear it was considered unacceptable and all preparations were made on the assumption that the retaliatory capability of a country was so great as to deter the attacker. This policy of deterrence was initially based upon the V-bomber force and became part of that process known as Mutually Assured Destruction, for which the acronym is aptly read as MAD. In the light of later attempts, by the United States, to establish the Strategic Defense Initiative, it is interesting to note that in the early 1950s that country was giving serious thought to placing the bulk of its defence effort into passive air defence against atomic/nuclear attack.

The growing interdependence of NATO members was also leading to questions of interoperability and commonality. This seemed fine in theory but not so easy in practice and it was a problem that has endured. Much NATO equipment was purchased from private, commercial companies and often where national tendencies could be sublimated, the more pressing ones of commercial expediency were not so easily dissuaded. Consequently, the overall pattern was the defence of Western Europe, with its frontier in Central Europe. The lesser role for the RAF, though some would argue that it was a primary role in a country which was

one of the exclusive nuclear club, was the defence of the V-bomber airfields.

These contrasting requirements had created a considerable sophistication in military thought and deed and it was becoming apparent that even the fast, high-flying jet bomber was now vulnerable to early detection and destruction by missile. Instead, it was recognised that advantage should be taken of approaching a target at very low level "under the radar", making use of ECM techniques and the cover of clutter that was still a problem despite MTI and the continuing improvements in signal processing techniques.

RESPONSE: AIRCRAFT & ARMAMENT

Armstrong Whitworth (Gloster) Meteor nightfighters

The versatility of the Gloster Meteor to be adapted for other roles is illustrated by the family of two-seat nightfighters developed and built by Armstrong Whitworth. By 1958, the last few squadrons of these remaining in Fighter Command were in the process of being phased-out, in favour of the Javelin.

Developed to Specification F24/48 from the ultimate day fighter variant, the Meteor F8, the nightfighter family comprised four major variants, the NF11 through 14. The basic modification involved a lengthened nose (from the T7 trainer variant) to accommodate both the second crew member and the wartime AI Mk X radar equipment. The wings reverted to the original span of the Mk I and the guns were moved from the fuselage to the wings. A T7 was completed as an initial prototype, but the first real NF11 flew on 31 May 1950. The first RAF unit to receive the type was No 29 Squadron at Tangmere, in January 1951. In all, some 338 NF11s were built for the RAF and 20 for export.

The Meteor NF13 was a "tropicalised" version of the NF11, differing only by having a cold air unit and a radio compass (with its associated loop antenna beneath the cockpit, behind the navigator). The maiden flight of the NF13 was made on 21 December 1952 and it served exclusively overseas with the RAF. Some 40 NF11s were converted to NF13 standard.

Although having an earlier mark number, the Meteor NF12 actually flew after the NF13, on 21 April 1953. It represented a progressive development of the NF11 and featured a smoother, longer nose, housing

Data

	Meteor NF12	Meteor NF14
Powerplant (common)	two Rolls-Royce Derwent 8 turbojets, rated at 3,700lb st	
Span	43ft 0in	43ft 0in
Length	49ft 11in	51ft 4in
Height	13ft 11in	13ft 11in
Wing area	374sq ft	374sq ft
Empty weight	12,292lb	12,620lb
Loaded weight	20,380lb	21,200lb
Maximum speed	500mph at sea level	576mph at sea level
(clean)	535mph at 30,000ft	535mph at 30,000ft
Time to climb	12min to 30,000ft	13.2min to 30,000ft
Service ceiling	40,000ft	40,000ft
Range	950 miles	950 miles
Armament (common)	four 20mm Hispano Mk IV cannon, with a total of 640rds	

the US APS-21 radar. It entered squadron service with Nos 25 and 85 Squadrons early in 1954. Armstrong Whitworth built 100 NF12s for the RAF.

The ultimate Meteor nightfighter was the NF14, considered by many to be the most aesthetically pleasing of all Meteors. It retained the APS-21 radar, but in a longer nose and fitted with a rearwards-sliding, clear blown canopy. Again, 100 were built for the RAF, the last of which left the production line in May 1955.

In 1956, Fighter Command possessed nine squadrons of Meteor NF12/14s and the last homebased air defence unit to give up its aircraft was No 72 Squadron, in June 1959. The last frontline operational NF14 sortie was flown by No 60 Squadron, from Tengah, Singapore, in April 1961. Conversions of the NF14, notably the target-towing TT20, continued to serve with the RAF in secondline roles until the mid-1970s.

Gloster Javelin

The Gloster Javelin had the dual distinction of being the RAF's first delta-winged aircraft and the first designed from the outset to be an all-weather fighter. It would gradually displace the radar-equipped Meteor night-fighters. In 1958, there were five operational versions of the Gloster Javelin in service with the RAF, plus the dual-control trainer version.

The specification to which the Javelin was designed, F4/48, led to an interesting "fly-off" between the Javelin prototype, then designated GA5, and the de Havilland DH110 (which later became the Sea Vixen and served with distinction in the Royal

Navy for many years). The first prototype GA5 made its maiden flight from Gloster's Moreton Valence airfield on 26 November 1951 and by 1952, had been selected by the RAF to meet its requirement.

This two-seat, twin-jet fighter adopted the delta-wing plan in order to offer a low wing-loading and give good high altitude performance. The large internal volume of the wing, together with the fuselage, offered space to house extensive avionic equipment and, also, a large fuel volume. The power-plant was a pair of Bristol Siddeley ASSa6 Sapphire turbojets, each giving 8,300lb of thrust. The use of a tailplane, in a "T" configuration above the fin, allowed landings to be achieved at near-normal angles of attack: most tailless deltas tended to land in a nose-high position. During the development phase, the delta configuration was refined, with a compound taper to the leading edge.

The large nose housed the air interception radar and during its progressive development, the Javelin was equipped with either the UK-built GEC AI17 or the AI22 (being the Raytheon APG-43 from the United States). The crew of two were housed in a tandem cockpit, the shape of which also evolved with the design. The armament of four 30mm Aden cannon was housed in the wings and the belly was "plumbed" to take two ventral fuel tanks.

The first production variant, the Javelin FAW1, entered RAF service with No 46 Squadron at Odiham in February 1956, and by August 1957 this unit had been re-equipped with the FAW2 version (essentially an FAW1 with the US AI22 radar in a shorter nose). A dual-control version with the radar removed, the Javelin T3, first flew in August 1956, entering service with No 228 Operational Conversion Unit (OCU) at Leeming in October 1957. The FAW4 featured an all-moving tailplane, but with the British AI17 radar. The first unit to equip with this version was No 141 Squadron at Horsham St Faith in February 1957.

For the FAW5, a new wing was introduced with increased fuel capacity, thus improving the already good endurance of the Javelin. This entered service with No 151 Squadron at Leuchars in May 1957. The FAW6 was the same airframe as the FAW5, but with the American radar. The Stradishall-based No 151 Squadron was the first unit to receive this type in October 1957.

By now the missile age was approaching and, for the FAW7, a major revision of the design was undertaken. The armament was improved by the addition of four underwing pylons, each carrying a de Havilland Firestreak infra-red, heat-seeking missile, and the gun complement reduced from four to two. The AI17 radar was installed. More-powerful ASSa7 Sapphire engines were adopted and four long-range drop tanks could be carried under the wings, in place of the missiles. The rear fuselage was length-ened, the trailing edges of the ailerons were thickened and the wing was fitted with vortex generators. The first FAW7 flew in November 1956 and the type entered service with No 33 Squadron at Leeming in July 1958.

The final production version, the Javelin FAW8, flew in May 1958, although it did not enter service until November 1959. This version was the first Javelin to be fitted with reheated Sapphires, offering 12,390lb of thrust. It was also equipped with the American radar, a Sperry autopilot, a drooped leading edge, dampers in the yaw and pitch axes, and extra vortex generators on the wings.

Later, in 1960, Glosters converted some 76 Javelin FAW7s up to FAW8 standard, these aircraft being re-designated FAW9 or, if fitted with in-flight refuelling probes, FAW9R. Javelin FAW9/9Rs of No 23 Squadron were the last of this type in Fighter Command, being withdrawn in November 1964. The Javelin continued in service with the RAF overseas until June 1967, when No 60 Squadron in Singapore disbanded.

In all 429 production Javelins were built, exclusively for the RAF, as follows:

Right: A Gloster Javelin FAW7, with dummy Firestreak air-to-air missiles and belly fuel tanks, of No 23 Squadron in company with a Hawker Hunter F6 of No 74 Squadron, armed with four 30mm cannon. These two aircraft emphasise the transition to a missile fighter era. (Crown Copyright)

Below: A formation of four Gloster Javelin FAW9, the ultimate variant of the Javelin line. Although seen carrying only two Firestreak missiles apiece, the aircraft could carry four altogether. (Gloster)

FAW1 – 40, FAW2 – 30, T3 – 23, FAW4 -50, FAW5 – 64, FAW6 – 33, FAW7 – 142 and FAW8 – 47. Some 133 of the fighters were built by Armstrong Whitworth.

Data: Javelin FAW7

Powerplant	two Bristol Siddeley Sapphire 203/204 turbo jets, rated at 11,000lb st
Span	52ft 0in
Length	56ft 3in
Height	16ft 0in
Wing area	925sq ft
Loaded weight	35,690lb (T/O clean), 40,270lb (T/O with 2 ventral tanks)
Maximum speed	709mph at sea level, 621mph at 45,000ft
Time to climb	6.6min to 45,000ft
Service ceiling	52,800ft
Armament	two 30mm Aden cannon, plus four DH Firestreak AAMs on underwing pylons, two per wing

Hawker Hunter

The Hawker Hunter is undoubtedly one of the world's classic fighter aircraft. Designed as a single-seat day fighter, it was progressively developed in that role and adapted successfully to advanced training, ground attack and fighter-reconnaissance roles. Beloved of pilots and proved in combat several times over, the Hunter was the mainstay of Fighter Command until the first Lightnings appeared. Although subsonic, the Hunter's handling qualities at all speeds were such that it remained an effective dayfighter from 1954 until 1960, and for 16 years beyond that date it served in the ground-attack role.

The Hunter began life as the Hawker P1067, having evolved from studies for a new interceptor begun in 1946. Three prototypes were ordered in 1948, at a time when the day and night/all-weather fighters were still seen as separate developments. A nimble single-seat interceptor was still required to complement the larger, two-seat, radar-equipped nightfighter. At the same time, Supermarine was developing the Swift – another single-seat dayfighter – as the Air Ministry's "insurance policy" against the failure of the Hunter. In the event, it was the Swift which failed.

The P1067, under the auspices of "Mr Hawker", Sir Sydney Camm, featured a swept wing, high-mounted tailplane, nose intake, twin 30mm cannon and was pow-

ered by the new Rolls-Royce AJ65, later known as the Avon. Specification F3/48, issued early in 1948, was found to be close to the P1067 and design work continued, to match one with the other. During the course of this work, the tailplane was moved lower, to the mid-fin position, the nose intake was transferred to the wing roots and the armament was doubled, with the gun-bodies and ammunition supply mounted in a detachable pack, which allowed swift rearming.

The first Hunter prototype, minus the guns, made its maiden flight from A&AEE Boscombe Down on 20 July 1951. Its three-year gestation from design to first flight was considered a long time by the standards of the day but, it must be remembered that the Hunter was a very different aeroplane to the

original P1067 concept. Test pilot Neville Duke expressed himself delighted with the new aircraft, remarking that it handled beautifully. The second prototype, with the gun-pack, flew in May 1952 and the third prototype, re-engined with the Armstrong Whitworth Sapphire engine and re-designated Hunter F2, flew in November 1952.

Production of the Hunter had been contracted before its first flight, with an order for 198 aircraft being placed in March 1951. This indicated the urgency with which the RAF required a modern interceptor. Even so, it was to be May 1953 before the first production Hunter F1s emerged, due to the need to fit a ventral air brake beneath the rear fuselage. The first RAF unit to equip with the Hunter F1, powered by an Avon

Avon RA7R, capable of developing 9,600lb. This aircraft, flown by Neville Duke, established a new World Absolute Speed Record of 727.6mph on 7 September 1953. A few days later it also established a 100km closed-circuit record of 709mph.

While the Hunter F1 and F2 were relatively short-range fighters, the Hunter F4 introduced increased internal fuel capacity and provision for underwing stores. The first F4 flew on 20 October 1954, powered by an Avon 113 or 114 engine, both of which were unaffected by surging when the guns were fired. This version entered RAF service with No 111 Squadron at North Weald in June 1955, followed by another eight squadrons in Fighter Command and 13 in RAF Germany.

The Hunter F5 was a development of the F2 but, essentially, a Sapphire-powered F4. This version beat the F4 to its first flight by one day and actually entered service ahead of the F4, going to No 263 Squadron at Wattisham in April 1955. The F5 also served with five other Fighter Command units, with aircraft of Nos 1 and 34 Squadrons being used operationally during the Suez campaign of 1956, operating from Nicosia, Cyprus.

The epitome of Hunter dayfighters was the F6 version which, as the P1099, first flew on 22 January 1954. Powered by the new Avon RA14 (Mk 203), initially rated at 10,500lb st but soon de-rated to 10,000lb st, the Hunter F6 was fitted with improved controls and ammunition-link "collector tanks" in two fairings on the underside of the gun pack. Later, the leading edge of the wing was extended in a "dog-tooth" to cure a tendency to pitch-up under high G-loadings at high altitudes and speeds. Some F4s were also retrofitted with the "dog-tooth" leading edge. Late production F6s were fitted with a flying tail, replacing the conventional tailplane/elevator configuration. These improvements gave the Hunter a new lease of life and it was from the F6 that the FGA9 and FR10 were later developed.

The first Fighter Command Hunter F6 unit was No 19 Squadron at Church Fenton, which took delivery of its aircraft in October 1956. By the end of 1958, the Hunter F6 had replaced all earlier variants in RAF service at home (a total of 14 squadrons), in Germany and had also been deployed to Cyprus. The improvements made on the Hunter F6 made it an ideal aerobatic aircraft and the famous "Black Arrows" and "Blue Diamonds" aerobatic teams, from Nos 111

Above: This fine Hawker study of the Hunter F6 shows the clean lines of a thoroughbred. The Hunter was, in many pilot's eyes, "the last gentleman fighter pilot's aircraft". (BAe)

RA7 rated at 7,500lb st, was No 43 Squadron at Leuchars in July 1954. It was soon found, in service, that the F1 could not fire its guns above a certain altitude, as this caused an engine surge. An altitude restriction was placed on the F1 to prevent the risk of engine "flame-out". As a result only two other units, Nos 54 and 222 Squadrons took the Hunter F1 into service.

This problem did not occur with the Hunter F2, powered by the Sapphire Mk 101, rated at 8,000lb st, but only 45 were built by Armstrong Whitworth. These aircraft entered service with No 257 Squadron at Wattisham in September 1954, followed by No 263 Squadron in February 1955.

The Hunter Mk 3 was a purely experimental aircraft, powered by an afterburning

and 92 Squadrons respectively, set the standards and established the tradition from which the "Red Arrows" of today take much pride. The all-black Hunter F6s of No 111 Squadron bought the Hunter aerobatic era to a highpoint at the SBAC show at Farnborough in September 1958, when they performed a 22-aircraft loop, a feat unsurpassed (at least to the author's knowledge) since.

Although not an interceptor, it is worth recording that a dual control trainer variant of the Hunter was developed, designated Hunter T7. First flown on 8 July 1955, it featured side-by-side seating with the nose being lengthened by 3ft and the armament reduced to two, later one, 30mm cannon. The first T7s entered RAF service with No 229 OCU at Chivenor in August 1958, with one or two examples later going to each of the operational F6 squadrons.

As has been already indicated, the Hunter was to serve as a ground-attack, fighter reconnaissance and advanced trainer aircraft with the RAF for many years. It also served with the Fleet Air Arm as the GA11

(converted from RAF F4s) and the T8 (essentially, a naval T7). It was also successfully exported to Abu Dhabi, Belgium, Chile, Denmark, Holland, India, Iraq, Jordan, Kenya, Kuwait, Lebanon, Oman, Peru, Qatar, Rhodesia (now Zimbabwe), Saudi Arabia, Singapore, Sweden and Switzerland. It remains a frontline fighter in at least four of these countries.

In all, a total of 1,985 Hunters of all marks were built, including licence production of 460 in Belgium and the Netherlands. Many of these aircraft were subsequently refurbished, upgraded and/or converted to different roles for their export sales. By any definition, the Hawker Hunter is a true thoroughbred.

Data: Hunter F6

Powerplant	one Rolls-Royce Avon 203 turbojet, rated at 10,000lb st
Span	33ft 8in
Length	45ft 10.5in
Height	13ft 2in
Wing area	340sq ft

Left: Showmanship par excellence at Farnborough in September 1958 with 18 Hawker Hunter F6s of No 111 Squadron ("The Black Arrows"). (BAe)

Order of Battle – September 1958

(extracted from SD161 Location of RAF Units, September 1958)

Fighter Command – HQ: Bentley Priory, Stanmore, Middx

No 11 Group – HQ: Uxbridge, Middx

Sqn	*Aircraft*	*Base*
1	Hawker Hunter F5/6	Stradishall, Suffolk
41	Gloster Javelin FAW4	Wattisham, Suffolk
46	Gloster Javelin FAW2	Odiham, Hants
54	Hawker Hunter F6	Odiham, Hants
89	Gloster Javelin FAW2	Stradishall, Suffolk
111	Hawker Hunter F6	Wattisham, Suffolk
228 OCU	Gloster Javelin T3 Gloster Meteor NF12/14	Leeming, Yorks
229 OCU	Hawker Hunter T7 DH Vampire FB5/T11	Chivenor, Devon

No 12 Group – HQ: Horsham St Faith, Norfolk

Sqn	*Aircraft*	*Base*
19	Hawker Hunter F6	Church Fenton, Yorks
23	Gloster Javelin FAW4	Coltishall, Norfolk
25	Gloster Meteor NF12/14	Waterbeach, Cambs
56	Hawker Hunter F5	Waterbeach, Cambs
63	Hawker Hunter F6	Waterbeach, Cambs
64	Gloster Javelin FAW7	Duxford, Cambs
65	Hawker Hunter F6	Duxford, Cambs
72	Gloster Meteor NF12	Church Fenton, Yorks
74	Hawker Hunter F6	Horsham St Faith, Norfolk
85	Gloster Meteor NF12	Church Fenton, Yorks

No 13 Group – HQ: Ouston

Sqn	*Aircraft*	*Base*
29	Gloster Javelin FAW6	Leuchars, Fife
33	Gloster Javelin FAW7	Leeming, Yorks (to Middleton St George 30 September 1958)
43	Hawker Hunter F6	Leuchars, Fife
66	Hawker Hunter F6	Acklington, Northumberland
92	Hawker Hunter F6	Thornaby, Yorks (to Middleton St George 1 October 1958)
151	Gloster Javelin FAW5	Leuchars, Fife

NB: RAF's first SAM unit, 264 Sqn, equipped with Bloodhound Mk 1, formed North Coates, Lincs, on 1 December 1958

Empty weight	14,400lb
Loaded weight	24,600lb (with drop tanks)
Maximum speed	715mph at sea level, Mach 0.95 at 36,000ft
Rate of climb	17,200ft/min (initial)
Time to climb	8min to 46,000ft
Service ceiling	51,500ft
Combat radius (clean)	318 miles
Endurance (clean)	1hr 18min (including 10min combat time at 46,000ft)
Range (with drop tanks)	1,840 miles (at 515mph)
Armament	four 30mm Aden cannon (in a removable pack), plus four underwing pylons for bombs, rockets or drop tanks

RESPONSE: AAA & SAMs

In the aftermath of the Second World War, Allied intelligence benefited greatly from the interrogation of German weapon technicians on their numerous missile projects. Work on missiles, thus, began almost as soon as hostilities ended and, initially, progressed at an easy pace. The advent of the Cold War, however, saw the new Russian threat emerge and missile development was accelerated.

The anti-aircraft missile or, to use the "new" terminology, surface-to-air missile (SAM), was probably the last of the new generation of missile weapons to be developed, together with their associated fire-control systems; acquisition (search) and tracking radars and command and control systems. The United States pioneered such developments, with the Nike Ajax system entering service in 1953, but the UK pursued its own investigations. These developments were industry-based rather than government-based, setting the precedent for the future. The first British SAMs were the Bristol/Ferranti Bloodhound and the English Electric (later BAC) Thunderbird. The latter was a totally mobile system which was developed for Army field use and, as such, does not come within the scope of this book.

Large calibre guns, particularly static emplaced systems, although improved by the addition of radar fire control systems, were on the way out. In 1958, a policy statement noted that there would be "no further attempts at a cannon solution for medium

or heavy anti-aircraft defence". With this decision, the Army's contribution to the air defence of Great Britain ceased. Smaller calibre, mobile gun systems were still considered tactically-useful but, in terms of national air defence networks, the traditional "ack-ack" gun was declared obsolescent.

Bofors 40mm L/70

This was was the improved postwar development of the, by-now classic, Bofors AA gun. It featured a longer barrel of 70- calibre and a more-powerful round of ammunition. The lethal radius of the shell was improved, the rate of fire doubled (by a redesign of the mechanism) and the powered mounting could be directly controlled from either radar or the predictor, with the option of visual engagement, as before.

Prototype weapons for the Swedish Army were tested in 1947, entering service a year later, and it was adopted by the British Army in 1953, alongside Fire Control Equipment No 7. The weapon entered service with the RAF Regiment, responsible for the air defence of RAF bases, in 1957.

Data

Calibre	40mm
Type of mounting	four-wheeled platform with outriggers
Weight in action	5.06 tons
Max elevation	90°
Effective ceiling	10,000ft
Weight of shell	2.2lb
Type of shell	HE
Muzzle velocity	3,280ft/sec
Rate of fire	240 rds/min

Right: The weapon which sounded the deathknell to AA guns was the surface-to-air missile (SAM). The RAF formed its first SAM unit equipped with the Bristol/Ferranti Bloodhound Mk1 in December 1958. This example was a "gate guardian" at Bawdsey for many years. (W. J. Taylor via Paul Jackson)

Left: As the Army foreswore their AA guns, the RAF Regiment retained the Bofors 40mm, in its L70 version (illustrated from the mid-1970s), for many years thereafter as light AA defences for airfields. (Author's Collection)

3.7in Gun Mk 6
Basically unchanged from the description in the previous "Snapshot". There had been minor improvements but the performance remained substantially the same. The 3.7in Mk 6 was declared obsolete in May 1959.

A new mounting with automatic loading, called "Longhand", had been developed. This version of the 3.7in system was the last British AA gun ever to be approved for service, in February 1957. Unfortunately, within days of its adoption, the first SAMs were introduced so Longhand never entered service. It had the same performance as the Mk 6, but with a rate of fire of 40 rds/min.

Data: see 1948 "Snapshot"

5.25in Gun Mk 1
As described in the previous "Snapshot", this weapon was on the way out. It remained in service until declared obsolescent in May 1959.

Data: see 1948 "Snapshot"

Bristol/Ferranti Bloodhound Mk 1
Development work on the Bloodhound had begun in 1949, under the codename "Red Duster", and, when it entered service with the RAF in December 1958 it was the first time, ever, that a complete ground weapons system had been placed in the hands of the RAF. Its operation was tied into the existing reporting and control system, the so-called Air Defence Ground Environment (ADGE), with RAF controllers deciding whether or not a target was to be engaged by fighters or missiles. Initial trials at Aberporth were very successful, with more than a dozen firings hitting their targets. First production deliveries began in 1957.

The Bloodhound was a winged, ramjet-powered weapon with four, detachable launch booster rockets with a proximity-fuzed HE warhead. Some reports suggest the development of a nuclear warhead for the Bloodhound but this has never been, officially, confirmed. Fixed site installation (typically 16 launchers to a squadron) for the zero-length launcher was on a turntable firing the missile at an elevation of 45°.

Targets were detected by a high power Vickers-Metropolitan three dimensional tracking radar, which was linked to a high data-rate Ferranti computer. Guidance to target was achieved by signals from an AEI Sting Ray (Type 86) target-illuminating radar being detected by a radar receiver in the nose of the missile. This information was converted to input the control surfaces, allowing the Bloodhound to steer an interception course.

The RAF was to equip 11 air defence missile units (Nos 62, 94, 112, 141, 222, 242, 247, 257, 263, 264, and 266 Squadrons) with the Bloodhound Mk 1 between 1958 and 1960, primarily in defence of V-bomber and Douglas Thor IRBM bases. Sweden ordered the system in 1958, followed by Australia in 1959. The Mk 2 version which superseded the Mk 1 from the mid-1960s was also adopted by the Swiss and Singapore Air Force.

Data

Powerplant	two Bristol Siddeley Thor ramjets plus four Gosling rocket boosters
Speed	Mach 2
Span	9ft 3.5in
Length	25ft (including boosters)
Service ceiling	not available
Range	43nm
Weight of warhead	not available
Type of warhead	HE

CRITIQUE

If the period between 1938-48 was described as transitional for the RAF, then 1948-58 may be considered one of consolidation and catching-up with yet a further transition coming towards the end.

The "consolidation and catching-up" element involved the introduction of swept-wing high-performance fighters with, as was noted in the previous "Snapshot", the acquisition from Canada of the Sabre F4. These were withdrawn from UK air defence units as the Hunter and Swift became available. As noted within its description, the Swift (intended as an insurance policy against the Hunter's failure) was the failure. The Javelin, to be the RAF's first missile-armed aircraft in later versions, began to replace the Venom and Meteor nightfighters from 1956 but, even in 1958, there were still a number of squadrons still using these first generation fighters.

During the early to mid-1950s, the development work which could have bought the British aerospace industry world reknown, to say nothing of orders, was beset by go-stop policies. Designs for high-speed interceptors from Fairey, Folland, Hawker and Saunders-Roe abounded. The reader is again referred to *Project Cancelled* for detailed histories. Let the Fairey FD2 Delta suffice as a brief example.

Construction work on the FD2 began in 1952 and with Peter Twiss at the controls, the aircraft's maiden flight was made in October 1954. By March 1956, Twiss had set the world's first four-figure speed record – 1,132mph at 38,000ft, exceeding the previous record held by the North American F-100 Super Sabre by more than 300mph. The next stage was the transition from experimental aircraft to operational fighter – the ER103/C – equipped with AI radar and wingtip-mounted Firestreak AAMs. Further paper developments were made, culminating in a bid for the RAF's OR329, calling for a two-seat, missile-armed Mach 2 fighter. The infamous Sandys White Paper of April 1957 killed the project dead.

The irony is, that in order to get around British supersonic flight restrictions, the FD2 was deployed to Cazaux, France, in late 1956 for further supersonic trials. The Dassault team there learnt much of delta wing aerodynamics and performance from this detachment which was useful for their own Mirage III project. The Mirage made its maiden flight just days after the FD2 returned home. It was later recorded that, when the Mirage was sweeping the world's fighter orders, Marcel Dassault remarked to a senior executive of a British aircraft manufacturer, "If it were not for the clumsy way in which you tackle things in Britain, you could have made the Mirage yourself".

The change in emphasis of the threat had much to do with the way the air defences were shaping. Although there is no doubt that a manned-bomber threat existed, the threat of nuclear-armed intercontinental ballistic missiles (ICBMs) was also rising. The need to defend against saturation attacks of Second World War proportions was dropping rapidly, hence the switch from AA guns to SAMs. By the early 1960s, the conviction that ICBMs posed the prime threat bought the number of air defence fighters to well below 100. More of this in the next "Snapshot".

While the authors of the 1957 White Paper on Defence were forward-thinking in their concept of missiles taking the place of manned aircraft, one cannot help but conclude that the technologists of the time over-sold the reality of achievement. While the developments were, indeed, being made, the reliability and accuracy of many systems proposed left much to be desired. History has since showed the concept of all-missile warfare to be flawed, despite the reality of a nuclear strike against Great Britain. The change of emphasis of the Royal Observer Corps as "fallout observers" is evidence enough of that fear.

The RAF air defence force in 1958 may have been numerically strong but it had lost the support of the RAuxAF in March 1957. New aircraft were coming along but so were the threats – both external and internal. Despite the forebodings of the Sandys White Paper, "push button" nuclear warfare, fortunately, did not materialise. By 1968, air defence would be on an upward trend again.

1968

Much of the 1960s was dominated by discussions over the whole future of air defence and its weaponry. The infamous 1957 Defence White Paper (*see also the section on the BAC Lightning*) had decided that the manned bomber was in eclipse and missiles were the future, against which there could be no method of defence except by the adoption of nuclear deterrence. The result was some confusion of thought. The reality was the continuing Cold War, which in terms of UK air defence was characterised by regular and persistent interceptions of Russian aircraft, over the North Sea, by RAF fighters.

The problem was basic. Conventional war was seen as a continuing risk and conventional methods were still being pursued, complete with radar warning systems and fighter control techniques that had already become established. The "unthinkable", for which the V-bomber force had been formed, depended partly upon psychology, and partly on the method of devising some element of warning that would not necessarily protect the target, but allow the necessary retribution to commence.

In 1968, the effects of this philosophy had reached their height although thoughts were beginning to turn away from a concept of "Mutually Assured Destruction" (MAD) to a more "flexible response". Air defence could, perhaps, be a distinct possibility. Even so, the RAF could, in this year, only muster a force of five frontline fighter squadrons, supplemented by a further two made up from Operational Conversion Units, plus two squadrons of SAMs.

This year also saw the start of the contraction of the Command system for the RAF when, on 30 April, Fighter and Bomber Commands merged to become Strike Command. What had been Fighter Command now became No 11 Group, with its headquarters at Bentley Priory, Stanmore. Its tasks were to give warning of any aircraft or missiles threat to the United Kingdom; to provide an air defence force and its associated control system wherever the need arose – including air defence for ships of the Royal Navy; and to exercise control of the United Kingdom's airspace in peace and war.

The air defence element of Strike Command is part of the unified system under the Supreme Allied Commander Europe (SACEUR), with the UK forming one of the four NATO air defence regions. It is a NATO requirement that commanders with responsibilities other than air defence shall appoint a deputy for air defence only. Thus, while the Air Officer Commander-in-Chief (AOCinC) Strike Command is the Air Defence Commander and Commander of

Below: Without a visual bombing capability, the Tupolev Tu-16 "Badger-C" was a pure missile-carrying aircraft, equipped to launch the AS-2 "Kipper" and, later, the AS-6 "Kingfisher". (US DoD)

the NATO UK Air Defence Region, he delegates his responsibilities for the direct day-to-day operational control to the AOC, No 11 Group. He retains overall responsibility for policy, planning, supervision and support of these forces.

The 1960s was the decade of the Lightning's pre-eminence in RAF service, although plans were in hand for the first Phantom unit – No 43 Squadron – to form in 1969, initially using the first aircraft to be handed over from the Fleet Air Arm during its run-down. For surface-to-air missile defence, the improved Bloodhound Mk 2 was now in service.

These improvements to the air defences of the UK were, in part, due to the NATO policy of Detente, Deterrence and Defence then in force. While *detente* sought to reduce tension by negotiation and general attitude between NATO and the Warsaw Pact, *deterrence* continued to be based on the ability of either side to survive a nuclear attack and still be able to retaliate with a threat of unacceptable damage to the opponent. The *defence* element, obviously, sought to provide sufficient forces to allow such an exchange to succeed.

The elements of both deterrence and defence were enshrined in a NATO strategy, "14/3", promulgated in 1967. In essence, this required NATO forces to have at their disposal a whole range of military capabilities, allowing an appropriate response to any level of aggression by the Warsaw Pact. As such, UK air defences were an essential part of that equation. The results of this policy, as it took effect, in terms of hardware and tactics, are described in the next "Snapshot".

THE THREAT

In 1968, the Cold War was at its height and there was no doubt that the Soviet Union was the perceived threat. As far as the UK was concerned, it was the long-range bomber force which comprised much of that threat; the ICBM being conveniently ignored for the purposes of air defence.

Of the three major types – M-4 "Bison", Tu-16 "Badger" and Tu-95 "Bear" – described in the previous "Snapshot", the "Bison" had been withdrawn as a bomber. The "Badger' and "Bear" had been in service a long time (and were to soldier on for another 20 years). However, although they gradually assumed less-offensive roles such

as maritime reconnaissance and ELINT (*EL*ectronic *INT*elligence), they continued to represent a real cause for concern.

The appearance in the early 1960s of the Myasishchev M-50 "Bounder" – a supersonic long-range bomber – caused many analysts sleepless nights, but in the event it was a failure and never entered service. The second Soviet attempt to produce a supersonic bomber – the Tupolev Tu-22 "Blinder" – was also to prove something of a disappointment. It did, however, enter production and some 250 were built. A much more refined version, eminently superior – the Tu-22M – was to come along in the late 1970s.

The saving grace of the Soviet long-range bomber force was the development of stand-off weapons, which meant that launch distances from targets became greater and the aircraft themselves were not so exposed to air defences as previously. This development saw a shift in manned bomber operations towards anti-shipping use.

Following the fall of Nikita Kruschev, the importance of the DA began to re-emerge. While not denigrating the primacy of the Strategic Rocket Force, strategists in the Soviet Union began to support the usefulness of long-range bombers. The commandant of the Gagarin Military Academy, Marshal S. A. Krasovsky, wrote in a thesis in the journal *"Miltary Thought"* in 1967:

"...aircraft also have an important role in the actions and combat operations of the ground troops and the navy.

More effectively than other services of the armed forces they can put out of operation very important fixed targets without destroying the entire objective, and they can also suppress many mobile and highly manoeuvrable targets."

He went on to suggest that, in the context of a war against NATO forces, the "Bison", "Badger" and "Bear", armed with either free-fall bombs or stand-off missiles, could reach most parts of the European continent, even if the United States was beyond their survivable range. Such thoughts were to prevail and new aircraft developed.

Also during this period, Soviet tactics did not envisage the long-range fighter escort mission: their longest-range fighters – the Sukhoi Su-15 "Flagon" and Yakovlev Yak-28P "Firebar" – were incapable of flying a mission further than 575 miles. As we shall see in later "Snapshots", fighters with the range to escort the bombers (assisted by

Right: Equivalent to the American B-58 Hustler, the Tupolev Tu-22 "Blinder-A" was equipped for conventional bombing, although later versions were configured for the AS-4 "Kitchen" air-to-surface missile. (TASS)

AAR) were to come into service. However, for the purpose of this "Snapshot", no fighters are included.

Having described the "Bison" fully in the previous "Snapshot", with no major improvements recorded over the past decade, it only remains to update the "Badger" and "Bear" and take a look at the "Blinder".

Tupolev Tu-16 "Badger-B/C"
By 1968, about 2,000 Tu-16 "Badgers" had been estimated to have been built, being standard equipment for both the Soviet Air Force and Naval Air Force. Apart from the initial "Badger-A", two more versions had been identified at this time: the "Badger-B" and the "Badger-C".

The "Badger-B" was essentially the same as the A-model but included provision to carry two of the swept-wing AS-1 "Kennel" anti-ship missile, guided by the I-band "Komet III" radar. The aircraft also introduced A322Z Doppler, the RV-10/17 radar altimeter and the SRZ-2 interrogator. In service with the AV-MF and, from 1961, the Indonesian Air Force.

First seen at the Soviet Aviation day display in 1961,the "Badger-C" was the second missile-carrier version ofthe *genre*. Its bomb-bay was rebuilt to house a single AS-2 "Kipper" anti-ship missile (similar to the US Hound Dog) in a semi-recessed position. The nose gun was deleted and re-designed to accommodate the "Puff Ball" missile acquisition system and A-329Z missile guidance system. The C-model had no visual bombing capability.

Data: see 1958 "Snapshot"

Tupolev Tu-22 "Blinder"
The West got its first sight of the Tupolev Tu-22 "Blinder" during the 1961 Aviation Day display, when a formation of 10 were seen. Similar in concept to, but not in the class of, the US B-58 Hustler, the "Blinder" was assessed at having ranges between 1,215nm to 3,510nm, depending on the authority.

Work on the "Blinder", with the manufacturer's designation Tu-105, began in the mid-1950s, with the aim of achieving the "Badger's" performance but with a greatly increased penetration speed and altitude. Thus an area-ruled shape was chosen, allowing supersonic dash with a minimum penalty for subsonic performance. The compound wing sweep began at the root at 70°, dropping to 45° at the tips. The twin engines, almost certainly the Koliesov VD-7/7F (based on the AM-3), were positioned in slim cowlings, mounted high on the rear fuselage to avoid the weight and drag penalties of long intake ducts. Defensive armament was reduced to a single automated tail turret with a single 23mm cannon.

Designated Tu-22 by the DA, the first version is thought to have flown in 1959 and, equipped for conventional bombing, was codenamed "Blinder-A" by NATO. However, following the decision to rely solely on missiles for strategic attack, many aircraft were transferred to the AV-MF. Later, the need for precision strike and missile-carrying re-emerged and the "Blinder-B"

appeared, with a bomb-bay modified to accept the AS-4 "Kitchen" air-to-surface missile. Some 170 were built, going to both the DA and AV-MF.

The AV-MF later took delivery of about 50 maritime reconnaissance/ELINT versions, the "Blinder-C". These offered payloads and in-flight refuelled-endurance compatible with the "Badger". Another version, the Tu-22U "Blinder-D", was built to incorporate a second (instructor's) cockpit, above and behind the standard (student's) cockpit, for use as an operational conversion aircraft.

Although not considered a success by the West, the "Blinder" did play an important role in providing European strike capability. It was also sold to Libya and Iraq, both countries having used the type in action, the latter against Kurdish insurgents and the former against Tanzania, in support of Uganda.

Data: Tu-22 "Blinder-A"

Powerplant	two Koliesov VD-7/7F turbojets, each rated at 30,900lb st (with reheat)
Span	78ft 0in
Length	132ft 11.5in
Height	35ft 0in
Wing area	1,650sq ft
Empty weight	90,000lb
Loaded weight	185,000lb
Maximum speed	920mph (Mach 1.4) at 40,000ft
Service ceiling	60,000ft
Range (combat)	1,750 miles (with full bomb load), including 250 miles supersonic dash
Armament	one 23mm NR-23 cannon

in a radar-directed tail turret, plus 17,500lb free-fall bombs for the "Blinder-A" or one AS-4 "Kitchen" nuclear missile recessed into the weapons bay for the "Blinder-B"

Tupolev Tu-95/142 "Bear-B/C/D/E"

Despite being an anachronism in its own lifetime (if one may mix metaphors), the Tu-95/142 series remains the only turboprop-powered bomber in production and service. The reason for this is simply its unmatched range.

In 1961, the Tushino display saw 15 aircraft to a new standard – Tu-95K "Bear-B" – equipped with a semi-recessed AS-3 "Kangaroo" air-to-surface missile in its fuselage bomb bay and the "Crown Drum" radar, operating in the low end of the I-band, in a nose-mounted "duck bill" radome. They retained all three twin-23mm cannon turrets and later models "sprouted" in-flight refuelling probes on the nose. Over the years, the AS-3 was dropped and some models were later seen with the AS-4. For the AV-MF, the "Bear-B" eventually sprouted many antennae and radomes for ELINT work, losing the upper-fuselage gun turrets.

The Tu-95KM "Bear-C" is essentially the same as the B-model but was built from new for multi-role tasking. First identified in 1964, this version, too, has been progressively modified over the years. One notable modification was the substitution of the "Bee Hind" rear warning radar for the "Box Tail" system.

The "Bear-D" is a re-build of the "Bear-A". First identified in 1967, it dates from the wholesale transfer of "Bears" from the DA

Below: Rebuilt "Bear-As" were transferred to the AV-MF from 1967 as platforms for provision of mid-course targeting information for missiles, being re-designated Tu-95 "Bear-D". (US Navy)

to the AV-MF. While not a combat bomber, the "Bear-D's" prime role is to provide targeting information to other weapons platforms (air or sea-based) and mid-course guidance for various anti-ship missiles in flight. As a secondary duty, the aircraft undertakes general maritime reconnaissance and ELINT tasks.

In place of the weapons bay is a large radome housing the "Big Bulge" I/J-band search radar, while a smaller J-band "Short Horn" is located in the nose. ELINT antennae and camera ports are located in the rear fuselage, while the mid-upper turret is deleted. Data transmission of targeting information to naval forces is by means of a secure A346Z J-band digital link.

The transition from the designation Tu-95 to Tu-142 appears to have taken place in the late-1960s and, although not the first of the series to carry the new designation, the "Bear-E" is known as the Tu-142R. Again it was a re-build of the A-model but specifically for maritime reconnaissance. The main difference between the "Bear-D" and the E-model is the bulged reconnaissance pallet over the weapons bay, housing seven optical cameras and, it is thought, either an infra-red linescan (IRLS) camera or a sideways-looking airborne radar (SLAR), or both. The smaller navigation radar, thought to be "Short Horn", is located under the glazed nose. Over the years, various combinations of ECM and ELINT antennae have been observed.

The progression of the "Bear" series is continued in the next "Snapshot".

DETECTION & IDENTIFICATION

As was mentioned earlier, for the concept of MAD to work reliance was placed, partly, on the method of devising some element of warning that would allow the necessary retribution to commence.

The United States had already begun to set up "chains" of early warning radars in the northern latitudes, covering the approaches to that continent. It was increasingly recognised that, although the famous "four-minute warning" was all that could be expected in the event of missile attacks, the Russians were still developing long-range, conventional bombers and these were likely to approach from directions other than that usually considered as the threat path.

The Royal Observer Corps had also changed in character and was increasingly

engaged in developing techniques of monitoring the after-effects of nuclear attack and the tracking of radiation levels across the country. Special Civil Defence command centres were established in selected underground sites. Typically one of these, in North London, was constructed under a block of flats, being capable of withstanding an attack and was provisioned to allow the inhabitants to survive for several weeks. In the event that the flats had been demolished, and thereby prevented egress, a long tunnel was run to an open area some distance away. Most chilling for the visitor was the provision of a small loudspeaker that transmitted a monotone, disruption of which indicated an incipient attack!

In the early-1960s the Americans had also accelerated efforts to increase the basic warning time and this could only be achieved by improved early warning. This was the role of the Ballistic Missile Early Warning System (BMEWS), two of which were already close to operation at Clear, Alaska, and at Thule, Greenland. Early in 1960, it was disclosed that approval was given for a third station, but this one was intended to be located in England. These systems had a range of some 2,800 miles, a mean power of around 2 Megawatts and a peak power of some 10 times as much. Contractors involved were General Electric, RCA and Western Electric, using combinations of FPS-49, FPS-50 and FPS-92 radars. It was all a long way, both in time and technology, from the Chain Home system of the 1940s. Considerable computational power, for that time, was used and the detection radars were backed by tracking radars, which were used to establish the missile's impact point with a high degree of precision.

The UK site was the subject of some deliberation and much speculation. Initially it was not even in the UK, Iceland being seen as the best choice, though this soon switched to Prestwick, Scotland, before being finalised at Fylingdales Moor in North Yorkshire.

The decade also saw the introduction in the UK of the US-supplied Douglas Thor intermediate-range ballistic missiles (IRBM) to RAF airfields stretching from Norfolk through Lincolnshire to Yorkshire. The technology was American, the man (and women) power was British and in the terminology of the day, the decision to launch would be a "matter for joint decision by the two governments".

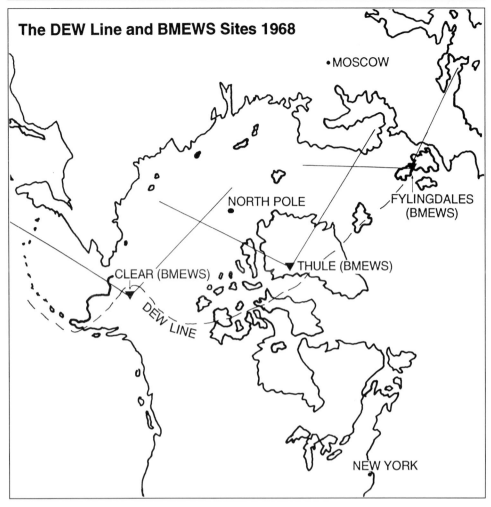

The DEW Line and BMEWS Sites 1968

•MOSCOW

NORTH POLE

FYLINGDALES (BMEWS)

CLEAR (BMEWS)

THULE (BMEWS)

DEW LINE

NEW YORK

Meanwhile, conventional exercises continued and the annual air defence exercises were conducted against a variety of "enemy" aircraft including Valiants, Vulcans, Victors and Canberras of the RAF, US B-66s and F-100s, Canadian Avro CF-100s (no relation to the US F-100 Super Sabre) and French Vautours. Significantly, the 1960 exercise, codenamed "Yeoman", saw the first use in an exercise, of the Firestreak AAM carried on a Javelin. It was also a period that saw a growing application of electronic jamming techniques which provided the associated command and control system with considerable experience.

The mix of missiles and aircraft was complemented by a mix of nationalities as NATO began to become a more cohesive force and despite the North Sea interceptions, the defence of the V-force bases and overall defence of the UK, the RAF's frontline was very much along the German border. This "internationalisation" of air

defence was the way of the future and some interceptor elements that had formerly been solely for national defence, were increasingly integrated under central control. The growing complexity of Command, Control and Communication (to be dubbed C^3 or "Cee Cubed" in the mid-1970s) was introducing other new methods and the evolution of a NATO Communications Satellite (Comsat) programme. The UK's network, to be named Skynet, was intended to be based initially upon a single synchronous orbit satellite supplied by the United States.

Meanwhile the so-called electronic revolution was gaining pace and both airborne and ground systems were becoming more capable, reliable and operationally effective. Early in 1968, the RAF accepted the first of the new Type 85 three-dimensional surveillance radar at Staxton Wold, North Yorkshire. At the time, it was the largest radar ever delivered to the RAF and had been developed by AEI (now Marconi

Radar and Command Systems). The official statement to the Press at the time stressed that the new radar would be integrated into the most modern civil air traffic and air defence system in the world. This underlined the growing acceptance of the civil Air Traffic Control system as a part of the national defence structure: after all, a long distance surveillance radar for an airport can just as well be used to detect an approaching bomber!

This fact had been recognised in 1962 when the UK made the decision to set up a joint civil/military ATC system which became known as the Linesman/Mediator concept. Linesman was the military side, which was intended also to provide an element of protection for the BMEWS system, by detecting hostile ECM aircraft as well as other forms of attack. Much dependence was to be placed on computers and displays, with a very large built-in redundancy to ensure a graceful degradation in the face of failure. The intention was for the system to become effective from 1971 onwards with an integrated Master Control Centre at West Drayton.

Automation was also making great strides and Marconi supplied S600 radars for an unmanned element in the NATO Air Defence Ground Environment (NADGE) chain, which was to stretch from Norway to Turkey. At that time (1968), it was considered that it was the first use of unmanned radar stations of such size and complexity in an air defence system. Computer-based systems in NADGE were expected to offer much better rates of response by reducing the reaction time of fighter elements, through the use of improved signal processing of the detected data. Of course, this implied a degree of complexity and it was significant that the cost inevitably increased, a pattern that would become familiar in the future.

Technology was making great strides in the airborne application and when the Lightning fighter entered service during the decade, it was fitted with a new radar and fire control system that had been developed by Ferranti. Designated AI23, the Airborne Interception Radar and Pilots' Attack Sight System created the convenient acronym AIRPASS and was one of the most advanced and versatile systems in the world.

Fitted in the Lightning's distinctive intake "bullet" fairing, the radar provided information to the pilot in basic form

Below: The original "Golf Ball" radomes of the three FPS-49 early-warning radars located at Fylingdales on the North Yorkshire Moors, as part of the BMEWS chain. These radars would provide the notorious "four-minute warning" of nuclear strike by Soviet forces. (Author's Collection)

enabling him to intercept the target and lock the radar beam. From then on, the radar automatically tracked the target and supplied information to the associated sighting system. Computer technology was the heart of the system, providing a high degree of automation. The whole operation from intercept to weapon deployment was completed without the pilot ever seeing the target but, if it should come into view, he could then take advantage of the normal visual sighting methods. An automatic warning device was used to inform the pilot when to break off the attack if there was a danger of collision with the target.

This growth in technology was to be the pace setter for the future. Another trend, discernible at this time, was the growing number of defence cuts and budget restraints that were to become a feature of all future equipment and re-equipment programmes. The Cold War was essentially a trial of intellectual strength through emerging technology and political chess playing.

Perhaps the real flavour of the times was to be noted in the 1968 version of the "Battle of Berlin". During a *Bundestag* meeting held in that city the previous year, Soviet aircraft had interrupted the session. To avoid a similar repetition in 1968, RAF, USAF and French aircraft were flown into the city with the express purpose of being used to fill the airspace and so inhibit penetration by Russian aircraft. The RAF provided two C-130 Hercules, three Pembrokes and two helicopters. Such outbidding of Soviet efforts was the basis of the economic attrition that characterised the years between 1946 and 1989 and which was eventually to lead to the economic ruin of the Soviet Union.

RESPONSE: AIRCRAFT & ARMAMENT

BAC Lightning

The BAC (formerly English Electric, now BAe) Lightning was the first and only British designed-and-built supersonic interceptor fighter to see RAF service. It saw its origins in the English Electric P1 high speed research programme (F23/49) begun in early 1949. Initial designs had been sketched from about 1947 by W. E. Petter, who handed on the work to Freddie (now Sir Frederick) Page later in 1949. The P1A made its maiden flight on 4 August 1954.

By 1953, the emerging high altitude bomber threat to the UK saw the need for a fast, quick-reaction interceptor crystallise. As the P1A was *in situ* in 1954, English Electric received a contract to build three P1Bs, the operational version of which was to be armed with two 30mm guns and a pair of de Havilland Propellers' Blue Jay air-to-air missiles (AAMs), subsequently named Firestreak. The P1B made its first flight on 4 April 1957 and on 25 November 1958 had the distinction of being the first British aircraft ever to attain Mach 2 in level flight.

On 4 April 1957 – the same day as the P1B flew for the first time – the Tory defence minister Duncan Sandys declared in the infamous White Paper entitled "Defence – an Outline of Future Policy", that the era of the manned interceptor was all but over. The exact wording in the document stated: "In view of the good progress already made, the Government has come to the conclusion that the RAF is unlikely to have a requirement for fighter aircraft of types more advanced than the supersonic P1 and work on such projects will stop." Surface-to-air missiles (SAMs) would replace the manned interceptor and the Lightning was to be the RAF's last such aircraft. The Lightning became the "stop gap" that stayed!

In the event, it took 31 years for the Lightning to be withdrawn from service (and, then, there were manned interceptors to succeed it). Therein lie the seeds of the Lightning's fate (see Critique for further comments), but we are getting ahead of ourselves.

The P1B Lightning (and the P1A before it) was of unusual configuration with a slim fuselage (almost totally re-designed from the P1A) and its twin Rolls-Royce Avon engines superimposed one above the other in the centre fuselage. This left no room for fuel in the fuselage and each wing only held 2,500lb (550gal) of fuel. This lack of fuel (and hence range) was to be a constant criticism of the Lightning for its whole career. The first development aircraft, virtually a Lightning F1, was fitted with 250gal (2,000lb) rear belly tanks which became standard on all aircraft. Powered by RA24R Avon 201 engines and with a total of 7,500lb (920gal) of fuel, there was just sufficient fuel to climb to 35,000ft, accelerate to Mach 1.5, make a one-pass stern interception and return to base, with 1,600lb (200gal) remaining.

A conical centre-body was inserted into the nose intake of the P1B to house the

Above: The first British supersonic fighter was the English Electric Lightning F1, armed with a pair of 30mm cannon and two de Havilland Firestreak infra-red homing missiles. Seven aircraft from No 74 Squadron are seen here performing an aerobatic routine break. (BAe)

Ferranti AI23 radar, while the cockpit was raised and faired into a dorsal spine which met the fin leading edge. The wings were highly-swept (60° at the trailing edge) with the ailerons across the wingtips. The tailplane was mounted low in the rear fuselage in order to overcome the transonic "pitch-up" which afflicted other British designs of the time with mid- or high tailplanes.

Production of the batch of Lightning F1 aircraft was ordered in November 1956, with an armament consisting of two 30mm Aden cannon in the upper nose and a "quick-change" pack beneath the nose for a second pair of Aden guns, the missile pylons and interface unit for the Firestreaks, or a pack of 48 x 2in FFAR (free-flight aerial rockets). The de Havilland Firestreak was an infra-red heat-seeking missile of the first generation and was only able to be successfully launched in a stern quarter attack.

The first production Lightning F1 flew in November 1959 and the first RAF unit to equip with the type, No 74 Squadron, was formed at Coltishall in June 1960. The RAF was, at last, into the supersonic fighter business. Moreover, the Lightning was the first RAF fighter to be designed as an integrated weapons system. The AI23 radar, known by its acronym of AIRPASS, allowed the pilot to search above and below the line of flight until he found the target on his radar screen. An automatic "lock-on" facility enabled the radar to track target movements. Raw radar

data was processed by onboard computers, allowing steering information to be displayed to the pilot. Once he had closed to within missile range (much greater than that of the guns), the heat-seeking homing head locked onto the target and the pilot instructed to fire the missile.

To enable the Lightnings to position themselves for the stern quarter attack, ground-controlled inteception (GCI) techniques were adopted. In this time of the Cold War, the Lightning was required to cover the North Sea area, intercepting any Soviet aircraft which might head towards the UK. Such long-range Soviet bomber or maritime reconnaissance aircraft were all subsonic. After scrambling, a pair of Lightnings would be split and take different directions towards the target, each aircraft coming in under GCI on one of the two stern quarters. Should the missile attack fail, it was then left to the guns to secure the kill. It was a vast improvement over earlier gun-armed Hunters and Javelins, as a tail-chase could be a long drawn-out affair, especially if the target had a tail-gun armament.

After 20 F1s, the F1A model was introduced, which differed by having the facility for air-to-air refuelling in the form an enormous probe which had to be fitted below the port wing and looked just like a medieval knight's jousting lance. It also introduced UHF radio and a rearranged internal equipment layout, which required a long external cable duct down the port fuse-

lage side. This model went to No 56 Squadron based at Wattisham, in December 1960.

This was followed in April 1958 by a second, larger, order for the Lightning F2 and its twin-seat operational trainer variant, the T4. The F2 model introduced Avon 210 engines with four-stage afterburning, a liquid oxygen breathing system, a revised "integrated" instrument panel, improved avionics and other changes. These aircraft were issued to Nos 19 and 92 Squadrons based at Leconfield in 1963, moving to Gutersloh as part of RAF Germany in 1965. The T4 was, essentially, a two-seat version of the F1A with a side-by-side cockpit a foot wider, full dual controls but only one Aden gun. It had been developed, initially, as the PII, from 1957.

By 1960, the effects of the "Sandystorm" were dying down and the authorities now felt it "unwise to predict, or attempt to predict, when manned fighters will finally go out of use". Thus, the RAF established its case for a second-generation Lightning. At the same time, de Havilland had been working on an improved missile, the Firestreak 4, allowing it to home onto infra-red emissions from head-on or other aspects. However, this missile, eventually known as Red Top, was so incompatible with the original

Firestreak equipment that it needed a new Lightning to carry it. Rolls-Royce, too, had continued to improve the Avon, coming out with the Avon 301 with a better afterburning system, delivering 12,690lb of thrust dry (ie, without afterburning) and some 16,300lb with reheat. This gave the Lightning a thrust-to-weight ratio of almost unity – not bad for a 1949 design.

So the Lightning F3 was born. The main external difference was a 15% increase in fin area, needed for Mach 2 performance, with a squared-off tip. It was, of course, compatible with the Red Top missile but it also was the first British fighter never to carry a gun armament – the twin 30mm Aden guns being deleted. The manufacturers (by now the British Aircraft Corporation – BAC) also developed an overwing hardpoint on each wing for fitting a pair of 260gal (2,100lb) ferrytanks, but these were not adopted by the RAF until the 64th Lightning F3. The first F3 flew in June 1962 and entered service with No 74 Squadron at Leuchars in April 1964. Eventually, it replaced all earlier models except for the two Germany-based squadrons. A two-seat version of the F3 was developed as the Lightning T5.

During 1963, the RAF formally told BAC that the Lightning was deficient in range, especially for overseas deployment,

Above: The second major production version of the Lightning to enter Fighter Command service was the Lightning F3 with the cut-off fin-and-rudder. Aircraft of No 29 Squadron are seen here at Akrotiri in Cyprus. The aircraft on the right is armed with Firestreak, while the second from the right has the improved Red Top missile. (Author's Collection)

and contracted with them for a modified fuel system of much greater capacity. The problem was not new to the manufacturers, who had been trying to get officialdom to accept that fact for six years. By the time the modified F3 appeared it had changed so much that the designation was altered from F3A (or F3ER for Extended Range) to F6, and the undelivered F3s were delivered as Interim F6s, with many changes. Ultimately, 14 F3s were brought up to F6 standard, in addition to the interim aircraft. The resulting Lightning F6 differed not only on the inside but also externally. The underside of the fuselage had been redesigned with a "bulge" to area-rule the surface for smoother supersonic airflow, with the original 250gal tank being replaced by a more substantial capacity 600gal (4,800lb) tank. This, in turn, sprouted two ventral fins to maintain yaw/roll characteristics at speeds beyond Mach 2, plus an airfield arrester hook. The wings, too, exhibited change with a new kinked leading edge, allowing extra lift for the greater take-off weight and over-wing pylon facilities for ferry tanks, while the flaps were made into integral fuel tanks, bringing total fuel capacity to just in excess of 1,250gal (10,000lb) giving some 40% more range. Finally, the RAF was made to see the error of its ways in deleting the guns, as a pair of 30mm Adens were reinstated in the forward part of the underfuselage bulge.

The first Lightning F6 flew in November 1965, going to No 74 Squadron, which deployed them to Tengah, Singapore, in 1967 where they were based until disbandment in August 1971. Eventually Nos 5, 11, 23 and 56 Squadrons in the UK all received the F6 version. Production of all Lightnings for the RAF is best summarised in the accompanying table.

In August 1967, the last production Lightning for the RAF was delivered and, in 1968, this type was the sole British air defence fighter. More of the Lightning's fortunes will be described in subsequent "Snapshots".

Data: Lightning F3/F6

Powerplant	two Rolls-Royce Avon 301 turbojets, each rated at 12,690lb st (dry) and 16,360lb st with reheat
Span	34ft 10in
Length	55ft 3in (including probe)
Height	19ft 7in
Wing area	460sq ft
Empty weight	(F6) 26,905lb
	(F3) 28,041lb
Loaded weight	(F6) 40,000lb
	(F3) 41,700lb
Maximum speed	1,500mph (Mach 2.27) at 40,000ft
Rate of climb	50,000ft/min (initial)
Time to climb	2.5min to 40,000ft
Service ceiling	70,000+ft
Range	800 miles (with ventral tank)
Armament	two Firestreak or Red Top AAMs (in a removable pack) or two retractable boxes, each housing 24 x 2in Mk1 spin-stabilised rockets; plus (on F6 only) two 30mm Aden cannon, with 130rds/gun, in forward section of ventral fairing

Handley Page Victor K1

Between 1960 and 1964, air-to-air refuelling (AAR) was an accepted part of the air defence world and the standard RAF aerial tanker was the Vickers Valiant, converted from the first of the RAF's three V-bombers. However, in 1964, fatigue cracks were discovered in the Valiant's wings and the fleet

---

RAF Lightning Production

Mark	No built
F1	20
F1A	24
F2	44 (30 rebuilt to F6 standards as F2A)
F3	70 (14 rebuilt to F6 standards)
T4	20
F3ER/Interim F6	16
T5	22
F6	39
	—-
Total:	255

was grounded and all had been withdrawn by May 1965. Although it had been planned to develop a tanker version of the Victor bomber in 1966-67, its emergence as a tanker was hastened by the Valiant tanker's swift demise. Fortunately, the second prototype Victor had already been equipped with two Flight Refuelling Mk 20B hose-and-drogue pods, one under each wing, and a single Flight Refuelling Mk 17 hose drum unit (HDU) in the fuselage bomb-bay, as a trials installation.

At very short notice, Handley Page undertook a "crash" programme to convert six Victor B1As to two-point tanker configuration, with just the Mk 20B underwing pods and bomb-bay fuel tanks. If the latter were removed, these aircraft could still be used as bombers and, so, were designated B(K)1A. However, they were assigned exclusively to the tanker role, entering service with No 55 Squadron at Marham in May 1965.

Once these six aircraft had been delivered, Handley Page began work on the three-point tankers with both the Mk 20B wingpods and the fuselage-mounted Mk 17 HDU. They also featured increased fuel tankage, improved communications and navigation aids, and underwing floodlighting for night operations. The first conversion, from a Victor B1 surplus to bomber requirements following the introduction of

the B2 variant, flew from Radlett in November 1965.

A total of 10 B1s were converted as the Victor K1 and 14 B1As as the Victor K1A. The first three-point tankers entered RAF service with No 57 Squadron at Marham in January 1966, becoming operational in June that year; with No 214 Squadron receiving its first aircraft in October 1966 and becoming operational in March 1967. By that time, No 55 Squadron had relinquished its tanker-training role to a dedicated Tanker Training Flight and became fully operational in the AAR role on Victor K1As.

The Victor saw its origins immediately after the Second World War, when Sir Frederick Handley Page instructed his designers to look at a jet-powered bomber to replace the Lincoln. An initial Operational Requirement of 1946 (OR230) was revised in 1947 and specification B35/46 was issued to industry. Handley Page revised their HP80 design to meet this revised specification. A formal contract for two prototypes was signed in 1948 and, in June 1952, (before the aircraft – now named Victor – had even flown) an order for 25 aircraft. The maiden flight of the Victor prototype was made on 24 December 1952. The first production aircraft flew on 1 February 1956 and the first RAF unit to receive the Victor B1 was No 232 OCU at Gaydon in November 1957. Obviously, full details of

Below: Although designed as a bomber, the Handley Page Victor was pressed into service as a tanker, following the "metal fatigue" problems of the Valiant K1s. This photo shows a Victor K1 of No 55 Squadron, with a pair of Flight Refuelling Mk20 aerial refuelling pods under the wings. Note the underwing markings to assist pilots in lining-up for "the prod". (Author's Collection)

the Victor bomber are not relevant in a book on air defence.

Although the Victor K1/1As gave sterling service, they were somewhat weight-limited in high ambient temperatures or when operating from high-altitude airfields. In those cases, to meet some operational tasks, it required two partly-loaded Victor tankers to launch on a sortie, so that one could top-up its tanks from the other before setting off for the "towline" to receive its "customers". This first version of the Victor tanker was operational until January 1977, when No 214 Squadron disbanded, when the K2 became available in sufficient numbers.

(See "Snapshot" – 1978 for details of the Victor K2)

Data: Victor K1A

Powerplant	four Armstrong Siddeley Sapphire 202/207 turbo jets, each rated at 12,690lb st
Span	110ft 0in
Length	114ft 11in
Height	28ft 1.5in
Wing area	2,406sq ft
Empty weight	90,000lb
Loaded weight	180,000lb
Maximum speed	Mach 0.9 at 40,000ft
Service ceiling	55,000ft
Range	2,500 miles
Armament	nil

IMPRESSIONS OF THE LIGHTNING

The Lightning was *the* fighter of the RAF from the mid-1960s through to the late-1970s. For this reason, these impressions of the "Electric Fighter" are carried in this "Snapshot".

When the English Electric Lightning F1A entered service with No 111 Squadron RAF in 1960 it was the *crème de la crème*. By the 1980s, as one pilot told me, it was "outsmarted by software". Derived from a high-speed research aircraft – the English Electric P1 – the Lightning works its pilot hard to achieve the results which today's air warfare demands. It had a modest armament of two Red Top infrared (IR) homing missiles and two 30mm Aden cannon and its fire control radar, the Ferranti AI23 AIRPASS, was valve technology. It was, by the end of its service, becoming a engineering nightmare. There were no line-replaceable

unit (LRUs) on this aircraft, which taxed the ingenuity of the "maintainers". Yet it was loved by all who flew and maintained it – and many more besides.

I have had a love affair with the Lightning – the sexiest of fighter aircraft – for 23 years. When did I fall? In September 1970, watching the late Sqn Ldr (then a Flt Lt) Russ Pengelly of No 23 Squadron flying a solo aerobatic sequence at the Battle of Britain air display at RAF Leuchars. The afterburner climb with which he began his display and his subsequent skill in throwing the aircraft around the sky left a lasting impression. The reality has all but gone but the memory of it will never fade.

In its day it was the best but, by 1988, even the Lightning "jocks" I spoke with were open in their praise for the F-15, F-16 and F-18 as examples of state-of-the-art technology. In almost every aspect, the Lightning could be found wanting: weapons capacity, fire-control efficiency, fuel capacity and endurance, crew workload and fatigue. It was, in its latter days, prone to fuel system unserviceability. (It must, however, be pointed out that on the day of my flight, three two-seaters were prepared against this eventuality but, as the exception which perhaps proved the rule, the one aircraft remained serviceable for all three flights that day!)

In one area alone could the Lightning still claim equality or, might one suggest – without breaking the Official Secrets Act – supremacy: performance! It flew at over twice the speed of sound (Mach 2.3) and could climb above 70,000ft. Perhaps it was these qualities that kept the Lightning's reputation as the years took their toll of attrition and technology left it behind. Despite several planned upgrades, which were never effected due to its "imminent withdrawal from service", the Lightning was always a "hot ship".

The consummation of my "affair" with the Lightning was a moment I will never forget, although she was a grand old lady at the time. Arrayed in the paraphernalia of modern jet flying – thick socks, thermal undies, G-suit, coverall, immersion suit, life preserver (still known as the "Mae West"), boots and "bonedome" – I clambered aboard XV328 (coded BZ of No 11 Squadron) at RAF Binbrook on a bright but windy January morning in 1988. Strap by strap, I belted the penultimate Lighting T5 two-seat conversion trainer to be built (first flown in 1966) to my backside. My pilot was

Wg Cdr "Jake" Jarron, "Boss" of No 11 Squadron. "By gum", my Yorkshire brain thought, "but it's cramped and whoever designed the cockpit had never heard of ergonomics!"

Once we were both strapped-in and the safety pins of our Martin Baker Mk 4 ejection seats (another aspect of 1950s technology never updated) removed and secured in their stowage, we listened, checks complete, for the R/T command to "scramble". Five minutes later, in the best fighter traditions, the order was received.

My moment of glory had arrived. The cockpit layout demanded that the righthand occupant of the side-by-side cockpit (your humble scribe) start the two Rolls-Royce Avon 301 series turbojets.

"Start – isolate" commanded Jake. I complied by reaching down between my legs and flicking a switch.

"Fire one" he continued. I pressed the "tit", pause – two – three. The engine turned and fired.

"Fire two." Again the second button was hit; again the second Avon growled into life.

"Off isolate" came the final command. I responded. Beneath and behind me, two old-fashioned turbojet engines, together capable of generating 32,600lb of static thrust with afterburning, idled, awaiting only the gentle touch of loving experience on the throttles to bring them to life.

We taxied out to the runway, pausing at the threshold to complete the final cockpit checks. Jake moved the throttles to 92% power...another pause and a quick visual check. He released brakes and into full cold (unreheated) power. The engine rpm and jet pipe temperatures were scanned and the throttles pushed "through the gate" into full afterburning power. There was a discernible "kick in the pants" as the afterburners came in and we roared down the runway. Rotating at 165kts we immediately retracted the undecarriage. Once "cleaned-up" we accelerated further. At 250kts the afterburners were cut and we turned towards the East Yorkshire coast.

Jake Jarron was busy with R/T conversations, first with Approach at Binbrook, then with Midland ATC (to pass through the civil airway) and finally with Boulmer

Above: The ultimate two versions of the Lightning, seen here in 1988. An all-grey Lightning T5 trainer, farthest from the camera (with the author in the right-hand seat), and the F6 interceptor, both from No 11 Squadron, the last RAF unit to fly the type. (John Green, REP-S/Crown Copyright)

Sector Operations Centre (SOC) to glean information of Bravo Mike, a Lightning F6 of No 11 Squadron who was to (unwittingly) act as our target. His real purpose (and ours) was to present a formation of F6 and T5 for the camera of John Green (an MoD photographer) in a Hawk chase aircraft, who was recording this event for posterity.

While this was going on, I was invited to peer into the radar B-scope through a rubber viewing shield, known by the pilots as "the boot". When I did this, I began to see what my informant on the ground meant when he referred to the Lightning as being "outsmarted by software". To anyone familiar with the current generation of airborne interception radar displays, this was positively prehistoric. No rotating green disc with neatly marked target blips here: just a square orange cathode ray tube with almost meaningless bars and circles and several traces.

Jake guided my eye to the blip which was, apparently, our target. It was 40nm to the northeast, he said. We "armed" our Red Top IR-homing missile and using mental arithmetic – so familiar to Jake but wildly incomprehensible to a mere amateur like myself – calculated the readings and translated them into directions and speeds to fly in order to bring us into our target's six o'clock. Initially he was above and to our left but gradually we manoeuvred round to come up on his seven o'clock to "launch"

the missile at about three nautical miles distance. We could have launched earlier but decided to confirm the target with a "vizident" first! It was only later that I learned we had been pulling four-and-a-half Gs on our final turn.

Once in company with Bravo Mike we settled down in a pair for the benefit of the camera, flying at 22,000ft and some 400kts. After 20mins the Hawk and the F6 broke off to rendezvous with a VC10 tanker aircraft, again for the benefit of the camera. We declined the tanker RV as, not having any fuel available to transfer to us, we had only 25mins fuel remaining and I was determined we should go supersonic before landing.

Turning towards Binbrook, we again cleared our route with Boulmer SOC and I was allowed to bring Bravo Zulu up to 30,000ft in order to begin our supersonic dash home. At the agreed height, we were flying at 95% power and then Jake cut in the 'burner again. For the second time, I experienced the feel of a "kick in the pants" as we accelerated through the sound barrier to Mach 1.3 and beyond. For a brief moment, the Mach meter read twice the speed of sound and then dropped back again.

All this time, control had remained with me, although Jake managed the throttles. I was getting the feel of the Old Lady and beginning to understand why the squadron pilots loved their "cabs". The Lightning is a responsive aircraft but (in what was virtually straight and level flight) I did not have to

---

Order of Battle – May 1968
(after merger of Bomber and Fighter Commands)

Strike Command – HQ: High Wycombe, Bucks (air defence assets only)

No 1 (Bomber) Group – HQ: Bawtry, Yorks

Sqn	Aircraft	Base
55	Handley Page Victor K1A	Marham, Norfolk
57	Handley Page Victor K1A	Marham, Norfolk
214	Handley Page Victor K1A	Marham, Norfolk

No 11 (Fighter) Group – HQ: Bentley Priory, Stanmore, Middx

Sqn	Aircraft	Base
5	BAC Lightning F6	Binbrook, Lincs
11	BAC Lightning F6	Leuchars, Fife
29	BAC Lightning F3	Wattisham, Suffolk
111	BAC Lightning F3	Wattisham, Suffolk
226 OCU	BAC Lightning F3	Coltishall, Norfolk
(65 & 145 Sqns)	& Lightning T4/5	
25	Bloodhound Mk 2 SAM	North Coates, Lincs
41	Bloodhound Mk 2 SAM	West Raynham, Norfolk

make many demands of her. After a two-minute supersonic dash, I began an economical descent towards Binbrook under Jake's guidance. Again, he cleared the transit of the airway and after this, Jake switched the radar to ground-mapping mode and the coast of South Humberside became recognisable.

Regrettably our fuel state did not allow any passes and breaks over the airfield and it was a sedate landing at 170kts, "popping" the brake parachute on contact with the ground. Rapidly decelerating along Binbrook's 7,500ft runway, Jake released the parachute and we taxied back to the apron. In making our post-flight checks, the anticlimax was an oxygen cock that did not want to be turned off. A friendly fitter reached in and, with an ease born of experience, flicked the switch.

My 36mins of sheer ecstasy had come to an end and I wrote myself into the history book as the antepenultimate journalist to fly Great Britain's only Mach 2 fighter. For me it was the end of an era. Only the memory remained...but what a memory!

RESPONSE: AAA & SAMs

By the 1960s, the Bofors 40mm L/70 was the only AA gun remaining in British service, specifically for low-level point air defence. The Bloodhound missile had taken over the medium-to-high level role and the Tigercat SHORAD missile was preparing to enter service.

BAC Bloodhound Mk 2

The rise and demise of the Bloodhound Mk 1 took place between 1959 and 1964, being deployed in defence of the RAF strategic nuclear deterrent V-Force bases. Eleven RAF squadrons (see previous "Snapshot" for details) were equipped with the Bloodhound Mk 1. Although, the Royal Navy's Polaris-equipped submarines did not take over the UK deterrent role until June 1969, withdrawal and disbandment of the squadrons took place between 1962-64, with Nos 62 and 242 Squadrons being the last Bloodhound Mk 1 squadrons to go in September 1964.

Development of the Bloodhound Mk 2 began in 1958, concentrating on better missile performance and lethality against lower-flying targets. The electronic counter-counter measures (ECCM) capability of the system was improved and continuous wave

(CW) radar replaced the older pulse Doppler system. The Mk 2 missile was now fully air-transportable as well as being used in fixed site installations.

The Bloodhound Mk 2 entered RAF service with No 33 Squadron at Butterworth, Malaysia in March 1963 and with No 65 Squadron at Seletar, Singapore in 1964, going on to equip Nos 25, 41 and 112 Squadrons in the UK in 1963, 1965 and 1964 respectively. The Mk 2 missile was exported to Sweden and Switzerland.

Shorts Tigercat

The Tigercat has the distinction of being the first mobile SHORAD system employed by the RAF. It is, essentially, a land-based version of the successful naval Seacat system, which began life in the late-1950s and

Below: The first of the low-level air defence (LLAD) missile systems to see RAF Regiment service was the Short Brothers Tigercat. Derived from the naval Seacat system, the missile was identical. (Short Brothers)

entered service on board HMS *Devonshire* in 1962. The missile is common to both systems. For the RAF, it represented an interim mobile system until Rapier was available.

Preparations to receive Tigercat began in February 1967 and the Tigercat Flight of No 48 Squadron RAF Regiment, based at Catterick, took part in live firing trials at Aberporth range in October-November 1967. The system was not, however, officially declared operational until September 1970 and still only comprised one flight of the four-flight squadron.

Tigercat was a simple system, capable of instant readiness. Once the target had been acquired visually, the missile is launched into the operator's field of view. Visual detection of the missile is assisted by the use of flares at its rear. He then directed the missile onto its target by line-of-sight by use of a thumb-controlled "joystick" which send radio commands to the missile to move its control surfaces as directed. The Tigercat system can be linked into either a TV or a radar guidance system. Marconi Radar supplied the ST850 radar which is employed in the enhanced version of Tigercat.

A Tigercat unit consists of the launcher trailer, the director trailer and two towing vehicles, usually Land Rovers. The detachment consisted of an NCO and four airmen. The system was, however, exported and remains in service with Argentina, India, Iran, Qatar and South Africa.

Data

Missiles/launcher	3
Type of mounting	two-wheeled platform with outriggers
Span	2ft 1.5in
Length	4ft 10in
Effective ceiling	9,000ft
Range	3.2nm
Weight of missile	206lb
Weight of warhead	37.5lb
Type of warhead	HE blast

CRITIQUE

It must be borne in mind that, by 1968, the UK air defence force was at its lowest ebb following the assimilation of Fighter Command into the new Strike Command. Yet even then, plans for future expansion and re-equipment were laid, based on the NATO strategy "14/3", promulgated in early 1967. If specific criticism is to be made of this decade it must, therefore, revolve around the way in which the Lightning fighter was procured and developed.

The fault lies not in the hands of the manufacturers but in the British Government (of both persuasions). The Tories chose to consider the Lightning not worth development, while Labour opted to procure the American F-4 Phantom II. Even then, they "muddied the water" by insisting on a 50% UK content (see next "Snapshot"). This led to a redesign to incorporate Rolls-Royce Spey engines and repackaged avionics from the cancelled TSR2 project. The chickens of this particular hen came home to roost in 1984 when, following the Falklands war, the RAF was forced to order 15 ex-US Navy F-4J Phantoms (assigned to the reformed No 74 Squadron) and create a new logistics chain to support these aircraft.

The Lightning was operationally successful but, politically, always about to be cancelled or withdrawn from service. By the time politicians and the RAF could see the way ahead, the die was cast. Potential export orders were given away to the the American Lockheed F-104G Super Starfighter and Monsieur Dassault's Mirage III. In the end, only 49 aircraft were sold abroad (35 to Saudi Arabia and 14 to Kuwait) out of a total of 312 built (not counting the 27 P1, P1A/B and P2 prototype and development aircraft and eight static test airframes).

Such development as was accomplished was only a direct result of RAF short-term requirements to solve particular problems at any given time in its history. By the time BAC (as English Electric had become) was allowed to get its act together and produced the multi-role Lightning, with increased range and provision for air-to-air refuelling, the market was all but gone and the two Middle Eastern customers (Saudi Arabia and Kuwait) were all that could be found. Even as late as 1985, it was hoped to sell refurbished Saudi aircraft to Austria but, alas, Sweden persuaded Austria that the J35 Draken was a better bet.

So much for the problems of Lightning development (or lack of it). On the wider front, NATO forces were beginning to promulgate the policy of Detente, Deterrence and Defence as outlined in the introduction to the next "Snapshot".

1978

The decade of the 1970s saw a subtle change in NATO thinking. This was a change in emphasis of the use of fighter aircraft, from interception and air defence to an air superiority and air defence role. This reflected a change in "nuclear thinking" from the tripwire response to one of flexible response. Undoubtedly this was evidence of a certain relaxation in international tension and a recognition of some small changes in what had previously been inflexible Soviet attitudes.

The year of the RAF's Diamond Jubilee saw improvements to the UK's air defence resources on the up-beat. The rapidly-obsolescing nature of the UK fighter force and early warning radar aircraft, combined with emerging new Soviet bomber designs (*see below*) had prompted a rethink of air defence plans in the mid-1970s.

The arrival of one squadron of Phantom FG1s in RAF service in 1969 showed the way ahead. Initially, RAF Phantom FGR2s were tasked with air-to-ground roles (as a "partial" Hunter replacement) but between 1974 and 1976 five more Lightning squadrons re-equipped with the Phantom FGR2s made available with the introduction of the Jaguar.

Also, the decade saw the arrival of the RAF's first airborne early warning (AEW) aircraft in the shape of the Shackleton AEW2. This role was taken over from the Royal Navy's Gannet AEW3s but, in addition to providing AEW over units of the fleet, it was also useful in improving the low-level radar coverage around the UK's Air Defence Interception Zone (ADIZ).

During this decade, the future air defence requirements of the UK were not ignored. Full scale development of the Air Defence Variant of the Tornado (formerly known as MRCA – Multi-Role Combat Aircraft) had been authorised in 1976, while the Nimrod AEW3 airborne early warning aircraft (to replace the interim Shackleton AEW2) had been ordered in 1977. An improved UK Air Defence Ground Environment (UKADGE) was also initiated during the mid-1970s. So, as it appeared on the surface, much-needed improvements were being initiated.

Yet, as the subsequent "Snapshot" will show, these improvements were not to be without their problems – in some cases, major problems.

THE THREAT

The Soviet Union and its Warsaw Pact allies remained the primary threat to the UK, through which some 40% of NATO reinforcements would be channelled in the event of a war on the Central Front in Europe.

By 1978, the DA was mainly equipped with an ageing and rapidly obsolescing force of bombers. Contemporary estimates put the

Below: A contemporary view of the Sukhoi Su-24 "Fencer-B" at a time when its designation was thought to be Su-19. Equivalent to the American F-111, it was designed to attack targets in Central Europe from bases in the western Soviet Union. (US DoD)

strength of DA at that time as some 250 Tu-16 "Badger" and 150 Tu-22 "Blinder" medium bombers; some 150 M-4 "Bisons" and Tu-95/142 "Bears", together configured for strategic bombing or missile launch; plus 120 of the latter two types reconfigured for aerial refuelling, ELINT or other ancillary roles. There were, however, two regiments equipped with some 70 Tupolev Tu-26 (Tu-22M) "Backfire" supersonic bombers.

Also in evidence was a new Frontal Aviation fighter-bomber, equivalent to the USAF's F-111, known as "Fencer". From the Sukhoi stable, it was originally thought to have been designated Su-19 but, subsequently, we know it as the Su-24. At this time, detailed information was scarce but it was considered that "Fencers" could just about target the UK from Warsaw Pact airfields in Central Europe and they were, therefore, considered a new threat to the UK defences.

As in previous "Snapshots", below are details of the new types in service and, in the case of the longer-serving aircraft, the improved versions which have appeared since 1968, with the exception of the "Bison" and "Blinder", which were covered in their entirety in earlier "Snapshots". As yet, no fighters (except "Fencer", which was really an interdictor) were then in service which could be used as bomber escorts against the UK.

Sukhoi Su-19/24 "Fencer"

Originally designated Su-19, the US Department of Defence began using the designation Su-24 from 1980. The application of an "F for Fighter" NATO codename – "Fencer" – is somewhat of a misnomer, as the aircraft does not carry any air-to-air weapons systems. It is, in fact, the equivalent to the US F-111 tactical interdictor, designed specifically for air-to-ground operations.

Design is understood to have begun in 1964, being first observed in 1971-72, with the first operational version, the "Fencer-B" entering service in 1976. The Su-19/24 was developed to give Soviet Frontal Aviation the ability to hit NATO targets in Central Europe from bases in the Western USSR, rather than operating from the crowded skies of its Eastern European Warsaw Pact allies, although from Eastern Europe it can reach the eastern parts of the UK.

The need to operate at night and in adverse weather dictated a more sophisticated avionics suite than that of the MiG-27

"Flogger-D" series. A terrain-avoidance radar, and a two-man crew were features of the new "Fencer". The benefits of variable geometry were now realised by the Sukhoi design bureau (with their "Fitter" experience, together with that of MiG's "Flogger"series).

The "Fencer-B" featured a deeply-dished lower skin to the rear fuselage box between the engine exhausts, plus a large brake-parachute housing. It was seen as an asset to Frontal Aviation resources and a potential threat against the UK.

Data: Sukhoi Su-19/24 "Fencer-B"
(as estimated in 1978)

Powerplant	two Lyulka AL-21F turbo jets, each rated at 17,200lb st dry and 25,000lb st with reheat
Span	56ft 3in spread 31ft 3in swept
Length	69ft 10in
Max T/O weight	68,000lb
Maximum speed	Mach 2+ at height
Range (combat)	200 miles (lo-lo-lo)
Armament	one 23mm six-barreled

GSh-23, plus nine stores pylons capable of carrying nuclear weapons, missiles of the AS-7 "Kerry", AS-10 "Karen", AS-11 "Kilter" and AS-12 "Kegler" type, plus bombs and rockets

Tupolev Tu-16 "Badger-D/E/F/G"

The Tupolev Tu-16 "Badger" series spawned a variety of versions, some of which were not bombers. These include the Tu-16R "Badger-R" for maritime/electronic reconnaissance, similar to the "Badger-C" but with a larger undernose radome and three ELINT radomes under the weapons bay, plus several camera positions.

The "Badger-E" is a photographic/electronic reconnaissance version, based on the "Badger-A". It houses a suite of cameras in the weapons bay plus two extra radomes under the fuselage. The Tu-16R "Badger-F" is similar to the E-model but with an ELINT pod under each wing. Later versions have several small radomes under the centre-fuselage.

The "Badger-G" is converted from the Tu-16KS "Badger-B" to carry two AS-5 "Kelt" missiles or (on the Tu-16K "Badger-G Mod") the AS-6 "Kingfisher" missile, while retaining the free-fall bombing capability. Fitted with improved avionics, including the "Short Horn" navigation/bombing radar. Both versions were delivered to the AV-MF (Naval Air Force).

Data: Tu-16 "Badger-G"

Powerplant	Two Mikulin RD-3M-500 (AM-3M) turbojets, each rated at 20,920lb st
Span	108ft 3in
Length	114ft 2in
Height	34ft
Wing area	1,772.3sq ft
Empty weight	82,000lb
Loaded weight	165,350lb
Maximum speed	652mph at 19,700ft
Service ceiling	49,200 ft
Range (combat)	3,885nm with a 6,600lb bomb load
Armament	Six 23mm AM-23 cannon

in forward dorsal, rear ventral and tail twin positions, plus a seventh, fixed, gun on the starboard nose. Up to 19,800lb of bombs, or (naval versions) stand-off air-to-ground missiles

Tupolev Tu-26 (Tu-22M) "Backfire"

American sources first acknowledged that the Soviet Union was developing a variable-geometry medium bomber in 1969, when it was assigned the NATO codename "Backfire". During the late 1970s and early 1980s it was surrounded in controversy which, even today (early 1993), has not been completely resolved.

The first controversy concerns the designation, which US sources have said is Tu-26. All Soviet references to the aircraft (including those at the SALT 2 talks) have called it the Tu-22M. Yet the aircraft is a new design and not a derivative of the Tu-22 "Blinder". According to Bill Gunston in *Aircraft of the Soviet Union* (Osprey, London 1983), his belief "is that Tu-22M was [the] swing-wing Tu-22 seen in 1969 and subsequently built in modest numbers". He also states that the original aircraft, "Backfire-A", was "believed to have [the] OKB designation Tu-136".

The logic of the Soviet reference to the Tu-22M designation leads on to the second controversy – that of the aircraft's intended role. The Soviet Union has always insisted the "Backfire" is intended for maritime and European strike missions, rather than for long-range strike against the continental United States. US sources have consistently maintained that the aircraft has strategic range, and this has led to reports that US estimates of "Backfire's" performance have been deliberately altered to suit the political line.

It is difficult to evaluate the pros and cons of this particular argument without hard data. However, the former Editor of *Jane's All The World's Aircraft* (JAWA), John W. R. Taylor, now Editor Emeritus and still responsible for the Soviet section of the book, has always maintained that the Soviet Union has always responded to his questionnaires for entries honestly. Thus, the JAWA 1991-92 listing of an "unrefuelled combat radius of 2,160nm" was taken as closest to the truth as was possible at the time. However, when the Tu-22M3 appeared at Farnborough in September 1992, it had a data board by the aircraft stating the combat

Above: A further conversion of the Tupolev Tu-16KS "Badger-B", the "Badger-G" version was given improved avionics and provision for two AS-5 "Kelt" missiles. The Tu-16K "Badger-G" Mod illustrated retained a free-fall bombing capability in addition to provision for the AS-6 "Kingfisher". (Flygvapnet)

Above: The advent of the Tupolev Tu-22M-2 "Backfire-B" gave the Soviet Union the capability to interdict the UK via the "back door" approach from the northwest. Free-fall bombs could be carried on external ejection racks under the engine intake ducts. (Flygvapnet)

radius of the aircraft to be 2,200km (or 1,188nm).

Both ranges certainly puts the UK within reach of "Backfire". As the late Air Chief Marshal Sir Andrew Humphrey, Chief of the Air Staff, said in December 1975, "Russian fast, wide-ranging and high performance aircraft like 'Backfire', armed with stand-off missiles, may soon become an even greater danger to allied shipping than the relatively slow-moving Russian submarines". As far as the UK air defence forces were concerned, "Backfire" was a threat capable of using the North Cape route to the North Atlantic shipping lanes or as a "back-door" through the UK air defences.

The main drawback to the Tu-22 "Blinder" was its poor cruise efficiency and long field length (for take-off), both of which are due to its wing being tailored to supersonic flight. The solution was, of course, variable-geometry wings, and so the advent of "Backfire" was no surprise. Believed to have flown in 1971, the first production model was the Tu-22M-1 "Backfire-A" and, as noted above, was only delivered in low numbers, sufficient to equip one squadron.

The first series production model, "Backfire-B", (Tu-22M-2 according to JAWA 1991-92) featured an increased wingspan over the A-model and with wing trailing-edge pods reduced to shallow underwing fairings. An optional nose-mounted flight refuelling probe is fitted, but usually the aircraft is seen without it. Initial production

aircraft were equipped for only one AS-4 "Kitchen" missile, semi-recessed under the fuselage, but later production aircraft had a pylon under each wing centre-section panel allowing a pair of "Kitchens" to be carried. Additionally, external stores pylons are frequently seen under the engine intake trunks of the aircraft. Like most Soviet bombers, a tail turret housing a twin 23mm cannon installation and fire control radar is carried.

The later "Backfire-C" will be discussed in the next "Snapshot".

Data: Tu-22M/Tu-26 "Backfire-B"

Powerplant	two unidentified turbofans (thought to be derived from the NK-144) each rated at about 45,000lb st
Span	112ft 6.5in spread 76ft 9.25in swept
Length	129ft 11in
Height	35ft 5.25in
Wing area	1.830sq ft
Empty weight	119,000lb (approx)
Loaded weight	286,600lb
Maximum speed	1,322mph (Mach 2+) at high altitude
Service ceiling	36,000ft+
Range (combat)	2,160nm (unrefuelled)
Armament	One or two AS-4 "Kitchen"

missiles and/or several AS-16 "Kickback" short-range attack missiles. Multiple racks for 12-18 x 1,102lb bombs. Plus two GSh-23 23mm cannon in a tail turret

Tupolev Tu-95/142 "Bear-F/G"

Extensively redesigned for the AV-MF as an anti-submarine warfare (ASW) aircraft, the "Bear-F" carries the bureau designation Tu-142 and has been in service since 1970. Although not a bomber-threat to the UK, these aircraft have been intercepted within the UK Air Defence Zone and, as such, are included here.

The Tu-142 features highly-cambered wings, double-slotted flaps, a 5ft 10in fuselage extension forward of the wings, an increased-size pressure cabin, an increased chord rudder and an increased size tail to the inboard engine nacelles to house a 12-wheel, main landing gear bogie. A navigation radar is housed in an undernose radome, while further aft but ahead of the forward weapons bay, is a large J-band over water search/surveillance radar. There is also a long fairing at the fin base, believed to house a magnetic anomaly detector (MAD).

There have been four further versions on the "Bear-F" theme, each being designated as Mod (Modification) 1 through 4. Mod 1 has the undernose radome deleted and, on some, the inner nacelles reverted to the earlier Tu-95 size. These were first identified in 1974. The Mod 2 (also known as the Tu-142M) is characterised by an exceptionally clean fuselage and a new, deeper (by 14in) cockpit, plus a drooped flight refuelling probe and a satellite communications antenna on the forward upper fuselage. The crew accommodation has been further improved, and is said by one source to be "palatial".

The Mod 3 version has the streamline pods on the tailplane tips removed and an prominent MAD fairing placed on the fin top, which is slightly higher. The aft weapons bay has been lengthened and has been modified to accept sonobuoys. In service since 1982-83, its is believed that earlier "Bear-Fs" have been bought up to this standard.

The Mod 4 variant is a Mod 3 with further improvements. On the nose is a thimble radome, presumed to carry either ECM or a terrain-following radar of some sort, plus a faired box under the nose housing a multi-sensor suite, including a FLIR and radar altimeter). On the forward port fuselage is an unidentified duct believed to carry cabling or an antenna of some description. To the rear, the tail observation blisters have been deleted and defensive ECM antenna attached. The "Bear-F" Mod 4 was first identified in 1986 and is believed to have entered service a year earlier.

The Tu-95 "Bear-G" is a bomber and ELINT conversion of the earlier "Bear-B/C" models, first identified in 1983. Retaining the original fuselage, it features the "duck-bill" "Down Beat" navigation and bombing radar on the nose for use with the AS-4 "Kitchen" missile, plus the thimble radome from the "Bear-F". There are large pylons on the inner underwing for the AS-4 "Kitchen" missile, plus an outerwing pylon which is

Above: As the Tupolev Tu-95 was developed, the Tu-142 variant came along for use as a maritime reconnaissance and strike aircraft. The "Bear-G", seen here, is converted from the "Bear-B/C" and is configured to launch AS-4 "Kitchen" missiles. (US DoD)

believed to carry chaff/flare dispensers. ELINT antennae have sprouted on the rear fuselage, while the ventral twin 23mm turret is retained. The tail gunner's position, however, has been deleted in favour of a VLF communications tailcone.

Data: Tu-142 (Tu-20/95) "Bear-F"

Powerplant	four 14,795hp Kuznetsov NK-12MV turboprop engines
Span	167ft 7.75in
Length	162ft 4.75in
Height	39ft 9in
Wing area	3,342sq ft
Empty weight	191,800lb ("Bear-F" Mod 3)
Loaded weight	407,850lb ("Bear-F" Mod 3)
Maximum speed	575mph at 25,000ft
Service ceiling	41,000ft
Combat radius	5,150 miles (on internal fuel)
Armament	two 23mm NR-23 cannon

(in tail turret), plus up to 22,000lb of ASW weapons in two (one reworked) internal weapons bay

DETECTION & IDENTIFICATION

Over the previous decade, electronic technology had continued to advance at a rapid pace, with Electronic Warfare (EW) benefiting from the lessons of the Vietnam War.

The UK's air defence still depended upon much the same philosophy that had always predominated, with detection, identification and location being the basis of tactics. It could also be said that EW was another aspect of this defence posture, with its ability to detect various sensors and to make use of the information to more effectively defeat enemy attempts at degrading the command and control structure. The RAF had been active in this type of electronic surveillance since the 1940s but most of the operations were, and still are, subject to a very high level of classification.

The Russians had wisely disregarded the trend towards "unmanned bombers" and by the early 1970s had long-range aircraft carrying stand-off weapons fitted with both conventional and nuclear warheads. In-flight refuelling gave an almost unlimited range and the UK became vulnerable to attack from aircraft from any quarter, rather than being preoccupied with threats from the Eastern Approaches.

This threat of massive, simultaneous attack from different directions, backed up by intense EW activity allied to electronic advances, led to the development of radar that combined the previously-separated functions of range, bearing and height into a single three-dimensional (3-D) radar.

A typical product of this period is the Plessey AR-3D. It generates very accurate height information and can discriminate between jamming and quiet aircraft at the same position, but at different heights. Precise target location is further enhanced by the use of pulse compression techniques. The increasing adoption of digital techniques also enhanced performance and reliability.

The escalating demands of air defence had led to the comprehensive UK Air Defence Ground Environment (UKADGE) system and, in the mid-1970s, NATO placed an order for new radar equipment at Saxa Vord, the RAF-manned early warning station in the Shetlands. The contract was open to international competition and was won by Marconi and Plessey. Significantly this order was placed with Marconi, for S649 search radar for azimuth and range location, with Plessey HF200s providing height finding. In view of the advent of 3-D systems this seemed to be something of a retrograde step, as a dual radar system can only concentrate on one target per height-finding element. In contrast, a 3-D radar can process multiple targets simultaneously. No official explanation was offered and, perhaps, it could be suggested that a multiple antenna site offers greater advantages of redundancy, during attack, than a single antenna site.

The decade also saw the entry of Marconi into the 3-D market with the introduction of Martello, which has a distinctively shaped antenna said to be more resistant to electronic countermeasures (ECM) than any previous design. This is largely due to the very low side lobes associated with the antenna, which are a susceptible area for interference by hostile measures.

Despite these innovations in ground-based radar, which provided good medium and high level coverage, it was obvious that low flying aircraft posed a considerable threat in terms of early warning. To overcome this problem a squadron of Airborne Early Warning (AEW) Shackleton aircraft was formed at RAF Kinloss. It is significant that a great deal of research work had been carried out in the UK on AEW techniques over the previous decade or so to fulfil a naval requirement. However, in 1965 the Royal Navy's aircraft carrier fleet was apparently axed and the need had evaporated.

As the American Boeing E-3A Sentry Airborne Warning and Control System (AWACS) emerged, consideration was given to a Franco/Anglo AEW land-based aircraft and when this foundered the possibility of using a Comet airframe with a suitable radar was mooted. Unfortunately, funding for the Comet conversion was frozen in 1971 and the experimental airframe reverted to normal use. Meanwhile, 12 Shackleton MR2s were fitted with a US General Electric AN/APS-20 radar which had been upgraded by the addition of a digital Airborne Moving Target Indicator (AMTI), of indigenous design and manufacture between 1972 and 1973. It should be noted that although this radar featured a shorter wavelength, hence less range, than the APS-120 then being fitted in the US Navy's Hawkeye, it did have the advantage of bringing the UK relatively up to date in AEW operations.

By 1975, the UK was once again looking ahead to the next generation of AEW and work was being carried out that would eventually evolve into the Nimrod AEW programme. This seemed to suggest a fairly early phase-out for the Shackleton AEW2, but history was to prove such an assumption wrong.

In some respects the answers to operational problems were still as indeterminate as they had been in the 1940s and this was particularly true of the Identification, Friend or Foe (IFF). Much of the equipment in use by NATO was now dated and even unreliable. For instance the Mk 10 had been in service for a number of years and its successor was still based on relatively old technology. When the interrogator received a reply it was still with a certain ambiguity. Was the reply genuine or was it simply an EW ploy, by an enemy that had gained access to the codes? Even in the event of no reply it still raised questions – is it hostile or has a friendly aircraft been jammed; is it using the wrong code or has it failed?. It is even possible that the system has been switched off to enable the aircraft to remain passive. Even when all of that is resolved, there still remained the question of NATO standardisation.

Much of the overall dilemma was due to funding and not a little to national interests, in which the operational solution was necessarily coloured by indigenous interests

and the sustenance of individual industry. Meanwhile, the comprehensive, all-round, UKADGE system was evolving with new technology in concert with other NATO systems and the French STRIDA air defence network. By this time the BMEWS system at Fylingdales was also superimposed upon the UKADGE, for despite its primary purpose of providing early warning of ballistic missile attack on the continental United States, it could also offer some measure of warning of similar attack on the UK.

Radar cover now extended over the whole of the UK up to some 40,000ft, using land-based radars. Additional coverage is provided by radars based in Iceland and Norway. Once the UKADGE detects an approaching target, the ability to rapidly determine its identity is vital. This is best done by a fighter aircraft which can make an initial engagement while still far out to sea. It was and is an awesome responsibility, for the system must be able to provide the earliest possible warning, rapidly distinguish friend from foe and then prioritise the reaction.

As the decade progressed, the ever-evolving electronic revolution created new systems of greater capability and, as the decade came to a close, plans were being drawn up for yet another updating programme for the UK's air defences.

RESPONSE: AIRCRAFT & ARMAMENT

Avro (later HSA) Shackleton AEW2
The Shackleton entered the air defence arena somewhat late in life. The first Shackleton GR1 flew in March 1949 (at which time the designator letters stood for General Reconnaissance, rather than the Ground-attack and Reconnaissance they stand for today). A lineal descendent of the Lancaster bomber, its role was maritime reconnaissance (MR) and this was clarified with the improved Shackleton MR2 version, which first flew in June 1952.

The life and time of the Shackleton in its maritime role and subsequent developments do not fit into this story beyond the very fact of its longevity. With the run-down of the UK aircraft carrier fleet initiated by the Labour Government (1964-70), the Royal Navy became concerned over the lack of airborne early warning (AEW) for the fleet. At that time (and until the withdrawal of the last conventional aircraft carrier,

HMS *Ark Royal*, in 1978), the RN's AEW force comprised the Fairey Gannet AEW3, fitted with the APS-20 radar developed by General Electric and Hazeltine. It was originally proposed to undertake licence production of the radar in the UK by Elliot Brothers (now GEC-Marconi Avionics). A subsequent cutback in the Gannet programme caused this proposal to be aborted, instead Elliot assumed responsibility for the UK support contract. Expertise gained in this role was fundamental to the later upgrading of the radar for the Shackleton AEW project.

To replace the capability, it was decided to refit 12 old Shackleton MR2C airframes with the APS-20 radar. In addition to providing AEW support to the RN, the aircraft were to be used to enhance the low-level radar coverage within the UK Air Defence Identification Zone (ADIZ).

Hawker Siddeley Aviation (into which Avro had been subsumed) undertook the conversion work, with the first Shackleton AEW2 (as the type was re-designated) flying on 30 September 1971. The modifications involved removal of the retractable "dustbin"-type search radar aft of the weapons bay, revision of the weapons bay (to carry search and rescue (SAR) stores, as the aircraft would be spending much of its time over water) and the installation of the APS-20 radar system, which includes a radome just forward of the weapons bay.

Included in the radar system was a UK-developed airborne moving-target indicator (AMTI) system and IFF system. With a shorter-wavelength antenna than the version of the radar then in production in the United States, the Shackleton AEW2 had a range of up to 100nm (for large targets). The three operator positions (radar operator, AEW operator and tactical co-ordinator – TACO) were situated just forward of the main wing spar (as it passed through the fuselage), and just aft of the navigator's position.

The RAF's Shackleton AEW2 equipped one unit, No 8 Squadron, and formed at Kinloss on 1 January 1972, moving to Lossiemouth later that year from where they flew for the rest of their RAF career. Typical sortie lengths were of 10hrs duration, although the Shackleton was capable of flying far longer.

Data: Shackleton AEW2

Powerplant	four 2,450shp Rolls-Royce Griffon 57A piston engines, each driving two, three-bladed, contra-rotating propellers
Span	120ft 0in
Length	87ft 3in
Height	16ft 9in
Wing area	1,421sq ft
Loaded weight	95,000lb (max T/O)
Maximum speed	300mph at 18,300ft
Service ceiling	25,700ft
Range	3,800 miles (at 200mph)
Armament	Nil, although SAR survival packs were carried

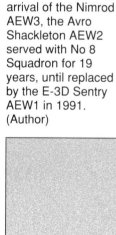

Below: Designed as an interim modification until the arrival of the Nimrod AEW3, the Avro Shackleton AEW2 served with No 8 Squadron for 19 years, until replaced by the E-3D Sentry AEW1 in 1991. (Author)

Left: Using APS-120 radars taken from the Fleet Air Arm's Gannet AEW3 aircraft, the displays on the Shackleton were far from "state-of-the-art" technology but, even so, in the hands of a skilled operator, could still be effective. (Tony Bobin/Crown Copyright)

BAC Lightning

The previous "Snapshot" has described the development and all versions of the Lightning fighters for the RAF. In 1978, only two Lightning units remained in RAF service – Nos 5 and 11 Squadrons – based at Binbrook. Despite their ageing weapons system (radar and missiles) and lack of range, they were still valued for their speed of reaction. Although the Lightning F6 was the prime version in service, many F3 versions also remained operational, together with the T5 for operational conversion of pilots.

Data: see 1968 "Snapshot"

Handley Page (HSA) Victor K2

The original plans for Victor bombers foresaw the use of surplus B2 airframes as aerial tankers. The Victor B2 was a more powerful aircraft, having Rolls-Royce Conway engines in place of the Sapphires and a greater wingspan of 120ft, allowing "hot and high" operations. A damaged Victor B2 was earmarked for conversion to K2 standard and plans were made for Handley Page to convert 21 B2/2Rs to K2 configuration in 1969-70 and eight SR2s in 1973.

However, in August 1969, Handley Page Aircraft went into voluntary liquidation (primarily as a result of rising costs of the

HP137 Jetstream programme) and although a rescue attempt was made, this, too, collapsed in February 1970. In the run-up to the demise of Handley Page, the MoD had made arrangements with Hawker Siddeley Aviation (HSA) to take over the product support of all Handley Page aircraft in RAF service and, by June 1970, all necessary jigs, tools and drawings, plus a number of senior staff, had transferred to HSA Woodford in Manchester.

At this time the 21 B2Rs earmarked for K2 conversions were stored in the open at Handley Page's Radlett facility in north London. A HSA field unit restored these aircraft to a condition to safely transfer them, plus a single B1 trials aircraft, to Woodford and all 22 aircraft were safely delivered by August 1970.

Meanwhile a revised design study for the K2 was undertaken by HSA and the Handley Page plan to incorporate wingtip tanks was dropped. The extended wingtip of the B2 was reduced by 1ft 6in in order to obtain bending relief on the wing, thus extending fatigue life. The location of the underwing pods was moved 2ft outboard in order to maintain the position of the pod, relative to the wingtip, the same as on the K1/1As. Finally, the ailerons were rigged at +2° from the neutral position, causing the aircraft to fly at a greater angle of incidence with only a slight increase in drag. Internally, many of the avionics systems were removed or changed as the Mk 1 aircraft had DC electrics and the Mk 2 an AC supply.

The fuel transfer equipment and tankage remained substantially the same as on the K1/1As. The Victor K2 has a seven-tank group in the fuselage, with a capacity of 4,500gals of kerosene; 10 wing tanks with a capacity of 4,000gals; plus two additional tanks in the bomb-bay, each with a capacity of 2,000gals.

The first Victor K2 conversion flew from Woodford on 1 March 1972 but, due to the many changes needed to individual aircraft to bring them to a common standard, the first K2 did not enter RAF service (with No 232 OCU at Marham) until May 1974. Five conversions were axed from the programme by the defence cuts announced in April 1975 and the only 24 Victor K2 conversions was delivered to the RAF. Of the three tanker squadrons in the RAF, only two converted to the K2: No 55 Squadron took their aircraft in July 1975, followed by No 57 Squadron, both based at Marham. The third unit, No 214 Squadron, disbanded with K1/1As in January 1977 as the last K2s were delivered.

Below: Powered by Rolls-Royce Conways, the Handley Page Victor K2 was a planned conversion from the B2/SR2 version, with the work being carried out by Hawker Siddeley Aviation. The fixed fairings over the upper wing trailing edge (used as fuel tanks) was the initial visual difference from the K1 version. This photograph shows a Victor K2 streaming all three drogues. (BAe)

(Details of Victor K2s from 1979 to 1993 can be found in the 1988 and 1993 "Snapshots")

Data: Victor K2

Powerplant	four Rolls-Royce Conway RCo 17 Mk 201 turbofans, each rated at 20,600lb st
Span	117ft 0in
Length	114ft 11in
Height	28ft 1.5in
Wing area	2,200sq ft
Empty weight	115,000lb
Loaded weight	223,000lb (max T/O) but could be up to 238,000lb after being "topped-up" with fuel once airborne
Maximum speed	640mph (Mach 0.92) at 40,000ft
Service ceiling	50,000+ft
Range	4,600 miles
Armament	nil

McDonnell Douglas F-4K/M Phantom FG1/FGR2

The F-4 Phantom II was the product of the McDonnell Aircraft Company (MACAIR – now part of the McDonnell Douglas Corporation) and was designed to meet a US Navy requirement. The maiden flight of the F4H-1 (as the Phantom II was originally designated) was on 27 May 1958. British involvement in the aircraft began in 1960, when the Royal Navy showed interest in the Phantom II as an alternative to the P1154, then being planned as the replacement for the Sea Vixen, as well as a Hunter replacement for the RAF.

With the cancellation of the Hawker P1154 RN in February 1964, the Royal Navy was left without a Sea Vixen replacement firmly scheduled. RN interest, fed by MACAIR marketing enthusiasm, led to the adoption of an idea for a "British" Phantom powered by a pair of afterburning Rolls-Royce Spey turbofan engines. A contract for two developmental YF-4Ks was placed with MACAIR on 1 July 1964, followed in September that year with a contract for two production F-4Ks, to be known as the Phantom FG1 in RN service.

Following the formation of the new Ministry of Defence in April 1964, pressure came to bear on the RAF to adopt the Phantom as its Hunter replacement in place of the P1154 RAF. The change of government in October 1964 led to a further re-evaluation. The new Labour Prime Minister, Harold Wilson, declared that the previous Conservative government's military aircraft procurement programmes were "vastly expensive" and "without cost control". He considered the time gap between the end of the Hunter's life and the projected in-service date for P1154 "to be that which no Government can ask either its service chiefs or its servicemen to accept".

The die was cast and, in February 1965, Wilson declared "it will be necessary to expand the late Government's purchasing programme for Phantoms and use this aircraft as a partial replacement for the

Left: The McDonnell Douglas F-4K Phantom FG1 was the first air defence variant of the type to enter RAF service, with No 43 Squadron (illustrated, intercepting a Tu-95 "Bear-D") in 1969. These were aircraft surplus to Fleet Air Arm requirements prior to delivery and were carrier-compatible. (Crown Copyright)

Hunter". (The term "partial" was important as it paved the way for development of the Harrier and Anglo/French Jaguar aircraft.) Formal contracts for production batches of both F-4Ks and F-4Ms (as the UK Phantom models were designated by MACAIR) were placed in July 1965. In all, 52 F-4K Phantom FG1 and 118 F-4M Phantom FGR2 aircraft were ordered.

As part of the UK-offset, the British Aircraft Corporation (BAC, now part of BAe) undertook manufacture of the rear fuselage, engine access doors and fin/rudder/stabilator assemblies, while Short Brothers built the outer wing panels. Other British companies involved in the industrial offset included Cossor Electronics (IFF system), Elliot-Automation (ASN-39A navigation computer, under Bendix licence), Ferranti (inertial navigation system and the AWG-11/12 fire control radar systems, under Westinghouse licence), Louis Newmark (AJB-7 all-altitude bombing computer, under Lear-Siegler licence), Marconi (AD470 HF/SSB and UHF comms set), Martin-Baker (Mk 5 ejection seats) and Plessey (PTR374 UHF/VHF transceiver and the Spey engine gas turbine starter). EMI Electronics supplied the recce pod for the FGR2 using equipment intended for the cancelled TSR2, but repackaged into a pod for the aircraft centreline hardpoint.

Taken all round, the Phantom was a vast improvement on existing British fighters. It had a multi-role capability with a modern radar derived from the Westing-

house AWG-10. The version for the F-4K was designated AWG-11 with the AWG-12 being the version for the F-4M. Thus, the RAF saw a return to the two-man crew of the Javelin days, although the RN's Sea Vixen already had two-man crews.

The AWG-11/12 was a pulse Doppler radar with pulse air-to-air search and tracking modes, detection and ranging modes, high- and low-level ground mapping facilities, navigation (which, coupled with the INAS, gave exceptional air-to-ground capability), terrain-clearance mode, beacon-homing, air-to-ground interdiction and bombing ranging modes, plus a variety of ECCM facilities. It also provided missile launch computations for the Sparrow medium-range air-to-air missile (MRAAM), together with semi-active illumination for the radar-homing missile.

Its armament was also a quantum jump. Instead of just two infra-red homing missiles and, maybe, 30mm cannon, the Phantom could accommodate four Raytheon AIM-7E-2 Sparrow III MRAAMs and four AIM-9D Sidewinder IC short-range air-to-air missiles (SRAAMs). Although there was no fixed gun armament, a centreline gun pod, the SUU-23/A, housing a 20mm GAU-4/A Vulcan cannon, was also procured. For its air-to-ground role, stores racks stronger than those available in the US were acquired, while EMI repackaged the reconnaissance equipment, originally intended for the TSR2, into a pod for carriage by the F-4M. American pattern 370

Below: The F-4M Phantom FGR2 differed slightly from the FG1 (see text) and was initially used for ground-attack duties. These aircraft were transferred to air defence from 1974. This 1984 view of a No 29 Squadron aircraft shows the later "air defence grey" colour scheme. (Author)

Left: The AWG-12 radar display of the Phantom FGR2, seen in stowed position, provided air-to-air search and tracking modes using pulse-Doppler techniques. By the end of its service life, a good crew could use the Phantom and its radar as effectively as current generation fighters. (Author)

and 600 US gal drop tanks were taken with the package.

The basis for the UK Phantoms was the US Navy's F-4J model, but modified to accept the Rolls-Royce RB168-25R Spey two-stage, by-pass turbofan engine. For this the air intakes, centre and aft fuselage, differ greatly. The "by-pass" function allows a percentage of the airflow entering the intake to be "siphoned-off" around the engine to provide air for boundary level control over the wings and also injection into the exhaust gases prior to initiating afterburning (or reheat). Once reheat is engaged, the by-pass air, containing more oxygen than the mass of air which has just travelled through the engine, offers a higher temperature in the jet pipes and, consequently, more thrust. However, to ensure sufficient air for the Spey at low speeds, each engine has two auxiliary air intake doors, one above (on the rear of the engine bay) and one in the belly. The main air intake features a movable ramp, which was modified to allow for the Spey's air requirements.

The Spey 201 (for the F-4K) was equipped with an airstarter needing an external power source; the Spey 202 for the F-4M was equipped with an electric starter which could be spun up on power from the aircraft's battery. Later the F-4K received the Mk 203 engine and the RAF's F-4M, the Mk 204 – both with rapid reheat lighting systems. Compared with the General Electric J79 engines of the US Phantoms, the Spey-engined versions offered a lower fuel consumption and an increased thrust at low level.

One feature unique to the F-4K, but not the F-4M, is the extra 40in extendible nose gear. The need for this is, basically, because of the shorter deck lengths (and consequently catapult lengths) of the British carriers. It gives the equivalent of an extra 11kts in wind-over-deck speeds, especially useful in the tropics where high temperatures and no wind are commonplace.

The reader may, at this stage, be wondering what an RN Phantom and an RAF ground-attack Phantom have to do with air defence. As the Wilson Government declared only one carrier (HMS *Ark Royal*) would be converted to operate Phantoms, the RN only required 29 of their aircraft to equip one operational unit, No 892 Naval Air Squadron (NAS), and one training unit, No 767 NAS. The balance were delivered to the RAF, with No 43 Squadron forming on the Phantom FG1 in September 1969 at Leuchars. Their eight-missile armament and longer range made them eminently more suitable as long range bomber-destroyers. The Lightning was an interceptor in classic sense, with light armament and shorter range.

As a "partial replacement for the Hunter", the Phantom FGR2s equipped several former Hunter squadrons, with the Harrier GR1 covering the balance. To cover these aircraft, No 228 OCU was formed at Coningsby in July 1970 with the "shadow" designation of No 64 Squadron. Once the

Jaguar GR1 came along, the Phantoms were progressively re-roled for air defence, replacing the Lightnings (except for Nos 5 and 11 Squadrons).

The first former Lightning unit to convert to the Phantom FGR2 was No 111 Squadron in October 1974 at Leuchars. The next unit to form was No 29 Squadron at Coningsby in early December 1975, followed by No 23 Squadron in late December, moving to Wattisham in February 1976, where it was joined by No 56 Squadron in June of that year. The revitalisation of the RAF air defence fighter force was complete for the time being.

Data: F-4M Phantom FGR2 (air defence role)

Powerplant	two Rolls-Royce RB168-76R Spey 202 turbofans, each rated at 12,250lb st (dry) and 20,515lb st with reheat
Span	38ft 4.9in
Length	57ft 7.1in
Height	16ft 1in
Wing area	530sq ft
Empty weight	30,918lb
Loaded weight	58,000lb
Maximum speed	1,386mph (Mach 2.1) at 40,000ft
Rate of climb	32,000ft/min (initial)
Service ceiling	54,400ft
Range	1,520nm (max – unrefuelled); 889nm (Intercept, with all three drop tanks); 318nm (QRA + centreline drop tank); 150nm (CAP – 3.26hrs on station, with all three drop tanks)
Armament	four AIM-7E-2 Sparrow or Sky Flash MRAAMs and four AIM-9D/L Sidewinder SRAAMs, plus one 20mm GAU-4/A Vulcan cannon in an SUU-23/A pod or a single 600 US gal drop tank on the centreline. Two 370 US gal under wing drop tanks could also be carried

IMPRESSIONS OF THE PHANTOM

While the Phantom's service in the RAF stretched from September 1969 to 1992, it was the fighter of the late 1970s and 1980s. In June 1977, the author paid a visit to Coningsby to fly with No 29 Squadron in the Phantom FGR2. This account, based on that originally published in *Defence* magazine in August 1977, early in the author's

career, offers a flavour of how the Phantom was perceived at the time and its applicability to the air defence role.

At the time of my visit to No 29 Squadron the unit was equipped with 10 aircraft and 14 crews, split into two Flights of seven crews. The roles of the squadron, as explained by its Commanding Officer, Wg Cdr Tim Elsworthy, were as follows:

1. *The Air Defence of the UK:* defending UK airspace, as tasked, in peace or war
2. *Interceptor Alert Force:* to provide aircraft and crews for QRA duties, as tasked
3. *Air Defence of the Fleet:* to provide protection for naval forces, as tasked
4. *Overseas Reinforcement:* to meet commitments and circumstances, as tasked
5. *The Anti-Fast Attack Craft (FAC) Role:* to train and be effective, using the SUU-23/A gun pod and the Sparrow missiles, against the emerging threat of FACs armed with anti-ship missiles
6. *Demonstration Flying:* to provide a formation or single aircraft for official presentations or public air shows, as tasked
7. *Trials:* to carry out operational and/or experimental trials of equipment or tactics, as tasked

Compared with the Lightning, I was told, the squadron was very impressed with the Phantom which offered twice the fuel and four times the armament. The crews considered the AWG-12 radar to be extremely effective and were impressed by the Phantom's low fuel consumption and increased low-level thrust.

Before briefing for the flight my pilot, Sqn Ldr Henry Lether, the squadron's Tactical Weapons Officer, expanded on the primary role of the squadron. The long-range, air-refuelled manned Russian bomber, mainly the "Badger", "Bear", "Bison" and the new "Backfire", carrying free-fall bombs or stand-off missiles, were expected to be the main target for the Phantoms. Of these aircraft, the "Backfire" was the one which caused the most concern. Sqn Ldr Lether echoed the Chief of the Air Staff's words in December 1976 which have been noted earlier in this "Snapshot". Using low-level, "back-door" tactics, they pose a new threat to UK airspace and it falls mainly to the AEW force and the Phantoms, with their look-down/shoot-down capability, to counter them.

Such long-range aircraft were expected to be destroyed before they could enter UK airspace. A recent development (at that

Order of Battle – Autumn 1978

Strike Command – HQ: High Wycombe, Bucks

No 1 Group – HQ: Upavon, Wilts (only assets relating to air defence shown)

Sqn	*Aircraft*	*Base*
55	Handley Page Victor K2	Marham, Norfolk
57	Handley Page Victor K2	Marham, Norfolk

No 11 Group – HQ: Bentley Priory, Stanmore, Middx

Sqn	*Aircraft*	*Base*
5	BAC Lightning F3 & F6	Binbrook, Lincs
8	Avro Shackleton AEW2	Lossiemouth, Morayshire
11	BAC Lightning F3 & F6	Binbrook, Lincs
23	McDD F-4M Phantom FGR2	Wattisham, Suffolk
29	McDD F-4M Phantom FGR2	Coningsby, Lincs
43	McDD F-4K Phantom FG1	Leuchars, Fife
55	Handley Page Victor K2	Marham, Norfolk
56	McDD F-4M Phantom FGR2	Wattisham, Suffolk
57	Handley Page Victor K2	Marham, Norfolk
111	McDD F-4M Phantom FGR2	Leuchars, Fife
228 OCU	McDD F-4M Phantom FGR2	Coningsby, Lincs
LTF *	BAC Lightning F3/T5/F6	Binbrook, Lincs

* Lightning Training Flight

AAA/SAM Units

Unit	*Equipment*	*Base*
85 Sqn RAF	BAC Bloodhound 2	HQ – West Raynham, Norfolk
	A Flt	West Raynham, Norfolk
	B Flt	North Coates, Lincs
	C Flt	Bawdsey, Suffolk
27 Sqn RAF Regt	BAe Rapier	Leuchars, Fife
48 Sqn RAF Regt	BAe Rapier	Lossiemouth, Morayshire

Left: This Phantom FGR2 (XV433 of No 29 Squadron) was the mount for the author's 1978 flight. Note the fin-top RWR fairing and the triple rear-view mirrors under the canopy frame to help cover the "six o'clock" position. (Author)

time) was their increased use of electronic warfare, in the form of ECM. The squadron, I was told, practised interception techniques under those conditions, with the assistance of the Canberra T17s of No 360 Squadron.

Of almost equal concern was the improved quality of Russian tactical fighters, such as the "Flogger", "Fitter" and "Fencer". Flying from bases in the Warsaw Pact countries, just behind the FEBA, eastern bases in the UK came within their range. The air defence force was having to develop its skill in "dog-fighting", as the likelihood of fighter-v-fighter conflict increased. To this end, they practised regularly with Hunter, Harrier and Jaguar aircraft.

Resplendent in the garb of the modern fighter pilot, Sqn Ldr Lether and I walked to our aircraft. Having gone through the complicated procedure of strapping a Phantom to my backside, we began the engine start-up procedure. With number one Spey "turning and burning" the second engine refused to light up. Declaring it unserviceable, we cleared our wingman to proceed without us in order that he would not miss the refuelling slot with a Victor tanker. We would follow in the reserve aircraft.

Some 20mins later we were ensconced in a second Phantom FGR2 (XV433) and taxying to the end of the runway. Following an afterburner take-off, we climbed to 3,000ft and headed towards our designated air training area over the Wash. We had missed our tanker slot, so would have to operate on our internal fuel alone. Once inside the training area we engaged reheat once more and, at 520kt, made a zoom climb to height, rolling out at 20,000ft some 40secs later.

Prior to the flight, I had been briefed on the basic use of the AWG-12 radar. On instruction from Sqn Ldr Lether, I now activated the radar and began searching for contacts in the "look-down" pulse-Doppler mode. Having made one contact, we investigated further to find another pair of Phantoms engaged in a similar training task to ourselves.

Meanwhile, under radar control from Neatishead, our wingman was being vectored towards us. Having made the rendezvous, we then split into our pre-briefed training mission – one-on-one fighter combat. For the first "attack" we were to act as a medium-level target for our wingman who was to fly at 25,000ft above the cloud. In the back seat, I kept a wary eye on the radar warning receiver (RWR) display, as well as

visually scanning the skies above. Picking up a visual contact to port, I suddenly felt my G-suit activate as we made a performance turn to try and evade our attacker. Seconds later I heard the words "Fox Two" come over the R/T and I knew we had been "hit" by a Sidewinder missile.

We joined up once before before splitting again. For the second time we were to represent an intruding aircraft but this time coming in low, under ground radar coverage and below cloud, at 250ft. After heading out to sea, we turned back and descended. Flying below cloud at 450kt, we gave our opponent a visually difficult target but, sure enough, his radar picked us up before we broke cloud cover. Coming at us from our "six o'clock", we broke left in an effort to avoid him. By now, despite the squeeze of the G-suit, I had picked him up visually at our "nine o'clock" just as he began a vertical "yo-yo" manoeuvre. This bought him to our deep "six o'clock" position once more and I heard "Fox One" called over the R/T. This time we had been "shot down" by a Sparrow missile.

It was now our turn to be the interceptor. To demonstrate the search capability of our radar, Sqn Ldr Lether set up a "canned" interception. Our target flew on a known heading of 250 degrees, while we flew at the crossing angle on a heading of 110-350 degrees. Operating the radar on Lether's instructions, I acquired the target at 20 miles and we manoeuvred ourselves to make a stern attack. As we approached the target, I changed scales on the radar display to a closer, 10 mile range, and, at five miles we got a "Viz Ident" (visual identification). Rolling in behind the target at three miles, we called "Fox Two" over the R/T – a simulated Sidewinder kill.

During this last engagement, a fuel-feed problem had manifested itself in our opponent's aircraft and it became necessary to return to base. During the return flight, our aircraft manoeuvred around the other Phantom, demonstrating the various battle formations, including the "tight fighting wing". Once back over Coningsby, we orbited the base while our wingman landed first. Our own landing was made a just over an hour after take-off. We touched down at 152kt, deploying the brake parachute at 145kt. Despite the mechanical problems encountered by two of the aircraft involved, the demonstration of the Phantom's ability as an air defence fighter had, to my mind, been most effective.

Over the years, the Phantom has stolen the hearts of every RAF pilot and navigator who has flown her. Perhaps the most suitable tribute to the "Phabulous Phantom" is one of many ditties sung by RAF aircrew over the years, which I understand had its origins with US aircrew during Vietnam. This particular risque chant was revealed to me during a "session" with Phantom aircrew in the Falkland Islands by Wg Cdr Steve Smyth in December 1991.

IRENE
Irene's her name, she's one of the best,
And every night, I give her the test.
The moon was out, the light was dim
And there she stood, so sleek and slim.
Well, I've seen her stripped, I've seen her bare,
I've seen her naked everywhere.
I felt her up, I felt her down,
I felt her all around and around.
I warmed her up as best I could,
And when I got in her, I knew she was good.
I rolled her over on her side
And on her back I also tried.
Irene's her name, she's the best in the land
SHE'S A PHANTOM JET IN THE FIGHTER COMMAND!

RESPONSE: AAA & SAMs

In the 1970s, the missile reigned supreme, with only a handful of Bofors 40mm L/70 guns remaining in RAF Regiment service for stop-gap LLAD duties. One unit of air-mobile Tigercat SHORAD missiles, modified from the naval Seacat system, was used for base air defence during the 1970s, pending the arrival of the Rapier system. The Bloodhound Mk 2 continued in the medium- to high-level role.

BAC Bloodhound Mk 2
Development of the Bloodhound Mk 2 was continuous, concentrating on even better performance and lethality. The ECCM capability of the system was further improved.

The first homebased unit to be deployed overseas, No 112 Squadron moved to Cyprus in 1969, disbanding in July 1975. When the UK withdrew from the Far East in 1970, No 33 Squadron disbanded at Butterworth, Malaysia, in January that year and No 65 Squadron handed over its equipment to the Singaporean Armed Forces in March.

At home, No 41 Squadron disbanded in July 1970 and from 1971, No 25 Squadron equipped with the Mk 2 missile, was deployed to RAF Germany, leaving only a Bloodhound Support Unit (BHSU) in the UK. The BHSU overhauled missiles from the Germany-based units but also included an Operations and Training Squadron.

The UK's air defences were without a medium-range SAM element until December 1975, when No 85 Squadron reformed using equipment returned from Cyprus, the Far East and the UK's BHSU (which then stood-down). Headquartered at West Raynham with "A" Flt, No 85 Squadron located its other flights at North Coates ("B" Flt) and Bawdsey ("C" Flt). A fouth flight, "D" Flt, had been formed to move to Coningsby but it never took place and "D" Flt remained at West Raynham. In 1977, it was announced that these Germany-based Bloodhounds would be brought back to bolster UK defence and that there would be a life extension programme for the Bloodhound.

Data: See 1968 "Snapshot"

BAC Rapier
Developed as a truly mobile LLAD system, the Rapier short range air defence (SHORAD) missile system was developed from the optically-sighted ET316 project, originally planned to complement the US "all-singing, all-dancing" Mauler system. When Mauler was cancelled in 1965 on cost grounds, the UK decided to develop the ET316 project further, as Rapier, to replace the Bofors guns. By using a frequency-agile radar, which became the Marconi DN181 Blindfire, an improved ET316 resulted, offering night and poor-weather capability in addition to optical engagements.

Below: The early success of the BAe Rapier LLAD system in trials lead to it being dubbed as more of a "hittle" than a missile by the RAF Regiment's Commandant General, AVM D. A. Pocock. This photograph shows a Rapier fire unit of No 63 Squadron, RAF Regiment, in a non-tactical position at Gutersloh in 1975. The operator's position is in the camouflaged bunker below and slightly to the right of the tree. (Author)

The Rapier SHORAD system used by the RAF Regiment is designed, primarily, for the point defence of airfields and other prime fixed-sites and is in service in its original towed configuration. The British Army uses it for high-value formation protection in both towed and Tracked Rapier form.

Towed Rapier consists of the launcher, equipped with four missiles, the search/surveillance radar and the IFF interrogation equipment; an optical tracker, which is sited a short distance away from the launcher on a tripod; and the system power supply, provided by a small generator carried on the launcher during movement.

The missile itself is derived from the naval Sea Wolf system and is powered by a two-stage rocket motor. It reaches speeds in excess of Mach 2 and can pull up to 20G. It contains a receiver for guidance commands, and servos for operating the missile flight controls. It has a small warhead activated by a crush fuze, and is treated, by operational units, as a round of ammunition.

According to Air Vice-Marshal D. A. Pocock, then Commandant-General of the RAF Regiment, in a paper published in *Aerospace* in December 1974, the Rapier missile "is, perhaps, more accurately described as a 'hittle'". He also stated "Experience and trials have proved that the combination of pin-point accuracy, plus kinetic energy equivalent to many kilogrammes of conventional explosive, are sufficient to ensure that even the toughest modern aircraft will not live to fight another day. Indeed, during trials even non-warhead [Rapier] rounds with telemetry heads destroyed Meteor target aircraft. This paper credits the system with a kill probability of "30cm at 6km range". His confidence in the system was proved during the 1982 Falklands campaign when official figures credited Rapier with 14 kills. (Subsequent research has thrown much doubt on this figure, caused by "the fog of war".)

The optical (ie, daylight) system is operated by only two men – the tactical controller and the tracker operator. The search radar alerts the tactical controller to the segment around the launcher into which a potential target is coming, having first interrogated the target automatically with IFF. He then alerts the tracker operator to the hostile target, who uses the optical lens to track the target, launching the missile when it comes within range. A collimated lens is then used to track the missile (from flares in the tail cone, ignited on launch). The missile

is automatically aligned to the line-of-sight. All the operator needs to do is continue tracking the target, as the fire unit computer automatically sends signals to the missile to maintain an interception course to impact.

The Blindfire radar-equipped system operates in a similar way to the optical system, except that following the surveillance radar alarm, the operator selects "radar". The Blindfire radar then slews to the target azimuth and carries out an automatic elevation search and locks onto the target. Once the missile is launched, the engagement sequence is fully automatic.

A towed Rapier system comprises two ¾ or 1-ton Land Rovers, one towing the launcher and a second with a trailer carrying nine reload missiles. The detachment consists of two NCOs and four airmen. With Blindfire, the third Land Rover tows the radar and, altogether, 17 reloads are carried between the vehicles. Rapier offers a wide variety of tactical employments. For base air defence, the RAF Regiment unit moves off-base to a pre-surveyed site, offering the best field of view and, also, easy concealment. Each Rapier squadron is organised into five main elements: the squadron headquarters, including all command and control elements; two Rapier flights, each with four fire units; a headquarters support flight; and an engineering flight.

The first RAF Regiment Rapier units formed from 1971 and, after working-up in the UK, deployed operationally to RAF Germany from 1972. These were No 58 Squadron (to Laarbruch) and No 63 Squadron (Gutersloh) in late-1974, followed by No 66 Squadron (Bruggen) and No 16 Squadron (Wildenrath) during 1975, forming No 4 Wing. Subsequently, a further two units (Nos 27 and 48 Squadrons) were formed within the RAF Regiment in the UK to provide base air defence for Leuchars and Lossiemouth, respectively, replacing the Tigercats of No 48 Squadron (see below).

Rapier has also been a successful export product, going to Abu Dhabi, Australia, Brunei, Indonesia, Iran, Oman, Qatar, Singapore, Switzerland, Turkey and Zambia. The units used to defend the USAF bases in the UK are owned by the United States but manned and operated by the RAF Regiment.

Data

Missiles/launcher	4
Diameter	5.2in
Length	7ft 4.5in
Type of mounting	two-wheeled platform

	with outriggers
Effective ceiling	10,000ft
Range	3.8nm
Weight of missile	88lb
Weight of warhead	1.2lb
Type of warhead	HE

Shorts Tigercat

The Tigercat had only a relatively short life with the RAF Regiment and was withdrawn from service with No 48 Squadron RAF Regiment in August 1978, when the squadron re-equipped with Rapier. The system was, however, exported and remains in service with Argentina, India, Iran, Qatar and South Africa.

Data: See 1968 "Snapshot"

CRITIQUE

This decade saw the RAF move into the second generation of fighter aircraft and air defence systems, albeit in fits and starts. Technology was moving in leaps and bounds and costs went through the ceiling.

The Lightning, deprived of any updating beyond that necessary to maintain air safety and minimal operational improvements, gave way to the Phantom, clearly "the best in the West" in its day. That said, the Phantom had to wait several years before assuming its air defence role. Despite being "50% British" in content, its cost was far higher that the USAF production variant of the time – the F-4E Phantom. These higher costs did not, necessarily, bring all-round improvement and, in the end, reduced the numbers bought.

This was to have its effect some years later, after the Falklands War changed the RAF's air defence commitments. I recall one RAF Phantom squadron commander explain the "foolishness" of the British Phantom purchase. We could have had far more aircraft (at a time when numbers mattered) had we opted for the "off-the-shelf" production aircraft, albeit wholly American. In the event, the RAF had to acquire 15 ex-US Navy aircraft during the 1980s, with a logistics support chain peculiar to the F-4J.

The advent of the Shackleton AEW2 was initially seen as an interim measure, but was to soldier on for 19 years. Although a series of new generation ground-based air defence radar began to be ordered by the end of this "Snapshot" period, the ground environment improvements (displays, software, communications and integration required to get the data where it was needed, fast) was to take much longer than anticipated.

Ground-based air defence weapons themselves were definitely improved with the adoption of the Rapier but, as events in the South Atlantic in 1982 and in the Gulf in 1991 were to prove, traditional anti-aircraft fire could still be an effective counter to air attack, even if it did not score direct hits.

Meanwhile the politics of mutual fear and distrust still were being peddled by both "sides". In reality things were beginning to thaw and many visitors from the West were taking holidays in the Soviet Union. Travel in the opposite direction was still strictly controlled, consequently the political message was more readily accepted in that region.

The consequences of an attack by ICBMs or the possibility of a defensive system were still a somewhat taboo subject though talks on their control were continuing. The defence plans of both sides were still heavily slanted towards manned aircraft. Consequently the use of Remotely Piloted Vehicles (RPVs), despite their success in Vietnam, seemed to lack the promise of earlier years. NATO was still looking at ways of modernising its forces while trying to achieve commonality in equipment standards, a quest that was to prove elusive in the light of national interests.

Russian emphasis was increasingly seen to hinge upon the provision of heavy lift capability and the provision of large fleets of assault helicopters, all grist to the mill of those obsessed with the great land war, so often prophesised for Central Europe.

However, much of the confidence of the West was based upon its undoubted advantage in certain key areas of technology, particularly avionics, munitions and training. Claims that Russian fighter pilots operated under a highly restrictive command and control organisation was often cited and seemed to be borne out by the shooting down of a Korean airliner a few years later. At the same time it should not be overlooked that during this period the Russians were introducing their own look-down, shoot-down radar that once again shifted the balance of opportunity.

Consequently the battle of excellence versus numbers continued and the defence industries flourished and would continue to do so for at least another decade.

1988

"SNAPSHOT" – 1988

Although it was not known in 1988, the Cold War was fast approaching its end. At that time, however, the basic protagonists were still NATO and the Warsaw Pact and, as such, improvements to the air defence of the UK continued as planned.

In this year, the Lightning finally gave way to the "Electric Flick Knife" (as some of the last Lightning pilots referred to the Tornado F3). Hawk trainers had been given a war role, armed with a pair of Sidewinder missiles and a 30mm cannon. The planned replacement for the Shackleton AEW2, the Nimrod AEW3 programme, ended in a final fiasco and was cancelled, the Boeing E-3D Sentry AEW1 having been ordered instead. The Victor tanker force (with its carefully-planned fatigue life much reduced by the demands of the 1982 Falklands campaign) was supplemented by 14 ex-civil airliners converted to tanker configuration: nine VC10s and six TriStar 500s. Meanwhile, the UKADGE programme ground slowly ever onwards, its in-service date slipping to the right yet again. The annual *Statement on the Defence Estimates* for 1988 provided a short essay outlining the *Official* view of the Air Defence of the UK. It is worthwhile reproducing it in full.

"1. The strategic position of the British Isles ensures that, in the event of a major conflict between East and West, we would be the prime target for attack. The destruction of our air defence assets, including aircraft, airfields and radar sites, would be among the enemy's first priorities as he sought to gain air superiority. Responsibility for the air defence of the United Kingdom rests with RAF Strike Command, which maintains a constant watch over the air and sea approaches to the United Kingdom, and holds aircraft on ground alert at all times ready to scramble and intercept intruders into the UKADR. In times of tension or war, continuous combat air patrols would be flown. Royal Navy ships with an air defence capability also contribute to our defences.

"2. In the event of conflict, NATO's own offensive operations could be expected to reduce the enemy's ability to attack the United Kingdom by destroying airfields and aircraft on the ground. But a substantial threat would remain from long-range bombers equipped with stand-off weapons. To deal with this, the RAF has developed the sophisticated system of layered defences illustrated [in the White Paper]. The first line of defence aims to detect and intercept hostile aircraft entering NATO airspace, destroying them before they approach their targets. In order to deploy these defences swiftly and effectively, a comprehensive NATO-wide command, control and communications system is vital. As part of this a new system, known as the improved United Kingdom Air Defence Ground Environment, will soon be operational, receiving information from a new generation of transportable radar; and airborne early warning will be much improved from 1991 onwards as the seven Boeing E-3s on order enter service.

"3. The responsibility for initial engagement of enemy aircraft would lie with the Tornado F3, armed with Skyflash medium-range and Sidewinder short-range air-to-air missiles. Two squadrons have been formed during the last year, and all seven squadrons will have entered service by the early 1990s. Supporting the Tornados would be two squadrons of Phantoms armed with Skyflash and Sidewinder, and an inner shield of Hawk aircraft equipped with Sidewinder. Air-to-air refuelling would enable most of our fighters to remain longer on patrol and operate further from their bases.

"4. Enemy aircraft that penetrated the outer defensive screen would additionally face attack by Bloodhound surface-to-air medium range missiles; if they survived they would be engaged by the shorter-range Rapier missiles and radar-directed Oerlikon guns that protect our most important airfields. In addition, passive measures, such as placing aircraft on the ground in hardened shelters and dispersing key assets, would help to reduce the damage inflicted. On the ground, defence of our air bases from terrorists or enemy special forces would be provided by RAF Regular personnel and six squadrons of the RAuxAF Regiment."

This essay is a concise statement of how the UK's air defences function. Let us now examine the elements in more detail.

THE THREAT

The Soviet Union, although under the more benign leadership of President Mikael Gorbachev who preached *glasnost* and *perestroika*, still maintained its strategic force levels. The older bombers were gradually giving way to the newer generation of long-range bombers, with a B-1B-equivalent – the Tu-160 "Blackjack" – under development, but at least Gorbachev was talking arms reduction and control with the West. He realised that the burden of the defence budget was a major constraint on his plans to modernise and revitalise the Soviet economy and raise living standards.

For defence spending to fall, the "high" temperature of the Cold War had to be lowered by reducing the likelihood of a nuclear exchange. The agreement on reductions and removal of Intermediate Nuclear Forces (INF) from the European theatre, signed in December 1987, proved that the nuclear threshold *could* be lowered. Strategic arms limitations and conventional force reductions in Europe were all on the table for dicussion.

Yet the reality of a threat to the UK (and NATO) still remained. According to the UK's *Statement on the Defence Estimates 1988*: "The substantial improvement in Soviet military capabilities over recent years has been made possible by the high priority given to the defence sector in the allocation of resources. Expenditure on defence has grown in real terms by about 50% since 1970. The share of national economic output allocated to defence, at 15% of gross national product, far exceeds that of any NATO country."

The airborne threat was clarified by figures published in the same document. From various comparative tables, it emerged that the Soviet Union had some 150 strategic (range over 2,970nm) bombers ("Bears" and "Bisons" equipped with freefall weapons) and a further 60 new "Bear-H" bombers equipped for launching the AS-15 air-launched cruise missile (ALCM) in their strategic forces. Long-range (540-2,970nm) INF forces, land-based in Europe from the Urals westwards, included 350 aircraft comprising a mix of "Badger", "Blinder" and "Backfire" bombers. The "Fencer" interdictor was included in the figure of 3,200 aircraft among the shorter-range (270-540nm) INF forces.

If the reader will accept that the "Bison", "Blinder" and "Moss" have already been described in full in earlier "Snapshots" and that the "Blackjack" will be covered in the next "Snapshot", the following data updates developments on the remaining threat aircraft. Also included for the first time is the Sukhoi Su-27 "Flanker", which is the first Soviet fighter to have the capability to escort medium- to long-range bombers against the UK.

Ilyushin A-50 (Il-76) "Mainstay"
Developed from the Ilyushin Il-76 "Candid" transport aircraft as a successor to the Tu-126 "Moss", the A-50 "Mainstay" is an

Left: Having experimented with airborne early warning and control with the Tu-126 "Moss", Ilyushin's AEW&C variant of the Il-76, codenamed "Mainstay" by NATO, could be used in support of aerial attacks on the UK. (333 Sqn, Luftforsvaret)

Above: A more contemporary view of the Sukhoi Su-24 in its Su-24MK "Fencer-D" version is identified by the wing fence above the inner pylon and a new radome and pitot tube design on the nose. (US DoD)

airborne early warning and control (AEW&C) aircraft, equivalent to the USAF E-3 Sentry.

The original Il-76 tranport version made its maiden flight on 25 March 1971. It is of high wing and T-tail configuration, with underslung engines, and in its military versions features a tail turret under the base of the fin housing two 23mm NR-23 cannon.

The A-50 "Mainstay" has a slightly lengthened fuselage, on which is located a large saucer-shaped rotating radome housing the AEW radar. It is equipped with a new IFF system, a comprehensive ECM fit and an in-flight refuelling probe. The base of the fin has been re-modelled to include an air intake, presumably to gather cooling air for the avionics associated with the AEW radar. The nose glazing has been faired-over and tail armament deleted.

It is assumed that "Mainstay" provides enhanced surveillance for air defence and, possibly, offensive operations. In 1988, it was estimated that a dozen "Mainstays" were operational throughout the Soviet Union.

An airborne tanker variant of the Il-76, designated Il-78 and codenamed "Midas" has also been developed. (See next "Snapshot" for details.)

Data: Ilyushin A-50 "Mainstay" (estimated on Il-76T)

Powerplant	four Soloviev D-30KP turbofans, each rated at 26,455lb st
Span	165ft 8in
Length	152ft 10.25in
Height	48ft 5in
Wing area	3,229.2sq ft
Max T/O weight	374,785lb
Maximum speed	528mph
Service ceiling	40,000ft
Range (nominal)	3,100 miles

Sukhoi Su-24 "Fencer"

By 1988, the "Fencer" had been firmly identified by the designation Su-24 and was credited as having twice the combat radius of action of the Su-17 "Fitter" with the same combat load. At this time it was estimated some 800 "Fencers" were in service, at least 500 of which had a strategic role, while one squadron's worth was also tasked with maritime reconnaissance in the Baltic Sea.

Following the A- and B-models, the Su-24 "Fencer-C", entering service in 1981, was an improved aircraft. The fin leading edge was extended, incorporating a small cooling intake, while a heat exchanger intake was positioned above the centre-section of the fuselage at the wingroot. A multiple air data probe unit in the nose replaced the single probe of earlier models. Forward of each wingroot were new triangular fairings also visible on the fin, near the tip. These are understood to be antennae for the aircraft's ECM equipment.

The Su-24M "Fencer-D" saw probe-and-drogue AAR facilities added to the aircraft. The nose is slightly lengthened, forward of the windscreen, while the chord of the lower fin is extended, giving a kink to its leading edge. There are large overwing "fences", becoming integral with the wingroot glove pylons, presumed to be capable of carrying Kh-29L laser- or Kh-29T TV-guided (AS-14 "Kedge") air-to-ground missiles, equivalent to the US Maverick type. Some undernose aerials are deleted, while a new "blister" housing an electro-optical sensor has been added to the rear of the nose-wheel doors. The multiple-headed nose probe has reverted to a single long probe. "Fencer-D" has been in service since 1983.

The Su-24MK "Fencer-D mod" is the "Fencer-C" bought up to D standards, but lacking wing fences and, in some examples,

AAR facilities. Some "Fencers" have been adapted to carry the UPAZ-A drogue AAR store for buddy-tanking operations.

The designation Su-24MR "Fencer-E" refers to the reconnaissance version of the "Fencer-D", with a navigation radar and sideways-looking airborne radar (SLAR) in the nose and ventral camera/IRLS housing, plus enlarged dorsal heat-exchanger air duct. It retains the capability to deliver air-to-ground weapons, although the gun is deleted. It is in tactical and naval use.

Data: Sukhoi Su-24MK "Fencer-D mod"

Powerplant	two Lyulka AL-21F turbo jets, each rated at 17,200lb st dry and 25,000lb st with reheat
Span	57ft 10.5in – 16° sweep 34ft 0in – 69° sweep
Length	80ft 5.25in (inc pitot tube)
Height	20ft 3.5in
Wing area	593.8sq ft – 16° sweep 549.1sq ft – 69° sweep
Empty weight	49,207lb
Max T/O weight	87,523lb
Maximum speed	Mach 1.35 at height, Mach 1.16, clean, at low level
Service ceiling	54,135ft
Combat radius	764 miles (lo-lo-lo) with 6,614lb of weapons and drop tanks
Armament	one 23mm six-barreled

GSh-6-23, plus eight stores pylons under fuselage, wing root and outer wings, capable of carrying a max weapon load of 17,637lb of nuclear weapons, missiles of the Kh-23M (AS-7 "Kerry"), Kh-25MR/ML (AS-10 "Karen"), Kh-58E (AS-11 "Kilter"), Kh-28 (AS-9 "Kyle"), Kh-59 (AS-13 "Kingbolt") and Kh-29T/L (AS-14 "Kedge") types, plus bombs and rockets

Sukhoi Su-27 "Flanker"

Development of this all-weather, counter-air fighter began in 1969. The prototype, designated T-10-1m, first flew on 20 May 1977 and several others followed. Its similarity to the MiG-29 fighter's configuration suggests that both aircraft were evolved from a common R&D programme, most likely the TsAGI Central Aerodynamics and Hydrodynamics Institute.

The prototype Su-27s, provisionally identified by the name "Ram-J" by the US DoD, were later codenamed "Flanker-A" under the NATO reporting system and featured curved wingtips, rearward-retracting nosewheel and twin fins mounted centrally over the engine housings. Development was not without its problems and it has since been revealed that two pilots were killed during the development programme.

A major re-design resulted in the first production model, the "Flanker-B", first flown on 20 April, 1981. The wingtips had been squared-off and the fins re-located outboard of the engine housings, while the tailcone was extended and the nosewheel re-located to retract forwards. This has become standard equipment in the Soviet air forces, being roughly the equivalent to the F-15 Eagle.

The US DoD suggests that the "Flanker-B's" thrust-to-weight ratio and manoeuvra-

Below: One of the first pictures of Sukhoi's Su-27 "Flanker-B", taken from a Norwegian P-3B Orion in 1987. It shows the aircraft armed with two short-burn AA-10A "Alamo-A" semi-active radar homing missiles under the fuselage, two short-burn AA-10B infra-red homing "Alamo-B" on the centre-wing pylon and a long-burn AA-10C "Alamo-C" under the engine duct. The outer-wing pylons can carry either a pair of AA-8 "Aphid" or AA-11 "Archer" close-range infra-red homing missiles. (333 Sqn, Luftforsvaret)

bility are much improved over earlier generations of Soviet fighters. It has a large pulse Doppler radar with look-down/shoot-down capability, with a reported search range of 130nm and track range of 100nm, and can be armed with up to 10 AAMs. First clear photographs of the Su-27, taken in 1986 by the Royal Norwegian Air Force, showed a "Flanker-B" armed with six AA-10 "Alamo" AAMs in three distinct versions: "Alamo-A" – semi-active radar homing, short-burn; "Alamo-B" – IR-homing, short-burn; and "Alamo-C" – semi-active radar homing, long-burn.

When used in conjunction with the Ilyushin A-50 (Il-76) "Mainstay" AEW&C aircraft, the "Flanker" has a formidable capability against low-flying aircraft and cruise missiles. With a combat radius on a par with the Tu-28P "Fiddler", it is well able to act as escort to bombers and long-range interdiction aircraft against targets in the UK.

In 1988, it was estimated that some 100 "Flankers" were in Soviet service. It is being used to replace many of the older MiG-21/23/25/27 and Su-15 aircraft in the Soviet inventory.

Data: Sukhoi Su-27 "Flanker-B"
(as estimated in 1988)

Powerplant	two Tumansky R-32 turbofans, each rated at 29,955lb st with reheat
Span	48ft 2.75in
Length	70ft 10.5in
Height	18ft 0in
Max T/O weight	44-60,000lb
Maximum speed	Mach 2 at height
Range (combat)	930 miles
Armament	one 30mm cannon in starboard wing root, plus up to 10 AAMs, including R-60/MK (AA-8 "Aphid") or AA-11 "Archer" SRAAMs and the AA-10 "Alamo" (of which there are three identified variants – see text) on pylons under the wings and fuselage. Alternatively, up to 13,225lb of air-to-ground ordnance can be carried in the secondary attack role

Tupolev Tu-16 "Badger-H/J/K"
The three versions of the Tu-16 "Badger" described in this section are all electronic warfare (EW) versions with specific tasks.

First observed in 1981, the "Badger-H" serves as an escort or stand-off EW aircraft. Its prime mission is to deploy airborne decoys, principally chaff, in advance of a missile-carrying strike force of bombers. It has the appearance of the A-model, with a glazed nose and chin radome, but in place of a weapons load carries multi-band receiving and analysis equipment, jamming and decoy-dispensing equipment for up to 20,000lb of chaff. It is also believed that flare ejection tubes are installed. Two "teardrop" radomes are located fore and aft of the bomb bay.

The "Badger-J" is an alternative EW platform, again to protect a strike force. The decoy dispensing equipment has been replaced by an enhanced receive/analysis/jamming ECM suite, including a large ventral "canoe" radome. This is surrounded by a number of heat exchangers and exhaust ports. Like the H-model, it has a glazed nose and some aircraft have been seen with large flat-plate antenna on the wingtips.

This trio is completed by an electronic intelligence (ELINT) version, "Badger-K" again retaining the glazed nose of the A-model. Among the variety of antennae associated with this task are two "teardrop" radomes located inside and forward of the weapons bay, with four small pods down the centreline ahead of the rearmost radome. This version is reported to have the largest fuel capacity of all "Badgers".

Tupolev Tu-22M-3 (Tu-26) "Backfire-C"
The advanced production version of the "Backfire" series, an example of the Tu-22M-3 was displayed at Farnborough in September 1992. First reported in 1980, the "Backfire-C" can be identified by its wedge-shaped air intakes, similar to those on the MiG-25 fighter.

This version is known to have been in service since 1985 in both the long-range bomber and maritime strike roles and is, to all intents and purposes, similar to the earlier models, except for the intake mentioned above and the lack of an in-flight refuelling probe.

Data: Tu-22M-3 (Tu-26) "Backfire-C"

Powerplant	two unidentified turbofans (thought to be derived from the NK-144) each rated at about 45,000lb st
Span	112ft 6.5in – spread / 76ft 9.25in – swept
Length	129ft 11in
Height	35ft 5.25in
Wing area	1.830sq ft
Empty weight	119,000lb (approx)
Loaded weight	273,373lb (max T/O)
Maximum speed	1.242mph at high altitude
Service ceiling	43,635ft Range (combat),

1,188nm (unrefuelled)

Armament one or three X-22 or AS-4 "Kitchen" missiles and/or several AS-16 "Kickback" short-range attack missiles. Multiple racks for 12-18 x 1,102lb bombs (to max of 10,886lb), plus two GSh-23 23mm cannon in a tail turret

Tupolev Tu-142 "Bear-H/J"

A new production model of the "Bear", the Tu-142K "Bear-H" is based on the F-model but with the shorter fuselage of the B/C-models and with the revised cockpit. Its main role is to act as a carrier for the AS-15 "Kent" air-launched cruise missile, six of which are understood to be housed on a rotary launcher in the bomb-bay. It is thought that underwing pylons inboard of the engines can carry a further four missiles (two per side).

Among the features of the "Bear-H" is a larger and deeper nose radome (thought to include terrain-following radar) and a small fin-top fairing. All ventral gun positions have been removed and the tail turret has a single twin-barrel 23mm cannon, in place of the usual pair. There are no ELINT blisters or camera ports on the aircraft. These new-build H-models were produced at Kuybyshev and achieved their initial operating capability in 1984. By the summer of 1988, some 70 aircraft had been built.

Based on the "Bear-F Mod 1", the "Bear-J" was first observed in 1986 and is understood to be for long-range communications duties with submarines, such as the US Navy's E-6A and EC-130 TACAMO. It is thought that the J-model is a conversion and can be identified by a long spike projecting from the fin-top and an underfuselage fair-

ing, presumed to be for a trailing wire antenna or, possibly, an in-flight refuelling buddy pack. Not an offensive aircraft as such, it is included for family continuity.

Data: See 1978 "Snapshot"

DETECTION & IDENTIFICATION

The early 1980s saw a massive escalation in defence spending in the United States and this was matched, to a degree, by other NATO nations. However, the sheer cost of advanced military systems still meant that there were often strict budgetary restraints, which meant that all spending was subject to a series of priorities which changed from time to time to reflect political trends. The UK began the decade with plans for a major updating of its national air defences. The new equipment included Tornado F2 interceptors, the Nimrod AEW3, new radars and extensive modernisation of command, control and communications equipment. The technological fall-out, in terms of both finance and technical complexity, was to last for the entire decade.

It was intended that the upgrading programme, known as the Improved United Kingdom Air Defence Ground Environment (IUKADGE), would offer new standards over some four million square miles of the UK air defence region. It was to prove a long and expensive programme which, eventually, was only partially operational by 1991, with the estimated cost of the complete programme being some £500 million.

By an evolutionary process, the 1940s "sector" philosophy had developed into a national Air Defence Operations Centre (ADOC) which had an overall view of the complete region. Tactical operations are conducted via Sector Operations Centres (SOC) and these are linked to Command and Reporting Centres (CRC) and Reporting Posts (RP). The RPs, equipped with three-dimensional (3-D) radars form the frontline in detection.

The development of highly-capable, transportable, ground-based radars allows them to be sited virtually anywhere in the country to improve their chances of survival in attack. Advances in telecommunications also ensured that they could be easily and rapidly connected to a national network of lines and exchanges. This ensures that they remain in contact even when some parts of

the network had been destroyed. It also implies a considerable amount of data handling and processing and this, once again, required a further advance in computational resources.

An invitation to tender against the RAF Air Staff Requirement (ASR888) for an Improved Command and Communication System (ICCS) to replace the existing Linesman, was issued in February 1979. The contract award to UKADGE Systems Limited (UKSL – a consortium comprising Hughes Aircraft, Marconi and Plessey), was "leaked" to the press in September 1980 with formal contract signature in March 1981 and a planned completion date set for August 1986.

Three new radars were used – the Marconi Martello (RAF designation – Type 91), General Electric GE592 (Type 92) and the Plessey Radar/ITT-Gilfillan AR320 (Type 93). All three types are transportable between operational sites. The new sensors and communications infrastructure were intended to provide a comprehensive, real-time picture of the region. It was a programme of some complexity and this was to prove problematical over the years ahead.

This increasing complexity and financial stringency was to prove to be something of a hallmark in the decade, the Nimrod AEW3 programme being another example of the technological innovative / cost / timescale, equation which proved difficult to balance.

In 1986, a Nimrod AEW3 made its first flight with improved radar equipment which the manufacturer, GEC Avionics, was confident would meet the UK's AEW requirement. It included a new computer which featured enhanced tracking software, twice as powerful as its predecessor; new antennae; a modified transmitter and a new system known as a vehicle correlator. The manufacturer was also anxious to emphasise that the Mission Avionics could be easily fitted in a wide range of other aircraft and, in acknowledgement of the growing strength of Europeanisation now becoming evident, these types included the Transall C-160 and Aeritalia G-222 transports. Working in partnership with Lockheed-Georgia, detailed designs had also been made for a palletised version to be used in the C-130. This latter teaming made a joint presentation to the French. Alas these plans came to nought.

Much was made of the earlier availability of the Nimrod AEW3 in comparison with its competitors. Yet the development programme seemed to drag on with the costs

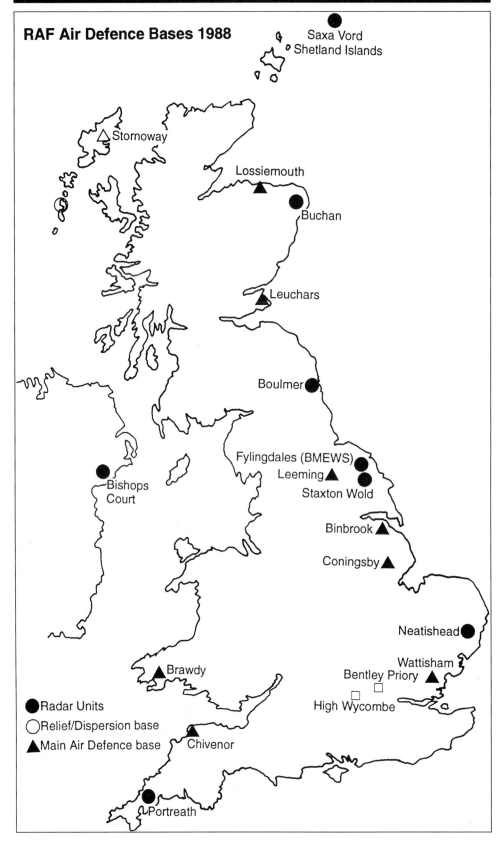

RAF Air Defence Bases 1988

Saxa Vord
Shetland Islands

△ Stornoway

Lossiemouth ▲
● Buchan

▲ Leuchars

Boulmer ●

Fylingdales (BMEWS) ●
Leeming ▲
Staxton Wold ●

Binbrook ▲

Coningsby ▲

● Bishops Court

Neatishead ●

Wattisham ▲
▲ Brawdy
Bentley Priory ☐
High Wycombe ☐

● Radar Units
○ Relief/Dispersion base
▲ Main Air Defence base

Chivenor ▲

● Portreath

rising and IOC constantly moving to the right. One of the main problems involved signals processing for the moving target indicator. The author was told by an industry source that this was known about from the early days in the programme. However, the project management – firmly in the hands of the MoD (PE) – left much to be desired with Ministry "red tape" and procedural wrangling causing delay upon delay, with associated rising costs. It was not until GEC Avionics was appointed prime contractor on the whole programme that the means to solve the problem were found. Alas, it was too little too late.

It must be said that, although admittedly a small airframe for the task, the Nimrod aircraft itself was not at fault. Technically, the solutions were in hand but, by then, the costs had risen to unacceptable levels. Much blame was heaped, unfairly in the author's view, on GEC Avionics. Certainly, the process of equipment procurement for the MoD was overhauled as a result of the Nimrod AEW3 "fiasco". After much political wrangling, Boeing eventually won the order to supply its E-3 Sentry AWACS aircraft, though involving a considerable offset agreement.

The choice of the Sentry was, it is said, the RAF's preferred option from the start. However, once the Sentry had been finally selected, it was not possible for the first of the new aircraft to be delivered until the early 1990s. Meanwhile, the venerable Shackleton AEW2 (an interim solution in 1972) had to soldier on, in declining numbers, while airframe attrition (in the form of advancing fatigue life and cost of maintenance) took its toll. This situation was exacerbated in April 1990 by the loss of one of these aircraft in a fatal crash in the Hebrides.

IFF remained an other area of discussion. Two systems were in use by the mid-1980s – Mk 10 and Mk 12. Both operate in a similar manner, but the future was to be served by the development of a standardised NATO Identification System (NIS), through a collaborative project including NATO members and France. The US share of the programme included Nunn Amendment funding. In February 1989, a contract was awarded to Bendix Communications Division for development of the Mk XV system which will be a secure, highly reliable system capable of operating in a hostile EW environment and to be interoperable with systems of other NATO countries. Cossor was awarded a contract to develop an interrogator side-lobe suppression amplifier for the new IFF.

The electronic advances had also affected the airborne radar, with solid state techniques allied to improved signal processing being used to create systems of considerable flexibility in compact dimensions. GEC Avionics (then Marconi Avionics) developed the AI24 Foxhunter radar, for the new Tornado F2, which features high pulse rate, pulse Doppler for long range search, tracking and attack, and short duration pulses for pilot-commanded dogfight modes. Ferranti Defence Systems of Edinburgh (now part of GEC-Marconi Avionics) provided the transmitter.

It was a complex system and the initial Tornado F2 airframes were supplied early, so that the radars were not immediately available. Some modifications were requested by the UK MoD, but details of this requirement were not released. Media reports of the time suggest that the problem was a case of receiver signal-to-noise ratio being too high.

Once again, it seemed that high technology was being problematical. But by 1988, following a period of discussion, agreement was reached on the total forward programme for the Foxhunter radar for the Tornado F3 (as the F2 ADV (Air Defence Variant)) had been re-designated, following airframe/engine improvements during development (*see section on "Response" in this "Snapshot"*).

The background to the Foxhunter radar, beset by problems in its early stages, makes interesting reading. When, in 1968, the RAF indicated its requirement for a Phantom replacement (ASR-395), an air defence variant of the MRCA (as Tornado was then known) was proposed and was enshrined in Air Staff Target 395 in 1971. Obviously, a new AI radar would also be required. The Airborne Radar Division of what was GEC Avionics (GAv – now part of GEC-Marconi Avionics) had been contracted to conduct a feasibility study for this radar in 1973.

Full scale development of this new radar began in 1976, with GAv working with the Royal Signals and Radar Establishment (RSRE – now part of the Defence Research Agency – DRA) at Malvern as technical authority. From the beginning of this cooperative effort between the two organisations, it was decided to opt for concurrent development and production. The penalty accepted for such a development programme was that early production radars

UK Air Defence Radar Cover

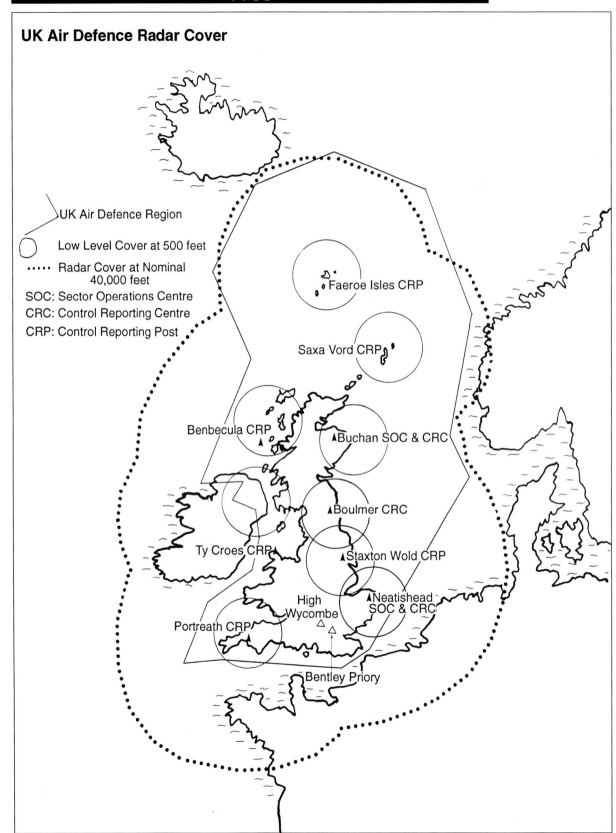

UK Air Defence Region

Low Level Cover at 500 feet

Radar Cover at Nominal
40,000 feet

SOC: Sector Operations Centre
CRC: Control Reporting Centre
CRP: Control Reporting Post

Faeroe Isles CRP

Saxa Vord CRP

Benbecula CRP

Buchan SOC & CRC

Boulmer CRC

Ty Croes CRP

Staxton Wold CRP

Neatishead
SOC & CRC

High
Wycombe

Portreath CRP

Bentley Priory

would have to be heavily modified as the programme gathered speed.

The problems which were to manifest themselves were exacerbated by the system of procurement for the radar. It was decided that, as in the case of the Nimrod radar system, AI24 would be Government Furnished Equipment (GFE). Thus, GAv was contracted by the MoD (PE) for the radar development and British Aerospace (BAe) for the airframe/weapons development. The system was further complicated by MoD (PE) subcontracting two important component parts of the radar, the travelling wave tube (TWT) to EEV and the parametric amplifier to Ferranti Manchester, who were instructed to deliver these to GAv.

In fact, the TWTs were to be supplied direct to Ferranti Edinburgh, a Marconi-appointed subcontractor which was manufacturing the transmitter/receiver section of the radar. The two GFE-contracted companies then supplied their parts, directly or indirectly to GAv, which assembled the radar system and in turn supplied it to BAe at Warton for installation in the Tornado ADV. A complicated procurement cycle by any description, which did not ease the project management.

However, with the dogged British tradition for making things work, the project proceeded. Paramount in the development was the need to ensure detection ranges were not limited by target altitude or enemy ECM. The requirement for a look-down mode against low level targets was, perhaps the most demanding.

The problems associated with AI24 Foxhunter stemmed from its apparent inability to detect fighter-sized targets at 100nm and subsequent delays in delivery to the Tornado F3 production line as GAv tried to solve the problems. It was not until the first W-standard radars reached the RAF's Tornado F2/F3 operational conversion unit that the message hit home.

The subsequent publicity, which saw Foxhunter dubbed as the "Blue Circle" radar, stems from the concurrent development and production approach to procurement. As the RAF found to its cost with the AEW Nimrod, modern weapons systems have complex components which must be able to work as efficiently in the system as they do individually.

By 1986, Foxhunter was underdeveloped, its combat capability limited (due to the emphasis on long-range detection) and it was late. Virtually every radar was "hand-built" to an evolving standard. The Nimrod AEW3 fiasco was hitting the headlines and GEC Avionics was being pilloried.

In August and September 1986, the RAF undertook a series of intensive flying trials to evaluate the status of the radar and identify the problems. Only three of these sorties were affected by radar unserviceability. The results of this evaluation led to a total of 53 problems being identified, not all of which were with the radar. As a result, the RAF convened a working party with BAe and GAv to consider a way of solving these problems. One interesting fact which emerged was that there was neither a technical specification for the radar nor an acceptance specification in place.

Meanwhile, during the spring of 1987, GEC-Marconi had quietly moved responsibility for Foxhunter from GAv to Marconi Defence Systems (MDS – now the third element of GEC-Marconi Avionics). This allowed airborne radar work to take place alongside the development of electronic warfare systems and missile seekers, recognising the importance of taking a total systems approach to the Tornado F3. It also provided a boost to company morale following the cancellation of Nimrod AEW3. With a new management team in place and regular input from the RAF's Tornado ADV Operational Evaluation Unit at Coningsby, things began to move. A company spokesman candidly told the author in 1988 that "If we'd had that sort of feedback (from the RAF) earlier, we'd have been aware of the problems earlier".

MDS became prime contractor for the radar, with Ferranti as its principal subcontractor. The UK MoD (PE) placed a new development contract with MDS and accordingly Marconi established a closer relationship with BAe – the Tornado F3's prime contractor – to ensure that all subcontractors on the radar were co-ordinated both in terms of specification and delivery schedule. By the time a new, fixed-price contract for the radar had been negotiated and signed, on 22 February 1988, MDS had put considerable amounts of its own money (declining to quantify the sum) and resources into the project, including computer-aided design, simulation and modelling facilities, to ensure the success of the programme.

A new and detailed specification was agreed for the contract, together with rigorous acceptance criteria; acceptance to be based on tests performed on the total

Tornado F3 weapons system in operationally-realistic manoeuvres. It is believed this is the first time such demanding and realistic tests have formed part of a contract for an airborne radar in the UK.

To return to those 53 problems, their scope covered the radar itself, the software, the HUD, the pilot's stick-top and the navigator's hand controller. Those relevant to the radar – 41 in total – were incorporated into the agreed specification for the new contract. The majority of them (31) were to be eliminated by the introduction of the Stage 1 radar; the remainder to be eliminated by Stage 2.

These improvements began to filter through and, in November 1988, when the author visited No 5 Squadron at Coningsby, they were equipped with aircraft fitted with interim Z-standard radars. Block 13 Tornado F3s, with the Stage 1 radar, were then expected to arrive in the early summer of 1989.

By the end of 1988, some 124 Z-standard radars had been delivered and from February 1989 into 1990, the RAF was to receive 76 Stage 1 radars, with the balance being Stage 2 from late 1990. The author was told that "at present, the Z-standard radar has a multi-track capability which will be, at least, doubled by the Stage 2 radar, with an improved raid resolution".

Flight trials of the Stage 1 radars were completed by the end of 1988. The operational benefits of this standard, which includes full HOTAS (Hands-On Throttle And Stick) control, mean there is a higher probability of successfully completing a beyond-visual-range (BVR) engagement – particularly holding lock-on while the semi-active Sky Flash MRAAM reaches the target. The radar incorporates additional scan patterns, improved target data and additional ECCM. The first Stage 1 radars were delivered to the BAe production line at Warton in November 1988, to satisfy an initial order for 24 Tornado ADVs placed by Saudi Arabia. For the RAF, the requirement was for the delivery of 76 Stage 1 radars by November 1990.

According to MDS, the Stage 2 modifications make Foxhunter "a real state-of-the-art multi-mode radar" due, mainly, to the inclusion of a new data processor based on the Motorola 68020 processor unit, also specified for the EFA radar and now undergoing flight trials. It allows improved acquisition and tracking with raid assessment and target data through automation of the system management and track-handling function.

With the processing power available, it will be possible to further improve the radar and discriminate the various engine "signatures" of potential targets, if software currently under development by MDS works out. To do this, modulations of returns from the harmonics of the first- and second-stage compressor blade passing frequencies are analysed. It is also possible, in theory, to incorporate information from the ARI1824/1 Hermes radar homing and warning receiver, another MDS product. This aspect also emphasises the importance of a systems approach in a programme such as this. This aspect could be incorporated into a Foxhunter mid-life update.

Automating the radar system further gives the navigator time to think tactics rather than spend time inputting data for the beyond visual range (BVR) phase of an attack. For instance, some 15 switch actions prior to missile-launch, required by the original specification, have now been eliminated. Looking to the future, the navigator should be able to make more use, via his plan situation display, of the tactics of a multiple fighter engagement, including use of Hawk T1As in their war-role as part of the Mixed Fighter Force. The aircraft becomes, in effect, a mini-AWACS.

The final standard of radar has more capability than earlier versions and was provided with a greater degree of automation of the radar function. This ensures a reserve of computing capacity to cope with the new weapons, communications and identification systems planned for current use and for future upgrades. By March 1988, nearly 100 production versions of the radar had been delivered and the production rate was expected to be some 50 per year, until RAF and export orders had been met.

Despite all its problems, the AI24 Foxhunter was the only wholly European modern pulse Doppler, look-down/shoot-down radar currently in operational service. Its long range search and multi-target tracking capability provides the vital BVR engagement option that is essential for modern air combat.

Returning to our main theme, there had also been a considerable amount of work carried out in the United States on very long range, ground-based radar commonly referred to as Over-The-Horizon (OTH). Similar work had been carried out in Australia and experimental sites had been established in both countries. In 1986, Marconi announced success in a new OTH radar in the UK. It was said that a combination of supercomputer, salinity of the sea and short-wave radio techniques had been brought together to see around the bend of the Earth's curvature. The radar uses a short-wave signal that, by virtue of the sea's salinity, adheres to the surface. Trials indicated that low flying aircraft could be detected up to 200 miles away.

As before, regular air defence exercises continued to be a feature of training and inter-service operational experience. In October 1988, seven NATO air forces took part in Exercise "Elder Joust", a three-day exercise involving some 130 aircraft carrying out interceptions, air-to-air refuelling and EW procedures. Significantly it was held concurrently with Exercise "Arc", the first jointly organised Anglo/Franco air defence exercise.

By the end of 1988, six out of 12 mobile radars for the UK system had been delivered and were operational. In the same period a Memorandum of Understanding was signed for development of a European Fighter Aircraft (EFA) to replace the Phantoms and complement the Tornado F3.

RESPONSE: AIRCRAFT & ARMAMENT

Avro Shackleton AEW2
During the 10-year cycle of this "Snapshot", the "interim" Shackleton AEW2 soldiered on with the RAF's No 8 Squadron, based at Lossiemouth in Scotland. It did its job as best it could with the increasingly obsolescing radar with which it was equipped, its performance being overshadowed by the NATO E-3 Sentry AEW force coming into action between January 1982 and April 1985.

This is not surprising as the whole system was pure 1950s vintage and, as an "interim" solution, only received minor upgrades. To fly with the Shackleton is almost akin to going back to the four-engined heavy bombers of the Second World War. (The Shackleton being descended in direct lineage from the Lancaster bomber.) Certainly the atmosphere inside the aircraft, as the author can attest having made one flight in the type, was noisey with the smell of leather crew seats omnipresent. The radar display imagery seemed light years away from that available to Sentry aircrews.

Data: see 1978 "Snapshot"

BAC Lightning F3/F6
The Lightning's inclusion here is a matter of record only. Its story has been told in earlier "Snapshots". The first of the two units to disband was No 5 Squadron in October 1987, followed by No 11 Squadron on 30 May 1988. It was a time of great nostalgia and the end of an era.

Data: see 1968 "Snapshot"

BAe (BAC/Vickers) VC10 K2/3
With the eventual retirement of the Victor tanker fleet in mind, the RAF was in need of a new tanker force. In April 1978, Air Staff

Right: A valedictory view of an No 11 Squadron Lightning F6 firing the very last Red Top missile to be launched on annual armament practise camp on 7 January 1988 closes the Lightning story for the RAF. (Flt Lt Ian Black RAF)

Requirement (ASR) 406 had been formulated and by July that year, BAe had been awarded a contract to convert nine former-civil VC10 airliners to a new tanker configuration.

The first prototype VC10 was an airliner (maximum capacity 151 passengers) for BOAC (now British Airways) and first flew on 29 June 1962. It featured swept wings, high-T tail and four rear-mounted Rolls-Royce Conway turbofan engines. The Super VC10 saw a fuselage stretch of 13ft, allowing a capacity of 163-174 passengers, depending on configuration, plus a fin fuel tank. It made its maiden flight on 7 May 1964.

The first of 14 VC10 C1 transports for the RAF flew on 26 November 1965 and featured the "wet" fin and uprated Conways of the Super VC10 with the fuselage, wing and empennage of the Standard version. An auxiliary power unit (APU) was installed in the tail-cone. It was configured for 150 passengers in rearward-facing seats, entering RAF service with No 10 Squadron in July 1966. (*See 1993 "Snapshot" for details of the C1(K) tanker conversion.*)

For the tanker role, the RAF had purchased five ex-BOAC Standard VC10s and four ex-East African Airways Super VC10s and, after conversion, were designated VC10 K2 and K3 respectively. The work involved in bringing these civil aircraft to military tanker configuration required the installation of five cylindrical tanks within the fuselage, each of 700gal capacity. The K2 models had to have part of the upper fuselage cut away to accept these, while the K3s had them installed via the freight door. After installation on the K3s, the freight doors were sealed. Aft of the flightdeck there is a small passenger compartment able to hold 18 (K2) and 17 (K3) support personnel for deployments away from base.

Both models are configured as three-point tankers, with a Flight Refuelling Mk 17B hose drum unit (HDU) installed in the lower rear fuselage, along with a close-circuit TV system, to monitor the approach of receiving aircraft, and floodlighting for night operations. Each outer wing, inboard of the ailerons, was fitted with a Flight Refuelling Mk 32/2800 refuelling pod, each with a capacity of transferring 2,800lb of fuel per minute, plus floodlighting. In addition, an in-flight refuelling probe was added to the nose, directly above the weather radar, to enable the tankers to receive fuel as well.

Avionics are of a similar standard to that of the RAF's VC10 C1 transports, with dual UHF/VHF and dual HF communications, ADF, IFF, Omega, TACAN and weather radar, with a Smiths Industries SFS6 flight system as standard. An APU is installed in the tail-cone to bring power support up to C1 standard.

The first conversion, a VC10 K2, first flew from BAe's Filton facility on 22 June 1982. First deliveries of the K2 to No 101 Squadron at Brize Norton were made in May 1984, with the K3s following from February 1985, the first K3 conversion having flown on 4 July 1984. The final delivery was made during 1986.

Below: The last of the first tranche of BAe (Vickers) VC10 tankers, a K3 version, seen trailing all three hoses from its wingtip FRMk32 pods and centre-line Mk17 HDU. (BAe Filton)

Above: Resplendent in its all-grey camouflage as part of the Mixed Fighter Force is this BAe Hawk T1A, fitted with underwing AIM-9 Sidewinder missiles and a 30mm gun pack under the fuselage. (BAe)

Data: VC10 K2/3

Powerplant	four Rolls-Royce RCo Mk 301 or Mk 550B turbo-fans, each rated at 21,800lb st
Span	146ft 2in
Length (excl probe)	158ft 8in (K2), 171ft 8in (K3)
Height	39ft 6in
Wing area	2,851sq ft
Empty weight	188,400lb
Loaded weight	314,000lb (maximum T/O)
Maximum speed	581mph (Mach 0.86) at 30,000ft
Service ceiling	42,000ft
Range	4,720 miles
Fuel Payload	with internal and supplementary tanks K2 – 20,737Imp gal; K3 – 22,609Imp gal

BAe (HSA) Hawk T1A

In October 1971, it was announced that the Hawker Siddeley Aviation (later British Aerospace) P1182 had been selected to replace Gnat and Hunter trainers in RAF service. An order for 176 Hawk T1 trainers (as the P1182 became) was placed in March 1972, with the maiden flight being on 21 August 1974. Deliveries of the Hawk to operational Flying Training Schools began in November 1976; others later went to the two Tactical Weapons Units (TWUs).

The Hawk is a swept wing, tandem two-seat advanced jet trainer with light strike capacity, powered by a Rolls-Royce/Turbomeca Adour turbofan. While the RAF aircraft only have three hardpoints – one under the fuselage for a belly gunpack and one under each wing – export models have always featured two hardpoints under each wing. The Hawk is considered a worthy successor to the venerable Hunter, with current sales (RAF and export) standing at 756, with further export orders in prospect.

In January 1983, BAe received a contract to fit 89 of the Hawks with the means to carry one AIM-9L Sidewinder AAM on the two underwing hardpoints. The aircraft of both No 1 and No 2 TWUs, plus the Red Arrows aerobatic team aircraft, were converted to Hawk T1A standard. Re-delivery of these T1A models was completed by May 1986. Of the 89 conversions, 72 were declared to NATO for a war-role of point defence and participation in the RAF's Mixed Fighter Force.

Data: Hawk T1A

Powerplant	one Rolls-Royce/Turbomeca Adour Mk 151 turbofan, rated at 5,200lb st
Span	30ft 9.75in
Length	36ft 7.75in
Height	13ft 1.25in
Wing area	179.6sq ft
Empty weight	8,500lb
Loaded weight	12,566lb (maximum T/O)
Maximum speed	661mph (Mach 1.2) in a dive
Rate of climb	6mins to 30,000ft
Service ceiling	50,000ft
Range	900 miles
Armament	one 30mm ADEN cannon in underbelly gunpack plus two AIM-9L Sidewinder SRAAMs, one under each wing

Handley Page (HSA) Victor K2

When first converted, the Victor K2s had already accumulated between 1,500 and 3,000 flying hours on each airframe. The RAF had planned for a minimum service life of 14 years for the K2. However, the needs of Operation "Corporate" – the Falklands campaign of 1982 – which saw aircraft from both Nos 55 and 57 Squadrons refuelling Hercules transports, Harrier attack aircraft, Nimrod maritime patrol/ASW aircraft and the Vulcan bombers which took part in the "Black Buck" raids on Port Stanley, took the usage of the Victors higher than planned. (While the RAF's tanker fleet was used in the South Atlantic, the USAF detached several of its Boeing KC-135 Stratotankers to the UK to cover the UK air defence tanker requirements.)

As a result, it became necessary to group the aircraft with the lowest fatigue lives in one unit, No 55 Squadron, and retire the longest-serving aircraft as they hit their fatigue limits. As the first Victor K2s were withdrawn, this policy saw the disbandment of No 57 Squadron in April 1986. Its place was taken by No 101 Squadron with converted VC10s (see above) and No 216 Squadron equipped with tanker conversions of Lockheed TriStars (see below), both types being ex-British Airways airliners.

In 1988, the Victor K2s of No 55 Squadron were the last of the V-force still in active service. While they had sufficient numbers with a useful fatigue life, the RAF intended to keep them in service.

Data: see 1978 "Snapshot"

Lockheed L-1011-500 TriStar K1/KC1

Following the Falklands campaign of 1982, the RAF's need for further air-to-air refuelling (AAR) capacity was recognised with the service purchasing six Lockheed L-1011-500 TriStar airliners from British Airways for conversion into tanker transports.

The prototype TriStar made its maiden flight on 16 November 1970. One of the first generation "wide-body" airliners, it had a seating capacity of up to 400 passengers, depending on configuration. Powered by three Rolls-Royce RB211 advanced turbofans (development of which bankrupted the original manufacturer), its engine configuration of two underwing and one mounted in the extreme rear fuselage with a fin-mounted air intake, was revolutionary. (The DC-10, from which the USAF KC-10 Extender tanker was derived, featured an all-through fin-mounted engine.) The long-range version of the TriStar, the L-1011-500, began flight-

Below: The RAF's ex-British Airways Lockheed L-1011-500 fleet has been converted to tanker/transports by the addition of two flight Refuelling Mk17T HDUs under the rear fuselage. This is the TriStar K1 version, shortly after conversion. (Marshall Aerospace)

testing in October 1978, entering British Airways service in 1979.

The conversion work began at Marshall of Cambridge in 1983 with work on two aircraft to a tanker/passenger K1 standard. This involved the installation of seven fuel tanks in the fore and aft baggage compartments, below the passenger floor, offering an additional 100,060lb of fuel; two Flight Refuelling Mk 17T HDUs in the lower rear fuselage, able to deliver fuel at a rate of 4,000lb/min at 50lb/sq in pressure; an inflight refuelling probe on the upper forward fuselage above the cockpit; and close-circuit TV for monitoring refuelling operations. The first of two interim K1s flew on 9 July 1985, followed by a further two aircraft converted to full K1 standard, all four aircraft being delivered to No 216 Squadron at Brize Norton by July 1986.

The final two ex-BA aircraft were converted to tanker/freighter configuration as the TriStar KC1. In addition to the K1 modifications, a 104in x 140in upwards-opening cargo door was installed forward of the port wing leading edge; the passenger floor was strengthened for high density loads, with all items (including passenger seating) being pallet-mounted on the cabin floor. The first KC1 was re-delivered to the RAF in December 1988 with the second following during 1989.

In 1984, a further three TriStar 500s were purchased from Pan Am of the United States. Pending planned conversion to K2 configuration, two were operated in the trooping role as TriStar C2s, to and fro between Brize Norton and Mount Pleasant in the Falkland Islands, where they are known affectionately as "Timmy". The third was maintained in storage with Marshall of Cambridge.

Data: TriStar K1/KC1

Powerplant	three Rolls-Royce RB211-254B4 turbofans, each rated at 50,000lb st
Span	164ft 6in
Length	164ft 2.5in
Height	55ft 4in
Wing area	3,541sq ft
Empty weight	242,864lb (in tanker role)
Loaded weight	540,000lb (maximum T/O)
Maximum speed	605mph at 30,000ft
Service ceiling	43,000ft
Range	7,013 miles
Fuel Payload	K1 – 213,240lb internal fuel plus 100,060lb in seven baggage compartment tanks

McDonnell Douglas F-4K/M Phantom FG1/FGR2

With the exchange of Phantom FGR2s for the FG1 model by No 111 Squadron complete by March 1980, very little happened to change the UK's Phantom air defence fleet until the aftermath of the Falklands campaign in 1982.

Following the liberation of the islands in June of that year and expansion work to the airfield at Stanley, a detachment of Phantoms FGR2s from No 29 Squadron was located "down south". The detachment was taken over in March 1983, by re-numbering No 23 Squadron, with No 29 Squadron taking over a number of No 23 Squadron's aircraft back in the UK. This left the UK air defences one squadron short and the F-4J(UK) – see below – was procured to fill the gap.

By November 1988, the threat in the South Atlantic had reduced sufficiently to allow No 23 Squadron to return to the UK, where it converted to the Tornado F3. The remaining Phantoms, now based at the new airfield at Mount Pleasant, were re-designated No 1435 Flight.

Meanwhile, further Tornado F3s were becoming available and, in May 1987, No 29 Squadron exchanged its Phantoms. The rundown of the Phantom force was, at last, beginning.

Data: see 1978 "Snapshot"

McDonnell Douglas F-4J(UK) Phantom

With the deployment of No 23 Squadron to the Falkland Islands in March 1983 a gap was made in the UK's air defence units. To plug the hole the RAF bought 15 surplus F-4J Phantoms from the US Navy, there being insufficient Tornado F3s available to form a replacement squadron.

As these aircraft were expected to have a relatively short RAF career, there was no major attempt to "Anglicise" the aircraft to achieve commonality with existing RAF F-4K/Ms. They retained the General Electric J79 turbojets and had their radars upgraded to AWG-10B standards. As a result, the aircraft retained their narrower fuselage cross-section and different air intakes. They were easily identified by the lack of the fin-top ECM fairing and the slightly different shade of Flint Grey in their camouflage.

According to the official method of aircraft nomenclature prevalent in the UK, these aircraft should have been designated

the Phantom F3. If one may be forgiven the cliche, "it is the exception that proves the rule", and the F-4J(UK) is how the type was officially known.

The 15 aircraft chosen for the RAF were completely overhauled at the NAS North Island, California, with the first F-4J(UK)s being delivered direct to Wattisham in August 1984 for service with the re-formed No 74 Squadron, otherwise known as "The Tigers". The remaining 12 aircraft had arrived on the unit by December that year.

Data: F-4J(UK) Phantom

Powerplant	two General Electric J79-GE-10 turbojets, each rated at 17,900lb st
Span	58ft 3in
Length	63ft 0in
Height	16ft 3in
Wing area	530sq ft
Empty weight	31,853lb
Loaded weight	61,795lb (maximum T/O)
Maximum speed	1,430mph (Mach 2.16) at 36,000ft
Rate of climb	49,800ft/min
Service ceiling	58,750ft
Range	900 miles
Armament	four AIM-9L Sidewinder

SRAAMs (two under each wing) plus four AIM-7 Sparrow or Sky Flash MRAAMs semi-recessed under the fuselage, with the option of a SUU-23 pod armed with a 20mm Gatling gun on the fuselage centreline

Panavia Tornado F2/F3

The Tornado Air Defence Variant (ADV), as it was originally known, was developed from the interdictor-strike (IDS) variant, or Tornado GR1 in RAF service, specifically for the RAF. Originally known as the Multi-Role Combat Aircraft (MRCA – sometimes cynically translated as "Must Refurbish Canberra Again"), it was christened Tornado in March 1969. One of its six specified roles was air superiority but it was the IDS version which was developed first.

British involvement in Tornado is based on participation in the tri-national holding company, Panavia Aircraft GmbH, a German company set up in 1969 to develop and build what was then MRCA. It is owned by British Aerospace (formerly the British Aircraft Corporation), Messerschmitt Bolkow-Blohm (MBB, now part of the Deutsche Aerospace grouping) and Alenia (formerly Aeritalia), with shares of 42.4%, 42.5% and 15% respectively. The RB199 turbofan engines were developed by Turbo-Union, a similar tri-national company, owned in the same proportions by Rolls-Royce, Motoren und Turbinen Union (MTU, also now part of Deutsche Aerospace) and Fiat Aviazione.

Structural design of the variable-geometry aircraft was completed in 1972 and the first of nine prototype aircraft, the German-assembled P01, made its maiden flight on 14 August 1974. While there was a production

Above: A Mc-Donnell Douglas F-4J(UK) of No 74 Squadron seen during Exercise "Elder Forest" in April, 1988, where it worked with Hawk T1As in the Mixed Fighter Force role. The aircraft is moving from its hardened aircraft shelter at Wattisham. (Author)

line for Tornado located in each participating country, there was no duplication of manufacture. Each company produced its own share and delivered the sub-assemblies to the three assembly centres. Production of the planned 813 aircraft is now complete, although 48 extra Saudi Arabian aircraft have still to pass through the line at Warton.

A more detailed history of the Tornado IDS and ECR development and their introduction into service with the RAF, Germany's *Luftwaffe* and *Marineflieger*, and Italian Air Force, does not concern this work and can be found elsewhere. Suffice it to say here that the RAF's first Tornado GR1s were delivered to the Tri-national Tornado Training Establishment (TTTE) in July 1980, with the first RAF unit, No 9 Squadron, becoming operational in June 1982.

The RAF is the only partner nation to require the ADV variant of Tornado, although Saudi Arabia took 24 export models. Air Staff Requirement (ASR) 395 issued in 1971 called for a long-range fighter with good loiter and endurance capability; the ability to counter mass raids; to be effective in a jamming environment; and to carry the range of weapons used on the-then current interceptor, the Phantom FG1/FGR2, – Sky Flash MRAAMs, AIM-9L Sidewinder SRAAMs plus an internal gun (missing from the RAF's Phantoms). Most important of all was the need to retain as much commonality with the Tornado GR1 as was possible. The RAF's initial requirement was for 165 Tornado ADVs.

Originally designated Tornado F2, the ADV is a minimal conversion of the IDS airframe. It is built, principally, of metal and is of cantilever, shoulder-mounted, variable-geometry wing with a single, sweptback fin and all-moving horizontal tail surfaces, known as tailerons. The forward leading edge sweep is 25 degrees, while in fully-swept mode it is 67 degrees. The twin RB199 turbofan powerplants have "bucket-type" thrust reversers.

The principle areas of difference lie in the fuselage length, the avionics and weapons system and the thrust of its engine. For the F2, the fuselage was lengthened by 4ft 5.5in with a small "plug" aft of the cockpit, to accommodate the Sky Flash missiles, and a longer nose radome. The fixed inboard portions of the wing are extended forward at the leading edge to give a 68-degree sweep and additional chord. The lengthened fuselage, apart from reducing supersonic drag compared with the IDS,

also allows more space for avionics and a further 200Imp gal of fuel.

A fully-retractable in-flight refuelling probe is situated on the port side of the forward fuselage (the IDS version has a bolt-on probe assembly on the upper starboard fuselage). A ram-air turbine (for emergency power) is installed, while the port 27mm cannon was removed.

On the avionics side, the terrain-following radar system of the Tornado GR1 has been replaced by the GEC Avionics (later transfered to Marconi Defence Systems – MDS) AI24 Foxhunter air interception radar system (the development problems of which were discussed in the previous section) plus a new Cossor IFF-3500 interrogator and radar-dedicated cold air unit. Foxhunter is a multi-mode, track-while-scan, pulse Doppler radar with FMICW (frequency-modulated, interrupted continuous wave). It is able to detect targets at distances in excess of 100nm and track several targets simultaneously.

There is an additional heads-down display for the pilot and a second Ferranti FIN 1010 inertial navigation system, plus new cockpit displays (with redesigned symbology) and an increase in computer storage capacity from 64K to 128K. A displayed data video recorder has replaced the navigator's wet-film display recorder, while the MDS Hermes modular radar homing and warning receiver has been added. There is also provision for the Joint Tactical Information Distribution System (JTIDS) data link to be installed in the future.

In addition to the single 27mm IWKA/Mauser cannon, the Tornado F2 (and F3) is armed with four BAe Sky Flash MRAAMs, semi-recessed under the fuselage, carried on Frazer-Nash launchers, plus two AIM-9L SRAAMs mounted on shoulder launchers either side of each inner, under-wing stores pylon (making four in all). It was planned that the Hughes AIM-120 AMRAAM would replace the Sky Flash and the AIM-132 ASRAAM would replace the Sidewinder.

The F2's powerplant is the Mk 103 version of the RB199-34R turbofan engine, with thrust ratings of between 5-10% (for both dry and reheat) of the GR1's Mk 101 engine (the figures for which are 9,000 and 16,000lb st respectively). The first of three prototype ADVs flew on 27 October 1979, while the first production Tornado F2 (a dual control version) flew on 12 April 1984.

The Tornado F3 is a result of the development of the F2 ADV pre-series aircraft to accept the increased-thrust Mk 104 version of the RB199 (with a further 7% improvement in engine ratings over the Mk 103). To produce the increased thrust, the afterburner section of the engine was lengthened by a further 14in, necessitating an equivalent stretch in the rear fuselage. At the same time, a Lucas DECU 500 (Digital Engine Control Unit) replaced the analog unit. These improvements were too late to be incorporated in the full production run of ADVs, so the first 18 aircraft were completed with the Mk 103 engines as the Tornado F2.

From aircraft 19, the appropriate airframe modifications to accept the Mk 104 engine were made. Additionally, an automatic wing sweep facility and an automatic manoeuvre device system was also installed. The resultant aircraft was re-designated Tornado F3 and all subsequent aircraft were to this standard. The first Tornado F3 flew on 20 November 1985.

It was planned that all 18 of the F2s were to be returned to BAe to receive all but the Mk 104 engine improvements, this version being known as the Tornado F2A. In the event, this did not happen and (as at January 1993) only two remain in use for test flying, one with BAe at Warton and one with the DRA Farnborough.

The RAF's first Tornado F2 unit, No 229 OCU (OCU), with the "shadow" designation of No 65 Squadron, was formed at Coningsby in November 1984. It received its first Tornado F3s in July 1986 and by December that year was fully operational on the type. All operational squadrons received the Tornado F3, with the first unit, No 29 Squadron, being formed in April 1987 and was declared operational in November. The second unit, No 5 Squadron, was officially formed on 1 May 1988. Both Nos 5 and 29 Squadrons are based alongside No 229 OCU at Coningsby.

The build-up of the Tornado F3 continued through 1988, with No 11 Squadron, the RAF's last Lightning squadron, converting in July and moving to Leeming where it was declared operational in November 1988. It was joined by No 23 Squadron, which formed in November 1988, although it was not declared operational until 1 August 1989. Details of the completion of the Tornado F3 build-up are in the next "Snapshot".

The author has been fortunate enough to fly in a Tornado F3 to see for himself the capability of the RAF's latest interceptor (*see next section*).

Data: Tornado F3

Powerplant	two Turbo-Union RB199-34R Mk 104 turbo fans, each rated at 9,100lb st (dry) and 16,520lb st with reheat
Span	45ft 7.5in (25 deg fully spread), 28ft 2.5in (67 deg fully swept)
Length	61ft 3.5in
Height	19ft 6.25in
Wing area	286.3sq ft
Empty weight	31,970lb

Loaded weight	61,700lb (maximum T/O)
Maximum speed	920mph (clean) or Mach 2.2 at altitude.
Rate of climb	N/A
Service ceiling	70,000ft
Radius of action	345+ miles (supersonic) 1,151+ miles (subsonic)
Endurance (est)	2hr CAP at 345-460 miles from base, including time for interception and 10min combat (without AAR).
Armament	four Sky Flash MRAAMs,

semi-recessed below fuselage, four AIM-9L Sidewinder SRAAMs, two on shoulder mounts on each inner wing pylon, plus one 27mm IWKA-Mauser cannon in lower starboard forward fuselage

IMPRESSIONS OF THE TORNADO F3

In November 1988, when the author was privileged to make his flight with No 5 Squadron, the Tornado F3 was the latest air defence interceptor to enter service with the RAF. The first unit, No 29 Squadron, had been declared operational a year earlier in November, 1987. The second unit to form, No 5 Squadron, is based at RAF Coningsby, Lincs, alongside No 29 Squadron and No 229 OCU , the latter with the "shadow" designation of No 65 Squadron (and is today known as the Tornado F3 OCU with No 56 Squadron as its "shadow" designation). Both No 5 Squadron and its former sister-unit at Binbrook, No 11 Squadron, were the RAF's last Lightning squadrons. The latter unit had already converted to the Tornado F3 and moved to RAF Leeming, Yorks.

Given that the Soviets would be expected to come in "large packages" by day or night, with EW support and the ability for self-defence jamming, this represents, for the RAF defenders, the equivalent of "looking for a needle in a haystack". Even with the slightly increased numbers of interceptors available with the build-up of the Tornado F3 fleet and improvements to the "defence in depth", it is unlikely that combat air patrols (CAPs) will consist of more than a pair of aircraft.

Sqn Ldr Clive Rowley, a flight commander with No 5 Squadron, explained to the author that, against the purely bomber threat, the RAF's aim is to destroy its enemy at beyond visual range (BVR) with its BAe Sky Flash semi-active AAM – known as "Fox One" in operational parlance – and

depart the vicinity, rapidly. The missile's advanced radar-proximity fuze offers a high probability of a single-shot kill against both subsonic and supersonic targets from high level down to the very lowest level.

Two basic types of attack are practised: the "bracket" and the "single-side offset". The bracket is a "pincer" approach against the enemy formation, with the pair splitting and coming at the formation at a slant angle, from both sides at once, and then turning to seek an opportunity to use their AIM-9L Sidewinder short-range IR-homing AAMs – "Fox Two". Dependent on weapons available and the size of the target formation, the Tornados may turn "down threat" to engage further targets. If, during any ensuing melee, a target crosses the Tornado's path, then the internal 27mm Mauser cannon allows a "Fox Three" (gunfire) opportunity. However, the Tornado is not an air combat fighter and, according to Rowley, "turning-and-burning is considered foolhardy in the extreme". Very simply, he would prefer to score "kills" in the BVR mode, effectively using hit-and-run tactics.

The single-side offset keeps the pair together on one side of the enemy formation but, again, they approach on the slant, launch Sky Flash BVR, and break away. The one tactic he cautions against adopting is the close-in attack which can leave the attacking fighter vulnerable to the radar-guided guns of the bombers or present a tempting target to any self-defence AAMs or forward-firing guns which aircraft, such as the "Fencer", might carry.

Where fighters are involved, the tactics are basically the same as for bombers but the paired, single-side offset is preferred. The Tornado aircrew with whom the author spoke preferred to approach these targets fast, engage the fighters at the greatest-possible range, invariably BVR, and break-away. Again, it was emphasised that the Tornado is not a close-combat fighter but, rather, a long-range bomber-destroyer.

The author was fortunate to be the first journalist to fly in an operational squadron Tornado F3 to see for himself the capability of the RAF's latest interceptor. On a sunny but incredibly cold day in November 1988, he presented himself at RAF Coningsby and was met by Sqn Ldr Clive Rowley, "A" Flight Commander on No 5 Squadron, which had only been officially re-formed on the Tornado F3 on 1 January that year, being declared Combat Ready on 1 May. (It was good to renew the acquaintance with Clive

Left: The first operational Panavia Tornado F3 unit in the RAF was No 29 Squadron, based at Coningsby, seen here four days before being declared to NATO air defence duties on 1 November 1987. (Author)

Rowley as he and the author had been at Bournemouth School together many years previously.)

Once escorted to the squadron's dispersal area, a collection of hardened aircraft shelters on the far side of the airfield, I was kitted out with the paraphernalia of modern fast-jet flying clothing: long johns, thick socks, polo-neck sweater, anti-g trousers, flying suit, one-piece immersion suit, life preserver (Mae West to the old-and-bold), boots, gloves and a Mk 4 flying helmet (otherwise universally known as the "bone-dome"). Once kitted out, Clive and I were able to talk about their aircraft, tactics and the planned flight for the next day.

Clive explained that the squadron was equipped with the latest standard Tornado F3s in RAF service. They were fitted with the current Z-list AI24 Foxhunter airborne interception radar and, as he emphasised, there were no longer any "Blue Circle" Tornados in the RAF. (A reference to initial Tornado F2/F3s being fitted with concrete nose weights, pending delivery of AI24.) The aircraft also have the current Operational Flight Programme (OFP) in the main computer and the latest software for the Missile Management System (MMS) plus full monochrome video recording facilities for the radar and the head-up display (HUD).

The Tornado, it was explained, is a highly-computerised aircraft, practically all its avionics having built-in test equipment (BITE) which allows the groundcrew to check systems fully before and after flight. Indeed, if the BITE does not show a "clean bill of health" on check-out, the aircraft is not flown, whether the air or ground crew find the faults themselves or not! However, the equipment is generally very serviceable and pre-flight aborts are not common.

The aircraft's performance and capabilities can be greatly improved by updating the on-board software. Changes are constantly being made to improve these. Clive volunteered examples of the rate of progress in this field. Since November 1987 (when the first No 5 Squadron crews began to convert onto type) they have experienced three changes to the OFP and two to the MMS software, which have altered controls and presentations and improved capabilities. Further software changes were, he told me, "in the pipeline" to further improve the OFP, the MMS, the radar data processor (RDP), the digital engine control unit (DECU), the command stability augmentation system (CSAS) and the spin prevention

and incidence limiting system (SPILS). The latter system will allow the aircraft to operate to its full aerodynamic limits safely.

"With the SPILS system", Clive told me, "it is almost impossible to 'depart' the aeroplane with mishandling. It does actually limit the [angle of] incidence the aeroplane can pull." Warming to his subject, he continued: "The SPILS is a completely carefree handling system – you can pull as hard as you want and you can do what you like with the controls. The system will prevent the controls from working if it thinks they shouldn't." By way of example, Clive explained it is impossible to perform the classic "slow roll" in a Tornado F3. "To do a slow roll, as you get round to the 90-degree bank point, particularly the latter part, you put on top rudder to keep the nose up. If you put top rudder on in the Tornado, it says 'no – you're cross-controlled, you don't want that'. You cannot actually do a proper slow roll on this aeroplane."

Although the squadron's aircraft are hardwired for the automatic wing-sweep (AWS) and manoeuvre devices system facilities, the software was (at the time of my visit) not yet available from BAe. The squadron expected its aircraft to be equipped with this facility by the first half of 1989.

The next tranche of aircraft to be delivered to Coningsby in mid-1989 were to be Block 13 Tornados with the improved Stage 1 AI24 radars. These aircraft have improved HOTAS controls for the pilot (using the same stick top as the F-18 Hornet and AV-8B Harrier GR5), an improved radar hand controller for the navigator and other minor systems improvements.

The next day, after taking almost 45min to "suit-up" in all the gear, I joined Clive and the other aircrew for our sortie brief. Conducted by the sortie leader, pilot Flt Lt Mick Mercer (teamed with Flt Lt Clive Duance as his "directional consultant") – callsign "Maple One" – we were briefed as a four-ship formation, splitting into two pairs to fight our little war and demonstrate the way in which the Tornado is operated.

Clive Rowley and I were to be Mick's wingman "Maple Two", while the second pair were crewed by "the Boss" – Wg Cdr Euan Black with Sqn Ldr John Middleton ("Maple Three"), and Sqn Ldr Rowley Tomlin with Flt Lt Mike Huffington as "Maple Four". It is interesting to note that officers Duance and Huffington were both "ab initio" navigators on their first operational tours. The remainder of the aircrew were either ex-Lightning or Phantom crews. The first 10 aircrew on No 5 Squadron had previous air defence experience on these two types or the Tornado GR1. After May 1988, a further four aircrews joined the squadron and these were all "first tourists" direct from the OCU.

The usual string of radio frequencies for ourselves and the various air traffic control authorities under whose control we would fly, together with weather conditions, air-space restrictions and diversions were disseminated. The scenario for the various combat air patrols was revealed as preventing a formation of "Fencer-Ds" from hitting a nuclear power station at Edinburgh. Our CAP rendezvous point was St Abb's Head and the CAP (Maple One and Two) was just inland of this. Maple Three and Four were to play the part of the "Fencers". Rules of engagement were then agreed as well as the universal disengagement call of "knock it off"!

We walked out to our aircraft which were sitting in one of the squadron's hardened aircraft shelters – referred to by all crews as HAS, pronounced "haz". Once in the HAS, while Clive made the external checks and signed the Form 700, my backseat "minder", Flt Lt Gerry Simm, made the navigator's front-seat checks and then, with external power fed into the aircraft, aligned the inertial navigation system (INS) – twin Ferranti FIN 1010 sets – by the two-minute rapid align mode, having had the statutory 12min full align prior to our arrival. I was then, strap by strap, connector by connector, "screwed into" Tornado F3 ZE763, coded "Charlie Delta".

While Clive strapped himself into the front and began his pre-start checks, I had an opportunity to take in my surroundings. The Tornado's rear cockpit is dominated by two cathode ray tubes (CRTs) for the radar and other displays but was still the most roomy "fast jet" in which I have ever flown. There was even a little "cubby-hole" in which to stow my camera. I took particular note of the IFF frequency dial, which I was to use later during the flight and satisfied myself I could set the codes as instructed. I also noted the switches to re-cycle the CRTs and computers, in the unlikely event we should experience an in-flight failure.

The external APU provided power to start the starboard engine which, by use of a cross-drive, was then able to start the port engine. Before doing this, however, the con-

trol surfaces on the wings – flaps, slats, spoilers, et al – were checked with the groundcrew, who were still connected by intercom line to the aircraft. The port engine was then started and the intercom line disconnected.

With a final reminder that the aircraft had a "command ejection" system, whereby if Clive felt that we and the aircraft needed to part company, by activating his own "bang-seat" I would be leaving the aircraft 0.4 of a second in advance of him, with the canopy closed. The wings were swept and we taxied clear of the HAS. Outside the wings went forward again. Pre take-off checks completed (usually called by the navigator with the pilot responding), on Clive's instruction I withdrew the ejection seat safety pin and stowed it safely in its appointed place on the canopy framing. The Martin-Baker Mk 10A zero-zero ejection seat was now "live". We checked in with air traffic control and awaited the order to taxi.

For a modern jet fighter, with both engines running, I was surprised by the relative "quiet" inside the cockpit. This feature of the Tornado design has been much publicised and I, for one, can vouch for its authenticity.

Once the order came we began to move forward, threading our way around the HAS complex, coming out behind "Maple One" heading towards the runway. At this stage the exhaust nozzles of the two RB199 engines were in "taxi" mode, to reduce the high residual thrust at idle, while the nose-wheel steering was in high gear. The planned pairs take-off was almost immediate, following the final checks. The engines were wound up to full cold power and a quick visual check of the engine instrumentation made. Clive gave Maple One a "thumbs-up" and engaged afterburner at 50% reheat. The leader, Maple One, tapped his helmet and then nodded. At this signal, Clive engaged 80% reheat and took the brakes off. We rolled forward and with the ASI indicating some 135kts, the nosewheel lifted and we took off at some 150kts. The undercarriage was immediately retracted and as our speed passed 215kts, we retracted the flaps and at 300kts cancelled the afterburner.

We climbed away as a pair to flight level 165 (ie, 16,500ft) on a heading of 340 degrees, heading north, and split to "battle" formation with about a nautical mile separation. Almost immediately we then closed up again to penetrate cloud. Although we could not see them, the second pair were "tied-on" behind, following us on their radars. During the transit north, we were under the control of Midland Radar and then handed on to Newcastle Radar for our descent to 6,000ft. At this stage, Maples Three and Four split away, preparatory to playing the role of "bad guys" while we continued up to an area northwest of Berwick-on-Tweed and set up our CAP which, due to the weather, was below the cloudbase at some 2,000ft.

At this point, it must be noted that one vital item in our aircraft was inoperative – the AI24 Foxhunter radar. As my flight was "unclassified", higher authorities had instructed the radar was not to be used on our aircraft. For the purposes of the exercise, the radar had "gone down" and we relied on information transmitted verbally over the RT – an artificial situation for my benefit only. In war, should this situation arise, there are pre-determined visual signals to use. For the record, however, the following description of the use of the radar is given.

As already noted, the navigator's station in the Tornado F3 is dominated by two side-by-side, multi-function CRT displays (MFDs) in the main instrument panel, with a number of key-pads below, offering a selection of display modes. The row of soft-keys under the MFD control the display; the row below those are hard-keys for basic mode options.

These key-pads are the interface between the navigator (effectively the Weapons System Operator – WSO) and the integrated navigation/attack system. The bottom line of alphanumerics on the CRT denotes soft-key functions, while the row above is the data readout/input line.

In the pilot's cockpit, a single cathode ray tube (CRT) – known as the electronic heads-down display – is available for displaying a repeat of either of the two WSO displays or the pilot's own attack format. Weapon-aiming and navigation symbology is projected on to the pilot's HUD, together with basic flight information symbology.

The navigator begins his search with the baseline computer-generated display of range/azimuth "search". The plots are displayed as short vertical lines plus a horizontal crossbar to indicate a confirmed IFF response. The target is designated by using the joystick to move a four-quadrant marker around the plot. The target will now be automatically tracked and the display format can be changed to "track-while-scan".

At the top of the screen, the aircraft's ground speed is shown, together with the aircraft heading and the height. Each confirmed track is displayed by a vector with either a number or letter coding. Numbers indicate friendly while letters indicate hostile targets crossing left-to-right. The boxed track indicates the target is being tracked by memory. The length of each vector is proportional to the target groundspeed and the direction is track relative to the Tornado F3.

The velocity/azimuth display shows target velocity up the left-hand axis while other axes are unchanged. Each target is shown as three horizontal bars, known as a "triplet", and the closeness of the bars indicates the distance to the target. The navigator can then look at a north-orientated battle plan – which the author was allowed to observe during the flight. This is basically a "window-on-the-world" plan view showing all radar and data-link tracks, plus the Tornado's position. It allows the navigator to select the first target for attack.

Moving to the attack display mode, the navigator selects his weapon – currently a Sky Flash MRAAM – and the target is illuminated by the Tornado's continuous wave (CW) signal. Further symbology is displayed on the screen: an "aim dot" shows the course to steer for a collision course with the target while a larger circle shows the allowable steering error (ASE), the diameter of which is dependant on the missile seeker gimbal limits and range to target. Launch success zones are shown on the right of the screen with maximum and minimum launch ranges. Memory tracking aids the re-acquisition of other targets after a launch, thus permitting a rapid sequence of attacks.

While the navigator is handling the weapon system, the pilot manages the attack sequence, re-designating if necessary. An air-to-air override switch on the throttles can be used if close-combat occurs. This throws all systems into the attack mode for instant reaction: the radar rapidly scans across the 20-degree HUD field of view, locking on to the first detected target and providing aiming cues for the Sidewinder SRAAM.

Compared with the now-ancient AI23 of the Lightning fighters, the AI24 Foxhunter, even before the Stage 1 and 2 improvements (now implemented), represents a great leap forward for the RAF air defender.

Meanwhile in the back seat, my two MFDs were displaying a repeat of the HUD symbology and the navigation plan situation. I had previously been shown how to move this around and change the range scale, so that Clive, when he called this mode up on his own CRT, had the required information. Adopting a one-minute racetrack CAP, we went into "battle" formation, flying at 2,500ft and at some 450kts. At Clive's instruction, I dialled up an IFF code into our transponder.

Maple One picked up our targets on the second turn-in and brought us in on a "sweep right" against them, calling "Fox One" on the leader. With no radar, the best we could do was use the Sidewinder acquisition round, carried as routine on training sorties such as this, and hope that the enemy IR signature would be picked up. Fortunately for Edinburgh, it was. Turning in low over the Northumbrian hills, we spotted an aircraft flashing in across our starboard quarter and we pulled round onto it, Clive using the boresight mode on his HUD and cueing the Sidewinder. The growl in my headset suddenly changed to a chirp and Clive called "Fox Two" on Maple Four. The engagement took as long to complete as you have taken to read this paragraph aloud.

Someone called "knock it off" over the RT and I reset the IFF dial. The four aircraft joined up in formation and headed east out over the North Sea to look for our tanker. Although we were not carrying drop tanks, and we had sufficient fuel to return to base then, we were intending to make a fast run and engage in further air combat. I had, anyway, requested a tanker "hook-up" to experience this aspect of Tornado operations. (Over the last 12 years, two previous attempts to experience air-to-air refuelling (AAR) had been aborted at the last minute – in flight – for operational reasons. Third time lucky, I hoped.)

Maple One conducted the RT communication with the tanker and discovered that, whereas on briefing we had expected a Victor K2, this had become a VC10 K2 of No 101 Squadron. It was on-line and trailing hoses from both its Mk 32 underwing pods. Maple One approached the starboard drogue. Even with a navigator in the back to monitor his approach, he did not connect first time. "Nervousness in front of an audience," chuckled Clive. He connected at the second attempt. We approached, and as I was too busy with my camera to offer any advice on the "hook-up", Clive fell back on his Lightning experience and connected the probe first time.

While the fuel flowed from tanker to Tornado, I gazed up at the enormous fin and up-swept tailplane of the VC10. It was a surprisingly smooth ride and, almost before I realised it, we had disengaged after taking on 3,000kg of fuel. Backing off, but formating to starboard of the tanker, the second pair came up to refuel. I was busy with my camera again.

The use of AAR for air defence forces has been SOP (standard operating procedure) with the RAF (and other air forces) for many years. The RAF has the technique down to a fine art and, while it is not without its pitfalls to the inexperienced, it is not a complicated procedure. The RAF (and virtually every other air force which has tanking capability, with the notable exception of the USAF) uses the "hose-and-drogue" technique, developed over the years by Flight Refuelling. The RAF's VC10 and TriStar tanker fleets are equipped with the company's hose drum units or Mk 32 pods.

Once we had all refuelled, our aircraft broke away and headed towards the lower levels. Clive had intended to demonstrate the Tornado's acceleration to me at low-level over the sea but the cloud base limited this to 2,000ft (which to an "air defender" is still "low-level"). Maple One tagged along, somewhat higher, monitoring the events below.

Slowing down to 350kts, with wings fully forward, Clive headed east over the North Sea as aircraft are not allowed to go supersonic while heading towards the coast. When ready, including a check with Boulmer radar, he moved the throttles forward into reheat and then combat power. This setting allows a little "extra" thrust to be used for a limited period of time, measured in minutes.

The acceleration was initially noticeable but as the speed increased and because of the lack of any visual references, it soon passed away. At 450kts, Clive swept the wings to 45 degrees, going to full 67-degree sweep at 550kts. At 700kts, with the Machmeter reading 1.15, he throttled back to idle. The Tornado was still accelerating and it took some time for the inertia to fall off and the aircraft to slow down.

As the speed dropped, so Clive bought the wings gradually forward. While having to do this manually, he told me it becomes almost "automatic" in his control actions. However, once the autowing-sweep is available, it will be one less "housekeeping" action to worry about in a combat situation.

So with the demonstration completed, we rejoined Maple One and set off down the North Sea to practice BVR interceptions, setting up a maritime CAP against Maple Three and Four. Again, I dialled up the IFF transponder code. With only one radar operational between the two of us, our effectiveness was limited but in two engagements we managed one "Fox Two". Visual contact, from my viewpoint, was always well after the shots had been called.

After two attempts at being the defender, we next became the target. It was pointed out, afterwards, that the only RWR contact the enemy should receive would be the lock-on from the AI24 radar and destruction of the target would then be some 10secs away.

Once again we became the hunters and in the ensuing interception, Maple Three passed Maple One before he could lock-on. The tactical situation then demanded he killed Maple Four, which was accomplished almost simulataneously by a "Fox One" from Maple One and "Fox Two" from us. Maple One then used the Tornado's acceleration to come up behind Maple Three to deliver another "Fox One".

At debrief, afterwards, it was explained that the intruders, flying at 4,000ft and some 560kts against an overcast sky, saw our single-side offset approach and cut in burners. Maple One's radar sorted the targets and although he thought he'd locked-on to the lead ship, it was in fact the wingman. In Maple Two, we were able to "fire" our Sidewinder from the beam in look-down/shoot-down mode. Clive explained the sequence of events.

"As the AIM-9 Lima variant of Sidewinder has virtually an all-aspect capability, I uncaged the seeker-head of the missile (in this case, of the acquisition round) by use of the Target Acquisition Enable button on the control column. This allows it to follow what it thinks it's targeting. A solid diamond appeared in the HUD, indicating a good lock-on (if it continues to track the target) and the growl in the headset turns to a chirp. Then you just pull the trigger and the missile is launched."

During our various combats, it was interesting to note that Clive's comment about not "turning-and-burning" was borne out. When turning we pulled a maximum of 4g, usually only 3 to 3.5g. Neither did we go visual until, as already noted, the missile shots had been called. I was assured that

events were not stage-manged for my benefit and I was suitably impressed.

So, with combat behind us and my breakfast still in my stomach, we began our return to base in an open "battle" card formation a mile square, to a pre-planned recovery position. While transiting back, the IFF code was returned to its original setting. After crossing the south Lincolnshire coast, we went into "arrow" formation for the run-in over Coningsby (at 400kts and 45 degrees of sweep). In turn, we broke to port and made our landing circuit.

There was to be a final demonstration of the Tornado's capability in store for me. We overshot the landing to allow Maples Three and Four to land and went around again. Clive put the wings forward as the speed reduced and made the final checks – flaps down, gear down. Full flap on "finals" – 180kts with some 10-15 degrees angle of attack – and made our final approach at 153kts.

In his final checks, Clive had pre-armed the lift-dump spoilers on the wings for activating on main-wheel impact. As we touched the ground, they deployed and as soon as the nosewheel contacted terra firma, Clive rocked the right-hand throttle outboard to activate the reverse thrust buckets on the engines, and wound them up to full cold power. Despite there being a 15kt crosswind over the runway, our landing was very stable and we "ground" to a halt within 2,500ft without recourse to the brakes. "No hassle," commented Clive laconically as we taxied forward. Later, he compared the worry-free landing characteristics, which he described as "one of the best parts of the Tornado". Landing the Lightning, at night on a short wet runway with a crosswind could be, he confided, "at the least, tricky, and at the worst, plain frightening. The Tornado makes it easy."

The port engine was shut-down as we taxied back to the HAS where we turned to present our tail to the doors. The wings were swept to 67 degrees and the tailhook (used for emergency arrested landings only) was lowered. Ejection seat safety pins were inserted while a winch cable was hooked onto the tailhook and the aircraft gently pulled back into the HAS. There the starboard engine was shut-down and the process of extracting myself from the back seat began. We had been airborne for 2hrs 20mins.

Of course, I had just flown a training air defence exercise sortie in the middle of the "raging peace". Clive explained the ways in which this sortie would have differed, had we been at war.

"Obviously when we scrambled to take-off, it would be at some sort of short notice. On arrival of the aircrew duty shift, they would go out to the aeroplane and check it all out, in its entirety in its shelter. Run the APU (auxiliary power unit), run one engine, check out the radar, the missiles. Everything would be up-and-running, the inertial 'navs' would be aligned. Everything would be made ready to go and then we close it all down, ready to start at a moment's notice. The crew then wait: either in the management cabin inside the HAS or, if required, at cockpit readiness. Either way we are listening to the telebrief, which is a land-line connecting us to our Wing operations centre or the SOC (Sector Operations Centre).

"We sit and listen for an incoming message, which would be something like 'Coningsby, Neatishead' and wait for the response. 'Neatishead, Coningsby – go ahead.' 'Coningsby, Neatishead – alert two Tornados.' At this point, our Wing operations centre allocates the callsigns for the next two guys who are due to go. They say 'Call-signs, five-one, five-two.' 'Roger' says Neatishead. 'Callsigns five-one and five-two ...' and they start giving you a scramble instruction.

"The moment they do, the pilots are out of the door of the management cabin (if they weren't already) and the navigators jot down the information. 'Callsigns five-one and five-two, you are to vector zero-six-zero, climb Angels one-five-zero, call Neatishead on TAD (a frequency code) one-two-six, back-up, zero-eight-seven, for CAP Foxtrot Four – scramble, scramble, scramble.'

"You start up – rapidly. In these circumstances, it would take you two or three minutes from being outside the cockpit to being ready to taxi; if you're inside the cockpit, even less time. You have already done all the checks we went through. The inertial 'navs' have been rapidly aligned, you start the engines, sweep the wings and then go. You are going to be airborne in 10-15 minutes-ish, less if you're in the aircraft. It depends on how far away you are from the end of the runway – taxying time is the major factor. The next difference is that you don't sit on the end of the runway doing engine checks. You turn on to the runway and do a rolling take-off and go. Most of our departures from the airfield on exercise or in war are reheat climbs away from the airfield. You get away quicker.

"As far as the sortie content itself is concerned, it's really not much different, to be honest. Once we're out there operating, like today, we do things pretty much the same as we do in a war scenario. We use the R/T a lot less – we do talk to GCI (Ground Controlled Interception) and each other but we keep it short and sharp. As far as ECM is concerned, one sort of jamming we expect to come up against is comms jamming. There probably isn't enough power (in the enemy ECM aircraft) for them to jam a lot of frequencies the whole time, powerfully. A better way for them to do it is to have a jammer that can find the frequencies being used and jam that frequency. So, if you chatter away on a frequency, they are going to find it and jam it. If you say things in short, sharp bursts, the chances are that they're not going to find out that frequency is in use.

"In a lot of what we do, we don't need to say anything at all. We can still get on and do the job; we're used to doing it without talking to one another. The other thing I can say, in general terms, is that we've got to have procedures so that we don't get shot down by our own side – aircraft or missiles."

"Once back on the ground," Clive concluded, "it is exactly the way we did it. We practice it every day, the way we do it in war. The 'hot winch' back into the HAS, one engine running (but shut-down once inside) and get back under cover as quickly as we can. We would leave everything running, with external power from the Houchin GPU [ground power unit] so that we can, as quickly as possible, get re-fuelled, re-armed and go again. There is no time limit between engine shut-down and re-start. No problems there. The one thing that does slow us down, at the start of the sorties, is that long time to align the inertial 'navs', but once it has had the full align it can be shut down and rapid-aligned again within seconds."

The lasting impression from my visit to, and flight with, No 5 Squadron was that, at last, the RAF has an interceptor that gives it effective reach out into the UK's air defence zone. Despite being unable to see the effectiveness of its radar for myself, one gets the impression from the aircrew that they are happy with the current standard and will be even happier when the Stage One modifications are incorporated. Stage Two mods should send them into raptures.

An aspect of the armament which gave me slight cause for concern: the need to use CW-illumination once a Sky Flash missile is launched, which must be locked-on to the target until missile impact. The anticipated advent of the AIM-120 AMRAAM in the mid-1990s, with its own active-seeker head, would have allowed a "fire-and-forget" operation. Unfortunately, in 1992, the MoD declared that the AIM-120 would not, now, be procured for the Tornado F3, due to the changing world circumstances and the need to save money. BAe has made an unsolicited proposal to upgrade the Sky Flash missiles to Active Sky Flash configuration, with a new seeker and electronics. As at July 1993, the outcome of this was unknown.

On the EW side, we enter contentious territory. The full ECCM capability of the AI24 radar was not explained to me, neither was the use of the ARI1824/1 radar homing and warning receiver. What I could not help but notice was the apparent lack of any chaff or flare dispenser visible on the Tornados which I saw at Coningsby.

One of the first items of equipment installed on the Tornado F3s deployed from the UK to Saudi Arabia in August 1991 was the Tracor ALE-40 chaff/flare dispenser, which was later changed to a Vinten VICON 78 Series 210 unit. Further details are carried in the 1993 "Snapshot".

From the aircrew point of view, the Tornado F3 is streets ahead of the previous genre. It is comfortable to sit in and the background noise is almost non-existent. The systems appear to work well and are respected by the crews. It is, in short, "user-friendly". However, one must add a proviso and that is the use of so much high technology – there are something like 19 on-board computers – and BITE might cause some embarrassment over logistics in a war situation. We have no doubt that the stringent peacetime safety margins (quite rightly observed) can be trimmed for operational use and there are "electronic shortcuts" which can be fed into the system to keep the aircraft flying in war.

Overall, the British taxpayers can rest re-assured that their new fighter is an effective weapons system for its task. Coupled with a highly-dedicated operational team of air and ground crew, it will do a good job. There are improvements already planned (an active missile – perhaps, further radar enhancements and the provision of a secure data link, to mention but three) and once these have been incorporated, the Tornado F3 will be an even better long-range bomber destroyer. The *Statement on the Defence Estimates for 1981* put an estimated price-tag of £314.3 million on the Tornado F2 (as it then was); in 1993 money this must be close to £17 million. Expensive it may be, but the Tornado F3 is surely an interceptor with impact.

IMPRESSIONS OF THE HAWK T1A

"Hostile, hostile – Jag!" The words came over the intercom from one of the two F-4J(UK) Phantoms of No 74 Squadron we were sharing the combat air patrol (CAP) duty with. Our Hawk immediately went into a 4g lefthand diving turn (called a conversion by the aircrew) heading towards the "Orange Force" Jaguar now clearly visible, streaking at low level towards the coast. Capturing it in our gunsight, we called "Fox 2" – a simulated Sidewinder missile launch – and another of today's "bad guys" was wiped off the tote board. I was experiencing the RAF's Mixed Fighter Force concept from the back seat of an Hawk T1A trainer (being flown in its point-defence role) over the North Sea during Exercise "Elder Forest" in April 1988.

Before recounting the experience itself, it is worth recording the details of the exercise. Designed to test the ability of the RAF to defend the UK from sustained air attack, Exercise "Elder Forest 88" was one of the largest air defence exercises to be mounted over Great Britain. Between 18 and 21 April 1988, aircraft from 10 nations operating from bases throughout northern Europe flew over 1,000 separate low- and medium-level sorties against RAF airfields, missile sites, radar stations and training ranges.

Defending these targets were all the UK-based air defence fighter squadrons (flying Lightning F6s, Phantom FG1/FGR2 as well as F-4J (UK) plus Tornado F3s), and the Tactical Weapons Unit (TWU) Hawks in their war-role and USAF F-5Es (more used to acting as "Aggressors") based at Alconbury in the UK. These "Blue Force" assets were supported by Victor K2, VC10 K2/3 and TriStar K1 tankers, Shackleton AEW2 and NATO E-3A Sentry airborne early warning aircraft. On the ground, Bloodhound and Rapier SAM units protected key installations. Even the Royal Navy lent a hand, providing two Type 42 destroyers to operate in their air defence role: HMS *Newcastle* to cover the northern sector of the North Sea, HMS *Southampton* to cover the southern sector.

Above: The BAe Hawk T1A of No 151 Squadron from Chivenor, in which the author took part in Exercise "Elder Forest" as part of the Mixed Fighter Force with No 74 Squadron in April 1988. (Author)

The "bad guys" (or "Orange Forces" as they are known in exercises) were drawn from RAF strike/attack squadrons equipped with the Jaguar GR1, Tornado GR1, Buccaneer S2 and Harrier GR3 as well as target facility squadrons equipped with Canberra B2, T17A and TT18. NATO air forces contributed aircraft for the strike packages as well. The long distances over unfamiliar territory was as good a training for them as it was for the RAF fighters. From Belgium came F-16s and Mirage Vs; Canadian CF-18 Hornets; Jaguars, Mirage F1s and Mirage IVPs from France; Alpha Jets, RF-4E Phantoms and Tornado IDS from Germany; F-16s and Drakens from Denmark; Dutch F-16s; Norwegian DA-20 Falcon ECM trainers; Italian PD-808 EW trainers; and from the USAF in Europe, A-10 Thunderbolts, EF-111A Ravens, F-111E/Fs and EC-130H Hercules.

The targets for the "Orange Forces" included all major fighter airfields and diversions in the UK, plus the radar stations and missile sites around eastern England and Scotland. Once they had "attacked" their targets, these strike aircraft continued to a variety of ranges to drop practice weapons and ensure full training value for the flight.

Organising a major "war" under peace-time constraints is a complex task and can take a team of staff officers anything up to two years. The purpose of the task must be identified and then the units, for whose benefit the exercise is arranged, allocated and advised. Rules must be written and directing staff at all levels appointed. After the event, the analysis of an exercise like "Elder Forest" also takes time, in order to extract the full implications.

Wg Cdr Tony Hughes-Lewis, who was responsible for the co-ordination of CINC UK Air and HQ Strike Command in all multi-role NATO and national exercises, was able to outline some immediate lessons which emerged. "The benefits of close liaison between the SOCs (Sector Operation Centres) and the Type 42 DDGs operating in the air defence role were highlighted," he told me, "and we will continue to refine the joint procedures which effectively extend the land-based Air Defence Ground Environment system."

"The SOC procedures are well established but need to be continually modified to allow not only for the air defence ships but also for the integration of MFF tactics and the introduction of the E-3 aircraft into RAF service." (The RAF aircraft, designated Sentry AEW1, are E-3D models, which are different to the E-3A used by NATO AEW Force.) Wg Cdr Hughes-Lewis continued: "The (NATO) E-3A in the exercise was most valuable and the MFF concept, once again, proved its worth as a means of concentrating forces within the UK Air Defence Region. The combination of the TriStar tanker and Tornado F3 made a most satisfactory debut in an operational environment," he concluded.

So much for the overview, back to the action. It was the last day of the "war", and I was acting the part of a re-inforcement Hawk pilot flying his first combat mission in a BAe Hawk T1A of No 151 Squadron. From No 2 Tactical Weapons Unit, RAF Chivenor, the Hawk was being used in its war role, theoretically armed with a pair of AIM-9L Sidewinder air-to-air missiles and a single 30mm ADEN cannon, but not carried in practice on this occasion. Together with a pair of McDonnell Douglas F-4J(UK) Phantoms of No 74 Squadron from RAF Wattisham, two Hawks from Chivenor were working as part of the MFF concept in defence of UK air space. After the action described above, we recovered to our CAP height of 6,000ft over Blakeney Point off the north Norfolk coast. I pondered that, for a trainer, this Hawk had effective teeth.

The concept of the MFF is a simple but effective use of available resources to increase the efficiency of the RAF's dedicated air defence force of Phantom FG1s and FGR2s, Tornado F3s and, until they were withdrawn (early in 1988), the Lightning F6.

Some 88 Hawk trainers have been given the capability to carry a pair of AIM-9L Sidewinder AAMs, in addition to their existing gun armament, being designated Hawk T1A. With no radar system they are, in effect, dayfighters in the traditional Second World War role, not unlike the Hunter F6. However, pair the Hawk with a radar-equipped fighter in a team, usually two Hawks to one fighter, and the air defence commander has increased his airborne assets considerably.

By using the fighters to detect "incoming strike packages" – during our sortie USAF A-10s, RAF Harriers and Jaguars – the fighters can launch their BVR AIM-7 Sparrow or Sky Flash radar-guided AAMs at the enemy interdictors, warn off the Hawks, who then turn (convert) onto the survivors. Being more manoeuvrable than, in this case, the Phantoms, the chances of attriting the enemy increases.

Should the enemy fly a covering force of escort fighters in advance of their strike aircraft, the Hawks can be converted onto the escorts, leaving the Phantoms or Tornados to deal with the more dangerous strike aircraft before they can deliver their ordnance. The beauty of the concept is that, once the inevitable dogfight has been resolved, the Hawks can return to the CAP rendezvous and pair off with the first radar-equipped fighters to appear and, thus, start all over again.

The MFF Hawk pilots are drawn from the TWU instructor staff for their war role and they all practise standard operating procedures (SOPs) with all types of fighter assigned to the Air Defence Force. These work down to basic airborne signals in the event of communications jamming from the enemy, using aircraft attitude to indicate the vector and direction in which to intercept.

The flexibility of operations is illustrated by the experience of the detachment operating from Wattisham the day before. Having been despatched on CAP, they were recovered to Coningsby (Tornado F3s) and Binbrook (Lightnings) and flew MMF sorties with all three aircraft types during the day. My pilot, Flt Lt Mark Tutton, had been airborne for a total of six hours during his day, only recovering back to Wattisham at the end of his last sortie. This, he told me, was typical when flying the MFF scenario.

The MFF concept is not new and can be traced back to the Second World War, when Hurricane nightfighters were paired with Blenheims equipped with early examples of airborne interception (AI) radar. During the late 1950s and into the early 1960s, radar-equipped Javelins supplied similar information to Hunter dayfighters.

Meanwhile, back on "Elder Forest", our collective tally appeared to be four Jaguars out of four: two to the Phantoms, one each to the Hawks. Later, on debrief, it appeared one Jaguar might have slipped through out net as both Phantoms apparently fired on the same aircraft. "C'est la guerre," one of the two Phantoms crews later remarked. He also noted that our confusion on debrief could have been clarified had we been operating in an Air Combat Manoeuvring Instrumentation (ACMI) range, all participants being equipped with ACMI equipment recording our every move for replay later. "This," he said, "is the beauty of ACMI".

Returning to the CAP location, we flew an elongated north-south "racetrack" circuit over Blakeney Point. Before turning south (away from the incoming raids), the Phantoms' radar checked the sky ahead for intruders. We also had communication with the SOC at Neatishead and although there was an airborne early warning E-3A Sentry operating over the North Sea, it was supervising a "live" search-and-rescue (SAR) operation for the crew of a Leuchars-based Phantom FG1 which had ditched the day before and was, thus, otherwise engaged.

Our next contact came some 15mins later, initially detected at 45 miles by one of the Phantoms, coming in at low level. On the next north-bound leg of our CAP it was identified as a pair of tracks at 30 miles and we descended to intercept. As we drew closer, it appeared we were offset slightly to the left of the pair of what were now identified as Harriers. One of them was dealt with by a "Fox 1" – a simulated Sparrow launch –

but one escaped. We were still expecting a second pair and the Phantoms left the Harrier, which had slipped through the first line of defence, to the Hawks – "easy meat" it was considered.

As we peeled-off onto the Harrier, a Tornado F3 – apparently totally unaware of our presence – appeared to port and began converting on one of the Phantoms. A timely call of "friendly, friendly" prevented "Blue Force" attaining an "own goal". The artificiality of the exercise accounted for the appearance of the Tornado, as in the "real thing" IFF would have identified us, one to the other.

In the meantime, we had come in on the Harrier's "seven o'clock" and Mark called "Fox 3", simulating a gun attack on the aircraft. I was too busy working my camera, weighing three times its normal weight as a result of g-forces from the manoeuvring to keep behind the jinking Harrier, to align my head with the gunsight and check. However, through the camera lens, we appeared to have been within range and on target for more than enough time for a real intruder to have been "splashed".

After just over an hour on CAP, with fuel running low, we handed over to another set of fighters and Hawks. Recovering to Wattisham, we made a straight-in long approach and landing. According to the exercise scenario, Wattisham had received a nuclear strike and we should have recovered directly into a hardened aircraft shelter (HAS) and donned NBC equipment on opening the canopy. As it was, we went "outside" the exercise after landing and stopped on the hardstanding outside a HAS. After walking through the "raging peace", as we re-entered the squadron's hardened operations centre, everyone inside was masked-up in NBC gear. The ENDEX signal was not due for another hour!

As far as the Hawk T1A's effectiveness as part of the MFF is concerned, its performance as a "force multiplier" had been ably demonstrated. It is, however, interesting to note a groundswell of opinion among the TWU pilots at that time. They would have been happier pursuing their war-role with the single-seat Hawk 200. As a great proportion of TWU work is conducted solo by the students, were this version of the Hawk to be procured by the RAF, the benefits to the MFF would be great.

Equipped with a lightweight radar and, having four wing pylons, the Hawk 200 can carry two drop tanks to allow a four-hour

CAP and using twin Sidewinder launchers on the outerwing pylons, the missile complement would be doubled. With the wingtip Sidewinder fit, six could be carried. However, the "must-have" requirements of other parts of the air defence force preclude the "nice-to-have" wishes of the Hawk MFF pilots, as there is only so much money allocated for the task.

RESPONSE: AAA & SAMs

It was the Falklands campaign of 1982 which saw the re-introduction of the AA gun into RAF service. Concerned over the threat of UK base security from Soviet *Spetznatz* special forces and/or fifth columnists, the RAF began forming Royal Auxiliary Air Force (RAuxAF) Regiment field squadrons on several bases from the early-1980s. The arrival of twin 35mm Oerlikon guns in the UK in early 1983, courtesy of General Galtieri, was taken to improve base air defence at minimum cost.

Meanwhile, missiles continued to form the major proportion of UK AAA. The first Bloodhound Mk 2s from RAF Germany had been returned to the UK in 1982. Having been successfully deployed and used in the Falklands campaign, the decision was made to improve the Rapier system and, in 1986, a contract to develop Rapier 2000 (Field Standard C) was given to BAe Dynamics Group.

Oerlikon-Buhrle Twin 35mm Type GDF

Having captured an almost-complete battery of twin 35mm Oerlikon GDF-002 air defence guns, together with quantities of ammunition, around Port Stanley airfield in June 1982, these "spoils of war" were returned to the UK. It was decided to refurbish and issue the weapons, together with the single Contraves Skyguard radar system captured intact, to the RAuxAF Regiment tasked with base air defence in the UK.

Subsequently refurbished by BMARC (now part of Royal Ordnance), the guns and radar were issued to No 2729 Squadron RAuxAF Regiment, based at RAF Waddington, together with Bedford TM 4x4 MMLC (Medium-Mobility Load Carrier) trucks. The unit was declared operational in April 1985. Although there was sufficient guns to form a second squadron, this would have required the purchase of a second Skyguard radar system. At this time there was not sufficient money in the appropriate

Left: One Skyguard radar was captured after the Falklands campaign and, in 1990, a second was acquired from Oerlikon-Contraves in Switzerland, allowing formation of a second squadron of twin 35mm Oerlikon AA guns. (Oerlikon-Contraves)

Order of Battle – 1988

Strike Command – HQ: High Wycombe, Bucks

No 1 Group – HQ: Upavon, Wilts
(only assets relating to air defence shown)

Sqn	Aircraft	Base
55	Handley Page Victor K2	Marham, Norfolk
101	BAC VC10 K2/K3	Brize Norton, Oxon
216	Lockheed L1011 TriStar K1/KC1/C2	Brize Norton, Oxon

No 11 Group – HQ: Bentley Priory, Stanmore, Middx

Sqn	Aircraft	Base
5	Panavia Tornado F3	Coningsby, Lincs
8	Avro Shackleton AEW2	Lossiemouth, Morayshire
11	BAC Lightning F6 (to May 1988)	Binbrook, Lincs
11	Panavia Tornado F3 (from November 1988)	Leeming, Yorks
23	Panavia Tornado F3 * (from November 1988)	Leeming, Yorks
29	Panavia Tornado F3	Coningsby, Lincs
43	McDD F-4K Phantom FG1	Leuchars, Fife
56	McDD F-4M Phantom FGR2	Wattisham, Suffolk
74	McDD F-4J(UK) Phantom	Wattisham, Suffolk
111	McDD F-4K Phantom FG1	Leuchars, Fife
228 OCU (64 Sqn)	McDD F-4K/M Phantom FG1/FGR2	Leuchars, Fife
229 OCU (65 Sqn)	Panavia Tornado F3	Coningsby, Lincs
79 1TWU	BAe Hawk T1A	Brawdy, Pembroke
234 1TWU	BAe Hawk T1A	
63 2TWU	BAe Hawk T1A	Chivenor, Devon
151 2TWU	BAe Hawk T1A	

budget. This was eventually resolved in 1991 – see next "Snapshot".

Originally developed by Oerlikon (now Oerlikon-Contraves) in the late-1950s, the GDF-002 system was introduced in 1980, comprising two 35mm KDB cannon, the cradle, two automatic ammunition feed mechanisms, the upper mount, lower mount and a Ferranti (now GEC-Ferranti) Type GSA Mk 3 sight, all mounted on a four-wheel towed carriage.

The guns are served by two operating crew and the system has a maximum elevation speed of 56deg/sec and a maximum traverse speed of 112deg/sec. They are capable of firing a range of ammunition including semi armour-piercing high-explosive incendiary (SAPHEI) and high-explosive incendiary (HEI) as well as training ammunition. The system is designed for use with either the Super Fledermaus or Skyguard radar fire control systems developed by sister company, Contraves.

Data

Calibre	35mm
Type of mounting	four-wheeled platform with outriggers
Weight in action	6.3 tons
Max elevation	92°
Effective ceiling	13,000ft
Effective range	2.5 miles
Weight of shell	1.21lb
Type of shell	HE
Muzzle velocity	3,850ft/sec
Rate of fire	550rds/min/barrel

BAe Bloodhound Mk 2

Following the departure of No 25 Squadron to Germany in 1971, the first of the

---

AAA/SAM Units

Unit	Equipment	Base
25 Sqn RAF	BAC Bloodhound 2	HQ: Wyton, Cambs
	A Flt	Barkston Heath, Lincs
	B Flt	Wyton, Cambs
	C Flt	Wattisham, Suffolk
85 Sqn RAF	BAC Bloodhound 2	HQ: West Raynham, Norfolk
	A Flt	West Raynham, Norfolk
	B Flt	North Coates, Lincs
	C Flt	Bawdsey, Suffolk
	D Flt	West Raynham, Norfolk
15 Sqn RAF Regt	BAe Rapier	Leeming, Yorks
19 Sqn ** RAF Regt	BAe Rapier	Brize Norton, Oxon
20 Sqn ** RAF Regt	BAe Rapier	Honington, Suffolk
27 Sqn, RAF Regt	BAe Rapier	Leuchars, Fife
48 Sqn, RAF Regt	BAe Rapier	Lossiemouth, Morayshire
66 Sqn ** RAF Regt	BAe Rapier	West Raynham, Norfolk
2729 Sqn RAuxAF Regt(V)	Oerlikon twin 35mm AA guns /Skyguard	Waddington, Lincs

Notes

* Until 1 November 1988, 23 Sqn flew McDD F-4M Phantom FGR2s from Mount Pleasant airfield, Falkland Islands; this detachment of four aircraft was then re-designated 1435 Flt on the re-formation of 23 Sqn with Tornado F3 in the UK

** These units allocated to defend USAF bases within the UK in time of war

Left: A field of BAe Dynamics Bloodhound 2 SAMs at an airfield "somewhere in the Eastern counties" of England stand guard against intruders. Although a replacement (known as MSAM) was planned, funding difficulties in the light of "Options for Change" looks likely to move this procurement to the right. (BAeD)

Left: The re-intro-
duction of "light flak"
into RAF Regiment
service was made
possible by the cap-
ture of sufficient
twin 35mm Oerlikon
AA guns at Stanley
Airport after the
close of the
Falklands campaign
in 1982. The guns
and their associated
Skyguard radar
were refurbished
before being bought
into service.
(Oerlikon-Contraves)

Germany-based Bloodhounds brought back
to bolster UK defence arrived home in
August 1981 and was based at Wattisham.
This unit, "C" Flt, was temporarily designated as "E" Flt of No 85 Squadron but
handed back to No 25 Squadron in 1983,
when the move of the whole unit was completed. The unit's HQ and "B" Flt were
located at Wyton with "A" Flt at Barkston
Heath and the Wattisham unit became "C"
Flt of No 25 Squadron once more.
Meanwhile, the assets of No 85 Squadron's
"D" Flt (scheduled to move to Coningsby
but which never did) were absorbed into
"A" Flt at West Raynham by September
1988, the flight formally disbanding in
March 1989.

Its sound original design has meant that
the Bloodhound Mk 2 missile was too-good-
a-system to discard and, has been described
in earlier "Snapshots", it has been continually updated. However, by 1985, the command and control system for the Bloodhound sites was somewhat long in the tooth.
Originally, missile status, targets and other
information was displayed on Second World
War-vintage table displays. Later, this was
superseded by perspex "tote boards" and the
judicious application of chinagraph pencils.
With the impending arrival of modern
ADGE and AEW systems, it was realised
that real-time information displays were
required if the system was to be efficiently
integrated into the new air defence network.

Nine Bloodhound missile flights were
split between two units, Nos 25 and 85
Squadrons (later to be consolidated on No
85 Squadron on 1 October 1989, when No
25 Squadron reformed at RAF Leeming on
Tornado F3 fighter aircraft). In order to
maintain efficient and effective control over
these sites, each with as many as eight
launchers, each Squadron and Flight operations room required an Automated Control
Room (ACR). After evaluation of four competing tenders, BAe received a £1.2 million
contract in July 1986. Hewlett Packard supplied their HP1000A processor for installation in the new control rooms, one in each
Squadron and Flight ACR, allowing full
redundancy.

At Flight level, the one console displays
operational status and engineering data
respectively, while at Squadron level there
are four consoles, permanently manned,
which give information on engagement status, tracking and engineering matters. Each
console has two screens: the larger one,
equipped with a tracker "roller-ball", dis-

plays a map of the UK airspace defended by
the Bloodhounds, together with the positions and tracks of potential targets,
together with the identities of the Flight
Launch Control Posts (LCPs) capable of
engaging them. Supplementary operational
data is presented on the lefthand side of the
screen in alphanumeric form. The smaller
screen, with a keyboard for data entry,
shows the engineering data.

Each LCP is now equipped with a
Ferranti Argus 700 computer. Real-time data
processing offers many advantages to the
self-contained Bloodhound LCP, including
the calculation of meantime before next
major service, out-of-service time estima-
tions and spares availability/location direc-
tories. The computer databases are also
"fully replicating" – any input information is
duplicated and stored by each of the proces-
sors.

The Bloodhound's primary means of
operation is by sector search, using the
Ferranti Type 86 "Indigo Corkscrew" Target
Illuminating Radar (TIR) which had replaced
the Marconi Type 86 "Blue Anchor" TIR in
1987. The TIR searches a sector allocated by
the SOC or squadron operations and details
of any targets are passed to the squadron
HQ. The Engagement Controller (EC) is
then allocated and authorised to engage the
target and the missile is fired.

Once launched, the missile flies ballisti-
cally for a few seconds until the boosters
burn out and are jettisoned. At this stage the
wings (which can be used in unison or dif-
ferentially to operate on the "twist-and-
steer" principle under positive G) unlock,
while the missile's receiver locks onto a target and it follows a climb-cruise profile
towards its target. Initially, the missile
homes in azimuth only before going to both
elevation and azimuth, respondiong to all
homing commands. As the missile closes on
its target, the proximity fuze senses the target and explodes the warhead. If, by some
chance, the target survives, the EC can
launch another missile.

A secondary mode of operation is provided by using voice control. Having identified the target and its track, the SOC passes
range and bearing by voice to the EC, who
directs the TIR to conduct a selected small
scan to acquire the target. After adjusting for
any jamming, the EC passes the TIR data via
the LCP computer to the missile launchers
which are then directed onto target azimuth
and run-up. Once the target echo is strong
enough, a "free to fire" signal appears on his

computer screen and the EC launches the missile.

Once a Bloodhound section has fired all its missiles, it is still possible to assist the air defence battle by broadcasting target details to manned fighters. This is known as the Target Information Service.

The first ACR was installed in November 1987 and the job was completed by mid-1990. This new automated command and control system was designed to provide maximum effectiveness for the Bloodhound Mk 2 system until it was finally replaced by a new weapon in the late 1990s.

Data: See 1968 "Snapshot"

BAe Rapier

In 1981 the United States ordered 32 Towed Rapier/Blindfire systems (28 operational fire units and four for training) to defend USAF bases in the UK, the first being handed over in 1983. They are manned by the RAF Regiment and tasked with the defence of seven bases: No 19 Squadron (located at Brize Norton, Oxon) to defend Upper Heyford and Fairford; No 20 Squadron (Honington, Suffolk) to defend Alconbury and Bentwaters/Woodbridge; and No 66 Squadron (West Raynham, Norfolk) to defend Lakenheath and Mildenhall. These three squadrons comprise No 6 Wing RAF Regiment and come under CinC RAF Strike Command, acting in his NATO capacity as CinC UK Air.

In November 1986, BAe Dynamics was awarded a contract to develop an updated version of Rapier – Field Standard C – which was based on the Rapier 2000 work, on-going as part of a continuous improvement programme for the MoD. The contract also covered initial production for three squadrons of the RAF Regiment and two of British Army of the Rhine's (BAOR) towed Rapier air defence batteries. *(For further details on the system, see the next "Snapshot".)*

Data: See 1978 "Snapshot"

CRITIQUE

By 1988, the upgrade of RAF air defences was well in hand. The Tornado F3 units were building-up, complementing the Phantom and Lightning squadrons, with the "Blue Circle" radar problems in the course of resolution, as previously described. Yet,

in October 1992, it was revealed by Malcolm McIntosh, the MoD Chief of Defence Procurement, that at one stage the performance of the AI24 radar was so poor that serious consideration had been given to scrapping the whole system and replacing it with the GEC Ferranti Defence Systems' Blue Vixen radar.

McIntosh was testifying to the House of Commons public accounts committee. At the same time he revealed that the whole AI24 Foxhunter radar programme (development and production costs) had reached just under £1 billion – as much as the abortive Nimrod AEW3 programme. The Blue Vixen refit idea was abandoned when it was decided that the Tornado F3 would not receive a full mid-life update. *(See the next "Snapshot" for details of the radar and defensive aids improvements made following the Gulf War in 1991.)*

During this decade, the UK's SAM defences had been reformed. Plans had been announced during 1987 for a significant increase in the number of Rapier fire units deployed at RAF stations in the UK. The intention was to increase the strength by 50% by the early 1990s through using existing manpower and fire units from the RAF repair pool. Additionally, some AAA (refurbished Argentine equipment) had been deployed.

The Nimrod AEW3 fiasco was finally over and the E-3D Sentry ordered. The new ground-based air defence radars were coming on stream, although some problems were being encountered with the reliability of the Type 93 systems. The only major problem remained with the ICCS element of IUKADGE, which was running late.

By the mid-1980s, it was apparent that the GEC-Plessey Telecom UNITER main access switches (equivalent to a civil telephone exchange) for voice/data interface between the various elements of the ICCS was running late, pushing completion to February 1987. Meanwhile, the three elements of ICCS were being brought together at a test installation at West Drayton. Hughes aircraft was providing the data handling system, Marconi the display/voice communications sub-system and Plessey the nodes of the digital data network.

By August 1986 the whole programme was being delayed, despite progress on the integration tests at West Drayton. By late 1987 the first items of hardware were moved onto the first site at Buchan and single-site acceptance tests started. System acceptance tests were scheduled for June 1988. It was during this period that the problems of software integration were becoming apparent. It took until early 1989 for the contractor, UKSL, to develop and begin implementation of the solutions to what, in fairness, must be said was a very complex systems integration problem which had never been attempted on such a scale before. The final resolution of the ICCS development is covered in the next "Snapshot".

Although the first signs of major changes in the European political arena were being recognised, Russia was still perceived as the major threat. The situation was not helped when analysts reported that Russian defence spending had increased and was considered to be some six to seven times the officially stated amount. Although trends in Soviet air power did not suggest as great an imbalance as its ground forces, compared to NATO, they still continued to pose a serious threat to NATO forces, with the expectation that it would increase in future years. Increased Russian interest was being seen in air-to-air refuelling capabilities, including the development of Il-78 "Midas" tanker aircraft.

Nevertheless for those who would listen, General Secretary Gorbachev increasingly mentioned "reasonable sufficiency" and an increasing willingness to consider arms reduction proposals. The more cautious were anxious to stress that this was all being said against a background of massive military modernisation programmes. Perhaps more significantly it was announced that Russian troops were to be withdrawn from Afghanistan.

Other straws were in the wind. Early in 1988, it was reported that the US armed forces were facing tough new budget restrictions. Ominously the proposals included plans to positively axe some projects, rather than allow them to "stretch out" over a period as had so often happened in the past. Also, military assistance programmes to more than 30 countries were to be ended because of budgetary constraints.

It was clear that financial considerations were beginning to colour the thinking of politicians and was an indication that the high spending days were in eclipse. Significantly, modernisation and updating were increasingly mentioned rather than brand new projects or major new programmes. One of the most important updates was the announcement in mid-1988 that a contract had been awarded to US company Raytheon to upgrade the Ballistic Missile Early Warning Radars at Fylingdales Moor. The completion date was expected to be September 1992.

Social pressures were also showing signs of influencing future military plans. In particular, moves were made to restrict low flying exercises over the Central European area. This was strongly resisted by the military who considered that contemporary simulators, in particular the visual systems, could not replicate the conditions to the degree required. These moves prompted the RAF to mount a well orchestrated PR campaign to sell the idea of low flying training to the general public.

Also in the training scenario was a proposal, by BAe, to develop an air combat manoeuvre (ACM) facility in the North Sea. The intention was to build the range as a private venture and then hire it out to the RAF, USAF and the Royal Netherlands Air Force. It certainly appeared attractive to the RAF; a dogfighting range close to its major fighter bases as well as a considerable saving over deployment to other, overseas ranges. Although there was some initial ambivalence over the idea it was eventually brought into operation.

Some programmes were being pursued more diligently and one of the most important of these, so far as the RAF was concerned, was the European Fighter Aircraft (EFA). In September 1987, the Chiefs of Air Staff of the four NATO countries involved (Germany, Italy, Spain and the UK) signed the European Staff Requirement for Development (ESR-D). This paved the way for the official go-ahead which was announced in April 1988. At the time, it was stressed that EFA was needed by the RAF to replace its air defence Phantoms and ground attack Jaguars and to complement the Tornado F3.

But greater changes were in the offing and just as the RAF was about to achieve a full modernisation, the premise against which their plans were drawn began to evaporate. The impact of this on the planned successor to the Phantoms and Jaguars, the EFA, was to cause problems in 1992. For this final part of the story, we move on to the concluding "Snapshot".

Left: This rear view of a Leeming Wing Tornado F3, seen prior to deploying to the Gulf in October 1990, is fully armed and modified for operations. Note the shoulder pylons for AIM-9 Sidewinder air-to-air missiles and, just visible beneath the rear fuselage, the chaff/flare dispensers added as part of the Gulf mods. (Crown Copyright)

Left: "Well Trousered!" The crew of the No 23 Squadron Tornado F3 model the latest in aircrew clothing during Exercise "Elder Joust" in 1990 with immersion suit, life preserver and G-trousers. They are fully protected against the NBC hazard and carry the AR5 respirator used on the ground between aircraft and protected building. (Author)

"SNAPSHOT" – 1993

The situation today is one of transition. On the one hand, the air defence improvements initiated during the Cold War are almost complete. The first IUKADGE station to be declared fully operational was Buchan in November 1992. On the other hand, the threat against which these plans were made has changed radically. The effect of this "Warm Peace" on all of Great Britain's armed forces was outlined in the MoD's document *Options for Change*, published in August 1990.

For the RAF, the withdrawal of Phantom fighters was accelerated, first from RAF Germany and then the UK-based air defence force, with the last unit, No 74 Squadron, disbanding on 1 October 1992. The Tornado F3 ("warts 'n' all" but improved after its operational experience in the Gulf) remains the UK's fighter force until the arrival of Eurofighter 2000, the renamed European Fighter Aircraft (EFA) programme. Tanker support for the fighters is being maintained (as the Gulf war added to the fatigue life usage of the Victor tankers) by the conversion of more dedicated VC10 tankers and the conversion of the VC10 transport fleet to act as tanker/transports.

The ground-based air defence element has changed with the rapid retirement of the Bloodhound SAM and disbandment of some RAF Regiment Rapier units. The Shackleton AEW aircraft had finally given way to the Sentry AEW1 in July 1991, while the new ground-based radars, including the new system at Fylingdales as part of the BMEWS chain, are available. All the air defence system needs now is for the remaining IUKADGE stations to be declared operational.

The above precis of the current situation may appear a mite simplistic but it must suffice due to the RAF's security restrictions and the changing nature of the times. The truth is that, while there was a definable threat, the response was measured and tailored to the costs available at any given time. Now, as will be seen in the next segment of this "Snapshot", the threat is less defined.

For the time being, the air defence of the UK is reasonably well placed and allows some margin for deployment to the fringes of NATO and totally "out-of-area" to meet the unexpected. It is against this changing background that the EFA was conceived, initially to complement Tornado F3s, but now – with "out-of-area" operations a distinct possibility – to virtually replace them.

The RAF's air defence role *per se* will not change but it will become more flexible, allowing assets to be deployed away from the UK to where they are needed. We may not, yet, have seen the reality of the whole of *Options for Change*.

THE THREAT

The major threat of an overwhelming attack on NATO Europe by the forces of the former Warsaw Pact has virtually vanished. While it is true that the Russian Federation itself presents a threat to the UK on paper, the reality of imposing a "capitalist" econ-

Right: By adding an aerial refuelling store beneath each wing, plus one on a stub pylon on the port rear fuselage, the Ilyushin Il-76 "Candid" transport has become the Il-78 "Midas" tanker. This aircraft was displayed at Farnborough in September 1992. (Author)

omy on the new republic has seen funding for the great military standing force slashed. The likelihood of a pre-emptive air attack on the UK has reduced tremendously but, as Russia and one or two of its new neighbours retain some teeth, it remains a scenario which must be guarded against.

As the events in the Middle East in August 1990 and the subsequent war against Iraq by the United Nations Coalition, led by the United States, proved, threats come from whence they are least expected. In the event, the threat of the Gulf War of 1991 was not, principally, of massive air attack but the use of tactical ballistic missiles carrying nuclear, biological or chemical (NBC) warheads. With the signature of the the second Strategic Arms Reduction Treaty (START 2) in January 1993, it must now be considered that a possible ballistic missile threat to the UK could come just as equally from a missile fired by a splinter group located in a southern Mediterranean or Middle Eastern country, as from Russia.

The deployment of US Patriot SAMs to Saudi Arabia and Israel was a direct response to the Iraqi "Scud" tactical ballistic missile threat. That such weapons were in the hands of so-called non-nuclear powers must serve as a lesson, the existing systems adapted to meet that threat and new sytems developed.

In the meantime, to round-off the continuity of previous "Snapshots", as far as an immediate air threat to the UK is concerned let us look at what was known as the Soviet Union, now called the Commonwealth of Independent States (CIS) and the new emerging republics of Eastern Europe. Five of the CIS states (Armenia, Khazakhstan, Kirgizia, Russia and Uzbekistan) have a collective security agreement which centralises ultimate control of forces and weapons. Separate bilateral treaties with Russia have been signed by Belarus (formerly Bylorussia) and Khazkhstan. Azerbaidjan, Moldova and Ukraine have declined to collaborate on collective security matters, while Georgia has not even joined the CIS. Estonia, Latvia and Lithuania are now totally independent, the withdrawal of Russian forces being imminent.

After the dissolution of the Soviet Union, the Russian Federation has maintained the five-arm structure of the former Soviet armed forces: strategic missile forces, land forces, air force, air defence forces and the navy. Although considered, plans to merge the air force with the air defence force have been abandoned. Under the Conventional Forces in Europe (CFE) treaty, Russia is allowed 3,450 fixed-wing aircraft, 890 armed helicopters and 300 naval aircraft.

The former Warsaw Pact states are now also newly independent of Russia and seeking co-operation with the West rather than confrontation. This effectively put the "start line" for any military action against NATO forces in general, and the UK in particular, some way eastwards.

Meanwhile, in what is seen as a "rapid re-wind" to pre-1914 political geography, the Balkans has once again become an area for concern. The emergence of ethnic groupings within and across the new boundaries give cause for concern. Yugoslavia has splintered, civil war is rife in Bosnia and what the eventual outcome may be is anyone's guess. Czechoslovakia has now split into two republics with the so-called "velvet divorce".

While no-one can argue that any of these new and re-created states appears to present a threat to Great Britain, the fact that British forces may end up in a shooting war (under a variety of scenarios) can only serve to emphasise that the forces available to the RAF must be capable of going anywhere and fighting whatever threat has appeared.

It is not the purpose of this book to catalogue the re-distribution of former-Soviet equipment. Let the Ukraine, which has emerged as one of the strongest air powers within the CIS, serve as an example. Under the CFE Treaty, the Ukraine is allowed 1,090 fixed-wing aircraft, 300 armed helicopters and 100 naval aircraft. Estimates in 1992 put the offensive strength of the Ukraine air force at 18 Tu-160 "Blackjacks", 24 Tu-95 "Bears", 220 Su-24 "Fencers" and a mix of 210 Su-27 "Flankers" and MiG-29 "Fulcrums", plus about 30 Ilyushin Il-78 "Midas" tankers, almost all of the former Soviet air force fleet.

What has become apparent is that, in efforts to obtain hard currency, the republics of the CIS and its former Warsaw Pact allies are prepared to sell their surplus military hardware, while developing and building improved or new systems to follow-on, although at a somewhat slower pace. So, to round-off the coverage of potential threat aircraft, as far as UK air defence is concerned, the known details of the Il-78 "Midas" tanker and Tupolev's Tu-160 "Blackjack" are recorded below.

Right: A close-up view of the fuselage refuelling store on the Il-78 "Midas" tanker shown at Farnborough in 1992. The drogue can be seen in the rear housing, above which are the signal lights for the receiver aircraft. Note the wing pylon and store visible in the lower right of the picture. (Author)

Ilyushin Il-78 "Midas"

Development of a probe-and-drogue tanker version of the Ilyushin Il-76MD "Candid-B" transport aircraft began in the mid-1970s. Designated Il-78 and codenamed "Midas", it is replacing the M-4 "Bison" in the tanker role. Although the type is known to have entered service in 1987, its first public appearance was at the 1992 Farnborough air show.

Essentially the same as the "Candid-B", the prototype of which first flew on 25 March 1971, it features three PAZ aerial refuelling pods, one mounted under each wing with the third on the port side of the rear fuselage. The guns in the rear turret have been removed but the location is retained as a flight refuelling observation station.

The reader is referred to the 1988 "Snapshot" for a general description and technical data of the "Midas", in its Il-76 "Mainstay" AEW&C guise.

Data: see 1988 "Snapshot" (under Il-76 "Mainstay")

Tupolev Tu-160 "Blackjack"

The most modern bomber to come from what we once knew as the Soviet Union, it is possibly the last. Looking not unlike the US B-1B Lancer, Tupolev's Tu-160 "Blackjack" was first observed on November 1981. It was officially revealed to the West in August 1988 when the former US Defense Secretary, Frank Carlucci, paid a visit to the Kubinka air base and inspected an example. A single aircraft was flown over Tushino airport on the Aviation Day flypast a year later. It is reported that the Tu-160

first entered service in 1988-89 at Priliuki in the Ukraine, which now has 18 "Blackjacks".

In August 1992, the last of some 40 Tu-160 "Blackjacks" was delivered from its Kazan production plant to the CIS air force base at Engels on the Volga river, in the Saratov region of Russia. Originally, the initial production run was expected to be about 100 bombers but, early in 1992, Russian President Boris Yeltsin ordered production to cease, as part of the country's contribution to disarmament.

The Tu-160 is a cantilever, low-wing, variable-geometry monoplane, some 20% longer than the USAF B-1B. In no way is it a "scaled-up" version of the Tu-22M (Tu-26) "Backfire". The wing-sweep is selected manually from 20° fully spread to 65° fully swept. The horizontal tail surfaces, unlike the B-1B's, are mounted halfway up the taller fin. The fixed wingroot sweep and engine installation are reminiscent of the Tu-144 "Concordski" supersonic airliner. The slim and shallow fuselage, with a slightly upturned nosecone, is blended into the wingroots and designed for maximum deflection of radar signals. It sits on a twin-nosewheel and bogie main undercarriage, each with three pairs of wheels. The four crew members each have an individual ejection seat and the pilots have fighter-type, single-stick control columns rather than yokes.

Although it had been assumed that the Tu-160's role was that of a high-altitude, stand-off bomber armed with AS-15 "Kent" air-launched cruise missiles (ALCM), it has since been revealed that it can also carry the AS-16 "Kickback" short-range attack missile

(SRAM), equivalent to the USAF AGM-69 SRAM. There are two 33ft weapons bays each capable of carrying AS-15 ALCMs, its supersonic successor AS-19 and the AS-16 SRAM.

As the AGM-69 is used for defence suppression along the path of a low-level penetration bomber, it may be assumed that the Tu-160 is capable of transonic penetration at low altitude as well as subsonic cruise/supersonic dash at about Mach 2 at 60,000ft. From this assumption, it then follows that the radar has terrain-following capability and that there is provision for in-flight refuelling.

Data: Tupolev Tu-160 "Blackjack"

Powerplant	four Soloviev Type-R tur bofans, each rated at 55,115lb st
Span	182ft 9in (spread), 110ft 0in (swept)
Length	177ft 0in
Height	42ft 0in
T/O weight	606,260lb (max.)
Maximum speed	1,240mph (Mach 1.88) at altitude
Service ceiling	60,000ft
Combat radius	4,535 miles (max un-refuelled)
Armament	Max weapons load of 36,000lb, consisting of free-fall bombs, 12 AS-16 SRAMs or six AS-15/AS-19 ALCMS

DETECTION & IDENTIFICATION

By the early 1990s, the process of modernisation and the integration of new sensors finally seemed to be coming to fruition, tending to confirm the assertion of the UK MoD that the RAF is now better prepared and equipped to defend the UK from air attack than ever before.

The UK Air Defence Region (ADR) stretches from the approaches to Iceland and Norway to the north, to the South-Western Approaches and as far out as the Scilly Isles – a long way from the southeastern sector considered to be the area of vulnerability in 1940. Ground radar stations now cover the area from sites at Saxa Vord in the Shetlands and Benbecula in the Outer Hebrides, to Portreath in Cornwall. All the information gathered from these is sent to the UK Air Defence Operations Centre (ADOC) at High Wycombe, Bucks.

The ADR is split into the North and South Air Defence Sectors, controlled by two Sector Operations Centres (SOC)/Command and Reporting Centres (CRP) located at Buchan and Neatishead, respectively. These, and the other Reporting Posts (RP) – see map on page 162 – all have local responsibilities but can control information from anywhere in the system with their standard equipment. A CRP/RP based on the Faroe Isles and manned by the Royal Danish Air Force also reports into the system. Communications is via a highly survivable digital system known as UNITER.

The core of ICCS is the two large databases from which operators extract the necessary information on which to base their decisions. The first is the Resource Data Catalogue which details weapons states and airfield availability. The other is the Recognised Air and Sea Picture which presents real-time information from all radar sources. These include data from the 12 core systems (four Type 91, two Type 92 and six Type 93 mobile radars), RAF E-3D Sentries

Above: Probably the last Russian bomber to be built for many years, this Tupolev Tu-160 "Blackjack" is seen here with wings extended forward for cruise flight. (Luftforsvaret)

Above: The new Raytheon three-dimensional, phased-array radar installed at the BMEWS site at Fylingdales on the North Yorkshire Moors. Note one of the old "golfball" radomes to the right of the picture. (Sgt Rick Brewell/Crown Copyright)

as well as the Royal Navy's Type 42 destroyers assigned to air defence. Other input can be taken, through separate buffers, from NATO ground-based sensors (notably Norwegian radars via ground links) and French, NATO and USAF E-3 Sentries.

As in previous "Snapshots", much of the activity has centred on shadowing Russian air traffic. Consequently the first notice of an approaching "visitor" is likely to come from Norwegian radar stations. This interoperability is vital and provided via the ICCS element of IUKADGE, which is linked into other NATO ADGEs. Inevitably this requires a high degree of command and control, with an emphasis on computational power and the original DAC Vax 785 machines were replaced by Vax 8650s.

The problems regarding the ICCS element of IUKADGE were chonicled in the previous "Snapshot". Between January and June 1989 an independent audit of the system was set up by the MoD. While admitting much was wrong, the report noted that the contractors, UKSL, had the solutions in hand. In July 1989 a Parliamentary written reply gave some indication of progress and a retrospective explanation of progress to date. In particular, and in reply to a question regarding in-service date, it was suggested that the ICCS was being progressively introduced over a number of years. Although some elements were already in service, official recognition was given to the fact that the system was late.

However the UK Secretary of State for Defence was pressed to confirm if consideration had been given to the use of a single software language, during the project definition stage. It was stated that initially consideration had been given to the use of CORAL 66, but a subsequent decision was made to obtain the maximum return from the NATO common infrastructure budget. This meant that the UK had to abide by the NATO rules of international competitive bidding, which precluded the specification of a single software language. To further compound the situation, NATO financial authorities insisted that existing NATO Air Defence Ground Environment (NADGE) software was to be reused wherever possible. With hindsight, it is easy to detect the seeds of future problems.

Growing concern led to further official disclosures in February 1990, when the UK Under-Secretary of State for Defence Procurement was briefed following indications of MoD concern over continuing slippage in the timescale and apparent lack of progress in addressing the problem. The situation was further exacerbated by various MoD attempts to "kick-start" the project and the decision by UKSL to resort to arbitration over alleged non-payment of sums due, said to be in the region of £50 million.

Two years later the situation looked a little healthier. A number of command and reporting posts and centres were up to operational standard while others were already

Left: The operations room of the new BMEWS site at Fylingdales is the antithesis of that used during the Battle of Britain in 1940. (Sgt Rick Brewell/Crown Copyright)

being used in training. Software considerations continued to dominate the programme and it seemed that a continual list of improvements were in process of compilation, including requirements for an enhanced training and simulation capability. To be fair it must be remembered that the software core of IUKADGE is one of the largest and complex systems in Europe. The requirement is challenging, calling as it does for all the posts to be linked with a variety of sites, sensors, aircraft and ships.

By November 1992, a UK Defence Committee report was able to state that encouraging progress had been made with a software system recovery plan. Following the successful completion of formal acceptance tests, the technical transfer of the basic system to the MoD took place in September 1991. This was several months earlier than had been anticipated and the system was handed over to the RAF on 1 July 1992.

Since then, the RAF has been involved with training and the gaining of hands-on experience. Inevitably a number of residual problems emerged and these were addressed by the manufacturer under the terms of the warranty. As is so often the case with military systems, work was also in hand to implement minor amendments to satisfy requirements that have arisen since the original contract was signed. All of these tasks were expected to be cleared by January 1993.

Finally, it could be announced that a phased plan had been compiled to bring the system into full operational use with the first station (Buchan) attaining its initial operating capability (IOC) in November 1992.

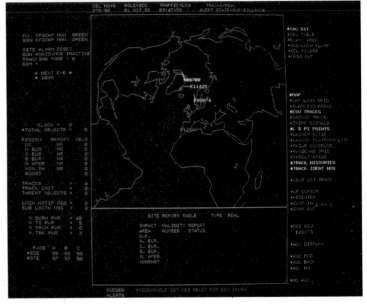

Above: A typical radar display provided by the new Raytheon BMEWS radar at Fylingdales. This picture has been sanitised for publication. (Crown Copyright)

Meanwhile work on systems hardware at the other sites continued into 1993, with Neatishead achieving IOC on 1 June.

The final element of the system – the ability to accept radar data from air traffic control radars through the National Air Traffic System – is scheduled for the turn of 1994-95. Rather more ominously, in view of past experience, the report also announced that detailed plans have been prepared for the regular updating of the system throughout its operational life.

The European AEW solution is firmly based on Boeing's E-3 Sentry with NATO, Great Britain and France all choosing the AWACS-derived aircraft. By early 1990, flight-testing had begun of the first of the

E-3D aircraft for the RAF. France ordered four similar aircraft and the flight-test programme reflected the common airworthiness elements of both the British and French fleets. Flight trials of mission equipment began later in the year, with deliveries to both nations beginning during 1991.

In 1992 it was announced that E-3 Sentries of the USAF and NATO were to receive an advanced passive sensor upgrade to permit positive identification of targets from their radar emissions. At the same time it was suggested that the RAF E-3D Sentry aircraft would be similarly modified, using equipment manufactured in the UK.

By late 1989, work had been completed integrating the RAF's existing datalink buffer sites throughout the UK into a single network. This makes possible the transfer, to command reporting centres, of relevant data received from AWACS aircraft by any site. Terminals at these sites can also exchange information with IUKADGE and with other air defence buffer links. Part of this work involved the supply of new workstation displays. Developed by Thorn EMI Electronics, these were among the first in-service systems to run entirely on Ada soft-ware.

At the end of 1989 it was announced that there would be a full system upgrade of the BMEWS site at Fylingdales, North Yorkshire. The station at Thule has already been upgraded, but the Fylingdales programme differs from the one in Greenland in that it has three antenna faces, mounted at 120° and capable of providing warning and tracking capabilities over a full 360° coverage. A requirement of the contract stipulated that all work on the facility infrastructure be undertaken by UK subcontractors, as a result of competitive bidding.

The modernisation of the Fylingdales BMEWS station has been a model of success. Construction work began in August 1989 and the new radar was installed late in 1991. Then began an intensive trials period, lasting for approximately one year, including extensive monitoring of adjacent emission levels following the standards laid down by the UK health authorities. The system was then extensively trialled by RAF crews, during operational training, prior to becoming fully operational in October 1992.

The new radar is a Raytheon FPS-115 Solid State Phased Array (SSPAR) system, comprising three 84ft diameter arrays. As noted above, this is the first large phased array system with three faces and is capable of tracking up to 800 objects simultaneously. Although the warning time of approximately 10mins is the same as with the earlier system, the radar resolution is much improved to enhance detection. The current secondary role of space surveillance is likely to become increasingly important in the years ahead. It will be considerable solace to environmentalists to note that the old "golf ball" radar site will be completely cleared and returned to its natural moorland state.

Although constructed as a joint venture between the UK and US governments, Fylingdales is very much under RAF command and control. The unit feeds information direct to the UK Government and British Military Command Centres, as well as to Command Centres in the United States. The site is also linked to the US Space Command Headquarters at Colorado Springs from where two other BMEWS sites are controlled: Thule, 600 miles inside the Arctic Circle in Greenland; and Clear, Alaska. The system has a secondary role of space surveillance which is likely to grow in significance in the years ahead.

Also in 1989, it was announced that the UK would co-operate with the US in a two-year joint trial (beginning in 1993) of a US Navy Relocatable Over-The-Horizon Radar (ROTHR) at a site in South Wales for the transmitter, the receiver and control station being sited at Cricklade in Wiltshire. This geographical isolation is a feature of bistatic radars and is to ensure electronic "silence" at the receiver while the transmitter is operating continuously. The trial was scheduled to begin in 1993. Cost was to be shared between the US and the UK with the latter covering some 90% of the projected cost of $90 million. Annual running costs were to be funded jointly out of RN and RAF budgets.

Below: The ICCS console provided by Marconi Radar & Command Systems for the Improved UKADGE system in service with the RAF. Again the difference between the 1940 control room and present day conditions is noted. (Marconi Radar)

It immediately attracted considerable opposition from environmental groups who had been equally vociferous over similar sites in the United States, while the use of Brawdy (South Wales) as one of the nodes in the US Ocean Surveillance Information System raised some queries as to the actual role of the radar. These queries were scarcely satisfied in a series of ambivalent Parliamentary answers when details of the agreement were announced.

Perhaps it was a combination of popular, public protest, political changes, a worsening economic situation or just the problem of requisitioning a very large area of land to establish the antenna arrays, that led to a quiet burial of the idea. The announcement, in early 1991, that the USAF was to scrap its own OTH-B programme also must have contributed to the decision.

This outcome was probably more symptomatic of the changing world and the realisation of changing military aims and requirements. A straw in the wind was noted in November 1990 when the UK Minister of State for the Armed Forces set out the allocation of certain types of equipment to be held by the UK following the signing of the Conventional Forces in Europe (CFE) Treaty. Clearly, political solutions were now becoming paramount, with an increasing tendency for the military to be curbed by financial rather than deployment considerations.

Meanwhile, the five-year period covered by this "half-Snapshot" must record the demise of an element of the UK's air defence which had served the country well since before the Second World War – the Royal Observer Corps. Since 1945, the ROC had become less of an air defence asset and more of an "Observer of Armageddon", being part of the UK Warning and Monitoring Organisation (UKWMO) under Home Office control, tracking fall-out after a nuclear strike. In effect, the ROC's prime role had become automated and the Home Office communicated this decision to the MoD in May 1991, although it did not become public until July. Essentially, the decrease in the perceived nuclear threat to the UK allowed the re-shaping of the Warning and Monitoring function and the UKWMO (and the ROC as its field element) would disband. The Corps ceased active training at the end of July and stood down from its operational role on 30 September 1991, with formal disbandment on 31 March 1992.

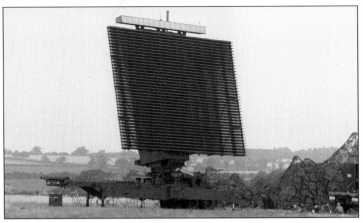

Thus, the five years of this final "half-Snapshot" have seen the arrival of the latest electronic detection system and the stand-down of the many pairs of "Mark One Mod Zero" eyeballs of the ROC. One cannot help but think that this is an asset wasted, however sophisticated the electronic means of detection have become. Yet, budgets and threats have to be balanced and money placed where the need is seen. This is exemplified by the Invitation to Tender for two new mobile tactical air defence radars for the RAF issued at the beginning of 1993.

Above: One of the three new transportable radar systems deployed as part of the Improved UKADGE system is the Marconi S723 Martello three-dimensional radar, known as Type 91 by the RAF. (Marconi)

RESPONSE: AIRCRAFT & ARMAMENT

BAe (HSA) Hawk T1A

While the Hawk T1A itself continues its war role as part of the Mixed Fighter Force, the training organisations in which they are located underwent significant changes during 1992 as part of the *Options for Change* reduction in UK armed forces.

No 1 Tactical Weapons Unit (1 TWU) at Brawdy was disbanded on 31 August 1992, and the duties of the TWU subsumed by No 4 Flying Training School (4 FTS) at Valley and by 2 TWU at Chivenor, now re-designated 7 FTS. Both are now under the control of RAF Support Command. The two previously undesignated training squadrons at Valley took over the "number-plates" of No 74 (the last RAF Phantom unit) and No 208 (one of the two Buccaneer units) Squadrons, becoming reserve squadrons. Meanwhile, Chivenor's Nos 63 and 151 Shadow Squadrons became Nos 19(R) and 92(R) Squadrons, respectively, being the two former RAF Germany fighter units.

Both Valley and Chivenor took on the dual role of advanced flying and tactical weapons training, under the description "mirror image". This training began in 1992 and is seen as another means of achieving economy within the defence budget.

Data: See 1988 "Snapshot"

BAe (BAC/Vickers) VC10 tanker series

The evolution and details of the VC10 K2/3 tankers was described in the 1988 "Snapshot". During 1990-91, the VC10 tankers which took part in Operation "Granby" were equipped with Marconi Defence Systems Sky Guardian 200 radar warning receivers (RWR). Following the Gulf War, these were removed from most of the aircraft, although it is understood that there is a programme underway to bring these back as standard equipment, rather than emergency fitments for the operational theatre.

However, as the Victor K2 fatigue life was rapidly running-out in 1990, BAe Commercial Aircraft Division was awarded a two-part contract to modify a further 13 VC10s to tanker configuration.

The first part of the contract, under Staff Requirement -Air (SRA) 415, called for the five remaining ex-BA Super VC10s stored at Abingdon to be converted to three-point K4 configuration. This involves the installation of a fuselage-mounted Mk 17B HDU and two wing-mounted Mk 32 pods plus a general refurbishment and update of the avionics to military standard, including air-to-air TACAN and a close-circuit TV(CCTV) monitoring system. Installation of JTIDS (Joint Tactical Information Distri-

bution System) equipment is planned for later. The first of these five "new" VC10 tankers flew on 29 July 1993 and with deliveries to No 101 Squadron at Brize Norton beginning in the autumn 1993.

The second part of the contract (under SRA416) involves fitting eight of No 10 Squadron's VC10 C1 transports with underwing Mk 32 pods, TACAN and CCTV. These dual-role two-point tanker/transports are re-designated C1(K), with an option on converting the remaining five transports in service. Neither the C1(K) or K4 conversions involve the fitting of additional fuel tankage. The first C1(K) conversion flew on 11 April 1992 and re-delivery to No 10 Squadron was scheduled for the end of the year.

On 19 February 1992, the Minister for Defence Procurement, Alan Clark, announced in the House of Commons that the RAF would take up the options to convert the remaining five VC10 C1s to tanker/transport configuration. BAe and Flight Refuelling received a contract to convert the aircraft, extending the original contract by a further two years to 1996.

As part of the *Options for Change* policy of retaining historic unit "number plates", No 241 OCU (for the VC10s) became No 57(R) Squadron (a former Victor tanker unit) in the middle of 1992.

Data: see 1988 "Snapshot"

Boeing E-3D Sentry AEW1

It will be recalled that the Shackleton AEW2 was purely an "interim" AEW aircraft

Below: The first VC10 C1(K) conversion, carried out by FR Aviation takes-off on a test flight from Bournemouth-Hurn airport. The aircraft carries a pair of FR Mk32B aerial refuelling pods under the outer wings. (FR Group)

for the RAF, being a 1950s-vintage airframe fitted with a 1940s-vintage radar. Its successor was to be the Nimrod AEW3, due to enter service in 1982. This programme was plagued by delays on the radar system and, in December 1986, the RAF placed an order with Boeing Aerospace for six E-3D Sentry AWACS (Airborne Warning and Control System) aircraft with an option on a further two. Later, one of the two aircraft options was exercised.

The E-3 is based on the classic Boeing 707 airliner airframe and was developed for the USAF during the 1970s. Two competitive radar systems, from Hughes and Westinghouse, were tested on two EC-137D prototypes in a competitive evaluation. The Westinghouse APY-1 radar was selected in October 1972. From aircraft No 25, the improved APY-2 radar was fitted.

The first of 34 production E-3As was delivered to the USAF in March 1977. NATO agreed to form a multi-national AWACS unit (but without the UK) and ordered 18 aircraft, the first of which was flown on 18 December 1980. After having its mission avionics installed by Dornier in Germany, it was delivered to the NATO AEW Force in January 1982, deliveries being completed by April 1985. All USAF and NATO aircraft were powered by four Pratt & Whitney TF33-PW-100/100A turbofans, rated at 21,000lb st each.

In December 1981, Saudi Arabia signed a contract for five E-3As to be powered by four GE/SNECMA CFM56-2A-2 turbofans, each rated at 24,000lb st. The aircraft for the RAF (and also France who ordered three, later increased to four, E-3Fs at the same time) are also powered by the CFM56. Externally, the RAF Sentries differ from USAF (apart from the engines) and Saudi aircraft by the addition of a SOGERMA in-flight refuelling probe (also on the French E-3F) and wingtip pods containing US Loral 1017 "Yellow Gate" ESM pods.

The first RAF E-3D Sentry AEW1 flew in September 1989, was fully-equipped by January 1990, and delivered to the UK in November 1990. The first aircraft to be accepted by the RAF was the second production model on 26 March, 1991. By August 1992, No 8 Squadron was declared fully integrated into the NATO AEW force, working alongside the NATO joint E-3A force from Geilenkirchen in Germany. Shortly afterwards, two aircraft were deployed to Italy in support of UN sanctions against Serbia and Montenegro. *(See following section for more details in "Impressions of the Sentry".)* Plans announced in the Defence White Paper of July 1993 indicate that only 6 E-Ds will be operational from the mid-1990s.

Data: Boeing E-3D Sentry AEW1

Powerplant	four CFM International (GE/SNECMA) CFM56-24-2/3 turbofans, each rated at 24,000lb st
Span	147ft 7in
Length	152ft 11in
Height	41ft 9in
Loaded weight	332,500lb (maximum T/O)
Maximum speed	530mph
Service ceiling	30,000+ft
Endurance on station	6hr at 870nm
Max endurance	10+hr (unrefuelled)

Handley Page (HSA) Victor K2

Between 1988 and 1992, the high-spot of the Victor's career was its involvement in Operation "Granby", tanking RAF strike and air defence aircraft during the Gulf War of 1991. Its use during this period brought its fatigue life down yet again (following the Falklands campaign – Operation "Corporate" in 1982). It will be finally retired in October 1993.

Data: see 1968 "Snapshot"

Lockheed TriStar tanker series

During the period covered by this "half-Snapshot", some of No 216 Squadron's TriStars operated in support of the RAF during Operation "Granby" in the Gulf. For this, two KC1s were painted in "desert pink" and equipped with radar warning receivers (RWR). Although it was planned for all RAF TriStars to receive the General Instruments ALR-66 RWR equipment, this programme has apparently stalled owing, it has been suggested, to a problem with the equipment.

Meanwhile, the fate of the the three ex-Pan Am TriStars, two of which were operating as C2 transports on the Falklands shuttle, was re-evaluated. It was originally planned to fit a Flight Refuelling Mk 32B pod under each wing but, due to aerodynamic problems and the proximity of the trailed drogue line to the aircraft's tailplane, the plan was abandoned for all the TriStars. Instead, starting with the third aircraft which was in storage, all three C2s will be bought up to the same avionics standards as

Right: This fine study of the present partners in RAF air defence shows a Boeing E-3D Sentry AEW1 of No 8 Squadron in company with a pair of Panavia Tornado F3 interceptors of No 5 Squadron. (Geoff Lee/BAe)

the K1s/KC1s and maintained in passenger configuration, being re-designated C2A.

The TriStar fleet, both tankers and transport versions, continue to be operated by No 216 Squadron at Brize Norton.

Data: see 1988 "Snapshot"

McDonnell Douglas F-4M Phantom FGR2

The five years between 1988 and 1992 saw the final run-down of the Phantom as part of the UK air defences. Discounting the withdrawal of the two RAF Germany Phantom FGR2 units, No 19 Squadron in December 1991 and No 92 Squadron in July 1991, and No 1435 Flight's exchange of Phantom FGR2s for Tornado F3s in July 1992, the run-down went as follows:

Operating a mix of FG1s and FGR2s from May 1988, No 43 Squadron flew its final Phantom sortie on 31 July 1989. Its partner at Leuchars, No 111 Squadron, "down-declared" from its NATO commitment on 31 October 1989, flying its last Phantom sortie on 31 January 1990. The Phantom Operational Conversion Unit (No 228 OCU/64 "Shadow" Squadron) disbanded on 31 January 1991, to be replaced for a 12-month period by the Phantom Training Flight, which disbanded in January 1992.

Of the final two UK Phantom units, No 56 Squadron disbanded on 1 July 1992, leaving No 74 Squadron, which had exchanged F-4J (UK)s for FGR2s in January 1991 to soldier on as the RAF's last Phantom squadron. The squadron was "down-declared" from NATO strengths on 30 September 1992 and disbanded shortly afterwards.

Data: see 1978 "Snapshot"

McDonnell Douglas F-4J (UK) Phantom

To maintain continuity between "Snapshots", it need only be recorded here that No 74 Squadron exchanged its F-4J(UK)s for Phantom FGR2s on 17 January 1991, after seven years useful service.

Data: see 1988 "Snapshot"

Panavia Tornado F3

To bring the re-equipment of the Tornado F3 force up to date, it must be recorded that although No 23 Squadron formed at Leeming in November 1988, it was not declared operational until 1 August 1989. The third unit of the Leeming wing is No 25 Squadron (formerly a Bloodhound Mk 2 SAM unit) which formed in July 1989 and was declared operational on 1 January 1990. This event marked the squadron's return to flying, having disbanded as a Javelin FAW9 unit in 1962.

The penultimate Tornado F3 base to re-equip was Leuchars in Scotland, where No 43 Squadron formed in November 1989 and became operational on 1 July 1990. Its partner unit, No 111 Squadron, re-equipped with the Tornado F3 in May 1990, took over QRA (Quick Reaction Alert) duties in December 1990, and was declared operational with NATO forces on 1 January 1991. By July 1992, the Tornado F3 had been deployed to Mount Pleasant in the Falkland Islands to replace the Phantom FGR2s of No 1435 Flt. The final change in the Tornado F3 organisation also came in July 1992. As part of the *Options for Change* review, No 229 OCU at Coningsby was re-designated No 56(R) Squadron.

Below: Down to earth, a Panavia Tornado F3 of No 23 Squadron outside its hardened aircraft shelter at Leeming during Exercise "Elder Joust" in April 1990. (Author)

Back-tracking slightly, the RAF was planning a further 15 Tornado F3s as part of the eighth batch of aircraft. However, following the cancellation of Oman's order for eight Tornado ADVs in 1990, the RAF was instructed to take over the airframes. To balance the equation, the 15 planned for Batch 8 was reduced to eight and then, in a move to balance the defence budget (felt possible by the lowering of East-West tension following the removal of the Berlin Wall) the decision was made, in June 1990, to abandon this final batch of aircraft (including 26 Tornado GR1s). Thus, the total number of Tornado ADVs ordered (including three prototypes and the 18 F2s) was 173. The final production aircraft was delivered to the RAF early in 1993.

In January 1991, the Tornado F3 went to war as part of the RAF contribution to Operation "Granby", perhaps better known as Operation "Desert Storm". The Tornado F3 had been the first RAF aircraft deployed

as part of Operation "Desert Shield" in 1991. A composite unit, comprising aircraft from Nos 5 and 29 Squadrons which had been preparing to return home from armament practice camp at Akrotiri in Cyprus, was put on stand-by and on 11 August 1991 it arrived at Dhahran in Saudi Arabia.

As the operations in the Middle East did not comprise part of the UK air defence, a full account of their war is left to those better qualified than myself to recall. The Tornado F3 did not actually fight an engagement with the Iraqis, although it did achieve some radar "lock-ons" which were almost immediately broken-off as the enemy turned tail. Suffice it to say that the aircraft made a valuable contribution to the air defence of Saudi Arabia and the protection of the attacking aircraft once battle had been joined.

What is more interesting, perhaps, are the improvements made to the aircraft before January 1991, which are today being

reflected in the aircraft defending the UK skies. Operation "Granby" was to shake off the deficiencies which had dogged the Tornado F2/F3 during its initial service, due to the poor performance of the early AI24 radars.

While the first Tornado F3s deployed from Cyprus were equipped with early "Type W" and "Type Z" radars, the RAF transferred 26 Block 13 "Stage 1" Tornados from Leuchars, where they had just been delivered, to Leeming for issue to No 11 (Composite) Squadron, prior to flying out to Dhahran to replace the initial aircraft.

The heart of the improvement was the "Type AA" radars with improved cooling and revised software (relating to improved close-combat capability and improved ECCM) as the original high repetition frequencies of the radar were optimised for its role as a long-range "bomber-destroyer". The Block 13 aircraft were equipped with an "F-18 style" top to the control column,

which concentrated all the short-range combat controls within the pilot's grip, an improved ARI18241/1 RHWR and a combat boost switch next to the throttle. This allowed an extra five per cent over the standard 9,105lb dry (un-reheated) thrust of the RB199 engines to be selected by increasing stator temperature some 20°C above the normal range, with the penalty of slightly reduced time between overhauls.

At Leeming a joint RAF/BAe working party bought all these aircraft up to what was known as "Stage 1 Plus" configuration. These included the addition of a pair of Tracor ALE-40 chaff/flare dispensers below the rear fuselage and a Philips-Matra Phimat chaff dispensing pod, located on the inner port pylon (usually used for a drop tank). Strips of radar-absorbent material (RAM) were added to the leading edges of the fins, wings (except for the di-electric panels covering the RHWR antennae) and weapons pylons. It is possible other signature-reduc-

---

Order of Battle – January 1993

Strike Command – HQ: High Wycombe, Bucks

No 11 Group – HQ: Bentley Priory, Stanmore, Middx

Sqn	Aircraft	Base
5	Panavia Tornado F3	Coningsby, Lincs
8	Boeing E-3D Sentry AEW1	Waddington, Lincs
11	Panavia Tornado F3	Leeming, Yorks
23	Panavia Tornado F3	Leeming, Yorks
25	Panavia Tornado F3	Leeming, Yorks
29	Panavia Tornado F3	Coningsby, Lincs
43	Panavia Tornado F3	Leuchars, Fife
111	Panavia Tornado F3	Leuchars, Fife
56(R)	Panavia Tornado F3	Coningsby, Lincs

(formerly 229 OCU/65 Sqn)

No 38 Group – HQ: High Wycombe, Bucks
(Re-formed 1 November 1992)

Sqn	Aircraft	Base
55	Handley Page Victor K2*	Marham, Norfolk
101	BAC VC10 K2/K3**	Brize Norton, Oxon
216	Lockheed L1011 -500 TriStar K1/KC1/C2	Brize Norton, Oxon

Support Command – HQ: Brampton, Cambs

Sqn	Aircraft	Base
74(R)	BAe Hawk T1A 4FTS	Valley, Angelsey
208(R)	BAe Hawk T1A 4FTS	

Sqn	Aircraft	Base
19(R)	BAe Hawk T1A 7FTS	Chivenor, Devon
92(R)	BAe Hawk T1A 7FTS	

AAA/SAM Units

Unit	Equipment	Base
15 Sqn RAF Regt	BAe Rapier	Leeming, Yorks
19 Sqn*** RAF Regt	BAe Rapier	Brize Norton, Oxon
20 Sqn*** RAF Regt	BAe Rapier	Honington, Suffolk
27 Sqn RAF Regt	BAe Rapier	Leuchars, Fife
48 Sqn RAF Regt	BAe Rapier	Lossiemouth, Morayshire
66 Sqn*** RAF Regt	BAe Rapier	West Raynham, Norfolk
2729 Sqn RAuxAF Regt(V)	Oerlikon twin 35mm AA guns /Skyguard radar	Waddington, Lincs
2890 Sqn RAuxAF Regt(V)	Oerlikon twin 35mm AA guns /Skyguard radar	Waddington, Lincs

Notes
* To be disbanded October 1993
** To receive the additional VC10 K4 variants in 1993
*** To defend USAF bases

---

ing measures were taken around the air intakes but details of these would not be discussed by the RAF. The "Stage 1 Plus" modifications were completed by changes to better adapt the aircraft to the higher temperatures in Saudi Arabia and included better air conditioning, anti-buckling canopy modifications and hot-weather tyres.

Later, in-theatre, the ALE-40s were replaced with a pair of Vinten VICON 78 Series 210 dispensers before hostilities commenced and the Phimat pod was removed to an undisclosed position on the aircraft. Despite some reports, the Marconi Sky Shadow ECM pod (used by the Tornado GR1) was not deployed on the F3. Also in-theatre, the RAF received supplies of the AIM-9M version of the Sidewinder AAM from the US, for use during "Granby" only. These "Nine Mikes" featured an improved IR seeker. During practice combat sorties in-theatre, it was found that by substituting the Tornado GR1's 1,500-litre external fuel tanks in place of the F3's 2,250-litre (known as "Hindenburgers") tanks, the F3's permitted manoeuvring limits were raised from 2.75G to 5G.

The improvements to the Tornado F3, as necessitated by the impending war, have given it a much better reputation. Paul Jackson, writing in *Defence* magazine in January 1991 (after a visit to Dhahran in December 1990) quotes Wg Cdr David Hamilton, who had just completed a three-month tour as the RAF's F3 squadron commander at Dhahran, as saying: "Stage 1 has transformed the aircraft by 50 percent". He added, "I'd like to stop off at Decimomannu [where the Tornado F3s had been practising air combat with Canadian CF-18 Hornets flying Iraqi tactics] and settle a few old scores".

On their return to the UK, it was decided that all Tornado F3s would be given a defensive aids package as soon as possible. Vinten was later contracted to supply the fleet with its VICON 78 Series 400 flare dispensers (two per aircraft), to carry eight CART CM 55mm Mk 1 infra-red decoy flares and an integrated control system. In addition, the Sidewinder AAM launch rails were to be equipped with the Swedish Celsius Tech BOL integral chaff dispenser.

Meanwhile, in March 1992, after an aborted Anglo-German development programme, the RAF settled on its replacement for the AIM-9 Sidewinder. BAe Dynamics (BAeD) was contracted to develop and produce the Advanced Short-Range Air-to-Air Missile (ASRAAM), based on the original AIM-132 ASRAAM but with a US Hughes seeker head. ASRAAM is expected to enter service later this decade. About the same time, the Government noted that the Tornado F3 force was not to be equipped with the AIM-120 AMRAAM (in place of Sky Flash) and BAeD submitted an unsolicited proposal to modify the existing Sky Flash missiles to Active Sky-Flash configuration. This had not been taken-up at the time of writing.

In the previous "Snapshot" it was mentioned that the Tornado F3 was wired to receive the US Joint Tactical Information Distribution System (JTIDS). The RAF has funding for 54 of these terminals, the first of which will equip a training flight with the OCU (now No 56(R) Squadron) at Coningsby. The remainder will be fitted to the aircraft of the Leeming Wing (Nos 11, 23 and 25 Squadrons), ahead of installation of JTIDS in equivalent USAF fighters. Further RAF procurement of JTIDS for Tornado F3s, the E-3D Sentries and some tanker types is planned.

As a fighter, the Tornado F3 got off to a unsuccessful start but, it must be said, it has come through the bad times and emerged as an effective long-range fighter. Unfortunately, the scenario for which is was designed changed at the wrong time. The need is now for a more agile air combat fighter – the European Fighter Aircraft (EFA) – and once EFA (or Eurofighter 2000 as it has now become) enters service at the turn of the century, it was announced in the Defence White Paper of July 1993 the Tornado F3 force is to be reduced by 13 aircraft or one squadron (No 23 Squadron from RAF Leeming).

Data: see 1988 "Snapshot"

IMPRESSIONS OF THE SENTRY

Airborne early warning (AEW) has become a vital component of modern air defence networks. The value of USAF and Saudi E-3 Sentry AWACS aircraft during the Gulf War proved the system's application worked for both offensive as well as defensive operations. In July 1992, the author was invited to join an operational sortie on board one of the RAF's E-3D Sentry aircraft.

Now possessing its full complement of seven Boeing E-3D Sentry AEW1 aircraft, the RAF's No 8 Squadron was officially declared to NATO duties on 5 August 1992. This event signifies that there are now sufficient crews declared operational on the type to allow the RAF Sentries to play an active part in NATO airborne early warning operational and training activities, working with the E-3As of the NATO AEW force and USAF E-3B/C Sentry AWACS. The RAF E-3D is considered by many to be the most sophisticated version of the Sentry in service today. Apart from being more fuel-efficient than its USAF/NATO counterparts, courtesy of the GE/SNECMA CFM56 turbofan engines (which are also on the Sentries used by Saudi Arabia and France), the combination of the Westinghouse APY-2 radar, with overwater capability, together with Loral 1017 Yellow Gate electronic support measures (ESM) is probably the best combination of warning sensors available for such an aircraft.

The RAF E-3Ds, in common with the French E-3F, are also equipped with a SOGERMA in-flight refuelling probe, while retaining the original boom-and-socket receptacle, allowing cross-operations with USAF tankers.

In a flight lasting over 10hrs, I was able to observe many aspects of the aircraft's role. Between the Sentry and its predecessor the Shackleton AEW2, the RAF has skipped a generation in AEW technology. Although based on the Boeing 707 airframe (with the RAF and French E-3s being the last 707 airframes to be built), as a platform it is streets ahead of the old Shackleton.

The flightdeck crew comprises two pilots, a navigator and flight engineer but it is the "back seat" mission crew who do the real work. Working from front to back these are the communications operator and the communications technician, sitting side-by-side. Their job is to put in place the plethora of radio and data links required to communicate with their "customers".

On the E-3D, the radio fit comprises three ARC-165 HF transceivers, two ARC-166 VHF transceivers (one mission-dedicated, one for the flightdeck) and six ARC-171 UHF/SATCOM transceivers (five mission, one flightdeck) – all from Rockwell Collins. In addition, there are two Magnavox ARC-187 UHF transceivers equipped with Have Quick ECCM modules.

The secure digital data links on board, to various NATO architecture and protocol standards, include: Link 4 (providing a one-way path to some US fighters with appropriate equipment); Link 11 (a two-way link to air, naval or ground stations); and Link 14 (a one-way path to ship or ground station). Link 16/JTIDS (Joint Tactical Information Distribution System) is now in the process of being "worked-up" on the RAF Sentries.

Link 16/JTIDS is a two-way link to air, naval and ground stations. Once the appropriate equipment is installed in the Tornado F3, the passing of target information back-and-forth will be much improved. Indeed, our aircraft was conducting JTIDS transmission trials with a ground station at West Raynham during the course of the flight. The JTIDS Class 2 terminals for the UK are being manufactured by GEC-Marconi Electronic Systems Corporation in the United States.

Aft of the comms section is the computer display technician with responsibility for the two IBM 4 Pi CC-2 high-speed computers with a storage capacity of 665,360 words (one monitoring the other); two digital multiplexers; controllers for the peripherals; three "very old" tape drives and one line printer.

In the main section of the fuselage are the nine Hazeltine high-resolution Situation Display Consoles (SDC) in three banks of three. The clarity of the colour displays has to be seen to be believed, although it took a good three hours for the author to absorb and understand the symbology of the processed radar returns from the Westinghouse APY-2 radar.

The exact range of the S-band APY-2 is, of course, classified but Westinghouse talks of "several hundred miles". Like any airborne radar its operation is restricted only by the curvature of the Earth but at 30,000ft, the radar horizon was some 285 miles (460km). The laws of physics being imutable, the higher you fly the greater the radar horizon.

There are several modes of operation for the APY-2, including two high pulse-repetition frequency (PRF), pulse-Doppler modes: PDNES (Pulse-Doppler, Non-Elevation Scan) which provides surveillance of aircraft targets out to the radar horizon but with no target elevation data; and PDES (Pulse-Doppler, Elevation Scan) giving the same area coverage but with target elevation data being determined by electronic vertical scanning of the radar beam.

Longer-range detection of medium- and high-altitude aircraft can be obtained by using the Beyond-The-Horizon (BTH) mode, in which pulsed radar without Doppler is used. This gives extended range coverage above the horizon where ground clutter does not occur. In BTH mode, a low PRF signal is transmitted and target returns provide range and azimuth information.

For maritime surface target detection, the Maritime mode uses a very short pulse width with a low PRF. This gives high resolution with a low clutter return. Further clutter-reduction is achieved by use of an automatically-applied adaptive digital processor.

In Passive mode the transmitter is shut down while the receivers and associated signal processing facilities continue to operate. This mode is particularly effective in adverse ECM conditions and permits hostile radar transmitters to be located while the E-3 itself operates under "radar silent" conditions.

The full capacity of all these modes can be enhanced by the sectoring of the radar's azimuth scan, which can have the 360-degree scan divided into as many as 32 individual sectors, each with its own scanning mode. Modes in any individual sector may be selected as required and if a brief "view" into any sector is desired, this is easily done.

It is also possible to "interleave" modes of operation. Thus, the PDES mode may be interleaved with the BTH or PDNES with Maritime. Targets can often be detected by both modes in this interleaved operation. This simultaneous multi-mode operation, combined with sectoring, provides high flexibility and the opportunity to match the radar to differing terrain environments or tactical situations.

On the forward bank of SDCs is located the fighter allocator flanked by two fighter controllers; on the second bank, facing the first, are the tactical director (the mission leader), surveillance controller and link manager; with the three surveillance operators (one of whom is dedicated to the ESM systems) on the third bank. Bringing up the rear is the radar technician at his own console.

On first appearance, to see the nine operators at the SDCs looks like organised chaos but over the course of the whole flight, the first impressions were deceptive. The level of cooperation between the various members from the tactical director downwards was, in fact, amazingly slick.

The surveillance controller takes the initial processed radar images and "cleans-up" the screen, tagging the tracks with whatever identity is required, for the tactical director who sees the big picture. The tactical direc-

tor then assigns the responsibility for the various elements of the particular task in hand to the appropriate specialists among his crew. Thus, he is able to deal with any "targets of opportunity" which occur during the operations.

An example of just such an unplanned event occurred during the flight. During a delay in a planned exercise to control an interception of Jaguar attack aircraft by Tornado F3 fighters, another formation of Tornado F3s appeared, early on their flight plan. Consulting with both Boulmer ground control and the airborne Sentry, it was agreed they could indulge in an *ad hoc* air combat manoeuvring exercise (or "dog fight"), during course of which there was a mid-air contact incident.

Fortunately the incident was not fatal, but in the minutes following the declared emergency it was possible to see the level of collaboration between the members of the team, dealing with elements of the emergency procedure. One could also see the emergency "squawks" of the two aircraft's IFF systems on the screen against their position tags. Both aircraft involved recovered safely to Newcastle airport.

Having dealt with the unexpected climax to our mission, it seems almost *passé* to record the real tasks. For the first part of the flight, we flew down to Lands End where, for two hours, we flew a "racetrack" pattern controlling the airborne element of "Thursday's War" for the Royal Navy's Flag Officer, Sea Training (FOST). Emphasising the importance of communications, it is interesting to note that there was a problem with one of the ships involved being tied into the Sentry's secure comms link, which was solved (at their end) an hour into the exercise.

Moving from Land's End towards Northumberland to position for the Tornado/Jaguar interception exercise mentioned above, the aircraft began JTIDS transmission trials referred to earlier in the article.

When the Jaguars finally arrived for their attack run, it was interesting to observe how the airborne fighter controllers (the weapons allocators) guided their aircraft onto the targets, passing on evasive measures initiated by the Jaguars.

The mid-air emergency bought the Jaguar exercise to an abbreviated end and, once the aircraft involved had landed, the Sentry moved further out over the North Sea to exercise its ESM/ECM equipment against a Norwegian Falcon 20 ECM aircraft. Although one was able to observe the exercise, the crew involved were not so forthcoming with their explanations as to what was happening, for security reasons.

Following this exercise, we turned back for home, landing at Waddington some 10hr 40min after take-off. One's impression of the whole system was that of an effective and invaluable aid to the conduct of both offensive and defensive air warfare. That was the message from the Gulf War, which saw extensive use of both USAF and Saudi E-3s. It is, however, comforting to see evidence of the system firsthand.

As these words were written, two RAF E-3Ds were deployed to Trapani, Sicily, later moving to Aviano, near Venice, to monitor sea and air movements in support of the United Nations sanctions against parts of the former Yugoslavia.

RESPONSE: AAA & SAMs

Oerlikon-Contraves Twin 35mm Type GDF
In order to increase the operational flexibility of the 35mm AA guns in service, No 2729 (City of Lincoln) Squadron RAuxAF Regiment, was split to form two units. The second unit, designated No 2890 Squadron RAuxAF Regiment, being formed on 1 October 1990. This unit took delivery of a second, new Skyguard radar from Oerlikon-Contraves in early 1991.

Data: See 1988 "Snapshot"

BAe Dynamics Bloodhound Mk 2
The reduction of East-West tension, following the break-up of the Warsaw Pact and then the Soviet Union, caused a great re-think in air defence circles. Despite having refurbished the Bloodhounds, the new circumstances caused a further re-think by the MoD.

In March 1990 it was announced that over the next year the number of Bloodhound flights would be reduced, concentrating on Wattisham, Suffolk, and West Raynham, Norfolk. Flights located at Bawdsey, Suffolk, Barkston Heath and North Coates (both in Lincolnshire) and Wyton, Cambridgeshire, were withdrawn to the two major bases, which were expected to "soldier-on" until 1995.

Later in February 1991, it was announced that "following a re-assessment of the cost-effectiveness of the RAF

Bloodhound air defence missile" they would be withdrawn from service altogether from 1 July 1991. At the same time it was revealed that a new medium-range SAM to replace the Bloodhound would be sought. This requirement is known as the Medium-range Surface-to-Air Missile (MSAM) and that it was required to be in service within five years.

Late in 1992, the MSAM decision slipped to the right, due to funding priorities. It is known that the Cardinal Points Specification, against which the bids have been made, requires eight key sites in Eastern England to be defended by the MSAM winner. Several threat "envelopes" have been described, involving saturation attacks by aircraft, combined with high-diving and cruise missiles, a heavy electronic warfare (jamming) environment and, possibly, an anti-tactical ballistic missile (eg, "Scud") capability.

Three main systems are being bid to meet the requirement: the GEC-Marconi/Eurosam SAMP/T (*Sol-Air Moyen Portée/Terrestre*), the Siemens Plessey/Hughes/NFT Advanced SAM (AdSAM, based on the Norwegian NASAMS project) and the Raytheon/BAe mix of Patriot with additional Rapier 2000 (Field Standard C) units as "gap-fillers".

The RAF's decision was originally due late in 1992 slipping to sometime in 1993. The original timescale for deployment of a MSAM slipped to the broad bracket of 1995-2005. The July 1993 Defence White Paper noted "there is no near-term requirement for a MSAM" and that the MoD is "now looking at the nature and timing of our longer-term needs"

Data: See 1968 "Snapshot"

BAe Rapier
During the period of this "half-Snapshot", the RAF Regiment added a further Rapier unit – No 54 Squadron – to its UK Rapier force. Based at Leeming, the new Tornado F3 base in Yorkshire, No 54 Squadron was formed on 1 October 1989 but, on 1 August 1990, this unit was re-numbered No 15 Squadron (following the disbandment of a Light Armoured Squadron). With No 27 Squadron at Leuchars and No 48 Squadron at Lossiemouth, this move completed the second three-squadron Rapier Wing tasked with base air defence in the UK. The other Wing was tasked with the air defence of USAF bases in the UK.

Below: Due to enter service this year, this picture shows the eight-round fire unit of the Rapier 2000 LLAD system, known as Field Standard "C" by the RAF Regiment. (BAe)

The further development of the Rapier system to Field Standard C (Rapier 2000 for export) was made against the Cold War scenario of a heavy ECM environment, multiple "pop-up" helicopter attacks, anti-radar missiles, and smaller battlefield targets (such as RPVs and cruise missiles). In addition, there was the threat of biological/chemical munitions (inhibiting crew operation) and the possibility of exo-atmospheric electromagnetic pulse (EMP) which would destroy unshielded electronic communications.

The new system comprises three towed units, all based on a common trailer: the missile fire unit (with the Mk 2 missile), the tracker radar unit and the surveillance radar unit. The missile fire unit contains eight ready-to-fire Rapier Mk 2 missiles, the electro-optical tracker, the missile command link and weapons system management computer. The Mk 2 missile features improvements including a combined armour-piercing and fragmentation warhead (although the semi armour-piercing warhead can also be used), a dual crush/proximity fuze and the increased range RO Thermopolae rocket motor digital autopilot, plus other minor improvements. The Mk 2 missile can be used just as easily by the older systems (Field Standards A and B).

The radar tracker unit is the Marconi Radar and Command Systems Blindfire 2000 able to operate in all weathers by day or night. The dual tracking system uses a Ferranti M700 processor, with frequency management software techniques to avoid jamming. Optical tracking is possible in similar conditions by use of the electro-optical IR-tracking unit, with a facility for remote siting of the viewing console. The surveillance radar from Siemens-Plessey Radar operates in the J-band and its advanced planar array offers a three-dimensional picture. It is integrated with current IFF Mk 10 and Mk 12 systems. By using a high elevation guard beam, when anti-radar missiles are detected, the radar transmissions are automatically stopped.

The first Rapier Field Standard C systems were scheduled to be officially handed over to the RAF Regiment (and the British Army) in the middle of 1993. Oman has already ordered the Rapier 2000 upgrade for its existing systems.

Data

Missiles/launcher	8
Span	1ft 3in
Length	7ft 4in
Type of mounting	two-wheeled platform with outriggers
Engagement zone	360° in azimuth, -5° to +60° in elevation
Engagement range	0.5nm to beyond 4nm
Effective ceiling	10,000ft
Weight of missile	94lb
Type of warhead	shaped HE charge and blast fragmentation, with impact and proximity fuzing

CRITIQUE

By the start of 1993, the impact of *Options for Change* and the down-sizing of the RAF was well in hand. The RAF's air defences are now at a peak of capability once more. While this is good news, the fact that the threats are now so rapidly changing means it is uncertain exactly what the air defences may have to cope with in the future. As outlined earlier in this "half-Snapshot", the Tactical Ballistic Missile may be more of a threat than manned aircraft or stand-off weapons. This eventuality may be being addressed (although with what priority is unknown) following deferment of the MSAM replacement for Bloodhound.

While all radar and C³ systems are modern, some specific systems may be required to address new "threat" if, indeed, it is considered a threat. With politicians and public alike anxious to see the so-called "peace dividend" in their pockets, defence spending is not likely to be increased in the near term. Priorities will have to be changed or capabilities discarded (whether in air defence, strike/attack, transport or maritime operations) if the quality of the lower quantity is to be preserved or increased.

The events of the last five years have shown that technology is delivering "the goods" but that it can also fall down. Systems are becoming so complex and sophisticated that it is not the hardware that is causing the delays but, rather, the software. When I tasked one industry source on this point, I was told, tongue-in-cheek, that to determine the real time taken for software development, take the original planned time and double it and then add-on the original figure, for good measure. Many a true word is spoken in jest, it is said.

What sometimes tends to be forgotten today is that development schedules are planned for just that purpose -development. If the latest fighter aircraft or missile does not perform perfectly first time, then the solution to the problem has to be found. That can take time and money. Even more time and money can be wasted if the project itself is not efficiently managed. By that I do not mean cut resources. Rather, it means the application of sound engineering principles, sensible accounting and a dose of old-fashioned common sense.

If the reader thinks I have just written what is "a blinding glimpse of the obvious", he would do well to remember the fiasco of the airborne early warning system being developed for the Nimrod. As a defence journalist who followed the twists and turns of this project, my opinion is that fault for the failure did not lie soley with the radar contractors. With no prime contractor responsible, the project was beset by the almost-mindless series of MoD committees and their associated "red tape".

One can also argue that, good as the Nimrod is as a maritime patrol aircraft, it was physically too small to handle the equipment and systems required for the complex AEW task. The reason Nimrod was chosen was that spare airframes were available. The Airbus A300 would have made a more sensible platform but that would have meant new airframe procurement at a time when money was seen as being better spent elsewhere.

The mistake of the Nimrod AEW was almost repeated with the Tornado's Foxhunter radar – the cynical codename "Blue Circle" has already been mentioned. However, rectification to the contracting system and project management allowed the technical improvements at the right time and the radar is now doing its job.

The delays which beset IUKADGE have also caused problems and, basically, have been down to the integration of various elements of the system, notably the Integrated Command and Control System (ICCS). In a written answer to the House of Commons Defence Committee's First Report on the 1992 Defence White Paper (November 1992), the official Ministry line was one of optimism. It began by noting that, in a previous answer, "encouraging progress was being made with the ICCS recovery plan drawn up by the system contractor, UK Systems Ltd".

The answer then goes on to record that "following successful completion of formal acceptance tests the technical transfer of the basic system to the Ministry of Defence took place on 27 September 1991, several months earlier than had been expected when the recovery plan was approved." It was still years later than *originally* planned. The statement records that the system was formally transferred to the RAF on 1 July 1992.

That may be have been the case, but the *complete* system was not, then, on line. "Since that date," the MoD's answer to the Defence Committee read, "the RAF has been training to take over the system operationally and obtaining hands-on experience. Residual problems that were thrown up in the extensive trials and work-up programme embarked on after acceptance are being dealt with by the manufacturer under warranty arrangements. Work is also going on to implement minor amendments to the system to satisfy requirements that have arisen since the original contract was signed and which are outside its scope (for instance, changes to the air safety regulations). All these tasks are expected to be complete by January 1993."

One must accept that this fine-tuning is both right and proper, yet the system was some seven years late. In many respects the delays to the ICCS element of IUKADGE could have prompted as much public concern as the Nimrod AEW affair. Bearing in mind the technology and methodology used in a systems integration of this complexity, delays were inevitable. One may, perhaps, suggest the development of the software should have been more tightly controlled at an earlier stage. It has also been suggested that the MoD could have been more helpful in communicating recognised problems to UKSL; the "hands-off" approach may well have been the reaction to "burnt fingers" acquired during the Nimrod AEW programme. Neither criticism can be laid at any one individual's door. It just took longer than anticipated to produce the solutions to the problems. As far as public interest was concerned, ICCS was well below the tip of the air defence iceberg. So, apart from the specialised defence press, there were few, if any, "investigative" stories in the popular press.

Even as these words were written, the future of the Tornado F3's successor – EFA – had been in doubt. In August 1992, Germany's Defence Minister, Volker Rühe, announced he would not proceed into the production phase of EFA and suggested that the changed strategic situation in Europe demanded a new solution. EFA was too expensive and designed against a defunct threat. This caused much annoyance to the UK and prompted a vigorous defence of the project at all levels at home. A four-nation industry study on how to reduce costs (and, consequently, capability) resulted in a proposed new variant, known as the New European Fighter Aircraft (NEFA) with a common airframe, system and engines (but with "mix'n'match" avionics and weapons).

At a meeting in Brussels on 10 December 1992, the Defence Ministers of the four partner nations were persuaded of the viability of the NEFA solution on grounds of its need – there being no better solution available in the timeframe – and cost -with savings of up to 30% being available. This has been achieved by re-thinking the production programme and offering a modular and less-sophisticated avionics

suite (notably the radar and defensive aids sub-system). To give the deal a cosmetic change, taking into account the further slippage of the in-service date to the year 2000, NEFA has been christened "Eurofighter 2000". This, together with the cost savings, was sufficient to convince Rühe to continue.

It may be said that, in the event, Volker Rühe has done the contracting European defence industry a big favour. With the cost reduced and its new name, Rühe can "sell" Eurofighter 2000 to the German public. Apart from safeguarding many thousands of jobs, the industrial base on which advanced combat aircraft are designed can be retained. With smaller production runs for the four partner nations and the flexibility to equip the aircraft with customised avionics and weapons systems, the potential for export might be better in the new circumstances.

With the project secured, British Defence Secretary, Malcolm Rifkind, has indicated that the RAF will receive the top-of-the-range EF2000 for an in-service date only four years later than originally suggested (but actually it is five) when the project was initiated in 1985. Thanks to Volker Rühe, it will cost the British taxpayer less than originally estimated.

In summary, 1993 sees the RAF in good shape to meet the pure air defence of Great Britain. There remains a threat which must be countered but, fortunately, it seems further away from our shores than it did three years ago. The "out-of-area" capability, as demonstrated during Operations "Corporate" (the Falklands campaign) in 1982 and "Granby" (the Gulf build-up and war of 1990-91) and the policing of air space over the former Yugoslavia and northern and southern parts of Iraq, clearly show the way.

The big conundrum is whether or not the UK armed forces can maintain the Government's commitments within its revised budgets. While no-one has specifically mentioned the 10-year rule as being in force (as it was in 1918 and 1945), it would be folly of the highest order to throw away such advances as have been made to offer a short-term saving. With prudent economies and some lateral thinking, the peace dividend can be delivered – but not overnight, as many people suspect.

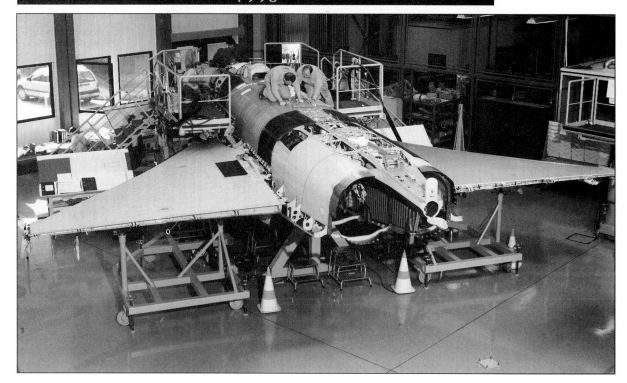

Left: The first Development Aircraft (DA-1) for the Eurofighter 2000 (formerly known as EFA) programme takes shape at the DASA facility in Manching, Germany. Note the considerable use of composite materials in the construction. (DASA)

Below left: This cutaway drawing shows the shape and elements of the construction of the Eurofighter 2000. The flight refuelling probe seen protruding from the forward starboard fuselage is retractable. (Eurofighter GmbH)

THE FUTURE

Although the development of the UK air defence system has been considered in 10-year "Snapshot" form, taking 1918 as the bench mark year, 1988 would seem, in retrospect, to mark a significant point in world history. It was the last full year of the Cold War. At the start of 1993, the "new world order" (whatever that means) had seen a rise in nationalism in areas of the world previously dominated by the former Soviet Union or its satellites.

By the end of 1989 the political map of Europe had been fundamentally altered and the whole concept of military response, created over the past 40 years, was no more. The events have been so momentous as to appear almost incidental, their full significance has yet to be appreciated and the effects will equally mark the next 40 years.

Military attitudes and funding are already changing and the electorates of Europe are anxious to enjoy the so-called "Peace Dividend". The old certainties have gone and are yet to be replaced with anything new or practical. In the interim there is likely to be a period of inertia, principle operational requirements will remain, although some may be severely limited in form. It is likely that a period of stagnation, not unlike those days of the 1920s, could afflict military thinking and planning.

The fiscal pressures on the RAF suggest that in the coming years various types of synthetic training systems would become popular. This will not always please the military who consider there is no substitute for actual flying experience. Typically, in early 1991, BAe brought its North Sea Air Combat Manoeuvring Instrumentation Range (NSAR) into full operation, having started operations in the previous September. The range is said to be one of the most advanced of its kind and the only instrumented Air Combat Range in the UK. It can be used by all RAF fixed-wing combat aircraft and by RN Sea Harriers. It has already been leased by other NATO air forces and Switzerland as well.

Another example of fiscal pressure was the consideration being given, in late 1992, to reduce the number of Tornado F3 squadrons assigned to UK air defence. The RAF admitted, then, that cuts were under review as part of a wider range of force cutbacks in the wake of the Soviet Union's disintegration. In the event, "Defending Our Future" – the statement on the Defence Estimates 1993 (HMSO, Cm 2270) noted that "with effect from 1 April 1994, a force of 100 Tornado F3 fighters will be fully capable of defending the United Kingdom's airspace and meeting our commitments to NATO's reaction forces ... a reduction of 13 aircraft." The White Paper went on to note that "the F3 force will be reorganised into six squadrons, rather than the seven at present. The Operational Conversion Unit (OCU) will continue to support the squadrons." As noted earlier, No 23 Squadron at Leeming has "drawn the short straw" and will be disbanded

Eurofighter 2000

In the meantime, by 1998, the Eurofighter 2000 (formerly EFA but still unnamed by the RAF) will have moved through its early stages having survived the crisis of 1992-93. Even so, assuming its progress continues to revised schedules (including a maiden flight now due in September 1993), the RAF will not receive Eurofighter 2000 until the year 2000 - five years later than originally scheduled!

The aircraft has its origins in the merging of three national "paper" projects – the UK's P.106 and P.110, with German (MBB) and Italian (Aeritalia) equivalents – to the Agile Combat Aircraft (ACA) of 1982. Supported only by the UK Government (although with Italian and some German industrial participation), this became the Experimental Aircraft Programme (EAP). Once the European Fighter Aircraft (EFA) was launched, the EAP became a realistic technology demonstrator for the programme.

The EFA is a canard delta, single-seat, twin-engined air combat fighter with a prime air-to-air role but capable of fulfilling air-to-ground missions. The basic design parameters were a basic mass empty weight of 21,495lb (9.75 tonnes), a thrust (per engine) of 20,250lb st (90kN) and a gross wing area of 538 sq ft (50 sq m). This was laid down in a European Staff development

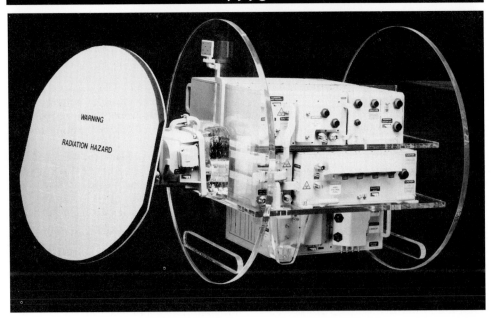

Left: A "space model" of the ECR-90 radar being developed for the Eurofighter 2000 by the EuroRadar consortium led by GEC-Marconi Avionics (formerly GEC Ferranti). (Via DASA)

target agreed in 1985 by the air staffs of Germany, Italy, Spain and the UK.

A four-nation consortium of the prime contractors (Alenia, British Aerospace, CASA and DASA, to use their present identities) was established in Munich in June 1986 and called Eurofighter/Jagdflugzeug GmbH, with an equivalent company – Eurojet – established to develop the EJ200 powerplant. The programme split agreed (based on the original numbers required) was 33% (250 each) to Germany and the UK, 21% (165) for Italy and 13% (100) for Spain. As with the Tri-national Tornado programme, a NATO agency was set up to manage the programme, known as NEFMA (NATO EuroFighter Management Agency).

The problems with Germany and the subsequent renegotiation of the programme, culminating in the December 1992 go-ahead for the re-named Eurofigher 2000, was covered in the previous "Snapshot".

The current status is that seven prototypes (known as Development Aircraft – DA) are being built. The first two aircraft, DA1 (built in Germany) and DA2 (built in the UK) are virtually ready to fly. These two aircraft will be powered by Turbo Union RB.199 Mk104E afterburning turbofans (from the Tornado, to reduce risk). DA3 (built in Italy) will be the first of the subsequent EJ200-powered versions. DA4 (a UK-built two seater) and DA5 (a German single-seater) will carry the full avionics suite of ECR-90 radar, DASS and IRST (see below). DA6 will be the Spanish-built aircraft and DA7 the last of the Italian ones.

As at July 1993, one of the two problems delaying the first flight of the Eurofighter 2000 has been solved. The Constant Frequency Generator (CFG) being developed by Ferranti-Bendix is to be replaced by an interim unit supplied by the US company Sunstrand. More importantly, the software for the Digital Flight Control System (DFCS) being developed by GEC-Marconi Avionics teamed with DASA (who are responsible for integration) is still being "tweaked". At the Paris Air Show in June 1993, a Eurofighter spokesman noted that this element was "taking longer than anyone thought" and that work proceeded "with extreme caution", bearing in mind the crash of the JAS-39 Gripen and YF-22 fighters. Taxying trials with both DA1 and DA2 have been conducted, with input into the DFCS software and the aircraft will fly when it is ready.

Despite continuing political debate, its ECR90 radar (led by the UK's GEC-Marconi Avionics, which has incorporated GEC-Ferranti Defence Systems) is the product of a European consortium offering the very latest in technology and automatic adaptive characteristics to enable it to carry out diverse tasks during a mission. While the RAF Eurofighter 2000 (and, hopefully, Italian and Spanish) versions of the aircraft will have this radar, Germany may opt for the Hughes APG-65.

Among the many other contracts awarded for the programme which, again, will equip the RAF version, was one for the development of a Passive Infra-Red Airborne Tracking Equipment (PIRATE) as the basis of a Forward Looking Infra-Red Search and Track System (FLIR-IRST). This five-year contract was awarded to EURO-FIRST, a consortium comprising FIAR (Italy), Thorn EMI Electronics (UK) and EUROTRONICA (Spain).

This type of equipment has long been a feature of Russian fighters, the dome-like sensor cover being a distinctive feature on the nose, forward of the canopy, of the MiG-29 "Fulcrum" and Su-27 "Flanker", for example. It is intended that the system will offer EFA either a multiple target detector and tracker capability, or as the infra-red equivalent of a TV camera producing a monochrome picture to assist in navigation, passive detection and as a landing aid under conditions of poor visibility.

The Defensive Aids Sub-System (DASS) was another major contract awarded in early 1992 to the EURODASS consortium, led by the UK's Marconi Defence Systems (now part of GEC-Marconi Avionics) and including Italy's Ellettronica. Germany had already opted to consider a less-expensive (and less capable) alternative and was then joined by Spain.

EURODASS is to develop a "core" DASS which is made up of fully-integrated electronic support measures (ESM), missile approach warning (MAW) and radar-jamming sub-systems, controlled by a dedicated

Defensive Aids Computer (DAC). The radar-jamming sub-system will use on-board transmission anntenae in the wingtip pods and will also feature a towed decoy, housed in the starboard wingtip pod. In addition, there will be a chaff and flare dispenser system (of a type unselected at the time of writing).

The Eurofighter 2000 will be armed with a single 27mm Mauser cannon (developed for the Tornado) internally and has 13 weapons stations under the wings (four under each) and fuselage (five) for 9,920lb (4,500kg) of stores. The RAF version will be armed with four Hughes AIM-120 AMRAAM BVR missiles and a pair of BAe Dynamics AIM-132 ASRAAM dogfight missiles.

The EJ200 powerplant has progressed well and is virtually ready for flight-testing. It is a fully-modular engine rated at (approximately) 13,490lb st (60kN) dry and 20,250lb st (90kN) with reheat. Its thermodynamic cycle is optimised for air combat, with a bypass ratio of 0.4 and a fan-pressure ratio of 4-4.2, plus a vari-cowl which is rotated up or down to increase or decrease airflow for specific flight regimes.

Among the many new technologies featured are digital engine control, wide-chord turbine blades of sungle-crystal metallurgy, powder metalurgy discs, lightweight compressor/turbine assemblies, integral blade/disc ("blisk") assemblies, convergent/ divergent exhausts nozzles and an integrated health monitoring system. An in-flight refuelling system is fitted as standard to all aircraft. At Paris in June 1993, Eurojet was claiming that the EJ200 had met all its development milestones to date.

As of June 1993, all the participants to the programme are re-orientating themselves in line with the agreement of December 1992, taking in revised schedules and consequent contract revisions. All this is expected by the end of 1993, when a better idea of the production numbers will have emerged. The RAF remains committed to its original 250 aircraft (although differing sources have suggested it could drop to 200 or rise to as much as 350). Germany is expected to order between 120-140 aircraft, while Italy looks like settling on 130 and Spain some 75 aircraft.

However, when considering 1998, Eurofighter 2000 remains in the future. Whether it will make the current first flight date of September 1993 will be known by the time these words are read. It has had its problems, technical and political, but the

Below: This "moody" view shows the second Eurofighter 2000 Development Aircraft (DA-2) taking shape at the Warton facility of British Aerospace. (BAe)

Above: The first British-built Eurofighter 2000 (DA-2) seen on the ground at Warton. First production aircraft are expected to enter RAF service in the year 2000. (BAe)

author remains convinced the programme will, eventually, succeed. If for no other reason than the money committed to date and the simple fact that there is no cheaper solution. No doubt "Their Airships" of the RAF are pondering on what name to christen the RAF's future fighter.

Whence the threat?

In retrospect the Cold War now seems to have been a period of stability. Both sides knew the rules and common defence industries flourished. In times past, arms races usually ended in conflict because the equipment had to be used to justify its replacement. The electronic revolution of the last 30 years made that a dated concept; system attrition is now created by advances in electronic technology which keep industry busy and the end user continually supplied with new, upgraded or enhanced equipment, to use the jargon of the times.

Those cosy days are past and it is becoming increasingly difficult to assess the future threats. In many cases the threat is seen as fairly minor conflicts reflecting the character of earlier European wars, using basic conventional weapons and capable of tying down large numbers of outside forces attempting to restore peace. Lesser conflicts, such as the UK has faced in Ulster for almost a quarter of a century, are another very real threat and capable of creating considerable problems of logistics, manpower and political will to address.

The Cold War certainties also offered many of the European members of the Western Alliance the chance to conveniently ignore the problems posed by ballistic missiles. An inability to offer any real defence and the reassurance of the MAD doctrine permitted a somewhat hypocritical attitude to be adopted. Because of their relative economic strengths, both the United States and the Soviet Union developed some aspects of an anti-missile defensive capability and the Americans are continuing work in this area of technology.

It would seem appropriate for Europe to reassess the risk of this type of attack. There is now a dangerously high rate of proliferation of ballistic missile technology in third world countries, with a particular risk emerging along Europe's southern and southeastern flanks. The threat of aerodynamic missiles is another consideration, for these are different from ballistic missiles and will require a suitable response. Whatever system may be selected to meet the MSAM (Bloodhound replacement) requirement will be given a degree of ATBM capability.

Europe should now be looking to the use of satellite technology for its future AEW role, possibly joining technological forces with the United States for the Global Protection Against Limited Strikes (GPALS) programme. A choice that could, in future events, prove to be as timely as the introduction of radar in the 1930s. Certainly the detection and identification tasks of the 21st Century must be based upon space platform techniques. In addition these sensors could be used to monitor a wide range of activities for early warning of natural disasters and, even, crop monitoring to improve their cost effectiveness.

Another emergent threat, just coming over the technological horizon, is that of microwave pulse weapons. Manufacturers are already used to producing various types of hardened circuits to resist the effects of the electromagnetic pulse generated by a nuclear explosion. However, pulse weapons would offer a wider range of applications, as well as precision and direction, that pose a very real threat against the basically vulnerable microchip.

Finally, probably one of the most far reaching developments of all has been the gradual rationalisation of the UK's military electronics industry as a result of take-overs and company re-alignments. Similarly, other European manufacturers have faced up to the future to create a stronger "European" complexion. Concurrently a number of European countries are coming ever closer

in both political and fiscal terms, despite occasional setbacks in a process that is now irreversible. At the end of the decade these trends may well ensure a greater European stability, in social and economic terms, than was ever achieved by the two disastrous "civil wars" that rent Europe during the first half of the 20th Century.

By 1998, we could well see the integration of the RAF air defence network and resources into a European-wide air defence system: smaller in its individual elements but larger in the scope of its overall capability and task. Whatever the fallout of the political and military changes still underway in 1993, there is no doubt that the RAF will have a part to play in air defence for many years to come.

Below: The venerable Avro Shackleton AEW2 makes a farewell appearance flanked by its successor, the Boeing E-3D Sentry AEW1, and a Panavia Tornado F3, the RAF's current interceptor. (Geoff Lee/BAe)

BIBLIOGRAPHY

J. M. Bruce, *The Aeroplanes of the Royal Flying Corps (Military Wing)*, (Putnams, London 1982)

Bill Gunston, *Aircraft of the Soviet Union* (Osprey Publishing, London 1983)

Major-General E. B. Ashmore, *Air Defence* (Longmans, Green & Co, London 1929)

Group Captain M. B. Elsam, FBIM, RAF, *Air Defence* (Vol.7 in Brassey's "Air Power: Aircraft Weapons Systems and Technology" series), (Brassey's (UK), London 1989)

John Bushby, *Air Defence of Great Britain*, (Ian Allan, London 1973)

Christopher Cole and E. F. Cheeseman, *The Air Defence of Britain 1914-1918*, (Putnams, London 1984)

Michael J. Gething, *Air Power 2000*, (Arms & Armour Press, London 1992)

Owen Thetford, *Aircraft of the Royal Air Force since 1918* (Putnams, London 8th Edition, 1988)

Ian V. Hogg, *Anti-Aircraft – A History of Air Defence* (Macdonald & Jane's Publishers, London 1978)

Peter Gray & Owen Thetford, *German Aircraft of the First World War*, (Putnams, London)

G. W. Haddow & Peter M. Grosz, *The German Giants – The German R-Planes 1914-1918* (Putnams, London)

Terry Gander, *Modern Royal Air Force, Encyclopaedia of the* (Patrick Stephens, Cambridge, 2nd Edition, 1987)

Bill Gunston, *Night Fighters – A Development & Combat History* (Patrick Stephens, Cambridge 1976)

John D. R. Rawlings, *Royal Air Force, The History of the* (Temple Press/ Aerospace Publishing, London 1984)

James J. Halley, *The Squadrons of the Royal Air Force* (Air-Britain (Historians) Ltd, Tonbridge 1980)

Air Vice-Marshal R. A. Mason and John W. R. Taylor, *Soviet Air Force (Aircraft, Strategy and Operations of the)* (Jane's Publishing Co, London 1986)

ed Robin Higham and Jacob W. Kipp *Soviet Aviation and Air Power – a historical view* (Westview Press, Boulder, Colorado, USA 1977 and Brassey's, London, UK 1978)

Bill Sweetman, *Soviet Military Aircraft (The Hamlyn Concise Guide to)* (Hamlyn Publishing Group Ltd/ Aerospace Publishing, London 1981)

INDEX